HROTSVIT OF GANDERSHEIM

Contexts, Identities, Affinities, and Performances

HROTSVIT OF GANDERSHEIM

Contexts, Identities, Affinities,
and Performances

Edited by
Phyllis R. Brown, Linda A. McMillin,
and Katharina M. Wilson

UNIVERSITY OF TORONTO PRESS
Toronto Buffalo London

ISBN 0-8020-8962-3

Printed on acid-free paper

National Library of Canada Cataloguing in Publication

Hrotsvit of Gandersheim : contexts, identities, affinities, and
  performances / edited by Phyllis R. Brown, Linda A. McMillin,
  and Katharina M. Wilson.

Includes bibliographical references and index.
ISBN 0-8020-8962-3

1. Hrotsvitha, ca. 935–ca. 975 – Criticism and interpretation.
I. Brown, Phyllis Rugg, 1949– II. McMillin, Linda A., 1959–
III. Wilson, Katharina M.

PA 8340.H76 2004   872'.03   C2003-905582-5

University of Toronto Press acknowledges the financial assistance to its
publishing program of the Canada Council for the Arts and the Ontario
Arts Council.

University of Toronto Press acknowledges the financial support for its
publishing activities of the Government of Canada through the Book
Publishing Industry Development Program (BPIDP).

Contents

HROTSVIT OF GANDERSHEIM

Contexts, Identities, Affinities, and Performances

Introduction

KATHARINA M. WILSON

Clamor Validus: **Legends, Drama, and Epic**

Born in the fourth decade of the tenth century, Hrotsvit lived and wrote in Gandersheim Abbey, in Saxony, during the abbey's golden age under Gerberga I's rule. Her name, which she translates as 'clamor validus' (Strong Testimony), expresses her poetic mission to glorify the heroes of Christianity, both secular and religious, and it echoes, perhaps even in a millennial, eschatological sense, the biblical identification of John the Baptist, the patron saint of her abbey, as 'vox clamantis' (voice calling out or proclaiming). Her heroes are the Ottos and the whole Liudolf dynasty and the saints and martyrs of Christianity. Writing in Latin, mostly in leonine hexameters and rhymed rhythmic prose, Hrotsvit chose hagiographic materials predominantly from the early Christian centuries for her legends and plays and contemporary and near contemporary events for her epics.

Her works are arranged in three books, organized generically and chronologically and delineated as such by prefatory, programmatic, and dedicatory materials. Book One contains the eight legends: *Maria, Ascensio, Gongolfus, Pelagius, Basilius, Theophilus, Dionysius,* and *Agnes.* Book Two contains the six dramas, based, formally she claims, on Terentian comedy for whose morally perilous but aesthetically alluring mimetic powers she wished to substitute the glorious and morally beneficial ideals of militantly chaste virginal Christianity. She chose the dramatic form, she argues, because the sweetness of Terence's style and expression attracted many (unsophisticated) readers who, in turn, became corrupted by the wickedness of his subject matter. It is in contrast to these readers that Hrotsvit presents herself as a privileged, capable, sophisticated reader, willing to brave the dangers of corruption in order to fulfil the programmatic mission of her name and give effective, persuasive, but also pleasing testimony for Christ, Christianity, and the world of monasticism.

Of her six plays two (*Gallicanus* and *Calimachus*) are conversion plays, two (*Abraham* and *Pafnutius*) depict the salvation of repentant harlots, and two (*Dulcitius* and *Sapientia*) deal with the martyrdom of three allegorical virgins during the persecutions of Diocletian and Hadrian respectively. Her two extant epics, finally, narrate the rise of the Ottonian dynasty (*Gesta Ottonis*) and the foundation of Gandersheim Abbey (*Primordia*). Throughout all her works Hrotsvit extols the ideals of monastic (especially eremitical) Christianity and exhorts her audience and readers to imitate and emulate her saintly models and examples.

New Testimonies: The Contents of This Volume

Approximately 1000 years after Hrotsvit of Gandersheim ceased to write in Saxony, a group of American scholars gathered in California to celebrate her life, her works, her accomplishments, especially her contributions to the world of letters. It was not an unusual gathering as far as the make-up of the medievalists was concerned, for the group included historians, literary scholars, linguists, classicists, theologians, and the like, but it was a rather unusual gathering for the longevity and spirit of cooperation among the participants. This was no random collection of Hrotsvit specialists delivering papers on diverse aspects of Hrotsvit research but a gathering of friends reuniting after two years of intensive work stimulated by the 1997 NEH Summer Institute directed by Jane Chance at Rice University, which focused on early women writers and included a week-long seminar on the Saxon canoness. Not surprisingly, therefore, the research shared and discussed at the conference resulted not in an amalgam of unrelated or tangentially relevant contributions to Hrotsvit scholarship, but in a cohesive, organic, and quite comprehensive investigation of Hrotsvit's art, her voice, and her world across the centuries.

The volume at hand presents that research in four sections. Section 1, 'Constructing a Context,' examines the historic, cultural, legal, and political contexts of Hrotsvit's works and locates her opus within the tenth-century aristocratic and clerical intellectual milieu. This section begins with Jay T. Lees's close analysis of the *Gesta Ottonis*, 'Hrotsvit of

Gandersheim and the Problem of Royal Succession in the East Frankish Kingdom,' in which Lees scrutinizes evidence of Hrotsvit's rather intricate understanding of the conflicting criteria for choosing a ruler in tenth-century Saxony. Lees argues that Hrotsvit shapes history so as to defend the Ottonian family's dynastic claim to the throne vis-à-vis the claims of individuals such as Otto and Henry I, privileging, thereby, the dynastic sources of legitimacy over individual claims. Hrotsvit's keenness is not limited to the political intricacies of Ottonian rule; she seems to be equally at home in legal matters as well. David Day's essay, 'The *Iudex Aequus*: Legality and Equity in Hrotsvit's *Basilius*,' focuses on one of Hrotsvit's hagiographic texts and explores the formidable legal acuity of the legend's Satan. Day argues that in *Basilius* Hrotsvit sophisticatedly details and ultimately resolves a complex tangle of promises and contractual obligations entered upon by the characters; that Hrotsvit thereby demonstrates a keen awareness of the principles of law and equity in tenth-century Germanic legal practice; and that she shows, perhaps, some familiarity with Roman legal concepts as well, especially the idea of the 'iudex aequus.'

Concern with outsiders or foreigners constitutes the subject of Linda A. McMillin's study, '"Weighed down with a thousand evils": Images of Muslims in Hrotsvit's *Pelagius*.' McMillin evaluates Hrotsvit's accuracy in describing her Islamic neighbours in Spain. The first Northern European to do so in the tale about the Cordoban boy-martyr, Pelagius, Hrotsvit combines fact and stereotype to present the formidable military and political threat of Islam while reassuring her audience that the power of the Christian God and his virgin martyrs will inevitably confound this new enemy. The section as a whole affirms a talented and singularly well-informed writer with clear a political and ideological agenda who placed her literary skills in the service of her patrons, both secular and religious, and used them in the glorification of her national and monastic identity.

Section 2, 'Forming Identities,' showcases the works of four scholars who contextualize Hrotsvit's works with respect to heroic, sexual, domestic, behavioural, linguistic, theological, and hierarchical aspects of early medieval and patristic literary traditions. Florence Newman's contribution, 'Violence and Virginity in Hrotsvit's Dramas,' leads us from the archetypal heroic to the ascetically heroic orientation of (female) virginal characters in Hrotsvit's works. She explores the dramas' preoccupation with women's bodies and the threats to those bodies, particularly the dangers to sexual chastity. Newman argues that Hrotsvit evokes the erotic in order to de-eroticize the female body and, thus, to affirm rather than condemn the achievement of Christian sanctity of the flesh. By sketching the various theological attitudes toward the body, Newman's work effectively contextualizes Hrotsvit's depiction of the corporeal as part of her celebration of the spiritual in the plays as she complicates and problematizes the virginal ideal and the body as the site of struggle and salvation. Children and family positions are the subject of Daniel T. Kline's essay, 'Kids Say the Darndest Things: Irascible Children in Hrotsvit's *Sapientia*.' By paying careful attention to Hrotsvit's Ottonian context and to the nuances of age and family position in the play, Kline offers a reconsideration of important questions of sexual violence, power, and the formation of a normative female Christian subject in Hrotsvit's works. No sentimental depictions of the innocence of childhood, he argues, the children in *Sapientia* enact the moral didacticism of the play and exemplify the value of Christian virginity while subverting the conventional masculine hierarchy, ultimately to question Sapientia's 'parenting toward death.'

Identity formation, in this case the desire for a transcendent identity, is the subject of Ronald Stottlemyer's essay, 'The Construction of the Desiring Subject in Hrotsvit's *Pelagius* and *Agnes*.' He argues that the attitudes and behaviour of Hrotsvit's heroic virgin martyrs in the legends allow Hrotsvit to mediate between the urgings of her own inward subjectivity and an objectified reality that would erase them. Concerns with sexuality, religion, and the self, addressed by all essays in this section, are persuasively linked to the political and ideological foci of the first section in the final contribution of section 2 by Ulrike Wiethaus, '*Pulchrum Signum*? Sexuality and the Politics of Religion in the Works of Hrotsvit of Gandersheim.' Awareness of the nexus of Saxon royal politics, religion, and sexuality, Wiethaus argues, and of Hrotsvit's identity as a woman, facilitates our understanding of positive ideas of sexuality and the way sexual transgressions function in Hrotsvit's works. On the one hand, Hrotsvit explores and even celebrates in her works the Christian patriarchal idea of womanhood defined as female strength in the service of male sexual ownership, female eloquence in the service of Christian ideology, female loyalty unto death to male authority figures who insist on their power over them. Her voice, in other words, comes at a price. Paradoxically, however, the essay concludes, Hrotsvit's self-definitions as author (and one may add, reader) in the prefatory texts build around inversions of these hierarchical systems.

While sections 1 and 2 contextualize Hrotsvit's texts and illuminate her art by analysing her awareness and use of intellectual, historic, religious, political, and ideological currents of her milieu and time, section 3, 'Creating Affinities,' explores other literary texts that inform Hrotsvit's works. This section begins with Robert Talbot's essay 'Hrotsvit's Dramas: Is There a Roman in These Texts?' in which he explores Terentian elements in the canoness's plays. The key to recognizing Terentian elements in Hrotsvit's dramas, he argues, is to notice how she converts them for use in her spiritual vision, noting especially her conversions of Terentian fathers into Roman emperors and spiritual fathers, and Terentian sons into young female Christian virginal females. Phyllis R. Brown's essay, 'Hrotsvit's Sapientia as a Foreign Woman,' traces Sapientia's characterization as a foreigner to biblical sources that help elucidate the antagonism between her Wisdom and Hadrian. Hrotsvit may simultaneously depict not only the present reality of Sapientia specifically, of women generally, and of foreigners finding their way in a man's world, Brown concludes, but also the promise of a better world made possible by Christ's incarnation, and of a salvation theology of equivalence over the creation theology of subordination.

In the third essay of section 3, 'Hrotsvit and the Devil,' Patricia Silber argues that, quite surprisingly, Hrotsvit's plays do not simply feature the devil in the guise familiar from patristic and apocryphal sources, that is, as the tempter always on the lookout for ways to outwit God's plan for redemption. Rather, as in later dramatic traditions, the human characters of her plays frequently are bent on perpetrating evil and are given attributes associated with the devil. Significantly, however, Hrotsvit emphasizes the comic rather than the threatening – in effect ridiculing the power of both the devil and his minions, and perhaps reassuring her audience, as she does in her legends, of the power of God and Christianity in the face of demonic enemies.

Section 3 concludes with a final intertextual study of Hrotsvit's art, Jane Chance's 'Hrotsvit's Latin Drama *Gallicanus* and the Old English Epic *Elene*: Intercultural Founding Narratives of a Feminized Church.' Chance suggests that the similarities between the two texts contribute to the growing understanding of feminization in the early church reflected by the reliance on female rather than male agency and on process as spiritual rather than martial.

Section 4, 'Conducting Performances,' is devoted to the exploration of Hrotsvit's theatre and theatricality beginning with Debra L. Stoudt's examination of the survival of Hrotsvit's plays and her dramatic fortunes in subsequent centuries. 'Hrotsvit's Literary Legacy' studies four nineteenth- and twentieth-century authors who took their inspirations from Hrotsvit's works. Stoudt analyses the ranges of these authors' debt to Hrotsvit as varying from mere inspiration to substantive use, and abuse, concluding with Peter Hacks's 'Rosie Träumt,' a fantastic mélange of four of Hrotsvit's plays inspired by the commemoration of the assumed anniversary year of her death. Janet Snyder's essay, '"Bring me a soldier's garb and a good horse": Embedded Stage Directions in the Dramas of Hrotsvit of Gandersheim,' turns to the probability of dramatic performance of the plays suggested by internal cues in the language. Snyder analyses direct statements in the plays about entrances, exits, recognitions, disguises, and actions that function to direct performance, much as a modern writer/director does.

Jane E. Jeffrey's wonderfully irreverent contribution, 'Dramatic Convergence in Times Square: Hrotsvit's *Sapientia* and Collapsable Giraffe's *3 Virgins*,' brings Hrotsvit's theatrical dramaticality right up to the second millennium. As she discusses the 1999 production of *Three Virgins* by Collapsable Giraffe (an adaptation of *Sapientia*), in a former sex superstore in Times Square, she suggests that a full millennium after Hrotsvit voiced her concerns on this matter, public rituals still debase women in ways remarkably similar to those Sapientia and her daughters experience in the play. Finally, the concluding essay of the volume, Michael A. Zampelli's 'Playing with Hrotsvit: Adventures in Contemporary Performance,' reflects on the successful February 2000 productions of two of Hrotsvit's plays at Santa Clara University. Zampelli, who directed the performances, explores the ways of performing these tenth-century comic dramas without undermining them with farce and, at the same time, highlighting their contemporary moral/religious relevance without insisting on any particular religious/political world view or shared certainty about the meaning of life.

Including discussions of politics, marriage, religion, personal and corporate (monastic/aristocratic) identity, as well as dramatic and legal acumen, this volume, thus, spans more than a thousand years and two continents in its scholarly focus of investigation, and it pays tribute to the richness, diversity, and relevance of Hrotsvit's art throughout the centuries. It does so employing a myriad of critical approaches ranging from feminist theoretical to historic and philological approaches of investigation.

Muliercula: The Construction Complex Voices

Who was Hrotsvit the author? Hrotsvit the dramatist? Hrotsvit the woman? Hrotsvit the Saxon? Hrotsvit the Benedictine religious? Hrotsvit the epic

historian? As an author, Hrotsvit's claim to fame stands fairly well established. Her linguistic polish, rhetorical ornamentation, sense of ambiguity, sustained irony, self-referenced authorial awareness, effective
didacticism, and multi-layered narration all have elicited at one time or
another either praise for her art or accusations that her works must be
forgeries. She is, indeed, a statistical anomaly. In a world dominated by
male, warrior values, with a male educated elite laying almost exclusive
claim to the written word, she wrote, she wrote prolifically, and she wrote
in competent, carefully ornamented Latin. Her dramas, in particular,
include fascinating experimentation with the genre. Generic hybrids in
good tenth-century fashion, they graft her hagiographic materials onto
dramatic form and create, thereby, the first known Christian plays. Clearly,
hers is a privileged voice but also a voice that came at a price: all her
saintly heroes (be they male or female) are paradigms of aristocratic and
clerical normalcy; all her heroes are paragons of the hierarchical aristocratic and ecclesiastic system of values; her constructions of female worth
are entirely orthodox and canonical. Where her gender makes itself
known is in the choice of materials and in the preponderance of female
protagonists in her texts; that is to say, while she does not reevaluate
behavioural desiderata for her female characters nor does she pay any
attention to individuals or groups of people either less fortunate than
she and her peers (there is not a single mention of the plight of the poor
or the existence of non gentility), vice, often coupled with paganism,
does become the almost exclusive prerogative of men, and her works
abound in exempla of female virtue, albeit traditional.

   Although Hrotsvit's originality, self-assurance, and even courage are
not necessarily gender-specific, she frequently ties them to, and skilfully
manipulates, gender identities. In the prefatory texts for example, she
carefully distances herself as reader/writer from the crowd of vulnerable
(because unsophisticated) readers when she proclaims her willingness to
brave the dangers of aesthetic allurements in Terence's wicked subject
matter in order to provide her readers with mimetically acceptable and
stylistically appealing exempla of Christian/monastic virtue. However,
her emphasis in that brave attempt is primarily placed on her individu-
ally: on her *qua* Hrotsvit not on her *qua* woman. At the same time, she
masterfully manipulates gender references and identities both to define
her authorship and to promote the idea of a gender- neutral ideal of
Christian monastic virtue.

   In addition to the conventional self-deprecatory references regarding
authorial deficiencies in style and diction (such as rusticity and lack of

ornamentation), Hrotsvit's prefaces also abound in the use of diminutives used as pejorative signifiers denoting the lack of grandeur, skill, and standing of both author and work. On reading retrospectively, however, we discover that these humility formulas and diminutives become self-confident assertions of authorial confidence and sophisticatedly ironic commentaries on the intersections of different ontological planes: it is not only Hrotsvit the writer who describes herself as 'muliercula' (little woman); she places that same term in the mouths of her pagan persecutors as well. In situations of grand heroism, as frail Christian virgins triumphantly humiliate their (male) persecutors and literally decimate pagan onlookers, the persecutors refer to them in these diminutives. Read analogously to Hrotsvit's self-referential statements of authorial intent and skill, these deprecatory phrases go well beyond the topoi and become assertions of confidence, or perhaps even attempts at transcending the traditional hierarchies of gender in ethical and intellectual categories.

We hope that this volume will succeed in anchoring Hrotsvit in her specific social, political, religious, and aesthetic milieu, and exploring her fortunes, and the inner world of her characters. We also hope that our tribute to her art, her keen awareness of contemporary issues, and her determination within the parameters of her monastic-aristocratic ideological constraints to provide her readers with a slew of exemplary female heroes and with literary acts of personal courage will contribute to the continued flourishing of her appeal to the twenty-first-century reader.

Texts and Translations

Throughout this collection of essays, citations of Hrotsvit's works are noted parenthetically and are from her *Opera Omnia*, edited by Walter Berschin (2001); translations are, whenever possible, Katharina M. Wilson's, published in *Hrotsvit of Gandersheim: A Florilegium of Her Works* (1998) or *The Plays of Hrotsvit of Gandersheim* (1989). The exceptions are translations of *Gongolfus*, *Theophilus*, and *Agnes* by M. Gonsalva Wiegand, from her dissertation 'The Non-Dramatic Works of Hrosvitha: Text, Translation, and Commentary' (1936); of *Gesta Ottonis* by Mary Bernardine Bergman, from her dissertation, 'Hrosvithae Liber Tertius: A Text with Translation, Introduction and Commentary' (1942); and occasional translations by contributors to the volume, as indicated.

SECTION 1

Constructing a Context

Hrotsvit of Gandersheim and the Problem of Royal Succession in the East Frankish Kingdom

JAY T. LEES

The *Gesta Ottonis,* which tells the story of Saxon rule in Germany from the accession of Henry I to Otto I's imperial coronation in Rome, is in many ways the most perplexing work of Hrotsvit of Gandersheim's literary oeuvre. It, even more than the *Primordia,* her history of Gandersheim, calls for placement within a historical context. While the poems and plays appear as stories Hrotsvit uses for dramatic and didactic purposes, and the *Primordia* tells a story close to the author's own heart, the *Gesta* versifies events of the recent past, events beyond the walls of Gandersheim. In this poem, Hrotsvit enters the political arena outside her abbey.[1] This essay focuses on a single issue, mentioned in Hrotsvit's *Gesta* in what seem to be rather simplistic terms, to demonstrate that the canoness has packed more meaning into her words than at first may appear and to show that she both grasped what was at stake and made a poetic case for what she deemed right.[2] The issue is that of legitimate royal succession in the East Frankish Kingdom.[3]

In the closing lines of the dedicatory prologue that Hrotsvit addressed to Otto I himself, she tells her ruler that she will recount his deeds up until the time of his imperial coronation in Rome in 962. However, Hrotsvit chooses to begin her poem neither with Otto's birth nor with his succession to the royal dignity in the East Frankish Kingdom in 936, but with the ascension of the ducal house of Saxony to the East Frankish throne in 919 when Otto's father, Henry I, became king. Thus the context into which Hrotsvit places Otto's imperial coronation is not merely that of his own *gesta* but that of the broader claim of the ducal house of Saxony to the East Frankish throne. That claim presented several problems concerning legitimate succession.

Since the middle of the eighth century, the Frankish Kingdom had been ruled by members of the Carolingian family. In the ninth century, the kingdom splintered into several parts due to its partition among the heirs of Carolingian rulers. In the eastern kingdom, the Carolingians maintained their hold on the throne until 911, when the last of that branch, Louis the Child, died without an heir. Faced with this extinction of the royal dynasty, nobles from Saxony, Franconia, Swabia, and Bavaria assembled and elected one of their own, Conrad of Franconia, as King Conrad I. Before Conrad died in 918, he may have designated Henry of Saxony as his successor. However, the next year only the Franconians and the Saxons elected Henry to succeed Conrad; Henry was recognized as king by all only after several years of squabbling. His son Otto succeeded him in 936 as Otto I; he is the subject of Hrotsvit's *Gesta*. Otto could claim the crown on the basis of having been chosen by his father and by a somewhat tenuous claim to be his father's oldest son.[4] However, past events had created precedents for other means of selecting rulers: election, designation of someone outside the ruling family, and partition of a kingdom among the sons of a ruler.

When the nobles chose Conrad I to rule the East Frankish Kingdom in 911, they were invoking a principle of election traceable to the Frankish invaders of the Roman Empire.[5] Even the Carolingian usurpation of the Merovingian throne by Pepin the Short was described by one chronicler as an *electio*, and election remained a part of the process of succession in Carolingian times.[6] Though an important part of succession, for the most part election was a formality in which nobles affirmed or acclaimed an uncontested claimant rather than 'elected' him.[7] With the extinction of the eastern Carolingian house in 911, however, the nobles faced several alternatives: go their own way with each ducal house choosing its own king, look west for a Carolingian (Charles the Simple was ruling in the West Frankish Kingdom, Louis the Blind in Provence), or choose one among themselves to replace the Carolingians. The significance of their choice to do the last of these and select the non-Carolingian Conrad as their king has been downplayed in recent historiography because he was a Frank and would rule under Frankish law like his predecessors. The choice was, in other words, a conservative one.[8] However, one can also argue that the significance of the 911 election for the future depended on Conrad's ability to turn it to the advantage of his own family by creating a new dynasty. His failure to do so allowed the principle of election to reassert itself, only this time the problem of such an election was demonstrated by its lack of unanimity and concomitant interducal strife.

The passage of the crown from Conrad to Henry also shows another possible determinant of legitimate succession. Widukind of Corvey, Liudprand of Cremona, and Adalbert, author of the 'Continuatio Reginonis,' all contemporaries of Hrotsvit, indicate that Conrad designated Henry of Saxony as his successor.[9] Earlier, Carolingian rulers had often designated successor sons for royal dignities, and Henry I would also do so in designating Otto as his successor. Conrad's designation was more dramatic as it called for moving the crown from one family to another.

The third principle of succession was that of partition of the kingdom among the sons of a ruler. This meant that on a royal father's death, kingdoms were inconveniently divided up to satisfy his male offspring.[10] Henry I had more than one son, and his decision not to partition his kingdom but to invoke the idea of an inalienable kingdom by declaring Otto his sole successor was without precedent.[11] Indeed, two of Henry's other sons did raise a loud voice of protest and more than one rebellion against their brother's pretensions.[12] In the early tenth century, the issue of succession was thus not simple. Claims of birthright, election, and designation competed with each other as factors to be applied in establishing the legitimacy of a candidate.

After Otto I became king in Germany in 936, his claim of legitimate succession did not go uncontested, as Otto's brother Henry tried on more than one occasion to overthrow his older sibling and take the crown for himself. Thus there were serious attempts to apply principles of succession which would undermine Otto's claim to the throne. Henry, however, was decisively defeated in 941. By the time Hrotsvit wrote the *Gesta* in the 960s,[13] Otto's personal claim was secure. So whatever Hrotsvit's reason for writing, it was not to enter an ongoing fray by defending Otto against his detractors. That battle was over. One may therefore suggest that Hrotsvit wrote the *Gesta* with an eye to the future.[14] Hrotsvit was a Saxon, almost without doubt a scion of a noble Saxon family;[15] she was a member of a Saxon religious foundation for women, a foundation created by the Ludolfinger family, which had produced Henry I and Otto the Great.[16] Clearly, it was in her best interests, not to mention those of her abbess Gerberga II and the other religious of Gandersheim, to see the Ottonian line continue. A glance at the past she was studying for her poem would have revealed the tenuous nature of the claims of German rulers since Louis the Child. Conrad I could not keep the crown in his own family; Henry I had immediately faced the refusal of the Bavarians and Swabians to participate in his election (the Bavarians went so far as to elect their own 'king');[17] Otto faced rebellions joined or led by his own relatives.[18] Otto was, in fact, the only son to succeed his father as king since Louis the Child, whereas the two other rulers since Louis had received the crown by election. Great as Otto was, there had been considerable questioning of and resistance to his claim to be the legitimate ruler.

Commentators on the *Gesta* have pointed out that Hrotsvit does not mention Conrad I but jumps right to the Saxons and Henry I.[19] This emphasis gives the impression that Hrotsvit is passively excluding Conrad. However, Hrotsvit is much more aggressive in her dismissal of the Franconian ruler. In fact, she begins her poem by wielding a verbal sword, namely the words *Postquam rex regum* (1), meaning 'After the king of kings' or 'When the king of kings' or with a poetic sense, 'Because the king of kings.' However translated, this phrase focuses the reader on what God did in the past, from which what proceeds will take its meaning. The sword cuts time, cuts history as it were. The *antequam* lies outside our purview, outside the meaning of the poem. Where the sword falls is thus profoundly significant, for the *antequam* will get no history from Hrotsvit.

The *postquam* refers to God's transfer of power over the kingdom of the Franks to the Saxon people:

> Postquam rex regum ...
> Iussit Francorum transferri nobile regnum
> Ad claram gentem Saxonum nomen habentem   (1, 3–4)[20]

So clean is Hrotsvit's cut in time that we are not told from whom or from what people the transfer is made. On which side of the *postquam* do the principles of designation (Conrad I's designation of Henry as his heir) and election (the election of Henry by several, but not all, of the dukes of the kingdom) fall? Of the accuracy of the accounts of Conrad's designation of Henry let it be said that there is considerable disagreement among historians.[21] We cannot be sure that Hrotsvit was aware of it, though its appearance in three contemporary accounts suggests strongly that it was well enough known for one searching out the history of Otto and his father to have heard it.[22] But it is impossible to believe that Hrotsvit was unaware of the election. It is therefore not just Conrad (and this whether or not Hrotsvit knew the story of the designation) but the election by the nobles that Hrotsvit removes from the reader's consideration. That election is replaced by another kind of election: God's.[23] Hrotsvit avoids a conflict between the notion that the nobles elected

Henry and that God elected Henry by beginning with the concept that God transferred power to the Saxon people rather than to one man.[24]

Historical scholarship has shown that Hrotsvit's allusion to power being transferred (*transferri*) to the Saxon people derives from the biblical passage in which Daniel says that God *transfert regna, atque constituit*.[25] What has gone unnoticed is that this reliance on biblical allusions continues as Hrotsvit proceeds to describe the Saxon people. She connects the worthiness of the Saxons to receive the right to rule with an etymology for the word *Saxon*. Widukind of Corvey also gives an etymology of *Saxon* by tracing it to the Germanic *sahs* meaning knife and therefore attributing to the Saxons' favoured weapon the origin of their name.[26] Hrotsvit, on the other hand, finds the meaning of *Saxon* in the Latin word *saxum*, a stone or rock. This etymology defines Saxons not in terms of an aggressive and violent nature, but rather in terms of resolute strength. Moreover, Hrotsvit brings the idea of a transfer of power by the King of Kings together with her presentation of the Saxons as 'rock':

> ... rex regum, qui solus regnat in ęvum
> Per se cunctorum transmutans tempora regum,
> Iussit Francorum transferri nobile regnum
> Ad claram gentem Saxonum nomen habentem
> A saxo per duriciam mentis bene firmam,   (1–5)

> ... the king of kings who alone reigns for eternity,
> Himself allotting the times of kings
> commanded that the renowned kingdom of the Franks
> be transferred to the illustrious Saxon people,
> who derive their name from rock because of their firm strength.

There is here a clear echo of Matthew 16:18 where Christ says to Peter, 'You are Peter (*Petrus*) and I will found my church upon this rock (*petra*).' This famous verse was used by the papacy to support its claim to primacy in the church since Peter supposedly died as bishop of Rome. Hrotsvit has taken this scriptural description of Christ founding an institution and applied it to the Saxons. Hrotsvit clearly wants to emphasize this institutional claim, not the claims of individual rulers.[27] According to her, the length of those rulers' reigns is limited by the eternal King, but the Saxons have been chosen to endure. As usual, Hrotsvit does not spell things out for the reader, but neither does she make difficult the leap to rendering her words something like, 'You are the

Rock (Saxons) and on this rock (*saxum*) I will found ... ' And here at the beginning of the poem one can already see its end, for as Peter moved to Rome so too will the Saxons with Otto's imperial coronation.

Hrotsvit deals with Henry I's succession in the next lines of the poem: 'Filius ...,/ Scilicet Henricus, suscepit regia primus' (6–7). This happens *postquam* God transferred authority to the Saxons. Hrotsvit's juxtaposition of *postquam* with Henry's succession is not merely the rendering of a chronological sequence of events: after God transferred ... then Henry took up ... Her *postquam* is causative, meaning 'since' or 'because': because God transferred power to the Saxons, Henry became king. Henry, she says, *suscepit* kingly authority. *Suscepit* can be translated in an active sense: Henry 'took up' royal authority. Here there is no need for an agent designating or electing Henry; he is his own agent. However, *suscepit* can also be given a passive sense: Henry 'received' royal authority. If we ask why Henry became king, the answer must be either that he took the royal throne because God gave authority to the Saxons or that by virtue of being the leader of the Saxons, he received it from God. God's choice of the Saxons is in either case the cause of Henry's succession, not just its chronological predecessor. There is neither room nor need to place a ducal election between God's granting power to the Saxons and Henry's taking the crown; nor is there a sense of Henry's being chosen on the basis of individual merits. While Hrotsvit will go on to praise the good qualities of King Henry, and as we shall see, she will not ignore election in the case of Otto I, the constitutive factor she emphasizes at the beginning of the poem is the election of the Saxon people by God, and whatever else Henry might offer, his sine qua non for holding power is, according to Hrotsvit, that he is a Saxon. Other criteria for succession are either left outside of the time frame of the poem (Conrad's designation) or removed from consideration (the ducal election). One should note that both designation and election could work to change a ruling house, and indeed, in the cases of Conrad and Henry they had done just that. While a ruler might use the fact of his designation or election to legitimize his own individual rule, for Hrotsvit the crucial issue is the legitimacy of a dynasty;[28] in the beginning of her poem she casts aside criteria for succession that could endanger an Ottonian royal monopoly.

Hrotsvit's justification of Otto's succession to the throne begins with her description of the three sons of Henry I. This passage appears straightforward enough. God granted King Henry and his wife the three sons Otto, Henry, and Brun

Ne post Henrici mortem, regis venerandi,
Imperium regni male surriperent scelerosi,
Hi sed regalis nati de germine stirpis
Rexissent regnum concordi pace paternum;
Quamvis dissimiles his servarentur honores
Binis regnanti subiectis scilicet uni.   (27–32)

so that after the death of the venerable King Henry,
wicked men could not seize power in the kingdom by evil means,
but that these born of royal lineage
would rule the paternal kingdom in harmonious peace,
although different honors would be destined for them,
two subject to the ruling one.[29]

A king without sons could be viewed as having been cursed,[30] and in her description of the fruitful Henry, Hrotsvit may well have meant to evoke his unfruitful predecessor Conrad in the mind of the reader: God's choice of the Saxons is apparent in the offspring of the present king; Conrad was a dead-end. This passage has also been seen as alluding to the principle of partition by which all the sons of a deceased king participated in ruling.[31] Hrotsvit does create a sense of the equality of the three brothers: All three are to bring peace to the kingdom, all three in some sense rule (*rexissent*). However, Hrotsvit had herself never experienced such a division of inheritance in the East Frankish Kingdom; she specifically speaks of the brother Brun as being earmarked for the clergy (53–60); and her poem as a whole overwhelmingly supports Otto's claim to rule the entire kingdom. Moreover, if Hrotsvit is referring to partition here, she has made an inadvertent and clumsy blunder for any mention of partition could potentially serve to undermine her real point, namely that Otto should rule the other brothers. Or is it that Hrotsvit is fully conscious of what she is saying and has some reason for describing the three as equals that has nothing to do with partition?

Hrotsvit goes on to relate that one of Otto's brothers himself became a potential usurper. This was Henry, later duke of Bavaria.[32] He was in a most awkward position at his father's death. Henry I played both on an idea of primogeniture, unheard of in earlier times when the kingdom was divided, and on one of designation by choosing Otto as his successor as early as 929.[33] With this designation, the principle of partition had fallen by the wayside. While to a great extent it was understood that Henry could not divide his kingdom at the expense of the nobility ruling in its various duchies, this left the son Henry with no claim to a royal inheritance.[34] However, a new justification was made for excluding the elder Otto from succession to the throne, namely that he was born while his father was only duke of Saxony, not king. In contrast, his brother Henry was the firstborn during Henry I's reign; he was born the son of a king. In seeking a rationale for succession in the East Frankish Kingdom, the claimants had no precedent except the election of Conrad I and the election and designation of Henry I, neither of which involved notions of familial succession. If the kingdom was not to be divided, the game of succession had to be played for the whole,[35] and the confusion wrought by conflicting filial claims opened the door to other rationales for succession.

Sources other than Hrotsvit tell us that the principle of being the first son born after the father had become king was used in support of Henry of Bavaria. Liudprand of Cremona, Hrotsvit's contemporary, says that Henry of Bavaria was urged to rebel against his brother by being asked if it were right that his father had favored Otto since 'you [Henry] were born to the royal dignity, [Otto] was not born in the same.'[36] Further-more, a later biography of Henry of Bavaria's mother Matilde alludes to Henry as being 'born to the royal dignity' (in regali solio natus) and 'born in the royal palace' (natus in aula regali).[37] Matilde's biography was written in the reign of Henry II, the grandson of Henry of Bavaria, and it shows that the notion scornfully presented by Liudprand, a de-voted servant of Otto, continued to resonate with the Henrican side of the family.[38] Conceivably, Hrotsvit, who does not mention the young Henry's claim, was nevertheless aware of it, and one of her goals in the *Gesta* was to undermine Henry's pretension by emphasizing the prin-ciple of clear-cut primogeniture unencumbered by the idea of being first-born to a reigning king.[39]

When Hrotsvit turns to the rebellions of Henry of Bavaria in the *Gesta*, she demonstrates considerable knowledge of the course of events but skirts the historical cause with recourse to the supernatural. It is 'antiqui ... inimici' (166 and 203), the ancient foe or wicked enemy, who insidi-ously provokes nobles close to Henry into giving him evil advice. How-ever, Hrotsvit describes this advice only by having the rebels tell Henry that he could receive the kingdom to rule by deposing his brother (219–20: 'Ipsorum votis sed plus parendo nefandis/ Susciperet regnum depulso fratre regendum'). This is not advice but a gross bribe, which fits uneas-ily with Hrotsvit's portrait of sly nobles coaxing Henry with flattery and winning him over with viciously delusive persuasions: 'Mulcentes nimium verbis ipsum male blandis' (216) and 'Qui male blanditis tandem victus suadelis' (220). These latter persuasions indicate Hrotsvit's conviction that the nobles convinced Henry not just that he *could* be king but that he *should* be king. The argument that Henry was born to a ruling monarch while Otto was not would have been a clever way to undermine Otto's claim to the throne with a point of fact. Indeed, it is an argument which, from Hrotsvit's perspective, might best be left unmentioned but at the same time could not go unchallenged. For the evidence that Hrotsvit was aware of this argument and attempted to counter it, we must return to the beginning of the *Gesta* and her presentation of Otto and his two brothers as harmoniously ruling the kingdom.

Hrotsvit's presentation of the brothers ruling together has been interpreted as referring to the custom of partitioning a kingdom, illogical as this is in the context of Hrotsvit's wish that Otto rule the other brothers.[40] However, if the passage is read not as a thoughtless parroting of the idea of partition but as a reaction to the young Henry's argument that by virtue of his royal birth he was more worthy than Otto to inherit the throne, then this statement shows Hrotsvit assaulting what for her would have been a dangerous idea by claiming the same dignity for all the brothers.

What is striking about Hrotsvit's further portrayal of Otto is her repeated insistence that he among the sons of King Henry is *primus*.[41] She says the three sons were given dissimilar honours, one to rule and the others to be subject to him, by calling Otto 'interquos primus' (33), among them the first. Widukind describes Otto's position vis-à-vis the brothers more clearly, calling him *primogenitus*.[42] Hrotsvit's use of verse may have forced her to be more succinct.[43] On the other hand, *primus* connotes more than *primogenitus*. It supports not only Otto's claim of being firstborn but suggests that he is 'first' in the sense of best or most suited to rule and links him to Henry I whom Hrotsvit also describes as being *primus* to rule.[44] Firstborn and greatest are, however, combined a few lines later when Hrotsvit describes Otto as 'Hic aetate prior fuerat, meritis quoque maior' (37), superior in age and greater in merits. When she introduces the young Henry it is with 'Post hunc Henricus fuerat feliciter ortus' (46: After [Otto], Henry was opportunely born), clearly establishing a ranking by birth. The point is made even more strongly when Hrotsvit presents us with Edith and Adiva, the two noble sisters sent by their brother King Athelstan of England to Henry's court. King Henry, says Hrotsvit, arranged for Edith to be betrothed to Otto, 'suo primogenito regique futuro' (70: his firstborn and the future king). In this line *primogenitus* is directly linked with succession to the throne. Also, one may note that Hrotsvit alludes to the notion that with this marriage Henry I designated Otto as his successor, but she touches on it ever so lightly. Designation is not what she wants to emphasize but that Otto was the first son given by God to the ruling Saxon family. The obverse is presented not with the young Henry but with Adiva, the younger sister who accompanies Edith, for Hrotsvit similarly ranks the sisters: '[Adiva] fuit ętatis meriti pariterque minoris' (113: [Adiva] was younger and therefore less meritorious). Here and with no reference to Henry, Hrotsvit again establishes a ranking by birth.[45]

With her description of Otto's actual succession to the throne Hrotsvit's emphasis on the firstborn continues:

> Quo nam defuncto regnum susceperat Oddo,
> Euisdem primogenitus regis venerandus;
> Et voto cunti iam respondente popelli
> Unguitur in regem Christo prestante potentem.   (128–31)

> With [Henry I's] death, Otto had taken up the kingdom,
> the venerable firstborn of the king,
> and with the responding prayer of the whole people,
> he was anointed into royal power in Christ's presence.

As presented by Hrotsvit, the constitutive factor in Otto's becoming king after Henry's death is that he is the firstborn. We note that Otto had taken up (*susceperat*) the kingdom, a clear echo of Henry's accession when he was the first who took up (*suscepit primus*) the kingdom. The sense here is that God's kingdom founded on the Saxons moves naturally by the principle of primogeniture from a ruler to his eldest son. 'Et voto cunti iam respondente popelli' (130) has been said to refer to an election.[46] While this may to some extent be true, Hrotsvit's use of the word *votum* lends considerable ambiguity to what actually transpired. *Votum* connotes a prayer or an oath of allegiance,[47] and attached as it is to *respondente* in a phrase modifying 'he was anointed into the royal power,' it conjures up the image of an acclamation or an affirmation rather than of an election. The nobles who 'elected' Otto in 936 can perhaps be glimpsed among Hrotsvit's *popellus*,[48] but no more than that. While anointing is introduced and may even be seen as constitutive ('Unguitur in regem ... potentem'), the one doing the anointing is not mentioned, only that the rite is done in the presence of Christ, which harkens back to the King of Kings transferring the kingdom to the Saxons.[49]

There is a defensiveness to Hrotsvit's repeated insistence that the firstborn of a king is especially meritorious and that a firstborn son should succeed the father. What provoked this, I would suggest, was the young Henry's claim that he was firstborn during his father's reign. Hrotsvit's counter is twofold: she accentuates firstborn without any qualifications or commentary;[50] then she gives no description or explanation of the rebellious nobles' deadly persuasions of the young Henry to oppose his brother.

Hrotsvit's silence on the rationale behind Henry's rebellions rings as loudly as her repeated affirmations that Otto was born first. When Hrotsvit shows Henry throwing his lot in with the rebels in order to take the throne, she gives no justification such as Henry's claim to being firstborn to the royal dignity. Indeed, she inserts her pious hope (*spero*) that Henry did not really mean it (223).[51] And as for Henry's last rebellion in 941, Hrotsvit skilfully tells her story while avoiding even mentioning Henry's participation. A possible reason for Hrotsvit's light touch in handling Henry of Bavaria's treacheries and rebellions is that she was writing at the request of her abbess Gerberga who was herself Henry's daughter.[52] However, Henry and Otto had got along quite well from 941 until Henry's death in 955. From the perspective of the mid-960s, it would be peculiar for Gerberga to have asked for a poem about her uncle Otto, meant merely to defend the reputation of her father, which by that time was not in need of defending. Though Henry's son and Gerberga's brother, Henry the Wrangler, was duke of Bavaria when Hrotsvit wrote the *Gesta*, Gerberga was abbess of a foundation of religious located not in Bavaria but in Saxony. Her foundation was under the protection of her uncle Otto, a king who had just become emperor and who had a son with every prospect of succeeding him. In these circumstances, there was no compelling reason for Gerberga to request a poem written in defence of her father. More likely, the abbess asked for a poem which would serve her and Gandersheim's best interest by supporting the line of rulers seated squarely in Saxony.[53] For this is what the poem does. We read Hrotsvit's description of Henry of Bavaria's rebellions as an overly kind, dutiful, and simplistic effort to protect her abbess's father by attributing his attacks on Otto to the bad advice of evil friends. But we should note that Hrotsvit salvages the reputation of Henry of Bavaria by eliminating the principle of succession for which, in rebellion, he stood.

It is not just the principle of 'first born to a reigning king' that Hrotsvit eliminates. In *Gesta Ottonis*, the loud voice of Gandersheim defends the dynastic claims of the Ottonians by ignoring Conrad's use of designation to select someone from outside the ruling family as his successor, reducing the elective principle of the dukes to an acclamation, and forcefully allying herself with Henry I's idea of an inalienable kingdom to be passed on in its entirety to his eldest son. Her poem communicates a sense that Otto's succession was an easy one made on the basis of a well-established principle of the divine calling of the eldest son. What she does not say is that that principle was far from well established when she wrote and that her poem was meant, at least in part, to make it paramount.

NOTES

I am grateful to the Graduate School of the University of Northern Iowa for funding this project. I would like to thank Julie Lowell, Katharina Wilson, and the readers at the University of Toronto Press for their helpful suggestions. Translations of Latin quotations are my own.

1 Eggert, 'Das Wir-Gefühl bei fränkischen und deutschen Geschichtsschreibern bis zum Investitur-streit,' 88–9.
2 On Hrotsvit's concern for the politics of her time see Homeyer, *Hrotsvithae Opera*, 392, 398–402; Pätzold, 'Hrotsvit von Gandersheim: Lebensnormen und Wertvorstellungen,' 25–6. On the *Gesta*, in addition to works cited in the following notes, see Kratz, 'The *Gesta Ottonis* in Its Contexts'; Kratz, 'The Nun's Epic: Hroswitha on Christian Heroism'; Wilson, *Hrotsvit of Gandersheim: The Ethics of Authorial Stance*, 111–42; and Kirsch, 'Hrotsvit von Gandersheim als Epikerin.' For political concerns found in other of Hrotsvit's writings, see McMillin, '"Weighed Down with a Thousand Evils": Images of Muslims in Hrotsvit's *Pelagius*' in the present volume of essays and Wailes, 'Beyond Virginity: Flesh and Spirit in the Plays of Hrotsvit of Gandersheim.'
3 The literature on succession in the tenth century is immense, not least because it ties in closely with the issue of the origins of Germany. In general, see the series of articles in Hlawitschka, ed., *Königswahl und Thronfolge in ottonisch-frühdeutscher Zeit*; for a pugnacious work of synthesis, see Brühl, *Deutschland-Frankreich: Die Geburt zweier Völker*. For some recent views, see Schneidmüller, 'Reich-Volk-Nation'; Springer, 'Fragen zur Entstehung des

mittelalterlichen deutschen Reiches'; the articles in Brühl and Schneid-müller, *Beiträge zur mittelalterlichen Reichs- und Nationsbildung in Deutschland und Frankreich*; and Keller, 'Entscheidungssituationen und Lernprozesse in den "Anfangen der deutschen Geschichte."' The most recent book-length treatment of Otto is Laudage, *Otto der Grosse*. For an influential comparison of Henry I and Otto I, see Keller and Althoff, *Heinrich I. und Otto der Grosse*.

4 It should be noted that Otto had an older half-brother, Thankmar, son of Henry and his first wife, Hatheburg. Hrotsvit never mentions Thankmar and gives the impression that Otto was the oldest son. While I will leave Thankmar aside in the present essay, I do believe that Hrotsvit alludes to him in the *Gesta* and in her veiled way deals with the complicated issue of half-brothers (one that touched not only Otto but his own son, Otto II). See Lees, 'Political and Dramatic Irony,' 799–801.

5 Hubrich, 'Fränkisches Wahl- und Erbkönigtum zur Merovingerzeit.'

6 Schlesinger, 'Karolingische Königswahlen,' 191–2, 196.

7 Keller, 'Widukinds Bericht,' 118–19; Tellenbach, 'Die geistigen und politischen Grundlagen der karolingischen Thronfolge,' esp. 190–9, 258–71.

8 Brühl, *Deutschland-Frankreich*, 403; Reuter, *Germany in the Early Middle Ages, c. 800–1056*, 135.

9 Widukind of Corvey, 'Res gestae Saxonicae,' 25–6, pp. 56–9; Liudprand of Cremona, 'Antapodosis,' 2.20, pp. 314–15; Adalbert, 'Continuatio Reginonis,' 919, pp. 192–3.

10 Schmid, 'Die Thronfolge Ottos des Großen,' 445.

11 Keller, 'Widukinds Bericht,' 118, points out that while this was new for determining a ruler, it conformed with ideas of inheritance in the East Frankish duchies.

12 Along with Henry of Bavaria (see n. 38 below), Otto's half-brother Thankmar would also lead a revolt. See n. 4 above.

13 Ernst Karpf argues for dating the time of Hrotsvit's composition of the *Gesta* to the period between ca. 965 and 968; see *Herrscherlegitimation und Reichsbegriff*, 115–18. This represents a revision of the traditional dating to 962–5. See Köpke, *Hrotsvit von Gandersheim* 87–9; Schütze-Pflugk, *Herrscher- und Märtyrerauffassung bei Hrotsvit von Gandersheim*, 64.

14 Keller, 'Widukinds Bericht,' 407; Leyser, *Medieval Germany and Its Neighbors, 900–1250*, 13.

15 Wemple, 'Monastic Life of Women from the Merovingians to the Ottonians,' 45.

16 Althof, 'Gandersheim und Quedlinburg'; Goetting, *Das Bistum Hildesheim 1*, 81–5.

17 Brühl, *Deutschland-Frankreich*, 419–27.

18 For overviews of the rebellions see Laudage, 'Hausrecht und Thronfolge,' 55–71; Althoff, *Die Ottonen*, 81–7; Laudage, *Otto der Grosse*, 110–19; and Kamp, 'Konflikte und Konfliktführung in der Anfängen der Regierung Otto I.'

19 Karpf, *Herrscherlegitimation und Reichsbegriff*, 119–20; Pätzold, 'Die Auffassung des ostfränkisch-deutschen Reiches,' 226.

20 For a similar interpretation of the beginning of Hrotsvit's poem, see Pätzold, 'Die Auffassung des ostfränkisch-deutschen Reiches,' 223.

21 See Brühl, *Deutschland-Frankreich*, 415, 421–2 with n. 78. Johannes Fried has forcefully questioned the historicity of the story of the dying Conrad designating Henry as his successor, not least because Conrad would have been abandoning his entire family's claim to the throne. See Fried, 'Die Königserhebung,' 281–6. Fried triggered a sometimes acrimonious debate over the trustworthiness of tenth-century narrative histories. See Keller, 'Widukinds Bericht,' 101–2 and esp. p. 247 n. 82, with a good bibliography of the debate, and more recently, Althoff, 'Geschichtsschreibung in einer oralen Gesellschaft.' For the purposes of the present study, the accuracy of the story of Henry's designation is not an issue. Whether the story was created from whole cloth or not, its presence in the accounts of three tenth-century writers indicates a belief that designation was a powerful means of legitimizing a ruler.

22 Keller, 'Widukinds Bericht,' 451; cf. Fried, 'Die Königserhebung,' 289–91.

23 Rörig, 'Geblütsrecht und freie Wahl in ihrer Auswirkung auf die deutsche Geschichte,' 82–3.

24 Karpf, *Herrscherlegitimation und Reichsbegriff*, 119–20; Pätzold, 'Die Auffassung des ostfränkisch-deutschen Reiches,' 226.

25 Daniel 2:21. Goez, *Translatio imperii*, 6–7, 90; Pätzold, 'Die Auffassung des ostfränkisch-deutschen Reiches,' 230.

26 Widukind of Corvey, 'Res gestae Saxonicae,' 1.7, pp. 24–5.

27 Karpf, *Herrscherlegitimation und Reichsbegriff*, 119–21.

28 Bornscheuer, *Miseriae Regum*, 179.

29 On this passage, see Leyser, *Rule and Conflict*, 16.

30 Schmid, 'Die Thronfolge Ottos des Großen,' 419–21.

31 Laudage, 'Hausrecht und Thronfolge,' 64; Leyser, *Rule and Conflict*, 16.

32 Glocker, *Die Verwandten der Ottonen und ihre Bedeutung in der Politik*, 53–80, 285–6. Henry became duke of Bavaria only in 947, but at times I will refer to him as such to distinguish him from other Henrys.

33 Schmid, 'Die Thronfolge Ottos des Großen,' 439–65; Keller, 'Widukinds Bericht,' 91–5, 109–20; Laudage, *Otto der Grosse*, 104–9; Althoff, *Die Ottonen*, 57–9; Leyser, *Rule and Conflict*, 15.

34 Schmid, 'Die Thronfolge Ottos des Großen,' 483–9; Brühl, *Deutschland-Frankreich*, 341, 461–2; Leyser, *Rule and Conflict*, 15; Laudage, 'Hausrecht und Thronfolge,' 56, 62–3; Keller, 'Widukinds Bericht,' 118–20; Springer, 'Fragen zur Entstehung des mittelalterlichen deutschen Reiches,' 418–19.
35 Laudage, 'Hausrecht und Thronfolge,' 62–3; Leyser, *Rule and Conflict*, 16.
36 Liudprand, *Antapodosis* 4.18, pp. 420–1: 'Rectumne patrem egisse rere regia tibi in dignitate genito non in eadem genitum praeponendo?'
37 *Vita Mathildis reginae posterior,* sect. 6, pp. 155–6; sect. 9, p. 161.
38 Schütte, *Untersuchungen zu den Lebensbeschreibungen,* 104–10.
39 The claim to being born of a ruling king can be compared to the Byzantine idea of *porphyrogenitus,* born to the purple, that is, born in the purple-walled birthing room of the royal palace. See Jakobs, 'Zum Thronfolgerecht der Ottonen,' 519. This is especially evident in the above phrases from the *Vita Mathildis reginae posterior.* However, since the *Vita* was written in the reign of Henry II, these passages have been seen as anachronistic propaganda meant to justify the crown going to the Bavarian family line. The idea of *porphyrogenitus* is, in this interpretation, viewed as only coming into play with the heightened Byzantine presence in the West when Otto II married the Greek Theophanu (972), which is to say, long after Otto's brother Henry's rebellions (Schütte, *Untersuchungen zu den Lebensbeschreibungen,* 104–5). The problem is that historians have gone the next step and argued that because the *Vita*'s emphasis on Henry's royal birth is problematic, the idea that he was the firstborn of a reigning king was not used to justify his rebellion.

This has been done at the expense of almost ignoring Liudprand (Leyser, *Rule and Conflict,* 16; Laudage, 'Hausrecht und Thronfolge, 61–2; Fried, 'Die Konigserhebung Heinrichs I,' 292 n. 108), who is quite clear about the advice Henry was given. Schütte calls for caution in trusting Liudprand and points out that Liudprand himself does not make the connection between Henry's being told he ranked ahead of Otto because he was born of a reigning king and the idea of *porphyrogenitus,* in spite of Liudprand's having defined the Greek term earlier in his book (cf. 'Antapodosis' 1.6–7, pp. 254–5 with 4.18, pp. 420–1). In my opinion, this fact more readily supports the accuracy of Liudprand's account than undermines it: one would not expect the conspirators to use the term (neither, by the way, does the *Vita Mathilde*). To say that Liudprand had no idea what rationale the conspirators used (or did not like the justification he heard?) and thus himself came up with the idea that Henry could claim a royal birth while Otto could not (which was the truth) begins to move us into the shadowland of deconstruction where Liudprand himself takes on a treacherous guise: Why create a plausible justification for the rebellion if he did not sympathize with it? No such complications arise if Liudprand reported what he and his contemporaries knew. Here see the comments of Keller, 'Widukinds Bericht,' 111–12, and esp. pp. 259–60 n. 199.

40 See p. 19 above.

41 Karpf, *Herrscherlegitimation und Reichsbegriff*, 121.

42 Widukind of Corvey, *Res gestae Saxonicae*, 1.31, pp. 62–3.

43 Karpf, *Herrscherlegitimation und Reichsbegriff*, 114–15.

44 See p. 18 above.

45 Lees, 'Political and Dramatic Irony,' 801–2.

46 Karpf, *Herrscherlegitimation und Reichsbegriff*, 121–2.

47 See Day, 'The *Iudex Auquus*,' in the present volume of essays.

48 Schütze-Pflugk, *Herrscher- und Märtyrerauffassung*, 66.

49 See Keller, 'Widukinds Bericht,' 107–8 (with n. 156), 257, who gives a similar interpretation of the 936 *electio* in Widukind.

50 See n. 4 above.

51 See Althoff, 'Geschichtsschreibung in einer oralen Gesellschaft,' 158–9.

52 Schütze-Pflugk, *Herrscher- und Märtyrerauffassung*, 62–3, 84; Althoff, "Gandersheim und Quedlinburg," 141.

53 Pätzold, 'Die Auffassung des ostfränkisch-deutschen Reiches,' 224–5. Althoff says that Hrotsvit's presentation of Otto stands as a warning to the ruler to be careful not to lose God's grace, and he concludes that the *Gesta* should not be seen as a work promoting the interests of the Ottonian house but as one promoting those of Gandersheim ('Gandersheim und Quedlinburg,' 141–4); see also Homeyer, *Hrotsvithae Opera*, 390.

The *Iudex Aequus*: Legality and Equity in Hrotsvit's *Basilius*

DAVID DAY

One of the stranger moments in Hrotsvit von Gandersheim's *Basilius* occurs as Proterius's servant brings the devil the 'letter of introduction' from his magician. Satan complains, oddly enough, '"Numquam christicole permansistis mihi fidi"' (83), '"Never do you stay faithful to me, you Christians"' (Wilson, *Florilegium*, 23); rather they take the benefits of his rewards and then run off to Christ, who promptly releases them from their obligations. Satan's focus on Christian 'faithlessness' to the devil is one of the most telling evocations of a question Hrotsvit explores throughout *Basilius*: what constitutes fraud versus faith in one's obligations to others? When is one justified in proving faithless to one's undertakings? These questions are raised repeatedly in the text as the characters enter into a complex of promises, obligations, and contracts with one another. In this essay, I shall examine these various undertakings and how they intersect with each other, together with the legal and equitable bases for the outcomes of each intersection. In exploring which of these obligations must be honoured and which may be justifiably avoided, Hrotsvit shows a sophisticated understanding of what is known in the common law as equity versus legality, equity being the set of precepts by which strictly 'legal' outcomes may be modified in the interests of manifest justice.

The first obvious undertaking or promise in *Basilius* is Proterius's commitment of his daughter to a life of religious seclusion with those 'consignate Christo' (31). Hrotsvit specifically identifies this as a 'votum' (34), a vow or promise made to a deity. She is also careful to point out that Proterius is rich, and his one child, a daughter, is his only heir:

'Unica feminei sexus proles fuit illi/ (Nec alius substantiole mansit sibi magnae/ Heres) (23–5); the daughter is thus identified as a potential heiress, and this perhaps explains why Proterius's servant seeks to have her lawfully, 'licito' (67, printed between 90 and 91), as opposed to simply seducing her. Indeed, Hrotsvit mentions that when Proterius gives in to his daughter, he grants her to the servant with a substantial dowry (131). Hrotsvit thus immediately introduces into her story an idea of property relations and transfers, making of *Basilius* more than a simple tale of morality and religious piety; the ideas of promise and consideration, major elements in the law of contract, are at once admitted as themes.

It is this specific promise of Proterius that Satan decides to thwart by arousing insane passion for the girl in the breast of Proterius's servant: 'fecit fervescere servum/ In supra dicte dementer amore puelle' (35–6). Interestingly, the servant's first response to the devil's promptings is to make yet another promise, this time to the magician, of gifts and gold, in return for his assistance in procuring the love of Proterius's daughter (43–5). The magician doubts his ability to deliver on any such contract, and so writes out the strange 'letter of introduction' to Satan, making yet another promise, this time of the servant's soul, if the devil can grant his desire (47–63). This leads the servant to Satan, who procures from him a specific, written promise of his soul in return for the daughter's love (96–8). Among this succession of attempted promises and contracts, Hrotsvit presents two that have so far become 'binding,' that is, in which the parties have agreed on the specific terms or come to a meeting of the minds: Proterius's vow of his daughter to a life of religious seclusion, and the servant's vow of his soul to the devil in return for the daughter's love. Both involve the transfer of the daughter's affections, and presumably of at least part of her 'property value,' to a second party to the contract. In the first case, these items are the subject of Proterius's initial promise; although the consideration for this promise is not stated, it certainly is implied in the value Proterius finds in a life of religious piety and virginity: he hopes to secure his daughter's salvation by such a course (26–32). In the second, they are the consideration by which Satan procures the promise of the servant's soul. The two contracts are obviously in conflict; one cannot be fulfilled without the other being broken. And yet of the two, the contract between Satan and the servant is actually completed: the servant promises his soul in return for the daughter's love, and Satan does in fact procure this consideration for him.

Christ will not allow this conflict to persist, however; Hrotsvit notes:

Tali coniugo Satane cum fraude peracto
Condoluit Christus mundi salvator amandus,
Quos pius effusa salvavit sanguinis unda,
Hostis sub diri vinclis captos retineri; (138–41)

When the marriage vows were taken, so fraught by the fraud of Satan,
Then it pained Christ the King, who salvation to us did bring,
That those whom he had saved and with his precious blood redeemed
Should in the enemy's chain as captive still remain.

(Wilson, *Florilegium*, 24)

The moment the daughter marries Proterius's servant, Christ prompts misgivings in her heart. She soon discovers that Proterius's servant has 'se quia serpentis iuri tradebat avari' (146) 'signed himself over to the greedy serpent's power' (Wilson, *Florilegium*, 25). In spite of his falsely swearing an oath to the contrary (161), yet another instance of a false promise, she demands he hear mass, knowing he cannot do this having forsworn Christ. She then appeals directly to Basilius, who takes the opportunity to ask the servant if he is willing to repent. The servant responds in despair of salvation:

'Si posset fieri, voluissem mente libenti,
Sed restat menti sceleris res facta volenti,
Me quia per literas hosti dederam male scriptas
Et nomen Christi caecato corde negavi' (181–4)

'I committed the crime of free will I signed
With my hand the letters that gave me to the fiend in fetters.
With my heart turned blind Christ's name I denied.'

(Wilson, *Florilegium*, 26)

Basilius assures the servant that he is not lost, because Christ, 'iudex mitissimus orbis' (187), the 'mildest judge of all' (Wilson, *Florilegium*, 26), never turns away a repentant sinner. There follows the episode of the servant's penance and the final dispute with the demon before the doors of the church; the devil's accusation of Basilius is interesting for its reliance on legal concepts of contract and ownership:

'Cur satagis proprium mihimet vi tollere servum,
Qui sua sponte meis submisit colla catenis?
Cartam percerte, mihimet quam reddidi ipse,
Tempore iudicii Christo monstrabo futuri.'   (244–7)

'How dare you say   you take my slave away
Who out of free will   submitted to my chains?
The written agreement   that he gave to me
I shall bring to show   on the final day of law.   (Wilson, *Florilegium*, 27)

The demon's complaint sounds very much like the reply a lawyer might make in court: he relies specifically on the written 'carta,' in which the servant signed away his freedom. However, Basilius has his answer ready: '"Ipsius Christi precepto, iudicis aequi,/ Reddere litterulas spero te protinus ipsas"' (249–50), '"By Christ's command, I trust, that equitable judge,/ You shall soon relinquish the letters that you hold' (Wilson, *Florilegium*, 27). Whereupon the faithful begin to sing and pray, asking for God's help, and 'cedidit scriptura dolosa/ Ante pedes sancti necnon pastoris amandi' (254–5), 'Anon the hellish writ/ Fell from above and lay right in the bishop's way' (Wilson, *Florilegium*, 27).

At first glance, this outcome would seem to bear out the devil's initial contention that '"Numquam christicole permansitis mihi fidi"' (82). He did, after all, have a contract with the servant, and Christ appears to be arbitrarily negating this promise in favour of Proterius's initial vow of his daughter to the church. However, Hrotsvit is careful to point out that the contract between the devil and his servant is 'scriptura dolosa' (254), cunning or deceitful writing, and she has earlier taken every opportunity to identify its author and his servants as frauds and cheats. The magician is 'perversus fraudis ... amicus' (46), 'perverse friend of fraud' (Wilson, *Florilegium*, 22); the devil himself is 'inventor ... fraudis' (74), 'author of fraud' (Wilson, *Florilegium*, 23); and when the demon first interposes himself between the servant and the church door, Basilius addresses him as deceitful thief, '"Inprobe fur"' (240). I contend that Hrotsvit is using these terms as more than just scornful epithets: she seriously means them to cast doubt on the legality of the devil's original contract with Proterius's servant. One must ask at this point on what bases such a determination of legality might be decided.

There are essentially three varieties of law which an author of Hrotsvit's historical situation and education could have had at least some exposure to. One is the Roman law of contract and obligations: even though

Hrotsvit lived well before the great twelfth- and thirteenth-century revival of Roman law, her skill as a Latinist and obvious erudition make it at least possible that she may have been generally familiar with some Roman legal precepts. There are also the rules of canon law. Although these had not yet been brought fully into conformity with the practices of Roman law as they would be by Gratian and the other later decretalists, canon law was already well developed by Hrotsvit's day and claiming for itself jurisdiction over delicts with a moral or spiritual component. Finally, one must look at the Germanic customary and statutory law that would have prevailed in tenth-century Saxony. Although there is little direct evidence of how this law worked in Hrotsvit's own day, some idea of its practice can be gathered by reference to the various Germanic legal codes predating the tenth century and also those such as the thirteenth-century *Sachsenspiegel*, which followed it.

Considering these areas of the law, how 'legal' are the outcomes of the story as Hrotsvit gives them? The central contract is the servant's written promise of his soul to the devil, and Hrotsvit provides us with a number of interesting details concerning this document. The writing with which the servant pledges his soul to the devil is variously characterized as 'literas' (183) (letters or writings), 'scriptura dolosa' (254) (wily or deceitful writing), and, always by the devil, as a 'carta' (94, 246), a written contract or charter. Hrotsvit's choice of this last term is extremely interesting because it matches the technical term for written documents by which contractual obligations were confirmed under Germanic law;[1] under the procedure of *investitura per cartam*, a written memorandum of one's obligations (the carta) was transferred to the other contracting party to seal the bargain.

This is precisely what the servant evidently gives to the devil, and the devil is very careful to use the proper term for the document any time he refers to it.[2] In his efforts to recover his 'property' from Basilius as the bishop leads the servant into the church, the devil is also acting in a legally proper form according to Germanic legal precepts. Although Germanic law was by modern standards 'loose' concerning the passage of rights in chattels to parties other than their owners, an owner could formally 'lay hands' (*anefang*) on his property when discovered in the hands of another,[3] and this is exactly what the devil does, seizing the servant by his left arm as he begins to enter the church, and demanding by what right Basilius now holds him. So far so good: Satan seems well within his legal rights.

This agreement, nevertheless, has a number of possible problems.

The most immediate one is its conflict with Proterius's promise of his daughter to the church. Hrotsvit uses the word 'votum' (34) – a vow or promise – when referring to this agreement. In Roman law and pagan religious practice, this term originally referred to a promise of a sacrifice or other benefit conferred on a deity in return for supernatural reward,[4] but in later medieval usage it came to refer to monastic vows more particularly,[5] and this is probably the meaning Hrotsvit is giving it here. Alan Watson contends the Roman 'votum' was analogous to the interlocking 'stipulationes' that developed in later Roman private law,[6] and if he is correct, the 'votum' was probably always seen as having a contractual character in spite of its arguably unenforceable nature. Proterius's promise is therefore prior in time to the contract between the servant and Satan, and Satan's agreement is fraudulent because it purports to give away that which is already promised to another – the person and property of the daughter.

There is also a problem with Proterius's agreeing to give his daughter to his servant at all. The terms used of the servant are quite consistent: he is almost always referred to as a 'servus,' a term meaning 'servant,' but also, significantly, 'slave' (35, 48, 96, 136, 177, 244). It is not clear whether Hrotsvit is consistently using the term with one meaning or the other, but she is certainly using it to point out his socially inferior position – this is brought out elsewhere in the text, for example, in the servant's knowing himself to be 'indignum' (39), 'unworthy' of such a union. The magician, moreover, doubts his ability to bind the lady over in affection to her 'servo' (48); the union is so unusual that it requires the intervention of Satan himself to be successful. Also, after the daughter tells Proterius of her love for the servant, it is clear that much of Proterius's horror flows not just from the forced violation of his prior pledge of her to the church, but also from the shame her ignominious union will cause to her family's reputation (133–7).

There is thus a strong focus throughout *Basilius* on the socially inappropriate nature of the marriage, and this disapproval is certainly reflected in some of the legal practices in or close to Hrotsvit's own time. If the servant is a slave or a freedman, such social disapproval would have been unequivocal. In Germanic law, both the Salic and Ripuarian Frankish codes punished marriage between a slave and a free woman, usually by making her a slave like her husband or sometimes by forcing her to choose between a loss of freedom or the death of her husband.[7] Under the provisions of Roman law, slaves were not even recognized as sui juris, and so were unable to contract marriages of any kind;[8] there were furthermore bars to socially 'unseemly' marriages such as those between daughters of senatorial rank and freedmen, which may very well apply in the case of Proterius's daughter and the servant.[9] It is true that later canon law mitigated these sorts of bars to some degree, recognizing marriages between slaves, for example, as James A. Brundage and R.H. Helmholz have shown,[10] but earlier bars to the union of slave or freedman and free persons of high rank underline the social and legal outrageousness of the servant's desire for Proterius's daughter and her willingness to be joined with him. Even if the servant is not an actual slave or freedman, the union of a woman of senatorial rank with a mere servant would have been socially irregular. As the marriage is the consideration for the servant's promise, this social and possibly legal irregularity speak to the contract's probable invalidity as well.

Furthermore, the servant's contract with the devil has yet another problem. Hrotsvit is very careful to point out the insane character of the servant's love for Proterius's daughter: it is 'dementer amore' (36), loving insanely; he is 'cecatus bachanti' (53), madly blind, and it is specifically Satan who has made him so (33–6). Under Roman law, and later canon law, persons with mental disabilities were not qualified to enter into contracts.[11] Satan's conduct is thus doubly fraudulent: he has not only made the servant crazy, but he has taken advantage of him by contracting with him after he is non compos mentis.

Yet another important flaw in the devil's claim to the servant's soul is perhaps set up in the prologue to the legend itself: in deflecting the reader's supposed reservations about her gender, Hrotsvit advises the reader to concentrate on praising Christ's mercy: 'Qui non vult digna peccantes perdere poena,/ Sed plus perpetuę conversos reddere vitę' (13–14), 'Who wants not that in due pain sinners their punishment gain,/ But eternal life He grants to the sinner who repents' (Wilson, *Florilegium*, 21). The phrasing of these two lines introduces at the legend's very start the idea of quid pro quo, of fitting payment for certain sorts of behaviours. Those who sin receive 'digna ... poena' (13), 'due pain'; those who turn to Christ, Christ rewards with eternal life: 'plus perpetuę ... reddere vitę' (14). As a pledge of Christ to humanity, this undertaking predates in time all those made throughout the rest of the legend, both Proterius's and the devil's. By turning to Christ and repenting, the servant avails himself of an absolute promise of salvation that the devil's fraudulent documents can never override. As C.W. Marx has recently shown, this basis for overruling the 'devil's rights' in the servant or any Christian is theological as well as legal. Patristic writers as early as Augustine had outlined various logical, equitable, and legal justifications for God overruling Satan's 'rights' in the souls of unredeemed humanity, most notably in this case what Marx calls the 'ransom theory': the idea that the devil effectively never had any right to humanity, but was acting as a servant of God, to whom humanity owed a debt because of original sin. This debt was redeemed or liquidated by Christ's sacrifice.[12]

All such justifications of the negation of the servant's contract seem to rely on a desire for equitability of outcome as opposed to strict legality. 'Equity' in common law usage refers to judicial practices and remedies designed to prevent or supplement legal outcomes that are somehow unconscionable, and it is historically inaccurate to apply it to Hrotsvit's legend without qualification and explanation. Pollock and Maitland note that in medieval common law practice, equitable considerations, especially the principles disallowing fraudulent contracts, were notable by their absence: the law was 'inclined to hold that a man had himself to thank if he is misled by deceit.'[13] But the severity of this tendency was combated by the principles of both Roman and canon law, which disallowed the static use of 'legal' structures and practices where they led to unconscionable results,[14] such as defrauding a contracting party of his property.[15] In England, the canonists' insistence on strict bona fides became a hallmark of equity practice in the later medieval courts of Chancery.[16] Recent work by legal historians such as Rebecca Colman has further suggested that the apparent rigidity of Germanic law was mitigated in practice by what might be considered 'equitable' considerations.[17] For example, in a trial by compurgation, a person already notable in the community as a fraud might well have difficulty locating the requisite number of oath helpers to assist him in prosecuting a claim for breach of contract. Certainly one would expect the devil to have these sorts of problems.

The distinction Hrotsvit draws between strict legality and equity of outcome is echoed, strangely enough, in much later medieval literature which almost certainly was not directly influenced by anything Hrotsvit wrote. I am speaking specifically of the 'debate of the devils' which occurs in Passus XVIII of the B version of *Piers Plowman*. Hearing of Christ's approaching harrowing of hell, Lucifer argues for his 'title' to the souls of the Patriarchs:

If he reve me of my right, he robbeth me by maistrie;
For by right and by reson the renkes that ben here
Body and soule beth myne, both goode and ille.

For hymself seide, that sire is of hevene,
That if Adam ete the appul, alle sholde deye,
And dwelle [in deol] with us develes – this thretynge he made.
And [sithen] he that Soothnesse is seide thise wordes,
And I sithen iseised sevene [thousand] wynter,
I leeve that lawe nyl noghte lete hym the leeste.   (274–84)

Another of the devils, though, doubts this argument: 'We have no trewe title to hem, for thorugh treson were thei dampned' (293). John Alford has convincingly argued that the impulse for setting aside the demons' 'legal title' to the souls is founded in the precepts of canon law, which required a good title at the taking of possession, regardless of other bona fides,[18] while W.J. Birnes has traced the same equitable principle to civil law practice.[19] Even though the legal results in *Basilius* are local and not directly related to larger issues of scriptural history, as are Langland's, Hrotsvit's conviction that strict legality must be set aside in cases of canon or civil law defined by 'equity' is very similar to that of the later English poet. C.W. Marx has identified probable bases for the disagreement in *Piers Plowman* in theological literature going back to at least Anselm's eleventh-century treatise *Cur Deus Homo*, which argues that because the devil originally defrauded humanity by leading them into sin, he has no true rights to their souls.[20] Of course, Hrotsvit's apparent portrayal of holy equity overcoming satanic legality in *Basilius* would predate Anselm's theological treatment of the same issue by several decades, perhaps indicating a more widespread prevalence of such ideas among Christian intellectuals in the tenth century.

I am not willing to go as far as Birnes and Alford do for Langland, and claim that Hrotsvit sees in the rigidity of strict legal practice the intractability of the Old Law, and in the flexible equity of civil or canon law the promise of the New.[21] For one thing, I am fairly sure the legal distinctions between 'civil' and 'canon' law were simply not that clear in the tenth century, certainly not so well defined that they could be subjected to a complex theological classification of this kind. Hrotsvit was not, after all, a lawyer, and in any case it would be another century or more before the systematic study of Roman civil law would become prevalent in western Europe or canon law would be systematized by the decretalists. It is fairly clear though that Hrotsvit displays a strikingly firm grasp of legal practice in the *Basilius*, and that she portrays a reliance on narrow definitions of 'legality' as a practice of the devil, while a reliance on broad principles of fairness and equity are characteristic of Basilius and

the servants of Christ. Her inspiration for these distinctions may have
been no more than the general Christian injunction to follow the spirit
rather than the letter of the law. But in making her case, she undeniably
shows a surprisingly precise knowledge of the civil and canonical law of
obligations as it existed in her own day.

In closing, I should like to simply note the marvellous effect this
application of law has to the text: it lends the futile frustration of the
devil a pronounced note of comedy, in every sense of the term. His
pointless plotting and ultimate discomfiture is of course funny: as always
in Hrotsvit, the bad guys lose, regardless of how sure they are that they
are playing, *this* time and for once, with a full hand. His inability to
prevail leads him to the sort of hopeless impotence we see Hadrian and
Antiochus display in *Sapientia* as the daughters of Sapientia frolic in their
torments: one cannot win against Christians because they are playing by
a new set of rules. And it also makes the text comedic in a more Christian
sense: the efficacy of Christian principles is upheld, and the promise of
an ultimately happy ending for those who observe them is triumphantly
and inevitably borne out.

NOTES

1 Huebner, *A History of Germanic Private Law*, 502.
2 A similar written instrument is used by the devil in Hrotsvit's *Theophilus* to
   secure the protagonist's soul, and as in *Basilius* there is considerable anxiety
   about securing the actual contract itself; in this case, Theophilus is concerned that the paper will be produced against him on the last day, much
   as the devil in *Basilius* threatens to receive final satisfaction on his contract
   on the day of judgment. In *Theophilus* as here, the usual term used to refer
   to the contract is 'carta,' but it is used with less precision by the demonic
   actors in the legend than in *Basilius*. Its character as a specifically legal
   document therefore seems to be less stressed. Both *Theophilus* and *Basilius*
   are, of course, among the earliest examples of the 'devil's compact' story, a
   family of works ultimately comprising among others *Faust*. For a full tracing
   of this literary history, see Rudwin, *The Devil in Legend and Literature*, 181ff.
   Elsewhere in this volume, Patricia Silber considers both legends in the
   context of conventional medieval depictions of the Devil.
3 Huebner, *A History of Germanic Private Law*, 411.
4 Watson, *The State, Law and Religion*, 41.
5 Latham and Baxter, *Revised Medieval Latin Word-List*, 517.

6 Watson, *The State, Law and Religion*, 41–2.

7 Huebner, *A History of Germanic Private Law*, 93.

8 Mommsen and Krueger, *The Digest of Justinian*, 1.5–6; Treggiari, *Roman Marriage*, 43.

9 Mommsen and Krueger, *The Digest of Justinian*, 23.2.44.

10 Brundage, *Medieval Canon Law* 14; Helmholz, *The Spirit of Classical Canon Law*, 68, n. 416.

11 Birks and McLeod, *Justinian's Institutes*, 3.19.8.

12 Marx, *The Devil's Rights and the Redemption in the Literature of Medieval England*, 9–11.

13 Pollock and Maitland, *The History of English Law Before the Time of Edward I*, 536.

14 Wolff, *Roman Law*, 70–9; Le Bras, 'Canon Law,' 351.

15 Vinogradoff, *Roman Law in Medieval Europe*, 75–7; Brundage, *Medieval Canon Law*, 70–1.

16 Plucknett, *A Concise History of the Common Law*, 614.

17 Colman, 'Reason and Unreason in Early Medieval Law,' 576.

18 Alford, 'Literature and Law in Medieval England,' 945.

19 Birnes, 'Christ as Advocate,' 72.

20 Marx, *The Devil's Rights and the Redemption in the Literature of Medieval England*, 18–19.

21 Marx does not even accept the idea that Langland's influences are legal as opposed to theological. He writes, 'The issue of the Devil's rights was first and foremost a theological one, and Birnes and Alford fail to consider the history of the doctrine of the redemption or the attitude to the Devil's rights in theology after Anselm' (109). However, as Marx shows in his consideration of texts such as the thirteenth-century *Conflictus inter Deum et Diabolum*, the theological refutation of the devil's rights often borrowed terminology and procedural detail from civil and canon law practice to structure the debate over the devil's *bona fides* (60–4). It would therefore appear that the theological debate itself borrowed heavily from the law, and that on this question the two disciplines were always closely intermingled. In considering the influences on a particular author's treatment of the issue, telling where one leaves off and another begins is probably not possible.

'Weighed down with a thousand evils': Images of Muslims in Hrotsvit's *Pelagius*

LINDA A. MCMILLIN

In the tenth-century world of Hrotsvit of Gandersheim, the successful growth of Islam around the shores of the Mediterranean represents a worrisome but distant threat on the edges of Northern European consciousness. Two centuries earlier, the most northern advances of the Muslims had been stopped by Charles Martel but it will be another hundred years before Western Europe organizes a significant counterattack in the crusades. In the centuries between these two military encounters, Islamic culture receives little attention in the writings of Northern Europeans. Rumours of Islamic atrocities toward Christians – in the East, on the seas, and to the south on the Iberian Peninsula – trickle north only sporadically. Yet one story, of a young Christian boy named Pelagius, executed in Cordoba in 925, reaches the ears of Hrotsvit at the court of Otto I. It becomes the only contemporary tale in her collection of eight saints' legends.[1]

Hrotsvit is one of the first Northern European writers to present Islam to her readers.[2] The remote location of Pelagius's martyrdom meant that she had to devote considerably more attention to the setting in this work than in her other stories and give her readers some information about their unfamiliar non-Christian neighbours to the south. Consequently, she includes a brief history of the Islamic conquest of Spain, a basic primer on Islamic culture, a summary of the conditions endured by Christians living under Islamic rule, and a scathing portrait of the Cordoban caliph, Abd al-Rahman III. This snapshot of life in al-Andalus is taken from a great distance and consequently is obscure and out of focus. Nevertheless, Hrotsvit constructs a surprisingly nuanced portrait of both the general history of Islamic Spain and the life of Christians living there. She conveys to her audience the real political and military threat of Islam to the Christian community. At the same time, she assures all that the Christian God and his young virgin martyrs will triumph over these latter day pagans as easily as the boy Pelagius can bop the great soldier/king al-Rahman in the mouth. As a result, Hrotsvit's Muslims – in particular al-Rahman – emerge as a combination of verity and political caricature, an enemy both fearsome and ridiculous who can ultimately be conquered by Christians of strong faith.

The Tale of a Spanish Martyr Heads North

The earliest Spanish account of Pelagius's martyrdom comes from the Cordoban priest, Raguel, who wrote his version of the saint's life based on the testimony of witnesses sometime before 967.[3] According to Raguel, Pelagius was sent from Galicia by his father at age ten to serve as a hostage in exchange for a clerical relative who had been on the losing side of a border skirmish between Christian and Muslim forces. After he had languished in prison for three years, Pelagius's exceptional beauty caught the eye of the Islamic ruler, who offered him a life of luxury in exchange for accepting the ruler's sexual advances. While choosing to preserve his virginity out of Christian conviction, Pelagius made a series of statements disparaging Islam. Consequently, he was tortured and killed. After 967, Pelagius's relics were transferred to Christian Leon (and even later to Oviedo) where he became a popular saint of the Reconquest.[4] His story was also celebrated in a Mozarabic liturgy dating to about the same time.[5]

It is highly unlikely that Hrotvit would have had any access to the Spanish accounts of Pelagius's martyrdom, in either the saint's life or the Mozarabic liturgy. There is no evidence that these texts travelled north of the Pyrenees until well after the tenth century.[6] Indeed, Hrotsvit and Raguel disagree on a variety of details of the saint's story. In Hrotsvit, Pelagius serves as hostage in place of his father rather than an uncle, is shot from a catapult, and beheaded rather than hacked to death, and undergoes a variety of postmortem tests to prove his sanctity rather than being instantly canonized. In an epilogue to the Legends, Hrotsvit herself confirms that her knowledge of Pelagius was not based on a written source: 'The order of events leading to Pelagius' martyrdom was told me by a certain man, a native of the city [Cordova] where Pelagius suffered, who assured me that he had seen that fairest of men and had true knowledge of the outcome of the matter.'[7] The most likely setting for such a conversation was the court of Otto I.

In the mid-tenth century, there were several diplomatic exchanges between Otto I and Abd al-Rahman III.[8] According to John of Gorze, who served as Otto's ambassador to Cordoba, a first round of correspondence between the two rulers in 951, initiated by Otto over the activities of Islamic pirates, was neither cordial nor successful.[9] However, by 956, Abd al-Rahman's ambassador, Bishop Recemundus of Elvira, had returned south from a successful visit at Otto's court and facilitated John's audience with the caliph. John's intention for the audience was to map out a treaty of friendship between the two kingdoms. However, his narrative ends before the outcome of these efforts was resolved. Recemundus's presence in Otto's court is confirmed as well in the writings of Liutprand of Cremona, who dedicated his 'Antapodosis' to the Cordoban ambassador.[10] While neither John nor Liutprand mentioned the Pelagius story in their writings, Recemundus included the saint's feast in a *calendarium* he wrote in 961.[11] Therefore, his sojourn at the court of Otto I presents us with at least one Cordoban native from whom Hrotsvit could have heard the martyr's tale. There were likely others as well, members of Recemundus's diplomatic party. While we cannot know with any certainty the name of Hrotsvit's source, there is no reason not to accept her word on how she became acquainted with Pelagius's passion.

Muslims and Pagans and Bears, Oh My!

While Hrotsvit's claim to an eyewitness source for the story of Pelagius rings true, this source does not seem to have schooled her in all the intricacies of Islamic culture and religion. Indeed, in her overall portrayal of her Muslim neighbours, Hrotsvit follows many of the popular but misguided stereotypes that will be a part of northern European literature for several centuries to come.[12] Like the later authors of the chansons de geste, Hrotsvit shows no understanding of the theological connections between Islam and Christianity. While such connections are recognized by some post-Crusade Christian polemicists who cast the Muslims as heretics, Hrotsvit's Saracens are 'perfida ... gens' (24), 'Deque profanato ... sacello' (41), 'a faithless tribe' who engage in 'cults of pagan worship' (Wilson, *Florilegium*, 29–30). Their religious practices parallel those of pagan Romans in early Christian martyr stories: 'diis auro fabricatis' (57), 'idols made of gold,' are central to their religion as are 'marmora comtus diademate ...veneratur ture' (65–6), 'images of marble...with jewels adorned...adored with frankincense' (Wilson, *Florilegium*, 30). To Hrotsvit, these practices make 'stulte sacris famulando novellis' (45), 'a foolish cult absurd,' and those who engage in this religion are 'perversus, vita rituque profanus' (33), 'quite perverse, in life and customs cursed' (Wilson, *Florilegium*, 30). Thus, without more sophisticated theological information, Hrotsvit casts the Muslims in the well-known general categories of pagan 'otherness.'

Despite their ridiculous religious practices, Hrotsvit's Muslims show remarkable military prowess. Consequently, they are a serious threat to the Christian West. Hrotsvit narrates the original conquest of Christian Cordoba, in which

> Perfida nam Saracenorum gens indomitorum
> Urbis Marte petit duros huiusce colonos,
> Eripuit regni sortem sibi vi quoque clari
> Extinxitque bonum regem baptismate lotum,
> Qui pridem merito gessit regalia sceptra
> Et cives iustis domuit quot tempora frenis.   (24–9)

> For the faithless tribe of unrestrained Saracens
> Fell upon the stout people of this town.
> They seized by force the reign of this glorious domain,
> And murdered the good king, who, cleansed by holy baptism,
> Held the royal scepter by right and with might;
> And ruled his men for long with just restraints and laws.
> (Wilson, *Florilegium*, 29–30)

This ability of Islamic forces to dispatch a Christian army quickly is repeated in her account of the reign of Abd al-Rahman III. The caliph boasts, 'Ullum nec tanta populum feritate refertum,/ Qui temptare suas auderet Marte catervas' (89–90), 'that no tribe was ever filled so with strength and valor/ That they would dare smite his army in a fight' (Wilson, *Florilegium*, 31). Hrotsvit claims that the Galicians are 'quite excellent in war.' Nevertheless, al-Rahman

> Tali cumque locum peteret pompa memoratum
> Et gentem primo temptaret denique bello

Extemplo tantum sortitur namque triumphum,
Ut iam bis senos una cum principe captos
Illaqueat comites artis stringitque catenis   (120–4)

He engaged the Galicians in a first encounter,
And promptly he chanced to gain and such a triumph obtain
That he trapped twelve nobles and captured their lord,
Seizing all these men and putting them in chains. (Wilson, *Florilegium*, 32)

Once again, Hrotsvit's Saracens anticipate those of the chansons de geste.

However, instead of being countered by even stronger Christian knights whose glory is only increased by defeating a formidable enemy, these Saracens win all the battles, reflecting an earlier historical reality when, despite Charles Martel, Christian victories over invading and raiding Islamic forces were few and far between. For Hrotsvit, al-Rahman is 'ductor barbaricę gentis' (32), 'the leader of the barbaric tribe,' and his followers are 'paganos' (39) who have 'barbarico ritu' (38), who 'fervebat dęmonis ira,/ Corde gerens veterem serpentis denique bilem' (97–8), 'pagans' with 'barbarian customs' who 'burned with demonic ire./ And in his heart, awake, was the bile of the ancient snake' (Wilson, *Florilegium*, 30–1). Hrotsvit goes so far as to instruct her readers:

Nullus pro meritis credat factum fore regis
Hoc, quod tam pulchra vincebat denique pompa,
Sed mage iudicio secreti iudicis aequo,
Ut populus tanto correptus rite flagello
Fleret totius proprii commissa reatus,
Vel quo Pelagius Christi pro lege necandus
Forte locum peteret, quo se morti dare posset
Necnon sanguineum pro Christo fundere rivum
Inpendens animam domino bene morte piatam.   (179–87)

No one, though, should credit this to the king's own merit,
That he should have succeeded in such a splendid way,
But rather the reason lies, and with God the Judge resides
Whose secret plan was either that this tribe, so chastised,
Should beweep the sins of which they all stood charged,
Or that Pelagius be killed for faith in Christ,
And might thus reach the spot, where to die was his lot,

And pour forth the waters there of his blood for Christ,

Giving his soul to God, made holy by his death.   (Wilson, *Florilegium*, 34)

Thus, the clearly dominant martial skills of the Muslims are still controlled by Hrotsvit's God and therefore, while a real threat to Christians,
are not a sign of moral or cultural superiority.

A third notable characteristic of Hrotsvit's Muslims is their greed: Abd
al-Rahman 'eripuit regni sortem sibi vi quoque clari' (26), 'seized for
himself the entire glorious and splendid Empire' (Wilson, *Florilegium*,
30). A few lines earlier Hrotsvit has specified the splendour of Cordoba's
wealth: 'Corduba famoso locuples de nomine dicta, / Inclita deliciis,
rebus quoque splendida cunctis' (15–16), 'Cordoba was its name; wealthy
it was and of fame;/ Well known for its pleasures and for its splendid
treasures' (Wilson, *Florilegium*, 29). That greed is a greater motive than
their desire to convert the Christians Hrotsvit makes explicit, writing:

Quo rex comperto non absque sui fore damno
Sensit, si cunctis pariter predivitis urbis,
Quam crebro validę cepit luctamine pugne,
Civibus excidium mortis conferret amarum.   (46–9)

The king having learned this, realized in full

That it would bring him harm if he did not change his mind

And put all wealthy people to death in this rich town

Which he had just captured in valiant fighting.   (Wilson, *Florilegium*, 30)

The Islamic leader's desire to destroy the faithful Christian population
of the newly conquered city is restrained by his desire for a wealthy
population that he could tax, unlike his Muslim followers. Thus Hrotsvit
emphasizes financial gain rather than religious toleration in the Islamic
practice of granting Christians protected minority status. Furthermore,
Abd al-Rahman III is 'regi ... avaro' (135), a 'greedy ruler' (Wilson,
Florilegium, 32), when he sets high ransoms for the captive Galician lords.
Even the fishermen who find Pelagius's corpse are motivated to recover
the body in order to sell it to the Christians. Such avarice is not a typical
part of the Western stereotypes of Muslims. However, for Hrotsvit, this
focus on wealth confirms the general ignominy of Islamic culture.

While greedy, fierce, and pagan, Hrotsvit's Muslim characters are not
uniformly unsympathetic. Some Muslims, especially rulers and above all
Abd al-Rahman III, are clearly beyond the pale; others, such as the

townsmen who visit the imprisoned Pelagius, can be merciful and generous. Hrotsvit writes, 'Illic ergo viri venerunt sedulo primi,/ Mulcendo
mentem iuvenis causa pietatis' (198–9), 'Hereto came eagerly the foremost men of town/ Moved by care humane, to soften the youth's grave
pain' (Wilson, *Florilegium*, 34). This first overture is motivated solely by
good will. Subsequently these men are so taken by Pelagius's beauty and
eloquence that 'animo miseranti/ Causa Pelagii suaserunt talia regi'
(208–9), 'with pity in their hearts, they pleaded with the king' on Pelagius's
behalf (Wilson, *Florilegium*, 34). Granted that their plan for Pelagius's
release – to have him become the king's lover – is easily recognized by a
Christian audience as not an acceptable alternative to imprisonment,
nevertheless, Hrotsvit presents these men as well-meaning rather than evil.

So too, the fishermen who find Pelagius's body, while quickly thinking
of the gold it is worth, are also moved by the sight of his mangled
remains. 'Rumpunt in tales miseranti pectore voces:/ "Heu, iacet exanimis
propriae spes unica gentis,/ Atque decus patriae tumuli sine sordet
honore!"' (338–40), 'Pity in their hearts, they pour forth these words:/
"Alas here lies dead the sole hope of his nation/ And the glory of his
land lies here without a tomb"' (Wilson, *Florilegium*, 38). These latter
Muslims know enough about Christian practice to recognize that a
headless corpse is likely to be the body of a martyr and valuable to the
Christian community:

'Nonne satis multis scimus nos vendere seclis
Semper sanctorum corpuscula passa virorum,
Quos capitis cedes monstraverat esse fideles?
Et quis laudabilis dubitet corpus fore testis,
Quod truncum misere capitis iacet absque decore?'   (341–5)

'Don't we also know that the remains of those
Whose decapitations prove them to be Christians,
Can easily be sold for large amounts of gold?
And who would doubt this to be the body of a martyr
Since the body lies, bereft of the head's glory?'   (Wilson, *Florilegium*, 38)

The residents of the monastery to which they bring Pelagius's body do
not greet the fishermen's hope of gold negatively. Rather,

Quod gaudens hymnis suscepit turba fidelis
Suavibus, exequias celebrans de more sacratas,

Largiter et precium nautis tribuit superauctum,
Ardescens sancti mercari corpus amandi.   (354–7)

The throng of the faithful received them rejoicing,
And with sweet hymns performed the sacred funeral rites
They paid generously a high price to the shipmen
Eager to buy the remains of the beloved saint.   (Wilson, *Florilegium*, 38)

These glimpses of sympathetic Muslims indicate Hrotsvit's awareness
that the relationship between Islam and Christianity in al-Andalus was
more complex than it might first appear.

Christian Life in Islamic Spain

While she is vague on theology, Hrotsvit's grasp of history is much
stronger. She begins her story of Pelagius with a brief account of the
Islamic conquest of the Iberian Peninsula. She presents a clear and
accurate chronology of events. Prosperous Cordoba had previously been
under Christian rule: 'Olim quae Christo fuerat bene subdita iusto' (19),
'Once this famous town to Christ in faith was bound' (Wilson, *Florilegium*,
29). The attack of the Muslims came suddenly and was immediately
successful. The result was a mixed population, 'paganos iustis inter-
miscendo colonis' (39), 'mixing his pagans with the faithful natives'
(Wilson, *Florilegium*, 30). Between this original conquest and her own
time, 'casibus his plures volvebat Corduba soles,/ Subdita per longum
paganis regibus aevum' (69–70), 'many years so passed, and amongst
vicissitudes/ Cordoba since that time was subject to pagan kings' (Wilson,
Florilegium, 31). Islamic aggression did not end with the conquest, however. The ongoing tensions between al-Andalus and northern Iberian
Christian kingdoms can be seen in Hrotsvit's account of the raid on
Galicia that resulted in the capture of Pelagius's father. The two kingdoms
did have a treaty but it was contested by Abd al-Rahman III who claimed:

'Sed, que Gallicios retinet fiducia captos,
Nescio, gratiolę respuant ut foedera nostrę
Et tandem veteris sint ingrati pietatis.'   (107–9)

'But what bold confidence drives the subject Galicians
That they would have foresworn and our treaties clearly scorn
Ungrateful for past kindness, I simply do not know.' (Wilson, *Florilegium*, 32)

His forces won the ensuing border skirmish and 'tunc restaurato rursus quoque foedere primo' (128), 'then, the treaty, too, was restored anew' (Wilson, *Florilegium*, 32). Hrotsvit has her basic historical facts straight: Galicia did have both treaties and several armed run-ins – some success-ful, some not – with al-Rahman in the 920s.[13] The subsequent ransoming of captives and exchange of hostages accurately reflects common prac-tice on both sides of the border.

While Islam is clearly a fierce aggressor in the conquest of Cordoba and is a continuous military threat to its northern Christian neighbours, Muslim attitudes toward Mozarabs, Christian peoples living under Islamic rule, are significantly less bellicose. 'Tolerant' is too strong a word, too fraught with modern connotations, to describe Islamic prac-tice. However, Christians (and Jews) were recognized as monotheists who worshipped the same God as the Muslims. Therefore, while they did not acknowledge the fullness of religious revelation given to Mohammed, Christians were not considered pagans, were not forced to convert to Islam, and could continue to practise their religion relatively unmo-lested. Such religious freedom is illustrated in Hrotsvit's account of Pelagius's postmortem adventures. The monastery where the saint is buried operates openly and publicly and is well known to Muslim citi-zens who seem to regularly aid the community in recovering the remains of executed Christians. A considerable throng of men visits the monas-tery to be healed by Pelagius's relics, and the ceremonies to test the religious merit of these relics are held publicly and without problem, though they do draw notice (366–71). Ultimately, this monastery is allowed to build 'mauseleo digne' (410), 'a worthy tomb' (Wilson, *Florilegium*, 40), for a person executed by the government. In such scenes Hrotsvit presents a robust Mozarabic Christian community operating with autonomy in an Islamic city.

A clearer description of official Islamic practice toward the Christians is included in Hrotsvit's first descriptions of life in Cordoba after the conquest. She records a pronouncement by the new ruler:

Ut quisquis regi mallet servire perenni
Et patrum mores olim servare fideles,
Hoc faceret licito, nulla post vindice poena   (52–4)

That whoever so desired to serve the eternal King
And desired to honor the customs of his sires,
Might do so without fear of any retribution.   (Wilson, *Florilegium*, 30)

As mentioned above, Hrotsvit sees the motivation for this decree to be greed rather than tolerance. Her judgment is not without merit – Islamic rulers could not tax fellow Muslims. Therefore, Christians and Jews were an important part of the tax base throughout the Islamic world. And Islamic indulgence of Christian religious practice was not without limits. Hrotsvit carefully lays out the boundaries of Christian religious freedom:

Hac solum caute servata conditione,
Ne quis praefate civis presumeret urbis
Ultra blasphemare diis auro fabricatis
Quos princeps coleret, sceptrum quicumque teneret,
seu caput exacto cicius subiungere ferro
Et sententiolam loeti perferre supremam.   (55–60)

Only a single condition, he set to be observed,
Namely that no dweller of the aforesaid city
Should presume to blaspheme the golden idol's name
Whom this prince adored or whoever else was king.
Or else, it was so willed, this man was promptly killed
And had to bear the sentence of punishment by death.

(Wilson, *Florilegium*, 30)

Despite the mistaken mention of 'idol,' Hrotsvit includes the most important constraint on Christian religious practice in Islamic culture. Blaspheming the 'name' of Mohammed was punishable by execution. Thus the Christian community of Cordoba had religious freedom but was heavily taxed and silenced. As a result for Hrotsvit, 'His ita digestis simulata pace quievit/ Obruta mille malis toties urbs nempe fidelis' (61–2), 'Following these decrees, calm in apparent peace/ The faithful city was weighed down with a thousand evils' (Wilson, *Florilegium*, 30).

Given Islamic law, Christian martyrdom in Cordoba was not automatic, not a matter of simply being faithful to Christianity. Rather, to be martyred, one had to go out of one's way to publicly insult Islam. Some Cordoban Christians did actively seek out such a death, especially in the mid-ninth century.[14] Hrotsvit alludes to these earlier martyrs:

Sed si quos ignis Christi succensit amoris,
Martiriique sitis suasit corrumpere dictis
Marmora, que princeps comptus diademate suplex
Corpore prostrato veneratur ture Sabeo,

Hos capitis subito damnavit denique poena:
Sed superos anime petierunt sanguine lotę   (63–8)

But those whom their desire for Christ's love set on fire,
And whom the thirst for martyrdom urged to insult and scorn
Those images of marble which, with jewels adorned,
The prince with prostrate body, adored with frankincense,
These men's bodies perished at the prince's order,
But their souls, purified, heavenward repaired. (Wilson, *Florilegium*, 30–1)

Leaders in both the local Mozarabic Christian community and the wider
Western Church viewed these saints with less favour, however, and eventually the papacy actively discouraged such Christian grandstanding in
Islamic countries. Hrotsvit seems to be aware of this controversy. On the
one hand, she clearly admires the ninth-century Cordoban martyrs and
may have purposefully constructed the details of Pelagius's death to
parallel those of the earlier saints – decapitation, the body cast into the
river.[15] On the other hand, Hrotsvit is careful to present Pelagius's tale in
such a way as to distance him from these earlier martyrs as well. He is an
outsider, not a local resident. He goes to Cordoba in order to spare his
father, not to seek martyrdom actively. He is passive and silent both in
prison and when first brought to court. His insult to Islam comes only
under duress, after he is physically embraced by the king (243–9). Nevertheless, it is for these insults made publicly at court that he will be
executed, as the king makes clear:

'Nostri blasphemos urget cultus cruciandos
Subdere mox morti ferro iugulosque forari,
Ni cedant et blasphemam respuant rationem'   (257–9)

'We kill those who assault and blaspheme our cult,
We subject them to death and pierce their throats with swords
Unless they cease their chant and their blasphemies recant.'
                                                          (Wilson, *Florilegium*, 36)

This proactive mandate for martyrdom is further punctuated when
Pelagius punches the king in the face. But Hrotsvit casts this aggressive
act as compelled by circumstance – Pelagius's self-defence of his own
virginity. It is not Pelagius who seeks out his death; rather he is a victim of
the evil Abd al-Rahman III.

The Evil Emperor

Abd al-Rahman III ascended the throne in Cordoba at age twenty in 912 CE. According to modern historians, his successful fifty-year reign was marked by an end to the civil war that had plagued al-Andalus and by the emergence of a strong, unified Islamic kingdom in the Iberian Peninsula. Al-Rahman is seen as the architect of this prosperity and his rule is considered the zenith of Muslim power in Spain. Al-Rahman was of mixed race – his mother was Frankish and his grandmother, Basque. While he swiftly and ruthlessly punished opponents, his policies toward Mozarabs were liberal. He not only guaranteed the rights of Christians to worship freely, he also allowed them to hold public office and serve in his government.[16] He had diplomatic ties with Byzantium, Italy, and, as mentioned above, Germany. In 929, he declared his autonomy from the caliphs of Baghdad and assumed the titles Caliph and Prince of Believers. This move gave him supreme civil and religious authority throughout al-Andalus.

Hrotsvit chooses to make this impressive historical figure the villain of her tale. Rather than the best of his dynasty, Hrotsvit sees al-Rahman as the worst:

> Donec sub nostris quidam de germine regis
> Temporibus regnum suscepit sorte parentum
> Deterior patribus, luxu carnis maculatus   (71–3)

> Then in our own days an offspring of that race
> Assumed in succession, the reign of his fathers.
> He was worse than they, and stained with wantonness.
>
> (Wilson, *Florilegium*, 31)

He embodies the epitome of all that is bad about Muslims. He shows his greed in the high ransoms he sets for the Galician lords, his bellicose nature in attacking Galicia, and his pagan sensibilities in his admitted idol worship. In each case, his vices are qualitatively worse than those of other Muslims. Not only is he greedy, he is duplicitous in negotiating Pelagius's father's ransom:

> Sed ducis est precium iussu regis duplicatum,
> Ultra quam propriis posset persolvere gazis.
> Cumque sui causa regi deferret avaro,

Quicquid habere domi sibimet suevit preciosi,
Casu condicti parvum puid defuit auri.
Quod rex sentiscens, fraudem quoque mente revolvens,
Dixit nolle ducem populo dimittere dulcem
Ni prius indictum plene solvat sibi censum
Non sitiens tantum precii, quod defuit, aurum,
Quantum rectorem populi gestit dare morti.   (133–42)

But on the king's demand, the duke's ransom was doubled,
To a sum exceeding what he could pay just then:
And when he bore as ransom to the greedy ruler
Whatever of treasures he could find at home,
By some mishap it was less than the demanded sum.
This the king declined, fostering fraud in mind,
And refused to return the sweet duke to his people;
Until, in full, he was told, he'd pay the required gold.
The king acted thus, not just in his greed
But in his desire strong to kill the nation's lord. (Wilson, *Florilegium*, 32–3)

His military prowess creates such arrogance 'Ut regem regum semet fore
crederet ipsum,/ Eius et imperio gentes omnes dare colla' (87–8), 'That
he even boasted to be the King of Kings/ And boasted that all nations
were subject to his rule' (Wilson, *Florilegium*, 31). And his religious
fervour extended to active persecution:

Sepius innocuo madefecit sanguine rura,
Corpora iustorum consumens sancta virorum,
Qui Christo laudes ardebant pangere dulces
Ipsius et stultos verbis reprehendere divos;   (81–4)

He drenched with guiltless blood, frequently the land
Ending holy lives, thus, of those just men,
Who were burning to chant the sweet praise of Christ
And were eager to denounce the king's own foolish idols.
                                        (Wilson, *Florilegium*, 31)

Hrotsvit's choice of villain would seem simply a correct reflection of
the historical record given the date of Pelagius's death, since 925 is
clearly within al-Rahman's reign. However, in the Spanish accounts of
Pelagius's martyrdom, the ruler remains anonymous. Hrotsvit purpose-

fully names al-Rahman in the text. Given his diplomatic exchanges with Otto's court, his name could have been familiar to her audience as well. Thus her naming is a bold move to satirize a contemporary political figure. Her reference to his claim to be 'King of Kings' could also reflect al-Rahman's title of Caliph. According to a contemporary chronicler, al-Rahman's practice was to use this title in all official writings.[17] Thus diplomatic correspondence with Otto would likely have included his broad claims to sovereignty. If so, Hrotsvit is clearly mocking al-Rahman's titles and rank. Hrotsvit further cast aspersions on al-Rahman's reputation in his taste for young boys. While the Spanish account of the Pelagius tale includes the seduction scene with the king, the king's vice remains unnamed and is contextualized as part of the general sexual excesses of the Islamic court as a whole.[18] For Hrotsvit, however, al-Rahman alone is 'corruptum vitiis ... Sodomitis' (205) 'stained by pederasty' (Wilson, *Florilegium*, 34).[19] Hrotsvit does acknowledge al-Rahman's military abilities. Yet even here she is able to turn the tables toward humiliation. While al-Rahman is successful in battle against the Galician, his lewdness first undermines his martial success: 'Ostentatque suum gemmato casside vultum,/ Ferrea lascivis inponens tegmina membris' (118–19), 'He displayed his face under his bejeweled helmet,/ Iron armor decking his wanton and lewd limbs' (Wilson, *Florilegium*, 32); later his face and beard are described mockingly: 'Sanguis ut absque mora stillans de vulnere facto/ Barbam fedavit necnon vestes madefecit' (274–5), 'The blood gushing forth from the inflicted wound/ Stained the king's beard and wetted all his garments' (Wilson, *Florilegium*, 36). A small Christian boy has managed to make the leader who holds him hostage after conquering his city look ridiculous. In his final scene, al-Rahman must get his henchmen to cut off this boy's head because the king's catapult, a state-of-the-art offensive war machine, is unable to inflict any harm on the heroic saint. Thus the greatest Muslim leader of Hrotsvit's day, with whom even Otto had to reckon, can be humiliated and defeated by one small but brave Christian boy.

Conclusion

In her account of the martyrdom of Pelagius, Hrotsvit presents her audience with an alarming view of their southern Islamic neighbours. Both in their military prowess and in their aggressive pagan otherness, Muslims are portrayed as a clear and present danger to Western Christendom. Hrotsvit's story is not overly alarmist, however. She is able to nuance her tale to reflect the uneasy economic and religious compromises of multicultural al-Andulusan society where a dominant Islamic ruling class sought to control a large Christian minority. This Christian church is under siege, 'weighed down,' but indomitable. Despite failed rebellions and unlucky border skirmishes, God continues to support and defend this community with the blood of virgin martyrs – a most powerful weapon. Like his sister martyrs facing Roman emperors, Pelagius is able to humiliate his royal enemy and expose him as a weak and silly buffoon. But by naming this particular buffoon al-Rahman III, Hrotsvit adds an additional layer of political satire to her work. Her audience can both laugh at and take comfort in this caricature of a real contemporary Islamic figure. One can wonder if Hrotsvit might even be casting some aspersions on the wisdom of Otto's attempts at international diplomacy. In any case, Hrotsvit's *Pelagius* succeeds as the best of 'cold war' propaganda – a cautionary tale about a real but rather distant enemy served a humiliating defeat by a mere boy and his all-powerful Christian God.

NOTES

1 Much attention has been paid to Hrotsvit's plays but little to the legends and even less to *Pelagius.* Marcelle Thiébaux, in her introduction to a translation of *Pelagius* in *The Writings of Medieval Women,* 171–219, briefly discusses the historical context of the work as does Enrico Cerulli in 'Le calife Abd al-Rahman III de Cordoue et le martyr Pelage dans un poème de Hrotsvitha.' See also Petroff, 'Eloquence and Heroic Virginity in Hrotsvit's Verse Legends,' in which Pelagius is used as one of three main examples, and chapter 1 of Jordan, *The Invention of Sodomy in Christian Theology,* 10–28, in which he analyses Hrotsvit's portrayal of the homoerotic episodes in the legend.

2 For more on medieval images of Islam in western Europe, see Tolan, *Medieval Christian Perceptions of Islam,* and his more recent *Saracens: Islam in the Medieval European Imagination.* Also available are Hill, 'The Christian View of the Muslims at the Time of the First Crusade'; Southern, *Western Views of Islam in the Middle Ages*; and Kedar, *Crusade and Mission.*

3 Díaz y Díaz. 'La pasión de S. Pelayo y su difusión,' includes an edition of Raguel. It is also available in *Acta Sanctorum,* Junii 7:183C–4F.

4 Jordan, *The Invention of Sodomy,* 23.

5 This is available in *Acta Sanctorum,* Junii 7:191B–7C.

6 Diaz y Diaz, 'La Pasion de S. Pelayo y su difusión,' 7ff.

7 Peter Dronke translates 'cuius seriem martirii quidam eiusdem, in qua passus est, indigena civitatis mihi exposuit, qui ipsum pulcherrimum virorum se vidisse et exitum rei attestatus est veraciter agnovisse' thus in *Women Writers*, 57.

8 See, in addition to Thiébaux and Cerulli, O'Callaghan, *A History of Medieval Spain*, 120, and Colbert, 'The Christians of Cordoba in the Tenth Century.'

9 John's account can be found in Pertz, *Vita Johannis Abbatis Gorziensis*.

10 Colbert, 'The Christians of Cordoba in the Tenth Century,' 384.

11 Ibid., 385.

12 Tolan, *Medieval Christian Perceptions of Islam*, xiv.

13 O'Callaghan, *A History of Medieval Spain*, 122.

14 For more on the martyrs of Cordoba see Wolf, *Christian Martyrs in Muslim Spain*.

15 In her introduction to the translation of Hrotsvit's *Pelagius* in *The Writing of Medieval Women*, 178, Marcelle Thiébaux makes this argument and speculates that Hrotsvit was even familiar with the writings of Eulogius, the chief hagiographer and apologist for the martyrs of Codoba who himself was later executed.

16 O'Callaghan, *A History of Medieval Spain*, 117.

17 Ibid., 118.

18 In *Christianity, Social Tolerance, and Homosexuality*, 194ff, John Boswell suggests that homoerotic relationships and activities were both common and socially accepted in al-Andulus; however, this view has been questioned by many and, recently, been effectively countered by Hutcheson in 'The Sodomitic Moor.' Nevertheless, the Western view that Muslims were likely to be sexually licentious (with an emphasis on sodomy) became an increasingly popular stereotype in the wake of the Crusades.

19 I agree with Boswell's assessment that Hrotsvit 'meant to make no theological statement about homosexual acts' (*Christianity, Social Tolerance, and Homosexuality*, 200). She does mean to insult al-Rahman, but her tone is no more condemning than in her other works in which pagan rulers lust after and try to seduce female Christian virgins – all such men are humiliatingly unsuccessful!

SECTION 2

Forming Identities

Violence and Virginity in Hrotsvit's Dramas

FLORENCE NEWMAN

'A key paradox of medieval hagiography,' according to Shari Horner, is that 'the bodies of female virgin martyrs are of primary importance in texts that purport not to be about the body at all.'[1] Other modern critics have noticed and sought to explain the hagiographers' inconsistency in focusing upon the corporeal ('breast, genital, gut, and all,' as Sheila Delaney succinctly puts it)[2] while celebrating the spiritual. Such explanations often acknowledge the sado-erotic appeal of sexually charged material for its audience. While not all of Hrotsvit's dramas are based upon the lives of female saints, they share with the saints' lives a preoccupation with women's bodies and the threats to those bodies, particularly – although not exclusively – to sexual chastity. Hrotsvit evokes the erotic, however, in order to de-eroticize the female body: the author's notorious dualism serves not to condemn and reject the physical (and, in the process to degrade women as the source of sexual pleasure and its concommitant guilt) but to affirm the achievement of Christian sanctity in the flesh. What appears to be the ultimate expression of the inconsequentiality of the body – Hirena's defiant response in *Dulcitius* to being consigned to a brothel, where her well-preserved virginity will be lost: 'voluptas parit poenam · necessitas autem coronam' (XII.3), 'lust deserves punishment, but forced compliance the crown' (Wilson, *Florilegium*, 51) – is in fact at the heart of the dramas' insistence on the virginal ideal. For it is only by means of the body and through its triumphs that union with God becomes possible.

Hagiography's ambivalence about the saints' physical life has aroused considerable critical discussion. Perhaps typical are the question and answer posed by Thomas Heffernan in *Sacred Biography: Saints and Their Biographers in the Middle Ages*. Heffernan asks, 'If the body is the locus of such "muck" [that is, the vileness and filth commonly mentioned in the *vitae sanctorum*], why did it take center stage in these sacred biographies?'[3] Heffernan proposes that inherent in the dualism of flesh and spirit is a conflict between 'pleasure derived from the body' and 'fear of the consequences of that pleasure'; the torture of female virgins at once titillated their audience with the spectre of bodily pleasure and instilled shame concerning human sexuality by debasing the object of desire.[4] Hrotsvit's *Dulcitius* would seem to illustrate precisely this arousal of the erotic impulse in order to punish it at its source. Dulcitius himself fantasizes, 'et vel optatis amplexibus me saturabo' (III.2), 'and satisfy myself in their [the three lovely maidens'] longed-for embrace' (Wilson, *Florilegium*, 47); finding the satisfaction of his desire illusory, he orders 'ut lascivae praesententur puellę · et abstractis vestibus publice denudentur · quo versa vice quid nostra possint ludibria experiantur' (VII), 'that they be led forth/ and that they be publicly stripped of all their clothes,/ so that they experience similar mockery in retaliation for ours' (Wilson, *Florilegium*, 49). The unsuccessful attempts to strip, prostitute, and burn the virgins' bodies and the successful penetration of Hirena's (by an arrow) conflate the sexual and the punitive. Likewise, the indignities inflicted upon Sapientia's daughters in the last of the plays – breasts severed, limbs lacerated, torsos grilled, broiled, flagellated and eviscerated – objectify the body in the first step, as it were, toward festishizing it.

But despite the potential of the dramatic form to enhance the sexually provocative aspect of hagiographical motifs, Hrotsvit's plays consistently deflect or deflate the 'sexing up' of their heroines. Thus Dulcitius's objectification of the three Christian girls – 'quam pulchrę · quam venustę · quam egregię puellulę' (II.1), 'how beautiful, how graceful, how admirable these little girls are' (Wilson, *Florilegium*, 47) – is rendered literal as he has them stowed away where the kitchen vessels are kept; his mistaking of the *vasa* for his would-be victims abruptly turns rape to farce. Although the resilience of Sapientia's daughters and their enthusiasm for, and invulnerability to, the various tortures they undergo may be only unintentionally comic, nonetheless, the pattern of escalating abuse on the part of the villains and unwavering good cheer on the part of the virgins, reiterated over the course of the play, dispels any sadistic pleasure the audience might take in observing physical suffering.[5] Fides tells Antiochus, 'Inviolatum pectus vulnerasti · sed me non lesisti · En pro fonte sanguinis · unda prorumpit lactis' (V.9), 'You have wounded my chaste breasts, but you have not hurt me. Look, instead of blood, milk gushes forth' (Wilson, *Florilegium*, 89). Spes mocks Hadrian: 'Decidentia frustra mei lacerati corporis · dant flagrantiam paradisiaci aromatis · quo nolens cogeris fateri · me non posse suppliciis lędi' (V.23), 'The pieces of my lacerated flesh give off this fragrant heavenly scent,/ forcing you to admit against your will that I cannot be harmed by your punishment' (Wilson, *Florilegium*, 92). Toward the end of the play, Hrotsvit juxtaposes the sexualized perception of Karitas with the Teflon asexuality she displays, when Antiochus says, 'Illa lasciva quam mihi cruciandam tradidisti puellula · me presente flagellabatur · sed ne tenuis quidem cutis summotenus disrumpebatur' (VI.1), 'That frisky little girl you gave me to be tortured was whipped in my presence, but not even the surface of her delicate skin was broken' (my translation).

The body nevertheless remains central to these dramas, with that importance concentrated in the virginal ideal perpetually at risk in the world Hrotsvit envisions.[6] The treatment of that ideal, while by no means programmatic, is relatively straightforward at the outset of the dramatic series and grows more complex over the course of the plays. The plot of *Gallicanus* is set into motion by the general's betrothal to Constantia, who has dedicated her virginity to God; her father must decide whether to sacrifice the temporal well-being of his empire by refusing his military commander or to sacrifice the eternal well-being of his soul by compelling his daughter to marry. The threat to Constantia's virginity is minimal, given that Constantius, unlike so many parents in saints' lives, supports the girl's vow of chastity. Constantia does aver that she would rather die than marry, however, and the firmness of her conviction leads to the conversion of Gallicanus and his daughters. Constantia's pivotal role is underscored by her hieratic prayer midway through the first half of the play:

Amator virginitatis · et inspirator castitatis Christe · qui me precibus martiris tuę Agnetis · a lepra pariter corporis et ab errore eripiens gentilitatis invitasti ad virgineum tui genitricis thalamum · ... · suppliciter exoro · ut Gallicanum · qui tui in me amorem surripiendo conatur extinguere · post te trahendo · ab iniusta intentione revocare suique filias digneris tibi assignare sponsas · et instilla cogitationibus earum tui amoris dulcedinem · quatinus execrantes carnale consortium · pervenire mereantur ad sacrarum societatem virginum · (V.2–3)

Christ, lover of virginity/ and inspiration of chastity,/ Thou who by the intercession of Thy martyr Agnes, healed me both from the leprosy of body and the error of paganism, and hast invited me to the virginal bedchamber of Thy mother ... I implore Thee, true wisdom, coeternal with the Father by whom all things were made,/ and by whose plan the Universe was created, ordered and weighed,/ that Thou revoke Gallicanus's intent, to try to quench my love for Thee,/ and call him to Thee./ May Thou also find his daughters worthy to be Thy brides, worthy of Thy trust./ Instill into their thoughts the sweetness of Thy love, so that despising carnal lust/ they may become worthy of joining the company of sacred virgins. (Wilson, *Plays*, 16)

Constantia invokes Christ as 'lover of virginity and inspiration of chastity' to check Gallicanus's wicked intentions and to infuse his daughters with such 'sweetness' of divine love that they will despise 'carnale consortium' and become worthy of joining the company of sacred virgins as Christ's brides. She alludes to the virgin martyr Agnes, who interceded to preserve Constantia's body and mind for the divine bedchamber. The language of love and matrimony suggests that while the Christian faith imposes a higher claim on the individual, one that transcends mere carnality, it is a claim made on both flesh and spirit. Similar language is given to Agnes herself in the *Legends*, prompting Elizabeth Petroff to observe that Agnes 'live[s] a remarkably sensual existence; virginity is not a negation of erotic desire, but a creative sublimation of it.'[7] Furthermore, the model of St Agnes, like other exemplars of 'heroic virginity,' reinforces the idea that the religious commitment of women especially was tied up with their bodies.[8]

The second half of the play obliquely mirrors the first; when the Roman persecution under Julian the Apostate falls upon John and Paul, Constantia's chamberlains, their steadfastness in faith brings about not only their martyrdom but also the conversion of the father and son who murdered them. The miracles performed by God to protect Constantia's chastity find their counterpart in the miraculous punishment of Terrentianus's son, which takes place at the tomb of John and Paul. Hrotsvit leaves no doubt that the body is crucially significant to saintliness when she has Terrentianus say:

Gratias regi aeternitatis · qui suis militibus tantum praestitit honoris · ut non solum anime gaudent in caelis · sed etiam mortua in tumulis ossa · variis fulgent miraculorum titulis · in testimonium sui sanctitatis · praestante domino nostro Iesu Christo qui vivit <et regnat deus in unitate spiritus sancti per omnia saecula saeculorum · Amen ·> (IX.2)

Praise to the Immortal King who bestows such honor on his soldiers that not only do their souls rejoice in heaven, but even their lifeless bones shine forth in the sepulchre, working miracles in testimony of their holiness, through the power of our Lord Jesus Christ, who lives and reigns one God in the unity of the Holy Spirit for ever and ever. Amen. (my translation)

For most early Christians, as Caroline Bynum has shown, concepts of the body were forged during the period of persecution, when the dissolution of the flesh in death was graphically realized by martyrs subjected to dismemberment and consumption by wild animals.[9] Tellingly, the first two of Hrotsvit's dramas, as well as the last, are set in the first century of the Christian era, one of the most prolific in its production of those saints and martyrs whose bodies testified both in life and in death to the veracity of their religious faith. *Dulcitius* most overtly demonstrates the degree to which, as Margaret Miles observes, the martyrs of hagiographical literature 'insisted on assimilating their bodies to the religious identity they had chosen and developed.'[10] In the play's opening lines, Diocletian decrees simultaneously the marriages of Agape, Chionia, and Hirena and their renunciation of Christ, to which Agape replies: 'nec ad negationem confitendi nominis · nec ad corruptionem integritatis · ullis rebus compelli poterimus' (I.2), 'we cannot be compelled under any duress/ to betray Christ's holy name, which we must confess,/ nor to stain our virginity' (Wilson, *Florilegium*, 45). The girls' mockery of Hadrian's paganism and their evasion of Dulcitius's embrace equally manifest the resistance to the world imposed upon them because of their belief in Christianity. In fact, the play portrays physical resolve as an extension of the believer's inviolate will: the three maidens first refuse to denounce Christ and then endure both sexual assault and torture to secure at last the martyr's palm and the crown of virginity, as Hirena specifies in her final speech: 'ego autem martirii palmam · virginitatisque receptura coronam · intrabo aethereum aeterni regis thalamum' (XIV.3). The physical threats against Hirena progress from death, to slow death, to rape – the last a fate which the persecutors assume to be 'worse than death' for Christian virgins.

As we have noted, Hrotsvit here appears to call into question the importance of physical *integritas* by having Hirena remain unphased by the prospect of being consigned to a brothel: 'Melius est · ut corpus quibuscumque iniuriis · maculetur · quam anima idolis poluatur' (XII.3), It is better that the body be dirtied with any stain than that the soul be polluted with idolatry' (Wilson, *Florilegium*, 51). However, when Hirena announces that rape holds no threat for her because 'nec dicitur reatus · nisi quod consentit animus' (XII.3), 'with neither [lust nor forced compliance] is one considered guilty,/ unless the soul consents freely'

(Wilson, *Florilegium*, 51), she echoes Augustine's insistence in *The City of God* that 'purity is a quality of the mind' and that

> corporis sanctitatem manente animi sanctitate etiam corpore oppresso, sicut amittitur et corporis sanctitas violata animi sanctitate etiam corpore intacto.
>
> Quam ob rem non habet quod in se morte spontanea puniat femina sine ulla sua consensione violenter oppressa et alieno conpressa peccato (I.xviii)[11]

> just as bodily chastity is lost when mental chastity has been violated, so bodily chastity is not lost, even when the body has been ravished, while the mind's chastity endures. Therefore, when a woman has been ravished without her consenting, and, forced by another's sin, she has no reason to punish herself.[12]

This 'spiritual definition' of chastity, as Clarissa Atkinson has shown, 'coexisted thoughout the medieval period' with the physical definition emphasized by St Jerome.[13] Identifying chastity as a quality of the mind does not negate the significance of the body but merely subordinates it to the will, which exercises its power over it and through it. Thus Augustine writes, 'Sit igitur in primus positum atque firmatum virtutem, qua recte vivitur, ab animi sede membris corporis imperare sanctumque corpus usu fieri sanctae voluntatis' (I.xvi), 'In the first place, it must be firmly established that virtue, the condition of right living, holds command over the parts of the body from her throne in the mind, and that the consecrated body is the instrument of the consecrated will.'[14] It has been pointed out that one consequence of Hrotsvit's locating innocence in the conscience of the woman raped is that dramatization of the innocent rape victim is virtually impossible, since the site of innocence (or guilt) is invisible to the viewer.[15] Hrotsvit solves the problem of dramatization by having Hirena articulate the principle of spiritual chastity and following almost immediately with the miraculous intervention of angels who whisk her bodily away to the nearest mountain top, an objective correlative of sorts to the saint's internal incorruption. For Hrotsvit, as for Augustine, 'ipsum corpus sanctificatur,' 'the body itself is sanctified,' 'cum immunditiae carnalium concupiscentarum non cedit,' 'by resisting the indecency of carnal desires' (I.xviii).[16]

The most peculiar of the plays in its treatment of the chaste ideal, but one crucial to our understanding of Hrotsvit's emphasis on the female body, is *Calimachus*. In the play, Drusiana's body continues to inspire lust and evoke divine protection, even after death. Like Constantia, Drusiana preferred death to loss of celibacy; in her case, God granted her wish, presumably as a means of fulfilling his salvific plan, since even death does not lessen her desirability or deter Calimachus from seeking his ruin through her.[17] The lifelessness of Drusiana's body not only portrays sexual desire in its most revolting and irrational form; it focuses our attention on the body *as* body. That Drusiana's corpse seems immune to decay suggests that the control over the flesh she exhibited throughout her earthly life continues by divine intercession once the soul has withdrawn;[18] moreover, the chaste condition Drusiana had maintained while alive God continues to maintain when she is dead. As Calimachus later reports at Drusiana's grave vault, a monstrous serpent poisons the servant Fortunatus, and Christ himself appears to Calimachus, sparks flying from his flaming face, to cover Drusiana's naked form respectfully and command, '"Calimache morere ut vivas"' (IX.13), '"Calimachus, die so that you may live"' (Wilson, *Florilegium*, 61). And in this sepulchral scene strewn with cadavers, several resurrections occur: first that of Calimachus, then Drusiana, then Fortunatus. These resurrections allow Hrotsvit to discourse on the relation of soul to body in Christian theology. Invoking God to revive Calimachus, St John states, 'Qui solus es id quod es · qui diversa duo sotians · ex hoc et hoc hominem fingis · eademque dissotians · unum quod constabat, resolvis · iube ut reducto halitu · disjunctaque compagine · rursus conliminata · Calimachus resurgat · plenus ut fuit homo' (IX.9), 'you who alone are what you are, who by mingling two different elements created man, and by separating those elements again dissolved that whole, grant that, his breath restored and the disjointed elements rejoined, Calimachus may rise up whole, as he was, a man' (my translation). Drusiana invokes God to resurrect Fortunatus:

> Divina substantia · quę vere et singulariter es sine materia forma · quę hominem ad tui imaginem plasmasti · et plasmato spiraculum vitę inspirasti · iube materiale corpus Fortunati reducto calore in viventem animam iterum reformari · quo trina nostri resuscitacio · tibi in laudem vertatur trinitas veneranda · (X.3)

> Divine Substance, who truly and singularly are without material form, who have made man in your image and breathed the breath of life into what you have made, grant that heat may return to Fortunatus's material body so that he may be formed anew a living being, and that our triple resurrection may be turned to praise of you, the revered Trinity. (my translation)

Only God exists without created form; it is the nature of humankind to combine form and spirit. Death dissolves that union, but resurrection restores it. Features of this episode – the broken tomb, the fiery messenger who intercepts those who approach it, the resurrections themselves – are reminiscent of Christ's Resurrection, and its stress on judgment, forgiveness, and punishment anticipates Resurrection on Judgment Day. We are inevitably reminded that the body, because of Christ's incarnation and physical suffering, is destined to be reunited with the soul for all eternity: 'It is sown a perishable body, it is raised an imperishable body ... it is sown a natural body, it is raised a spiritual body' (I Cor.15: 42, 44) – but body it is and will be.

The theology of human nature and the promise of resurrection explain, at least in part, Hrotsvit's preoccupation with chastity and with the threats and displays of violence common to the genre of saints' lives. Only by resisting physical temptations and enduring physical afflictions can the believer demonstrate her adherence to the truth of the Christian faith and thus merit supreme reward. Augustine ends *The City of God* by establishing precisely such a connection between the martyrs, miracles, and the resurrection of the flesh: the miracles of the martyrs, he argues, attest to the reality that 'Christus resurexisse in carne et in caelum ascendisse cum carne' (XXII.ix), 'Christ rose in the flesh and ascended into heaven in the flesh.' He continues, 'Pro ista fide mortui sunt qui haec a Domino impetrare possunt propter cuius nomen occisi sunt' (XXII.ix), 'For this faith they died, and they can now obtain these blessings [i.e., miracles] from the Lord, for whose name they were slain.'[19] The saints underwent death because they believed that their bodies would be resurrected; the miracles they perform confirm the validity of their belief:

> Dicendo enim vera passi sunt, ut possint facere mira. In eis veris est praecipuum quod Christus resurrexit a mortuis et immortalitem resurrexionis in sua carne primus ostendit, quam nobis adfuturam vel principio novi saeculi vel huius fine promisit. (XXII.x)

> It was for speaking the truth that they suffered; and because of this they have the power to perform miracles. And among all the truths they speak, this is the most important: that Christ rose from the dead and first displayed the immortality of that resurrection in his own body, and promised that it would come to us at the beginning of the new age or (which is the same) at the end of the world.[20]

Even prior to death, Hrotsvit's heroines exhibit miraculous power over their bodies and those of others, proving the strength of their faith and the truth of Christ's promise.

In *The Resurrection of the Body in Western Christianity, 200 – 1360*, Bynum provides a context for Augustine's comments in the 'early exhortations to martyrdom' that 'both express in graphic ... prose the suffering entailed and offer hope of resurrection as a protection against it.' She goes on to observe that 'resurrection was finally not so much the triumph of martyrs over pain and humiliation as the triumph of martyrs' bodies over fragmentation ...'[21] Sheila Delany has traced Augustine's influence at the other end of the medieval period on the legendary of the fourteenth-century friar Osbern Bokenham. Bokenham's depictions of the 'fragmentation and reconstitution' of women's bodies in his saints' lives, Delany states, reflect his larger concern with 'Christian eschatology, death, and resurrection.'[22] For example, as an Augustinian friar, Bokenham had particular reason to view the hagiographical motif of dismemberment in light of Augustine's teaching that 'the resurrected body would be the same body as during life, complete in all its parts, lacking only concupiscence and corruption.'[23] The emphasis on resurrection theory, though strongest in the later Middle Ages, originated during the patristic period, and Augustine's doctrine dominated from the sixth century on.[24] It is no accident that at the centre of Hrotsvit's dramatic sequence we should discover the miracle of Drusiana's resurrected form, alive, intact, testifying to God's power in and over the created world.

Subsequent plays complicate and problematize the virginal ideal and the body as the site of struggle and salvation. *Abraham* and *Paphnutius* both feature women who have prostituted themselves, illustrating the very opposite extreme from the models of feminine chastity represented earlier. These plays illustrate the forgiveness of God, extended even to those – *especially* to those – who have failed the tests of virtue attendant to life in this world. *Abraham* most obviously employs Christological themes to recall the good Shepherd's redemption of his lost lambs. In these plays, promiscuity becomes the paradigm of all human sinfulness, just as virginity had epitomized the successful struggle against forces both mundane and diabolical. The antidote to spiritual pollution is physical mortification. Mary adopts a hair shirt and continuous vigils and fasts; Thais is confined for three years to a narrow cell filled with her own excrement. Here Hrotsvit seems most disparaging of the body and most conventionally misogynistic about women's concupiscence. Thais, it is said, 'non dignatur cum paucis ad interitum tendere · sed prompta est omnes lenociniis suę formę illicere · secumque ad interitum trahere' (I.24), 'is not satisfied with leading only a few men to damnation/ but is ready to ensnare all men with the allurement of her beauty and drag them along with her to eternal perdition' (Wilson, *Plays*,102). In Mary's case, it appears certain that her wilful capitulation to lust has irrevocably altered her status in God's eyes. Effrem promises her:

> Si incorrupta et virgo permanebis · angelis dei fies aequalis · quibus tandem stipata · gravi corporis onere abiecto · pertransies aera · supergradieris ęthera · ... zodiacum percurres circulum · nec subsistendo temperabis gressum · donec iungaris amplexibus filii virginis · in lucifluo thalamo sui genitricis · (II.5)

> If you remain incorrupt and a virgin, you will be the equal of God's angels; accompanied by them, having thrown off the burden of the body, you will traverse the sky, surmounting the ether ... and you will pass through the circle of the zodiac, not slackening your pace until you are embraced in the arms of the Virgin's Son in the lustrous bridal chamber of his mother. (my translation)

After her defection, according to Abraham, she 'se corruptam sensit,' perceived herself corrupted or marred, and after hearing of her self-castigations, Effrem remarks that she punished herself, 'Nec iniuria · huiusmodi namque ruina · toto lacrimarum fonte est lugenda' (III.5), 'Not without reason, for her ruin must be mourned/ and with great outpouring of tears deplored' (Wilson, *Florilegium*, 70).

Nonetheless, Hrotsvit implies that just as the choices the will makes through the body can cause the soul's damnation, those same choices can elevate the soul to that purity requisite for union with the divine. Abraham receives two visions that foretell Mary's fate: in the first, a hideous dragon seizes and devours a little white dove; in the second, Abraham crushes the dragon under his feet and the same dove darts away. The escape of the dove is reminiscent of the ascent Effrem had predicted for Mary if she preserved her virginity. The vision reported by the hermit Paul at the end of *Pafnutius* is even more suggestive: 'Videbam in visione lectulum candidulis palliolis in cęlo magnifice stratum · cui quattuor splendidę virgines pręerant · et quasi custodiendo astabant ·' (XI.2), 'I saw in my vision a splendid bed in the heavens, adorned with white hangings and coverings, around which were four radiant virgins who stood there as if they were guarding it' (my translation). Paul assumes that this beatitude is prepared for his holy father Antonius, but a celestial voice tells him, '"Non ut speras Antonio · sed Thaidi meretrici servanda est haec gloria"' (XI.2), '"This glory is not reserved, as you believe, for Antony, but for the prostitute, Thais!"' (my translation). The bed, the white linen, the heavenly setting, the splendor – the bed chamber of the divine bridegroom inevitably comes to mind. In some of the stories of Mary Magdalen (of whom Thais's experience and Mary's name are evocative), physical integrity is restored to the repentant prostitute.[25] Susan Haskins reports that in the thirteenth century Margaret of Cartona, a devotee of Magdalen who had lived with her lover and bore a child by him before her conversion, claimed to have heard the voice of Christ telling her, 'Your contrition and sorrow will restore to you your virgin purity'; Christ adduced as precedent Mary Magdalen: 'After the Virgin Mary and Catherine, the Martyr [of Alexandria], there is none above Magdalen in the choir of virgins.'[26] Hrotsvit does not go so far; or, perhaps, she goes farther, by indicating (in the words of Joan Cadden) that 'the essence of virginal purity [exists] in spite of the absence of physical virginity.'[27] The fervency and fidelity of these sinners' love for God, combined with their penitential suffering, earns the same portion of honour as those, like Antonius, who remain steadfast in their faith.

Abraham and Pafnutius are set in the fourth century, when the foundations of Christian monasticism were being laid by the eremetic fathers; Antonius himself was considered the 'first' among hermits and his legend the inspiration for a new type of hagiography celebrating sainthood achieved not by violent execution but by voluntary and life-long ascesis.[28] In choosing to link the stories of Mary and Thais with those of Gallicanus and Agape, Chionia, and Hirena, Hrotsvit underscores the historical progression by which monasticism succeeded martyrdom as the ideal imitatio Christi:[29] the 'bloodless martyrdom' whereby monks and nuns rejected the world and sacrificed themselves completely to God was no less difficult or deserving than the spectacular passiones of the original saints. Furthermore, Hrotsvit implies that the common denominator between the two forms of Christian perfection is the arduous but ultimately achievable struggle to bring the body through its earthly trials to its spiritual destination.[30]

In the last of her plays, Sapientia, Hrotsvit returns to the early period of Christian oppression when the forces brought to bear on the body originated externally rather than as acts of self-denial. Nevertheless,

Hrotsvit emphasizes the volition involved: the martyrs seek out their own persecution, arriving in Rome to evangelize the pagan populace, and they eagerly embrace whatever grotesque tortures Hadrian sends their way: Fides jumps into a pot of wax and pitch prepared for her; menaced with flogging, Spes says, 'Hanc pietatem exopto · hanc lenitatem desidero' (V.19), 'But *this* is the kindness I desire; *this* is the mildness I hope for' (Wilson, *Florilegium*, 91). The virgins' invulnerability to pain may seem to cancel any admiration of their courage, fortitude, and patience, but that invulnerability manifests not only the impotence of their enemies but also the firmness of their will. Bynum refers to this phenomenon as the 'anesthesia of glory' by which the impassibility promised to the body in the final resurrection is anticipated physically by the martyr undergoing affliction.[31] Throughout their progress toward death, the three sisters and their mother have their eyes on the prize. Sapientia says to her three daughters, 'Ad hoc vos materno lacte affluenter alui · ad hoc delicate nutrivi · ut vos cęlesti, non terreno sponso traderem · quo vestri causa socrus aeterni regis dici meruissem' (IV.3), 'It was for this that I nursed you with my milk flowing free;/ it was for this that I carefully reared you three;/ that I may espouse you to a heavenly, not an earthly bridegroom and may deserve to be called the mother-in-law of the Eternal King thereby' (Wilson, *Florilegium*, 87). Later Spes cries to Karitas, 'nitere · constanti fide imitari sorores · ad cęli palatium precedentes' (V.26), 'Follow in firm faith the example of your sisters, who precede you to Heaven's palace' (Wilson, *Florilegium*, 92). Sapientia adds, 'sperne presens utile · quo pervenias ad gaudium interminabile · quo tui germanę fulgent coronis · illibatę virginitatis' (V.29), 'Spurn the comfort of this life/ so that you may reach never-ending joy, where your sisters already sparkle, radiant with the crowns of untouched virginity' (Wilson, *Florilegium*, 93).

The continuum between the earthly ordeal endured in the natural body and the heavenly reward to be received in the spiritual body is emphasized by the concluding scene, in which Sapientia prepares for burial her daughters' remains: 'Flosculos uteri mei · tibi terra servandos committo · quos tu materiali sinu foveto · donec in resurrectione maiori reviridescant gloria' (IX.1), 'I commit to you, Earth, the flowers of my womb. Guard them in your earthen lap until in glory they bloom afresh/ after the resurrection of the flesh' (Wilson, *Florilegium*, 95). Tellingly, Sapientia's companions refuse to leave her until she herself has expired and they can inter her body as well. Her closing, rhapsodic prayer offers a synopsis of church doctrine regarding Christ's dual nature, incarnation, and promise of resurrection:

ut nullus in te credentium periret · sed omnis fidelis aeternaliter viveret · mortem nostram non dedignatus es gustare · tuaque resurrectione consumere · Te etiam perfectum deum hominemque verum · recolo promisisse omnibus qui pro tui nominis veneratione vel terren̨e usum possessionis relinquerent · vel carnalium affectum propinquorum postponerent centen̨e vicissitudinem mercedis recompensari · et etern̨e bravium vit̨e debere donari · (IX.6–7)

Thou hast not refused to taste death for us, only to destroy it by rising again from the dead./ Very God and very man,/ I know that Thou hast said that Thou wilt reward a hundredfold/ all of those who gave up the hold/ of worldly possessions and earthly love for the worship of Thy name,/ and Thou has promised to the same/ to bestow upon them the gift of life everlasting. (Wilson, *Florilegium*, 96)

The image with which the prayer concludes – that of the martyred girls singing a new, joyful song as they follow the Lamb among the other maidens – segues into the verse paraphrase of St John's *Apocalypse* that immediately follows the plays in the Emmeram codex (Munich, Bavarian State Library Clm 14485). St John's vision, which was understood in the Middle Ages as simultaneously a prophecy of the future and a revelation of God's eternal present, fulfills the promise of bodily resurrection at the heart of Christian belief and brings full circle the story of resolve and resistance begun with Constantia.

In Hrotsvit's dramatic series, the female body is frequently the occasion of sin – for Gallicanus, for Dulcitius, for Calimachus, for Thais's many lovers, for Thais and Mary themselves. It is even more often the target of abuse, sexual and otherwise. The body holds such prominence not, as one might assume, because the plays seek to exploit the erotic aspects of women's sexuality, but because, for the author, the body is the locus of that dedication, struggle, victory, and reward made possible by God's habitation of the flesh and his desire to redeem it.[32] The theology of the body informing the plays is applicable to both women and men; Hrotsvit's view of virginity, Petroff observes, 'is not gender-linked.'[33] Nonetheless, in the dramas women almost exclusively demonstrate and express the dominance of the will over the body faced with temptation and peril. Given that most women are inherently physically weaker than most men, female characters provide Hrotsvit with a rich opportunity to illustrate one of her favourite biblical themes: 'God hath chosen the foolish things of the world to confound the wise; and God hath chosen

the weak things of the world to confound the mighty' (I Cor. 1:27). In
this sense, perhaps the plays provide proof of Duncan Robertson's statement that 'the "weaker" sex performs brilliantly under torture,' thus
more effectively displaying the absolute conquest of 'immaterial, divine
power over the material world.'[34] But God does not act alone: the power
of the feminine mind collaborates in that conquest.

Throughout the dramas, Hrotsvit summons up the traditional association of women with the body, which ordinarily connotes irrationality,
sensuality, and inferiority, as a means of illustrating the spiritual strength
women exercise through the body. Constantia has no concerns about the
prospect of living celibately in the same household as her former suitor,
whereas Gallicanus hesitates. Pafnutius fears that Thais's delicacy will
cause her to break under the harshness of her penance; instead, he finds
that she prefers her filthy cell to the soft uncertainties of the outside
world. Sissinus thinks Hirena will be 'abominably defiled' by forced
prostitution; the young virgin is confident that she cannot be sullied
unless her *animus* consents. While the female body is so often considered
a liability in the quest for holiness, the women in Hrotsvit's plays are
capable of almost anything they put their minds to – including mystical
marriage with the risen Christ.

This affirmation was no doubt welcome to Hrotsvit's original audience, assuming it was the nuns of Gandersheim Abbey. They are, the
dramas imply, the direct successors of the virgin martyrs: their commitment to chastity and religious service will also earn them a place among
the white-robed company who follow the Lamb. The choice to dramatize
the struggles of the faithful against the powers of this world has implications for the playwright as well. In order to fulfil her intent of employing
Terence's dramatic style to exalt religious virtue, Hrotsvit tells us in her
preface to the plays, she was compelled ('cogente') by the conventions of
the genre to contemplate and articulate 'that detestable madness of
unlawful lovers and of their evil flattery' (Wilson, *Florilegium*, 41): 'Hoc
tamen facit non raro verecundari · gravique rubore perfundi · quod
huiusmodi specie dictationis cogente detestabilem inlicite amantium
dementiam · et male dulcia colloquia eorum ·' (4). She goes on to make a
statement that seems to refer equally well to her heroines' ordeals and to
her own successful effort to wrest the Terentian form to moral purposes:

quanto blandicie amentium ad illiciendum promptiores · tanto et superni
adiutoris gloria sublimior · et triumphantium victoria probatur gloriosior
presertim cum feminea fragilitas vinceret · (5)

'because the more seductive the unlawful flatteries of those who have lost their sense,/ the greater the Heavenly Helper's munificence/ and the more glorious the victories of triumphant innocence are shown to be,/ especially/ when female weakness triumphs in conclusion.' (Wilson, *Florilegium*, 41)

However her compositions measure up to those of her predecessor, for Hrotsvit the labour has been worthwhile, because she has worked within the constraints of dramatic poetry and yet avoided ('abstinendo') the pernicious allurements of the pagan writers ('perniciosas gentilium delicias,' 9). Analysing Merovingian hagiography, John Kitchen has remarked on the importance of the authors' prefaces for understanding what the writers themselves saw as the meaning of their *vitae*.[35] In the preface to her plays, by casting her work as the dangerous exposure of herself to the seductions of the Terentian form, Hrotsvit reinforces and enacts the process of triumphing through trials of fortitude and piety necessary for the saints' ultimate reward.

NOTES

1 Horner, 'The Violence of Exegesis,' 22.
2 Delany, *Impolitic Bodies*, 106.
3 Heffernan, *Sacred Biography*, 282.
4 Ibid.
5 In *Impolitic Bodies*, Sheila Delany points out that decapitation alone distinguishes the virgin martyrs from the cartoon character Roadrunner (71). The literary pattern of the saint's life is by definition comic, culminating in, ideologically speaking, the happiest of endings. For modern readers, stories of the saints may be 'comic in the common sense meaning of the word as well as in the more literary meaning,' as Carolyn Walker Bynum has said of texts and pictures concerned with the reassemblage of bodies at the general resurrection in *Fragmentation*, 25.
6 In 'Beyond Virginity,' Stephen L. Wailes argues that virginity is not of major interest to Hrotsvit: sexual subject matter is only tangential to the larger theme of 'the conflict of flesh and spirit' (3). While I disagree with Wailes on the relative importance assigned to sexuality in the plays, I share his belief that the sexual elements are part of Hrotsvit's larger vision of human nature and that the theme of the dramas is not virginity for virginity's sake. Wailes also recognizes the relevance of Augustinian thought for the devel-

opment of Hrotsvit's ideology of flesh and spirit, although he draws upon different passages of *The City of God* in making his case.

7 Petroff, 'Eloquence and Heroic Virginity,' 236.

8 Miles, *Carnal Knowing*, 75.

9 Bynum, *Resurrection*, 58.

10 Miles, *Carnal Knowing*, 54.

11 The Latin text of *The City of God* is from the Loeb Classical Library seven-volume edition (Cambridge: Harvard University Press, 1957–72), with roman numerals indicating book and chapter number. Delany, *Impolitic Bodies*, points out the same Augustinian allusion in Bokenham's fourteenth-century version of the life of St. Lucy: 'never shall the body be defiled without the assent of the soul' (117).

12 Augustine, *City of God*, trans. David Knowles, 28.

13 Atkinson, '"Precious Balm in a Fragile Glass,"' 132–3; see also Newman, *From Virile Woman to WomanChrist*, 30.

14 Knowles's translation, 26. In defining virtue as a quality of the mind, Augustine follows a widespread philosophic tradition reflected in the Stoics and Neoplatonists (cf. Marcus Aurelius, *Meditations* 2.1, 8.27; Plotinus, *Enneads* I.4.7.8 ff.; Boethius, *The Consolation of Philosophy* I. pm. 4, II. pr. 4). Augustine avoided the more dualistic tendencies of this tradition (i.e., the body as the prison of the soul) by stressing that the body is a good created by God for the soul's use and that the love of the soul for the body is natural and eternal. See Gilson, *The Christian Philosophy of Saint Augustine*, 60–1, 167.

15 Sperberg-McQueen, 'Whose Body Is It?' 54.

16 Knowles's translation, 27–8.

17 Wailes, 'Beyond Virginity,' suggests that Drusiana is sexually tempted by Calimachus and that God takes Drusiana's life in order to save her from suicidal despair (14–15). Wailes's analysis of this scene answers a number of questions, such as why Drusiana protests so vociferously that she feels nothing but disgust for Calimachus and why God's intervention on her behalf differs from his miraculous preservation of women's chastity elsewhere in the dramas. It is worth noting that Augustine's comments on the inviolability of the will in *The City of God* arise precisely in his discussion of women who committed suicide in order to avoid rape, mistakenly, according to Augustine, since the victim of assault remains innocent while the suicide is guilty of self-murder (I.xvii). I believe we must accept at face value, however, Drusiana's plea that Christ speed her death to prevent not *her* ruin, but that of Calimachus: 'Iube me in te Christe · ocius mori · ne fiam in ruinam delicato iuveni' (IV), 'Help me, O Christ, therefore, with

my plan / and permit me to die so that I won't become the ruin of that
charming young man' (Wilson, *Florilegium*, 57).

18 Caroline Bynum has demonstrated how consistently bodily incorruption is
offered as proof of holiness in the Middle Ages: 'The claim that all or part
of a saint remained incorrupt after burial was an important miracle for
proving sanctity, particularly the sanctity of women' (*Resurrection*, 326; see
also, *Fragmentation*, 187). Such miracles were especially associated with
women saints, she speculates, 'because both medical literature and misogynistic tracts characterized the female body as more changeable than the
male' (*Resurrection*, 221). Of major relevance to Hrotsvit's treatment of the
body not only in the dramas but in the legends is the continuity Bynum
describes between the physical purity attained by asceticism during life and
the 'jewel-like' glory assumed by the saint's remains in death (ibid., 113–
14): the body of a saint 'had begun to be a relic while still alive' (ibid., 200).

19 Knowles's translation, 1047.

20 Ibid., 1049.

21 Bynum, *Resurrection*, 45, 50.

22 Delany, *Impolitic Bodies*, 124.

23 Ibid., 125.

24 Ibid., 126–7.

25 Newman, *From Virile Woman to WomanChrist*, 176–7.

26 Haskins, *Mary Magdalen*, 184–5. Margaret also received a vision in which
she saw the Magdalen 'surrounded by angels and dressed in a robe of silver,
with a crown of precious jewels upon her head,' the robe and crown earned
(by her victories over temptation, and by the penance which she imposed
upon herself' in the desert (187). Haskins proposes that Mary Magdalen
came to occupy the place in the heavenly hierarchy abandoned by the Virgin when her perfection raised her above the realm of ordinary women:
Magdalen became 'a model for mere mortals who could sin and sin again
and yet through repentance still hope to reach heaven' (141).

27 Cadden, *Meanings of Sex Difference in the Middle Ages*, 264.

28 Robertson, *Medieval Saints' Lives*, 26, 76–87.

29 Sticca, 'The Hagiographical and Monastic Context of Hrotsvith's Plays,' 13.

30 In *Pafnutius*, Hrotsvit expresses this goal as the 'harmony' of body and soul,
a concord disrupted when Thais puts her body in service to the world. See
Chamberlain, 'Musical Learning and Dramatic Action in Hrotsvit's
Paphnutius,' 331–4.

31 Bynum, *Resurrection*, 45 nn.95, 96.

32 Demers, '*In virginea forma*,' reaches a similar conclusion, though for differ-

ent reasons, arguing that Hrotsvit's characters have not 'simple-mindedly rejected or written off the body' but validate it through the 'ecstatic intensity and power of their praise' (57). Speaking more generally, Bynum in *Fragmentation* admits that in Western religious history the 'body was not always a friend or a tool or a gateway to heaven,' yet is struck by 'the extent to which female bodily experience was understood to be union with God' throughout the medieval period (236).

33 Petroff, 'Eloquence and Heroic Virginity,' 230.
34 Robertson, *Medieval Saints' Lives*, 53.
35 Kitchen, *Saints' Lives and the Rhetoric of Gender*, 139.

Kids Say the Darndest Things: Irascible Children in Hrotsvit's *Sapientia*

DANIEL T. KLINE

To judge from the frequency with which they appear in her work, Hrotsvit of Gandersheim is fascinated by children and childhood – its social dynamics, physical instabilities, and developmental possibilities. Many of her plays and legends focus on children and youth, the fragility of their lives, and the need to find meaning in their deaths, even the social necessity and theological exigency of their deaths. Hrotsvit's re-sourceful, sassy, and irascible children are like the 'litel clergeoun' of Chaucer's *Prioress's Tale*, who sings incessantly and perhaps inappropriately where he ought not to. One of the best examples of Hrotsvit's portrayal of children, and the focus of this essay, is the play *Sapientia*. However, in contrast to the stereotypical Jews who are offended by the child's song and viciously silence the little boy in Chaucer's story, Hadrian, the pagan emperor in *Sapientia*, attempts to coerce Fides, Spes, and Karitas, Sapientia's three young daughters, to worship or even to recognize the pagan gods verbally. Hrotsvit's *Sapientia* thereby stages a series of oppositions: youth and age, child and emperor, male and female, Christian and pagan, verbal licence and physical mastery. While Hrotsvit's plays have been analysed for their gender dynamics, theological implications, monastic ideals, and Ottonian contexts, the representation of childhood and the dynamics of age have yet to be considered fully in relation to other key themes.[1] My contention in this essay is that careful attention to the nuances of age and family structure leads to a reconsideration of important questions of sexual violence, the exercise of power, and the construction of gender, which, in turn, lead to a consideration of Hrotsvit's representation of children generally.

Context

Katharina M. Wilson notes that the royal abbey at Gandersheim was not simply the modern stereotype of a cloistered, isolated environment but was a cultural crossroads, and 'like the other great medieval monasteries it functioned as a school, hospital, library, political center, house of refuge, and center of pilgrimage.'[2] Gandersheim's close relationship to the Ottonian court has been well documented, as has the context of papal politics, imperial rule, and Christian apologetics in which Hrotsvit's plays are embedded.[3] Hrotsvit flourished at Gandersheim during the period in which the abbess was Gerberga II, who around 965 commissioned the *Carmen de Gesta Ottonis Imperatoris* or *Gesta*, a Christian epic depicting Otto I as the ideal Christian ruler.[4] Otto III's death in 1002 ended the Ottonian dynasty, plagued as it was by internal intrigue and external attack. Throughout the dynasty, monastic institutions like Gandersheim often became involved in larger political struggles as a result of their wealth and prestige. On the one hand, noble families used religious establishments as ways of preserving wealth and caring for the upkeep and education of their daughters, as well as forestalling political alliances through sequestration of their daughters and keeping the land and wealth necessary for dowries.[5] On the other hand, the imperial family began to recognize that land given over to a monastery with papal privileges was lost to them, and as a result, in the eleventh century Emperor Henry II required that widows and daughters marry.[6] At the same time, the bishops of Hildesheim attempted to exercise episcopal control over Gandersheim and put the female establishment under male jurisdiction.[7] Significantly, Hrotsvit entirely ignores the place and influence of the Hildesheim bishops in her *Primordia Coenobii Gandeshemensis* or *Primordia*, the history of Gandersheim from its founding in 852 until 918.[8] Interestingly, the effect of Hrotsvit's *Primordia*, according to Thomas Head, was to celebrate the inseparable linkage of the Liudulfings and Gandersheim, 'two lineages, or families,' one royal, the other religious, and both noble[9] – exactly the opposite of Sapientia's response in rejecting Hadrian's offer to join her family to his under his royal but pagan sponsorship.

Gandersheim, like other medieval monastic institutions, had as one of its main purposes the education of noble youth, especially daughters, and had as one of its primary means of stability the inclusion of new members. Women could enter the cloister at any time in their lives, but many came as young children or even infants: oblates were given to the religious house by their parents; novices could be selected because of their intellectual precocity or religious piety; and daughters might be placed into the convent to provide for their well-being or to militate against alliance through marriage. Hathumoda, Gandersheim's first abbess, entered religious life at age five and became abbess of Gandersheim at twenty-six; Emperor Otto II's daughters Sophia and Mathilda entered Gandersheim at age eleven, when their peers were getting married.[10] If Hrotsvit's plays were read or even performed at Gandersheim or the Ottonian court – and there is now no longer any reason to think that they were not in some way represented, either by reading or performance[11] – then it is certainly possible that oblates, novices, students, and young noblewomen, exactly the age and status of the young girls in *Sapientia*, were also part of the audience. The representation of childhood offers insight into the didactic aims of the play and the ideological effects of the representation of age, for it is upon the bodies of the virginal young that Hrotsvit inscribes a hagiographical discourse of youthful resistance to aged power, feminine opposition to masculine domination, and Christian triumph over secular authority. In short, *Sapientia* elucidates the ideological effects created in a specific historical and cultural context by representation of age in relation to gender and power.

Family

Mirroring the sometimes precarious social and political situation of Gandersheim during the Ottonian empire, *Sapientia*, more properly called *The Martyrdom of the Holy Virgins Fides, Spes, and Karitas*, opens with the collision of two incompatible and contesting social systems: the masculine pagan Roman hierarchy of Hadrian, Antiochus, and their minions and the feminine and very Christian domestic clan of Sapientia (Wisdom) and her three young daughters, Fides (Faith), Spes (Hope), and Karitas (Love). Reversing the trajectory of Matthew's birth narrative in which wise men from the east make a pilgrimage to Bethlehem to meet the newborn Jesus and then raise the suspicion of Herod, the local ruler (Matt. 2: 1–12), Sapientia ventures to Rome on a missionary endeavour and arouses the concern of the emperor Hadrian. Antiochus, Hadrian's spymaster, views the foreign woman and her daughters as dangerous to the stability and tranquility of Rome because Sapientia 'hortatur nostrates avitos ritus deserere · et christianę religioni se dedere' (I.5), 'exhorts our [Roman] citizens and clients/ to abandon the ancestral and ancient rites/ and convert to Christianity' (Wilson, *Florilegium*, 82) and because under the influence of their Christian teachings, which Hadrian compares to a mortal plague, Roman women refuse to sleep or to eat with their husbands. From the outset of *Sapientia*, the menace of potential civic strife is figured as domestic discord, specifically in the lack of male access to the female body, in the loss of male prerogative over the individual household, and in the threat to the patriarchal lineage of the Roman *civitas*. Sapientia's matrifocal family, lacking the *pater familias* of the ancient household, threatens the very nature of the patriarchal Roman state, especially since as a noble widow she wields both power and wealth.[12]

When Sapientia and her daughters are first brought before the emperor, Antiochus wants to force their cooperation, but Hadrian asks, 'Quid si illas primule aggrediar blanda alloquutione · si forte velint cedere?' (III.3), 'What if I mollify them first with flattering speech?/ Perhaps they will then give in, one and each' (Wilson, *Florilegium*, 83). Hadrian appeals initially to Sapientia, 'Illustris matrona blande et quiete ad culturam deorum te invito · quo nostra perfrui possis amicicia' (III.3), 'Noble lady, I invite you amiably and kindly to worship our gods and so enjoy our friendship' (Wilson, *Florilegium*, 83). When Sapientia rejects his offer, he says, 'Adhuc mitigato furore · nulla in te moveor indignatione · sed pro tua tuique filiarum salute · paterno sollicitor amore' (III.4), 'Having controlled my anger, I am not indignant but am concerned with fatherly care/ for you and your daughters' welfare' (Wilson, *Florilegium*, 83). The emperor offers to complete Sapientia's 'headless' family as both friend and father and proposes, in effect, to supply the social and domestic amenities that the foreign woman and her daughters need to be placed in the highest echelons of Roman society. In the emperor's view, his offer of friendship would restore Sapientia to 'claritas ingenuitatis' (III.6), 'the splendor of your noble ancestry' (Wilson, *Florilegium*, 84), co-opt the threat she poses to the empire, and integrate her and her daughters into Roman society. Attempting to put himself in the position of the ancient head-of-the-household, the *patria potestas*, with the power of life and death over those in his family, Hadrian extends the offer of his patronage, but the Christian women are already pledged to Christ, and as Fides says, 'Pro ipsius amore sponsi · promtę sumus mori' (IV.4), 'For the love of that Bridegroom we are prepared to die' (Wilson, *Florilegium*, 87). The implication, of course, is that Sapientia and her daughters are members of a spiritual family whose values oppose those of the empire and whose authority exceeds the emperor's own. This family of Christian women does not need a man to lead them or a place in the civic hierarchy.

Language

The opening of *Sapientia* not only contrasts two different social alignments; Hadrian's first interrogation of Sapientia also reveals two separate axes of communication, two different discourses working along different lines of orientation: a masculinized (vertical) hierarchical discourse of physical power articulated by the emperor and his minions and the feminized (horizontal) discourse of spiritual affiliation among equals. On the one hand, the emperor attempts to incorporate Sapientia and her daughters into the patriarchal hierarchy with offers to act as their benefactor and father. Their refusal then prompts the emperor to escalate the violence of his threats against the Christians, with his language proleptically enacting the coming torture. On the other hand, Sapientia and her children boldly undercut the emperor's authority by fearlessly talking among themselves outside of Hadrian's hearing and understanding. Simply put, the emperor, whose word is law, must contend with a competing discourse and is put into the unconventional position of being ignored: Sapientia and her daughters overlook his physical presence, disregard his verbal commands, and minimize his political authority.

In fact, when Sapientia rebuffs the emperor's offer of friendship and relation, the struggle between Hadrian and Sapientia and her children becomes a conflict over language. When Sapientia is first brought before the emperor, Antiochus warns her that she must 'mitiga effluentiam verborum' (II.2) and 'pręcogita quid loquaris' (III.1), 'Bridle your tongue' and 'be careful of what you say' (Wilson, *Florilegium*, 83), but the mother and her daughters openly mock the emperor in his presence. Even after three days in prison to reconsider their refusal to honour the Roman gods, the mother and daughters are still defiant, and Antiochus asks the emperor, 'Cur dignaris cum hac contumace verba miscere · quę te insolenti fatigat praesumptione?' (V.3), 'Why do you deign to exchange words with this impertinent woman who keeps insulting you with insolent glee?' (Wilson, *Florilegium*, 88). In Fides's view, the emperor is a fool, and to Hadrian Fides's speech is 'murmuras subsannando' (V.4), 'mumbling in derision' (Wilson, *Florilegium*, 88). Although explicitly the little girls are punished for their insolence, in effect, the Christians and pagans do not speak the same language. In response to Antiochus's assertion that Fides must be mad to insult Hadrian so, Fides replies, 'Dixi

· et dico · dicamque quamdiu vixero' (V.5), 'I have called him a fool,/ I now call him a fool/ and I shall call him a fool/ as long as I live' (Wilson, *Florilegium*, 89). Finally Hadrian commands, 'Duodecim centuriones · alternando · scindant flagris eius membra' (V.6), 'O brave centurions, come to the fore/ and avenge the insults that I bore' (Wilson, *Florilegium*, 89). However, as the emperor's language extends into action, the scenes of torture become a theatre of testimony. Although Hadrian clearly believes that the vengeance wrought by his brave centurions will affirm his power and authority, instead, ironically, Antiochus articulates the depth of the girls' resistance with his remark, 'O utinam possit ullo coerceri modo' (V.9), 'O, would that she could be somehow coerced!' (Wilson, *Florilegium*, 89). Fides's speeches then confirm that she cannot be coerced. In an inversion of the paradigm of torture explicated in Elaine Scarry's influential *The Body in Pain*, the torturer gives credence to the victims' expressions of Christian truth instead of the victim confirming the torturer's inculpatory narrative.[13]

Age

The incompatibility of the pagan and Christian discourses and their relationships to the daughters' bodies is further emphasized in Sapientia's disquisition upon Boethian arithmetic principles, for Sapientia's math lesson encapsulates the play's key insights. The emperor is, in effect, a poor reader and a poor interpreter, for he neither recognizes the allegory of the girls' names nor fathoms God's wisdom that is at the root of Sapientia's lesson, as Sapientia specifies:

> In hoc laudanda est supereminens factoris sapientia · et mira mundi artificis scientia · qui non solum in principio mundum creans ex nihilo omnia in numero · et mensura et pondere posuit · sed etiam in succedentium serie temporum et in aetatibus hominum miram dedit inveniri posse scientiam artium · (III.22)

> Praise be thereof to the supreme wisdom of the Creator/ and to the marvelous science of this world's Maker,/ who not only created the world in the beginning out of nothing and ordered everything according to number, measure, and weight,/ but also in the seasons and in the ages of men gave us the ability to grasp the wondrous science of the arts. (Wilson, *Florilegium*, 86)

Each facet of Sapientia's mathematical discourse is, in effect, an interpretive guide to Christian mystery. Not only does Sapientia's arithmetic lecture defy gender stereotypes by putting scientific wisdom in the mouth of a woman, but the effect of this mathematical discourse is to render the universe itself legible, readable, and coherent given the right exegetical key.

Furthermore, her daughters' bodies and physical beings – quite literally their ages and the numerical relationships among them – are exactly that interpretive guide. The 'ages of men' unlock the 'science of the arts,' which in turn reveals the divinely ordained order of the world. The symbolic associations of the girls' ages and theological implications of the female trinity of daughters extends into the play's structure. The trinitarian number is echoed by the three daughters, the three figures in the furnace heated for three days, the daughters' burial three miles outside of Rome, and Sapientia's three-day mourning period after their death. Additionally, as noted by Wiles, 'The dramatic action too has a neat mathematical structure ... The first daughter undergoes four tortures, the second three, the third two – leaving the finale to Wisdom [Sapientia] who has undergone the supreme single torture of losing her children.'[14] This progression from four to one is itself trinitarian, in which the three daughters are of a single mind, will, and purpose with the mother.[15]

Likewise, it is essential to recognize that these are the bodies of youngsters – ages eight, ten, and twelve.[16] Sapientia's children are not, strictly speaking, fully developed women; they are, with the exception of Fides, prepubescent bodies lacking secondary sex characteristics; they are bodies in transition. Their ages are not accidental: seven was typically considered to be the end of the first period of life (*infantia*), in which a child was held to be a reasonable creature, and twelve was the age of female marriageability, when a daughter could begin adult responsibilities. The range of ages from eight to twelve therefore is generally representative of childhood per se, specifically marks the transition from *infantia* to *puella*, and in the Middle Ages, those years were typically a period of intensive education for children of noble families. Like the Christian ideal propagated by institutions like Gandersheim, Sapientia's 'parenting toward death' has taught her children not to value the pleasures of the material world; rather, as she instructs Karitas toward the end of the play, 'sperne presens utile · quo pervenias ad gaudium interminabile · quo tui germanę fulgent coronis illibatę virginitatis' (V.29), 'Spurn the comfort of this life/ so that you may reach never-ending joy, where your sisters already sparkle, radiant with the crowns of untouched virginity' (Wilson, *Florilegium*, 93). At the same time Sapientia's teaching constructs the body as a malleable object serving the propagation of Christian doctrine. Despite the horror of their ordeals, each child denies feeling any pain; their bodies, horrifically inscribed by the instruments of torture, become texts to be auto-explicated; rather than sites of abuse, they are gospel texts to be read by the faithful for the conversion of the pagan, and as sites of education, they convey the continuity of a chaste matrifocal community through the malleable and precarious period of childhood.

The deepest truths of Christianity are present, therefore, within Sapientia's family, in the very arithmetic structure of and relationships among the daughters' ages and ordeals. Finally, Hadrian and Antiochus's inability to follow the logic of Christian apologetics in the math lesson confirms their stupidity in the daughters' eyes and creates the stunning spectacle of three young girls freely sassing and insolently lecturing the most powerful male on the planet, the emperor of Rome. Rather than being an untidy addition to the play or extraneous didactic lesson for the edification of the audience, Sapientia's math lesson foregrounds the centrality of age as a hermeneutic category in which body and language, power and knowledge, meet.

Flesh

However deficient they may be in physical strength, economic resources, or social backing to challenge Rome directly, Sapientia and her young daughters nevertheless successfully subvert the pagan state with the only tools at their disposal: their voices, their bodies, and their beliefs. It is in the interplay of body and voice that Hrotsvit fashions the children's martyrdom. Each child's ability to gloss the body – that is, interpret its signs and inscriptions – increases as Hadrian's ability to interpret those same bodies decreases; simultaneously, Hadrian increases his abuse of the youthful bodies as his ability to read them – and read beyond them – decreases. In his encounter with Sapientia and her daughters, both Hadrian's language (his ability to persuade those inferior to him) and his literacy (his ability to interpret their bodily signs) fail, even as he extends his coercive language into the physical realm by treating the young girls' bodies as books upon which his text of physical mastery can be written. The girls' wounds become the script with which Hadrian attempts to inscribe unambiguously his masculine privilege and social superiority.

Sapientia, however, reads her daughters' bodies differently and instructs them each in Christian exegesis of the body; their young bodies become a kind of palimpsest in which Christian hagiography supersedes Hadrian's peremptory inscription of his power. Sapientia's mathematical lesson for the emperor in a sense adumbrates her subsequent martyrological instruction for her girls, highlighting for viewers or readers of the play the significance of her 'parenting toward death.' In this process, details of Sapientia's child rearing are recounted during their martyrdoms, even as the physical atrocities attempt to sever the girls from each other and destroy the physical and emotional ties between them and their mother. When Spes asks her mother to support them with her prayers, Sapientia replies that she prays incessantly 'quam inter ipsa crepundia · vestris sensibus non desistebam instillasse' (IV.2), 'that you persevere in your faith, which, from your earliest childhood on, I tried to instill in your minds without any rest' (Wilson, *Florilegium*, 87). Karitas responds, 'Quod sugentes ubera in cunabulis didicimus · nullatenus oblivisci quibimus' (IV.3), 'We will never forget what we learned in our cradle suckling at your breast' (Wilson, *Florilegium*, 87). Sapientia then reminds her daughters, 'Ad hoc vos materno lacte affluenter alui · ad hoc delicate nutrivi · ut vos cęlesti non terreno sponso traderem · quo vestri causa socrus aeterni regis dici meruissem' (IV.3), 'It was for this that I nursed you with my milk flowing free;/ it was for this that I reared you three;/ that I may espouse you to a heavenly, not an earthly bridegroom and may deserve to be called the mother-in-law of the Eternal King thereby' (Wilson, *Florilegium*, 87). In effect, according to Stephen Wailes, 'the drastic and prolonged cruelties in *Sapientia* reflect the crisis of the empire that this play embodies,' for the play 'shows the process of change in the Empire, its Christianization, as the three young women remain steadfast, and more importantly, their mother, the genius of their faith, survives them to celebrate their martyrdom within the new Roman community she has created.'[17]

Martyrdom

In each daughter's case, the miraculous and divine attributes of the tortured body are prefigured in dialogue. In particular, Sapientia repeatedly emphasizes her daughters' youthfulness with a view toward subsuming their physical age to the demands of their miraculously painless martyrdom: 'Vincite infantilis teneritudinem aetatulę · maturi sensus fortitudine' (IV.1), 'Overcome the softness of your tender years by strength of mature reflection' (Wilson, *Florilegium*, 87), she exhorts her children.

Each martyrdom follows a similar structure: the emperor's demand for conversion is met unblushingly by childish resistance; the child's commitment to martyrdom is encouraged by her mother; and then each child in turn exhorts her sibling toward perseverance in her physical ordeal. While the expression of bodily mastery extends from Hadrian to the girls, from the emperor as false father to the loyal Christian daughters, the paths of Christian authority and bodily exegesis extend from mother to daughter: the pagan emperor's offer of fatherhood has no effect on their determination. 'Pro ipsius amore sponsi · promtę sumus mori' (IV.4), 'For the love of that Bridegroom we are prepared to die' (Wilson, *Florilegium*, 87).

First, Fides's martyrdom begins with her refusal of Hadrian's command, 'Fides intuere venerabilem magnę Dianę imaginem · et fer sacrę deę libamina · quo possis uti eius gratia' (V.4), 'Fides, look with respect upon the venerable image of great Diana and bring offerings to the holy goddess so that you may possess her favor' (Wilson, *Florilegium*, 88). Her tortures gradually escalate as punishment for both her brazen speech and her insults to the emperor. During the interrogation, Fides murmurs under her breath about Hadrian's foolishness, particularly his inability to understand the pagan image before him: 'Quid enim stultius · quid insipientius videri potest · quam quod hortatur nos contempto creatore universitatis · venerationem inferre metallis?' (V.5), 'For what is more foolish, what can seem more stupid than your command to show contempt for the Creator of all and venerate base metal instead?' (Wilson, *Florilegium*, 88). Antiochus and Hadrian do exactly that as they fail to see beyond Fides's physical ordeal to the imperturbable truth of her faith. As she dies – and it is a lingering death – Fides encourages her younger siblings, 'parate vos ad tolerantiam futuri certaminis' and 'Este obtemperantes monitis nostrę sanctę parentis · quę nos hortabatur presentia fastidire · quo meruissemus aeterna percipere' (V.14), 'prepare yourselves to bear the impending strife' and 'Obey the admonitions of our saintly parent who has always exhorted us to despise this present world so that we may deserve to attain the Eternal Kingdom' (Wilson, *Florilegium*, 90).

Next, with Spes, Hadrian again attempts to temper his language and woo the child with 'paternal affection,' even to the point of promising, 'Depone callum pectoris · et conquinisce turificando magnę Dianę · et ego te proprię prolis vice excolo · atque extollo omni dilectione' (V.17), 'Lay aside this callousness of heart and relent; bring incense to the great Diana. Then I will adopt you as my own child/ and cherish you with all my heart' (Wilson, *Florilegium*, 90). Instead of inserting herself into the emperor's family and good graces, Spes scorns the emperor and Antiochus, barking contemptuously, 'Paternitatem tuam repudio' (V.17), 'I don't want you for my father!' (Wilson, *Florilegium,* 90). Spes offers her final prayers as her tortures are escalated until she is silenced. Her beheading finally severs the mechanism of speech and resistance, but not before Spes encourages her younger sister to follow her elder sisters' examples.

It is finally in Karitas's martyrdom that the problem of the young girls' irascible language is presented most succinctly and directly. Hadrian, pushed to the limit of his endurance, says simply to Karitas, 'Karitas · saturatus conviciis tui sororum · nimiumque exacerbatus sum prolixa ratione earum · unde diu tecum non contendo · sed vel optemperantem mei votis ditabo omnibus bonis · vel contraluctantem afficiam malis' (V.31), 'Karitas, I have had more than enough! I am fed up with your sisters' insults and I am rather exasperated with their drawn out arguments; I will therefore not contend with you for long, but reward you richly with goods if you obey, and punish you if you disobey' (Wilson, *Florilegium,* 93). And now his command is reduced from words and deeds to two words: 'Dic tantum · "magna Diana"' (V.32), 'Simply say "Great Diana"' (Wilson, *Florilegium,* 93). The struggle between the young girls, their mother, and the Roman emperor is no longer a matter of accepting Roman imperial sponsorship, performing pagan sacrifices, or acceding to the demands of civic ritual; it boils down to two simple words: 'Great Diana.' It is a battle over language, and, of course, power. Testifying to the solidarity of purpose she shares with her mother and siblings, Karitas refuses the emperor, who himself complains, 'O iniuria · quod a tantilla etiam contempnor homullula' (V.34), 'How insulting to be held in contempt by mere a child' (Wilson, *Florilegium,* 93). Karitas replies, infuriatingly, 'Licet tenella sim aetate · tamen gnara sum te argumentose confundere' (V.34), 'I may be young in years, yet I am expert enough to confound you in argument' (Wilson, *Florilegium,* 93). As Karitas's ordeal hastens to its ending, her youthfulness is continually emphasized as she uses language to expose the ineffectualness of Hadrian and his pagan power structure. Karitas teases him, saying, 'O iudicem inpotentem qui diffidit se absque armis ignium · octuennem infantem superare posse' (V.35), 'What an impotent judge, who cannot overcome an eight-year old infant without the force of fire!' (Wilson, *Florilegium,* 94). Antiochus calls her 'illa lasciva ... puellula' (VI.1), 'that petulant little girl' (Wilson, *Florilegium,* 94), when he describes the flogging and burning which could not hurt her but hurt five thousand of Hadrian's men. As she is

tortured, Antiochus recounts, 'Ludens inter flammivomos vapores vagabat
· et illaesa laudes deo suo pagebat' (VI.2), 'Playfully she walked among
the flame-spewing vapors, quite unhurt,/ and sang hymns of praise to
her God' (Wilson, *Florilegium*, 94). Three men in white accompany Karitas
in the blaze, while the onlookers stand amazed, in a scene reminiscent of
the famous story of Shadrach, Meshach, and Abednego and an angelic
fourth figure in Nebuchadnezzar's flaming oven (Dan. 3). Like the three
Judaic youths who defied a royal decree to worship an idol and were
thrown into an oven without injury, so too Karitas defies the emperor
and frolics playfully, untouched by the flames.

Like Shadrach, Meshach, and Abednego, who refused to worship the
pagan statue because of their Jewish faith, Sapientia's daughters are
asked but scorn to pledge fidelity to – or at least to acknowledge and thus
identify with – the goddess Diana in an act of Roman civic commitment.
Hrotsvit's choice of Roman deities here is not random. Diana is, after all,
goddess of the hunt, the moon, and not unironically, virginity. In other
words, the young girls are asked to pledge fidelity to a goddess whose
explicit values are congruent with their own but whose civic orientation
and spirituality are incompatible with their beliefs. Therefore, the problem is not so much one of ends as of means: a pagan or non-Christian
system of belief, even when it shares the same values as Christianity, is
emphatically not the moral equivalent of Christian belief, in Hrotsvit's
hagio-historiography. And the means to that desired end, virginity, does
not capitulate to the civic ideal but opposes secular social mores through
the process of martyrdom. For the unmarried Christian female, death in
the face of non-Christian authority does not result in fragmentation or
isolation but rather assimilation into a different and infinitely better
family structure.

Conclusion

It is usual in scholarship on Hrotsvit now to understand that her writings
rather uncomplicatedly support the Ottonian imperial project.[18] Marla
Carlson states that Hrotsvit's martyrdoms are devoid of any subversive
political component and actually strengthen the creation of what Foucault would call 'docile bodies' who ascribe to conventional power relations: 'by erasing pain from her representation of martyrdom, Hrotsvit
appropriates the voice of the victim to serve as a sign of the Imperial
Church's power, and her dramatization of *passive* female triumph serves
to reinforce male strength in action.'[19] What emerges from these scenes

of martyrdom in *Sapientia* is more than an either/or struggle of Christian fidelity against secular authority or masculine domination over feminine weakness. The characters' lack of pained expressions or pathetic sentiments in *Sapientia* does not minimize the violence of Hrotsvit's representation of tortured little girls, nor does the daughters' physical acquiescence to (irresistible) masculine brutality equal passivity. Fides, Spes, and Karitas are unrelentingly verbally active and oppositional, in a word, *childish*. They listen to their mother, follow her instructions, and make fun of the male authority figure, Hadrian. Rather than falling into any simplistic cultural polarities like male/female or flesh/spirit, the struggle in *Sapientia* is multidimensional and mapped onto differing forms of affiliation: a matrifocal foreign family versus a patriarchal political hierarchy, with the audacity of youth over against the stolidity of age. The Christian daughters make a fool of the powerful Roman emperor. Rather than supporting an imperial project unequivocally, *Sapientia* would seem then to criticize the alliance of political policy and spiritual objectives on the Roman model, for the childish Christian girls refuse even to acknowledge a Roman goddess who shares their commitment to virginity. It is the daughters' youthfulness and not only their gender that brings their strategies of resistance into high relief.

The refore, the violence against these girls is heightened by the youthfulness of their bodies, and despite each child's claim that she feels no fear, the description of the tortures, combined with their severity and prolongation, cannot be ignored. After her breasts are mutilated, Fides is also flogged, flayed, grilled, boiled, and finally beheaded. These abuses in total are less suitable for martyrdom and more closely related to preparing a meal for a feast, making Fides a kind of reverse Eucharistic transformation: the body of Faith has become a meal to be consumed by the Christian audience as a sign of their own fidelity to doctrine. The triumph of the young women in their painless ordeal is a graphic reminder of the gospel paradox that 'the last shall be first and the first last' (Matt. 19:30) and the dominical saying that unless one becomes as a child one cannot enter the kingdom of heaven (Matt. 18: 1–5). Fides, Spes, and Karitas not only frustrate the personal and political authority of the emperor, they also spiritually surpass their own devout mother Sapientia, whose final words to Karitas are, 'et cum Christo iungaris in cẹlo · memento matris · iam patrona effecta te parientis' (VII.2), 'and when you are united with Christ in Heaven, remember your mother, having been made patron of her who bore you' (Wilson, *Florilegium*, 95). And in the mechanism of their resistance and triumph – their irascibility, insults, petulance, *sotto voce* murmurings – in short, in their language, I think we hear 'clamor validus Gandersheimensis,' the 'strong voice of Gandersheim,' offering a vision of female affiliation in the face of male violence and exhorting her noble community, which includes females across the entire lifespan, to resist political coercion. Hrotsvit puts this blessed impudence in the mouths of girls and grants the power of resistance to the voices of the young.

At the same time, the degree to which the girls' language conveys a sense of individual subjectivity and personal agency is limited. Although Fides claims, for example, that she will jump into the burning liquid prepared for her torture of her own free will ('Sponte insilio' V.11), her language and her will, like her sisters,' is as much *imitatio* of her mother's dogma as it is *elocutio* of an inner life. As Karitas, the youngest sister and the last to die, explains:

> Ego quidem et sorores meae · eisdem parentibus genitae · eisdem sacramentis imbutae · sumus una eademque fidei constantia roboratę · quapropter scito nostrum velle · nostrum sentire · nostrum sapere · unum idemque esse · nec me in ullo umquam illis dissidere · (V.33)

> I am born of the same parents as my sisters, imbued by the same sacraments, strengthened by the same firmness of faith. Know, therefore, that we are one and the same in what we want, what we feel and what we think. In nothing will I differ from them. (Wilson, *Florilegium*, 93)

Despite their different ages, the three daughters are also, in a sense, undifferentiated. In essence, the girls' language is not their own; it is their mother's, making them closer in character to the Prioress's little boy who learns the *alma redemptoris* by rote than to Virginia in the *Physician's Tale*. By the end of *Sapientia*, Hadrian appears to be little more than the agent of the girls' martyrdom in a scenario envisioned by the mother; although for different purposes, Sapientia desires her daughters' deaths as fervently as Hadrian and Antiochus. Sapientia's threefold purpose in coming to Rome, 'Nullius alius rei nisi agnoscendę veritatis causa · quo fidem quam expugnatis plenius ediscerem · filiasque meas Christo consecrarem' (III.7), 'For no other matter/ but to be a witness to truth, to understand the faith, which you persecute, better,/ and to consecrate my daughters to Christ' (Wilson, *Florilegium*, 84), ultimately will allow her to occupy the powerful and privileged position of 'socrus aeterni regis' (IV.3), 'mother-in-law of the Eternal King' (Wilson,

Florilegium, 87). While physical martyrdom flows from Hadrian to the girls, Christian teaching moves from the mother to her daughters: each daughter comforts the mother; the mother exhorts each child; and finally, each daughter urges the next to remain faithful to the death. These words of fidelity to a mother's teachings extend beyond the dramatic context into the audience at Gandersheim and particularly to the girls of the audience – oblates, novitiates, pupils, and daughters all.

Nonetheless, that triumph comes at the price of three particularly brutal martyrdoms. A provisional analysis of Hrotsvit's representation of children militates against the interpretation of Hrotsvit as an uncomplicated Ottonian apologist. However, let it not be said that Hrotsvit presents a rather modern, sentimentalized view of childhood – quite the contrary. Hrotsvit's representation of children is situated at several complicated interrelations. While I find compelling Stephen Wailes's recent comment that *Sapientia*, like *Gallicanus* and *Passio Sanctarum Virginum Agapis, Chionię, and Hirenę*, is 'political, a plain fact to which virtually no comment has been directed,' I find his separation of Hrotsvit's dramas into the 'Imperial Plays' and the 'Plays of Sexuality' to be problematic, for it is precisely at the intersection, rather than the disjunction, of power and sexuality that Hrotsvit's children find their troubling and troublesome place.[20] In 'an age when young people were universally considered to be primarily instruments of family policy,'[21] to use McNamara's apt phrase, the choice to marry or to remain a virgin was both sexual and political, as the unmarried noblewomen in Gandersheim knew well. To marry at a father's command for the social advancement of one's family or to join a husband's lineage in order to extend it through bearing children carried both sexual obligations and political responsibilities, as the young women educated at Gandersheim also knew well. Thus, the youthful transgressions of Fides, Spes, and Karitas in the face of royal prerogative reflect the risks of intermarriage, of blending family lineages, in short, of being a young noblewomen in the Ottonian period, while their own and their mother's willingness to sacrifice themselves for the purity of their beliefs and the maintenance of their own moral pedigree and family history bespeaks the 'crueel corage' described by Barbara Newman.[22] Yet this maternal courage comes with a high price, for the final image of Sapientia mourning the death of her children among a community of grieving women was all too common in the medieval period. While loved by their parents – or at least by their mother and appreciated for their inherent nobility by Hadrian, a potential step-father – Sapientia's daughters are also, in a sense, expendable.

However, in Sapientia's final prayer for her daughters' salvation, Hrotsvit clearly focuses on the Christian moral of the play, the necessity of Christian virginity for her historical and cultural moment, rather than a sentimentalized depiction of childhood. That is why the daughters are insistently allegorical figures – Faith, Hope, and Charity are tortured in the presence, and for the benefit, of Wisdom. Thus, the paradoxical logic of the Christian gospel – the translation of bodies into texts and the allegorical idealization of children to illustrate the paradox of losing one's life to find it – is itself never free from violence, even as the gospel narratives themselves are never free from violence. Parenting toward death, whether Christian or not, is sensible from this privileged theological perspective, but I am not sure that makes it right.

NOTES

1 In 'Beyond Virginity,' Stephen L. Wailes discusses Hrotsvit's dramas as enacting the struggle of the flesh and spirit; in 'Impassive Bodies,' Marla Carlson attends to the gendered audience dynamics of Hrotsvit's Ottonian context; in 'Re-Viewing Hrotsvit,' Sue Ellen Case sees in Hrotsvit a feminist forerunner who has the potential to subvert patriarchal power.

2 Wilson, *Hrotsvit of Gandersheim: The Ethics of Authorial Stance*, 148–9.

3 The following paragraphs on the historical background of Gandersheim and the Ottonian Empire draw from McKitterick and Reuer, *The New Cambridge Medieval History*, 3:233–66; McNamara, *Sisters in Arms*, 176–229; Sticca, 'The Hagiographical and Monastic Context of Hrotswitha's Plays'; Wemple, 'Monastic Life from the Merovingians to the Ottonians'; and Head, 'Hrotsvit's *Primordia* and the Historical Traditions of Monastic Communities.'

4 Wilson, 'The Saxon Abbess: Hrotsvit of Gandersheim,' 35.

5 Head, 'Hrotsvit's *Primordia*,' 152.

6 Wemple, 'Monastic Life,' 42–3.

7 See McNamara, *Sisters in Arms*, 203–29, and Head, 'Hrotsvit's *Primordia*.'

8 In 'Hrotsvit's *Primordia*,' Thomas Head summarizes the purposes of etiological narratives like Hrotsvit's *Primordia*: 'The story which Hrotsvit's audience would have heard or read shared three specific themes in common with most foundation narratives: first, the attempt to link the religious community to powerful patrons, both secular and sacred; secondly, the establishment of legal precedent for the community's rights; and thirdly, the demonstration of the continuity of the present community with its heroic past' (148).

9 Ibid., 148–9.

10 McNamara, *Sisters in Arms*, 189; Wemple, 'Monastic Life,' 43 and 45.

11 Scholarly opinion has shifted since Peter Dronke's observation, 'It is considered scholarly to add that Hrotsvitha could not have intended her own plays for performance – at most, for reading aloud at mealtimes in the convent refectory' (*Women Writers in the Middle Ages*, 55). The opinion that Hrotsvit's plays were not performed, a view made suspect by recent performances, including the workshop performances at the 1997 National Endowment for the Humanities Summer Institute, 'Literary Traditions of Medieval Women' at Rice University, and the performances at Hrotsvit 2000, Santa Clara University, owes more to the relative inability of scholars to place Hrotsvit into a coherent evolutionary paradigm of dramatic development in the West than it does to the intrinsic characteristics of the texts themselves or the historical situation in tenth-century Saxony. See Witt, 'Canonizing the Canoness,' and Michael Zampelli's essay in this volume.

Most recently, Wiles, 'Hrotsvitha of Gandersheim: The Performance of Her Plays in the Tenth Century,' surveys the internal and external evidence offered by Hrotsvit's texts and the history of Gandersheim, other medieval (including tenth to twelfth century) dramatic spectacles, and the modern history of Hrotsvit performances. He makes the provocative suggestion that Hrotsvit's plays are more likely 'the encoding of a dramatic event; that the texts were performed first and then processed by the scriptorium in order that they could be read by scholars and incorporated in a manuscript' (135), and that 'Hrotsvitha must have written her plays in prose dialogue for a male cast' (139) because her plays called for the profligate display of the female body.

12 An accessible study addressing these issues is Gardner, *Women in Roman Law and Society*. Gardner writes, 'A legitimate child was, from birth, subject to the control (*potestas*) of the father ... [and the] father was the head of the *familia*, the basic Roman social and property-owning unit. The *familia* under his control consisted of his children, whether living with him or not; his sons' children, if any; his wife, if married with *manus* [lit. *hand*, or in the power of the husband]; and his slaves ... The *familia*, obviously, could include several nuclear families, living apart (those of married sons), as well as daughters married and living in families belonging to other *familiae*. At the death of the *pater*, the children and wife cease to be *alieni iuris* (subject to another's' control) and became *sui iuris* (independent)' (5–6).

13 Scarry, *The Body in Pain*.

14 Wiles, 'Hrotsvitha of Gandersheim: The Performance of Her Plays,' 141.

15 Hrotsvit's entire oeuvre is now well known for its structural and numerical

parallels. For a full accounting of number symbolism in Hrotsvit and an analysis of the mathematics lesson in *Sapientia*, see Wilson, 'Mathematical Learning and Structure in the Works of Hrotsvit of Gandersheim.'

16 One exception to scholars' lack of attention to the dynamics of age and childhood in Hrotsvit is the treatment of the contemporary martyr Pelagius. See McMillin, '"Weighed down with a thousand evils,"' in the current volume: 'Thus the greatest Muslim leader of Hrotsvit's day, with whom even Otto had to reckon, can be humiliated and defeated by one small but brave Christian boy' (53).

17 Wailes, 'Beyond Virginity,' 12.

18 Peter Dronke writes, 'In her dramas especially, Hrotsvitha, like the Ottonian family, wanted to replay the Roman world in a Christian mode ... [and] in her poetic legends and plays, too, Hrotsvitha was aware of helping to refashion, for the Ottonians, a culture worthy of the role they had chosen – worthy of Charlemagne, of Constantine, and of the myth of Rome' (*Women Writers in the Middle Ages*, 59–60). Stephen L. Wailes states, 'With the abbess's [Gerberga's] close connection to Otto I and his court, and with the special relationship of Gandersheim to the Ottonian dynasty, there can be no doubt that imperial politics were a subject of deep Christian interest for Hrotsvit and her circle' ('Beyond Virginity,' 25), and Marla Carlson notes about *Sapientia* specifically, 'The absence of pain on the part of Hrotsvit's stage martyrs supports a system of signification vital to the Ottonian imperial project, as system wherein military victory is a sign of divine favor ... For members of this [female] audience ... the reading practices reinforced by rituals such as ordeal add another message, equally useful, "Do what the Imperial Church tells you to do, because the Church knows what God means"' ('Impassive Bodies,' 485).

19 Carlson, 'Impassive Bodies,' 487. Michel Foucault discusses the creation of 'docile bodies' in *Discipline and Punish*. While Carlson associates the absence of the daughter's pain with the tenth-century practice of judicial ordeals, Florence Newman, in 'Violence and Virginity in Hrotsvit's Dramas' in the current volume, understands the girls' imperviousness to torture as a proleptic enactment of the impassibility of the resurrected body: 'The body holds such prominence in these plays not, as one might assume, because they seek to exploit the erotic aspects of women's sexuality, but because, for the author, the body is the locus of that dedication, struggle, victory, and reward made possible by God's habitation of the flesh and his desire to redeem it' (71).

20 Wailes, 'Impassive Bodies,' 6. See especially essays by Linda McMillin and Florence Newman in this volume.

21 McNamara, *Sisters in Arms*, 190.
22 Barbara Newman writes, 'What I shall call the "maternal martyr" paradigm emerges as a tenacious literary convention that duplicates tendencies in the cult of Mary, but also responds to potent social forces acting on medieval mothers, especially young widows. The maternal martyr is a woman whose holiness is enhanced by her willingness to abandon her children or, in extreme cases, consent to their deaths as the Virgin did to Christ's. As a consequence of this renunciation, she is delivered from family ties and enabled to live for God alone' (*From Virile Woman to WomanChrist*, 77).

The Construction of the Desiring Subject in Hrotsvit's *Pelagius* and *Agnes*

RONALD STOTTLEMYER

In his classic study *Women Writers of the Middle Ages*, Peter Dronke offers a particularly valuable insight into the writings of Hrotsvit of Gandersheim: he notes that Hrotsvit's works provide illuminating glimpses into her interior life if we read her attentively for 'indirectly autobiographical moments,'[1] that is, for those moments when her irrepressible wit erupts into the text. What initially makes Dronke's remark about Hrotsvit's 'autobiographical moments' intriguing is the historical context in which she was working. As a tenth-century dramatist, hagiographer, and poet, Hrotsvit is writing two centuries before medieval people are supposed to have had the first intuitions of personal subjectivity in matters of political consciousness, literary authorship, and religious self-examination.[2] Yet the evidence of Hrotsvit's self-awareness in various texts, a subjectivity that she unabashedly terms 'clamor validus Gandeshemensis,' intimates that she is writing from a subjective position a good deal more individualized than one might expect from a religious composing didactic works in the tenth century. While it would be anachronistic to propose that Hrotsvit exhibits a modern sense of self in her writings – that is, a sense of unique personality, of distinctive individuality – it is nevertheless impossible to read her writing as essentially anonymous. In fact, Hrotsvit refers to herself by name no less than six times in her works.[3] At the same time, her adroit use of the linguistic conventions of narration, ironic treatment of medieval literary topoi, and deft handling of rhetorical devices create a highly nuanced persona. Thus, the voice emerging from her prefaces, authorial commentary, and impersonation of saintly martyrs in the legends – a voice at once coy, anxious, ironic, ingratiating, passionate – exhibits a range of inflections suggestive of a fully developed literary personality, what we today would call an 'author.'[4]

As a young canoness associated with Gandersheim, a small, richly endowed convent that enjoyed unparalleled intellectual, religious, and political autonomy during the Ottonian empire, Hrotsvit had access not only to academic resources needed for a fine education, but also to the intellectual and artistic culture necessary for her literary development.[5] Peter Dronke even suggests that Hrotsvit may have received instruction from Rather of Verona, the great scholar and prose stylist whom Otto I invited to court to tutor his younger brother Bruno.[6] Tantalizing as Dronke's suggestion is, in her preface to the legends Hrotsvit herself graciously acknowledges indebtedness to two influential mentors as she was struggling to become a writer:

> Primo sapientissime atque benignissime Rikkardis magistrẹ ... · deinde prona favente clementia · regiẹ indolis Gerberge cuius nunc subdor dominio abbatisse · quẹ aetate minor · ut imperialem decebat neptem · scientia provectior aliquot auctores quos ipsa prior a sapientissimis didicit me admodum pie erudivit· (*Liber Primus, Praefatio,* 7)

> I was first taught by Riccardis, the wisest and kindest of teachers ... and then, finally, by my lady of high station/ Gerberga of royal blood, my merciful abbess, under whose rule I now live. She is younger in years than I, but as befits the Emperor's niece, more advanced in learning./ It was she, who, other authors concerning/ continued my instruction/ offering me an introduction/ to the works of those writers whom she herself studied with learned men. (Wilson, *Florilegium,* 19)

Important as her mentors were to her literary education, they do not of course explain the particular creativity of her legends any more than does her study of Terence explain her highly original plays. Nor does she give enough details about the instruction she received from Rikkardis or Gerberga to illuminate how she developed the sophisticated persona voicing the legends. The self-confident, eloquent voice narrating the heroic stories of Pelagius and Agnes seems to have been shaped, psychologically and artistically, more by Hrotsvit's identification with the medieval ideal of the charismatic saint than by her learned mentors.

Mikkel Borch-Jacobensen's conception of the role that identification plays in the construction of a subject, however, illuminates the reciprocal relationship that exists between Hrotsvit's persona and her legends. The desiring subject, as he theorizes it, develops from one's identification with the desirable:

> Desire (the desiring subject) does not come first, to be followed by an identification that would allow the desire to be fulfilled. What comes first is a tendency toward identification, a primordial tendency which then gives rise to a desire ... Identification brings the desirous subject into being, not the other way around.[7]

Hrotsvit's choice of holy virgins for subject matter in many of the plays and legends clearly suggests her identification with these exemplary people, an identification that gradually becomes realized not only in her highly idealized, vividly described lives of eloquent virgins and martyrs but also in the construction of her own communal identity as a hagiographer writing the interior life of desire in the tenth century.

The eight narratives that constitute the legends – *Maria, Ascencio, Gongolfus, Pelagius, Theophilus, Basilius, Dionysius,* and *Agnes* – serve the conventional didactic purpose of saints' lives – that of presenting heroic narratives about exemplary Christians to inspire readers to live virtuous lives. More particularly, Hrotsvit's legends also exhibit, as Katharina Wilson points out, the character of moral exhortation typical of tenth-century hagiography:

> The legends usually begin (or occasionally end) with a statement or exposition of doctrine which, in turn, is exemplified by a hagiographic tale, used as apodeictic proof of the initial assertion. They are also punctuated by doxological and devotional authorial asides emphasizing their relevance of the doctrine to narrative action, and they frequently end or begin with prayers. In her exemplificatory use of hagiography as well as her utilization of Eastern sources, Hrotsvit stands in the mainstream of tenth-century conventions.[8]

Where Hrotsvit's saints' lives begin to take on a distinctive quality is in the allegorical spareness of her characterization. In restricting her description of the saints' personalities to the moral qualities each exemplifies, Hrotsvit simplifies them, transforming each saint into an emblem of religious desire, thus giving herself latitude for amplifying their desirability.

Over the years, readers have frequently commented on the liveliness of Hrotsvit's characterization in the legends, a dramatic treatment in sharp contrast to the perfunctory efforts of less inspired compilers of saints' lives in the Middle Ages. Helena Homeyer, for instance, notes that an anonymous Carolingian writer, using the same model for a legend of Agnes as Hrotsvit did, told the saint's story in a dull, perfunctory way: 'The character of the epic is dry and austere, the construction less dramatic in comparison to the poetry of the nun' (my translation).[9] The source of Hrotsvit's liveliness may be found in the creative approach she takes to her material. As well as experimenting with what Wilson calls generic hybrids in all of her works,[10] Hrotsvit also made some of the first literary constructions of individualized subjects in the legends indirectly through her prefatory essay, through her authorial commentary in the narratives, and through her impassioned impersonation of the virgin martyrs Pelagius and Agnes.

By including both male and female subjects, who are ethereally beautiful, precociously eloquent, and spiritually heroic, Hrotsvit is defining her young protagonists according to the highest spiritual ideal to which a medieval Christian may aspire – the virgin martyr. While Hrotsvit does not exhibit in her writings a 'new sense of spiritual and psychological change, of intention, and of personal responsibility,' which Caroline Walker Bynum finds central to the twelfth-century discovery of individuality,[11] she does display in her portrayal of these saints an identification with their perfection that helps her mediate between her own desire for an authorial identity and the social constraints of her religious vocation. Moreover, the narrator's commentary on the martyr's eloquence, courage, and alterity in these legends seems a voicing of Hrotsvit's own desire for a transcendent, saintly identity.

One of the first indications of subjectivity comes from the preface to the legends. Although we might expect a depersonalized, third-person voice introducing the legends, what we hear instead is a first-person narrator making a plea for tolerance of her various shortcomings as a writer, especially in matters of prosody and poetic style:

> Hunc libellum parvo ullius decoris cultu ornatum sed non parva diligentia inlaboratum omnium sapientium benignitate offero expurgandum eorum dumtaxat qui erranti non delectantur derogare sed magis errata corrigere · Fateor namque me haut mediocriter errasse non solum in dinoscendis syllabarum naturis verum etiam in dictionibus componendis · pluraque sub hac serie reprehensione digna latitare · sed errores fatenti facilis venia · viciisque debetur pia correctio · (*Liber Primus, Praefatio,* 1)

> I offer this little book,/ small in stylistic merits, but not small in the efforts it took/ to the good will of the wise/ for correction and advice; at least to

those who don't enjoy to rail/ against authors who fail,/ but, rather, prefer to correct the work's flaws. I do confess/ that my failings are rather more than less/ in the handling of meter, style, and diction,/ and that there is much in these works warranting correction./ Yet, the one admitting openly her failing/ should find forgiveness prevailing/ and her mistakes deserve kind help. (Wilson, *Florilegium*, 19)

These lines function as the familiar humility topos, a plea for the reader to overlook the work's stylistic inadequacies and refrain from censuring the writer who has erred. A closer reading reveals that the passage resonates with the irony that frequently undercuts much of the apparent humility of authors using the topos. The resulting voice is one of a self-possessed writer.

The first-person, present indicative verbs that govern the two sentences of the passage – 'offero' (I offer) and 'fateor' (I confess) – immediately establish deictically a persona performing actions in the act of speaking.[12] The rhetorical complexity of the passive participle construction that characterizes the first sentence of this passage – the parallel yet antithetical 'parvo ullius decoris cultu ornatum sed non parva diligentia inlaboratum' – suggests the work of a skillful writer, one who self-consciously uses rhetorical figures while supposedly entreating readers to overlook her inadequacies in poetic style. As the sentence concludes, the irony deepens. On one level, Hrotsvit is petitioning the good will of her wise readers to help her correct her faults. But at the same time, the 'I' voice of the passage is clearly manipulating their attitudes toward her work by assigning them identities as talented writers while castigating any who would belittle her writing. After entreating her readers not to belittle her for her errors, Hrotsvit's persona then confesses her inadequacies of poetic craft and seeks their forgiveness and corrections. The sense of agency exhibited in the persona's apparent anxiety about her writing skills signals Hrotsvit's need to establish her own authorial authority as a conscientious stylist in a work that she was probably commissioned to write. More important, the passage's sophisticated rhetoric and pervasive irony also suggest that she is actually using the humility topos to draw attention to her talents. Her plea for a tolerant reading of her prosody and poetic style seems almost a challenge to readers to find flaws in her craft. In using the topos to foreground her talents, Hrotsvit is engaging in a literary tradition that extends from classical literature to the present.

In the sentences that follow, Hrotsvit defends her authority to use apocryphal sources upon which to base her saints' lives. Once again, she relies upon her superb rhetorical skills to manipulate her readers' attitudes, this time to defuse any blame that might be directed toward her for 'crimen praesumptionis iniquae':

> Si autem obicitur quod quedam huius operis · iuxta quorundam estimationem sumpta sint ex apocrifis · non est crimen presumptionis inique sed error ignorantię quia, quando huius stamen seriei · ceperam ordiri · ignoravi dubia esse in quibus disposui laborare · At ubi recognovi pessumdare detrectavi · quia quod videtur falsitas · forsan probabitur esse veritas · (*Liber Primus, Praefatio,* 3–4)

> When, however, the charge is raised/ – or at least by some so appraised – / that parts of this work's discourses/ are based on apocryphal sources,/ I must reply/ and hereby testify/ that it was not a misdeed of presumption/ but the innocent error of flawed assumption,/ because when I first started to weave the strands of these works, I was not aware that some of my sources met with doubt;/ and when I did find this out,/ I still decided not to suppress them because what appears to be false today/ may perhaps be proven true another day. (Wilson, *Florilegium,* 19)

The passive and impersonal construction of the opening subordinate clause – 'Si autem obicitur' – not only politely keeps her detractors anonymous, but also blunts their criticism with the conditional 'si.' At the same time she contextualizes her use of apocryphal materials with a qualification followed by another passive, 'iuxta quorundam estimationem sumpta sint ex apocrifis.' The most important details that emerge here, however, are the narrator's attitudes toward using her sources after she learned that they were suspect: 'I still decided not to suppress them because what appears to be false today/ may perhaps be proven true another day.' This firm refusal to undo the work she has begun clearly contradicts the deferential tone of the previous paragraph, suggesting that she is a writer with a clear sense of what she wants to do in her narrative and an awareness that attitudes and opinions about the reliability of written sources change over time. Thus although earlier in the paragraph she denied that using an unauthorized source for her saints' life was 'a misdeed of presumption,' she goes on to aver that the difference between truth and falsehood can be difficult to discern.

In making her cavalier observation about using apocryphal materials, Hrotsvit is expressing a strength of mind that many of her readers would likely have found either headstrong or laudable, depending upon the orthodoxy of their beliefs. Taking such liberties with such a legendary figure as Agnes insinuates not only that Hrotsvit has a well-developed sense of self as a thinker and writer, but also that she has specific ideas about how she wishes to construct Agnes's character. Moreover, the degree to which Hrotsvit made substantive changes in the Agnes legend – which Elizabeth Petroff identifies as giving Agnes more autonomy about making choices, providing her with more opportunities to express herself eloquently, and inventing dramatic scenes to realize ideas about Agnes's character from the source, the pseudo-Ambrose letter[13] – suggests that she wanted to depict Agnes as a fully developed, heroic, and eloquent character, a Christian martyr who would inspire veneration. Most importantly, however, Hrotsvit's comments about sources here seem to be inviting readers to decide for themselves what is the truth in particular legends and who has the authority to declare it. Even at the Benedictine monastery of Gandersheim, which enjoyed considerable intellectual freedom under Otto I, the expression of such an opinion from a young canoness must have sounded bold.

Whatever her specific attitudes toward her sources may have been, Hrotsvit defines herself in the preface through the subject role of hagiographer. This role was an important one for medieval religious communities, requiring the hagiographer to be more than merely a chronicler of a holy person's life. In fact, as Thomas Heffernan suggests in *Sacred Biography*, 'the sacred biographer's primary mission in writing the life is not to render a chronological record of the subject's life ... but rather to facilitate the growth of a cult.'[14] The imperative of transforming the holy person into a cult figure naturally suggests an imaginative treatment of her or his biography, one that foregrounds the mystery of sanctity. At the same time the text itself must officially articulate the community's appreciation of the holy person's life as a revered document:

> For the Christian sacred biographer, this mission means stressing the encomiastic aspects, the *ethos*, of the subject's life. Such a task involves a considerable degree of interpretation, and it is an interpretative process which – if the life is to gain adherents for the cult figure – must accomplish two vital objectives: it must complement and satisfy the specific community's understanding of this holy person, and it must establish the text itself as a document worthy of reverence, as a relic.[15]

While most of the assertions Hrotsvit makes about her difficulties in writing and desire for help in correcting errors may be dismissed as calculated attempts to garner sympathy from her readers, it is also possible to read them as mirroring genuine anxieties she has about her skills and reputation as a writer of saints' lives. The specific criticisms she levels at her own work – her problems with prosody and achieving a decorous poetic style – indicate that she is comparing her abilities with a poetic ideal she would like to achieve – in short, becoming a writer who masterfully produces works distinguished by a graceful facility with language, the *eloquentia* required for a revered religious document.

Hrotsvit's desire to fulfil this particular role is significant since it constituted one of the highest ideals to which a medieval Christian could aspire. As Brigitte Cazelles observes, a hagiographer was thought to fulfil a sacred office in the medieval church:

> The ability to speak to God and to speak of God is reserved for the select few: the saint, because of his closeness to God and because he writes down his own story; the pope, who as the most eminent representative of the temporal Church, orchestrates the mediation between the saint and the faithful; and the hagiographer, because of his religious and cultural training.[16]

In striving to excel as a hagiographer, particularly as a hagiographer who opens her book with the subject of the Virgin Mary's sanctity, Hrotsvit appears to be constructing her own identity as a person privileged to speak of saints and God. The compositional history of the legends and the prefatory statements that accompany them suggest, furthermore, that she gradually became confident about filling the role of hagiographer.

Initially, Hrotsvit compiled the first five legends (*Maria, Ascensio, Gongolfus, Pelagius,* and *Theophilus*) into what she termed a 'libellus' (a small book), or an 'opusculum,' (little collection) in her preface. This designation suggests both the brevity and, ironically, the insignificance of her work. Elsewhere, she uses the frail woman topos in a plea for tolerance of her stylistic lapses:

> Quamvis etiam metrica modulatio femineę fragilitati difficilis videatur et ardua · solo tamen semper miserentis supernę gratię auxilio, non propriis viribus confisa · huius carmina opusculi dactilicis modulis succinere apposui · (*Liber Primus, Praefatio,* 8)

> However difficult and arduous and complex/ metrical composition may appear for the fragile female sex,/ I, persisting/ with no one assisting/ still put together my poems in this little work/ not relying on my own powers and talents as a clerk/ but always trusting in heavenly grace's aid/ for which

I prayed,/ and I chose to sing them in the dactylic mode ... (Wilson, *Florilegium*, 19–20)

Sometime later, she composed the last three legends (*Basilius, Dionysius,* and *Agnes*) and added them to the collection along with a another dedication to her abbess Gerberga. The tone of this new *Prologus ad Gerbergam Abbatissam,* however, is openly confident, even joyful:

En tibe versiculos, Gerberg, fero, domna, novellos
  Iungens praescriptis carmina carminulis,
Qualiter et veniam meruit scelerosus amandam
  Congaudens modulis succino dactilicis;
Spernere quos noli, nimium cum sint vitiosi,
  Sed lauda miti pectore facta dei!

                              (*Liber Primus, Pars Posterior, Prologus II*)

Behold, I bring to thee, Gerberga, my Lady, new verses, /
  thus adding songs to the songs I have been commissioned to write, /
and how a wretched sinner won loving forgiveness,/
  I joyfully sing in dactylic strains;/
Do not spurn these, even though they be exceedingly crude,/
  but do thou praise with gentle heart the works of God.

                              (Wiegand, 192)

This short dedication opens with an exclamatory offering of her new poems to Gerberga, accompanied by a joyful reference to the wretched sinner saved by divine grace in the legend that follows, *Basilius*. To end, Hrotsvit makes only a perfunctory use of the humility topos – 'Spernere quos noli, nimum cum sint vitiosi' (Do not spurn these, even though they be exceedingly crude) – enjoining her abbess instead to praise the works of God: 'Sed lauda miti pectore facta dei!' (but do thou praise with gentle heart the works of God). She has by now abandoned the elaborate self-deprecation of the preface to the first five legends to become 'the Strong Voice of Gandersheim.'

More important, the passionate language we find throughout the legends suggests that Hrotsvit's composition of them rises out of a psychological need she had as a medieval woman to escape, artistically at least, the inferior subject position to which women were usually assigned. Although Hrotsvit and other religious women in her community enjoyed a rare autonomy in their social, intellectual, and artistic lives within the royally protected principality of Gandersheim, they cannot have escaped knowing about the virulent misogyny of the Middle Ages, an ideology driven by the conception of woman as an intellectually inferior, spiritually corrupt, and physically weak creature. This awareness of the dominant culture's antifeminism became for some medieval women – Hildegard of Bingen, Mechthild of Magdeburg, and Hadewijch of Brabant, for example – a powerful motive for self-definition through artistic creation. If the wry, calculating voice we hear in the preface to the legends is any indication of Hrotsvit's sense of self, then it seems inescapable that she was one of the earliest medieval writers in Europe to filter out the negative images of women found in patristic texts to emphasize women's spiritual equality with men. In doing so, she also exploited the rich possibilities for sublimated self-creation that hagiography makes possible.

Two of the eight legends she wrote – *Pelagius* and *Agnes* – provide especially useful insights not only into medieval constructions of virginity, but also into the particular kind of interior desire that Hrotsvit gave herself artistic permission to speak of. Virginity, as Joan Cadden has argued, was a composite religious value for the Middle Ages:

> In its most literal form it was the absence of the experience of intercourse.
> In its most heroic form it was a source of Christian martyrdom. It was an
> active expression of love of God, a vehicle of humility, a token of the
> rejection of the world, and a representation of mystical purity.[17]

Hrotsvit's depiction of Pelagius's and Agnes's struggles and triumphant deaths certainly exhibits this complexity in her conception of heroic virginity. Both are heroic, humble, otherworldly, and mystically pure in their active love of God. Their bodies are also beautiful and their speech is persuasively fluent. By focusing so prominently on her protagonists' physical beauty and eloquence, Hrotsvit appears to be extending the religious signification that virginity had for the central Middle Ages, adding physical attractiveness and eloquence to the requisite supernatural powers and spiritual worth. Certainly, her virgin martyrs' beauty and gracious language complete their spiritual attractiveness.

Likewise, in constructing these two appealing adolescents as subjects for her exploration of virginal martyrdom, Hrotsvit seems to be expressing her religious desire as fundamentally androgynous, a rapturous identification with an unstained corporeal beauty that is both male and female. Moreover, by underscoring her male saint's beauty and her female saint's courage, she is interrogating essentialist depictions of male and female values, thereby asserting spiritual equality and reifying, at least in these two legends, the spiritual promise of Galatians: 'in Christ there is no male nor female' (Gal. 3. 28).

What we should note initially about Hrotsvit's construction of the desiring subject in *Pelagius* and *Agnes* is the artistic freedom she exercises in both. As she makes clear in the preface, she does not feel constrained to strive for historical accuracy, for painstaking adherence to the facts of her texts. She seems much more interested in having the narrative authority to make her characters what she believes they should be. Although it is probably anachronistic to claim that she is experimenting with the hagiographical romance, a generic hybrid that developed in France three centuries later, it is nevertheless certain that she is taking considerable liberties with her sources. Hrotsvit seems to have made these changes to serve her desires for impersonating a very particular kind of heroic, virgin martyr. This particular kind of martyr – one who is, for the most part, serenely detached from the distasteful details of corporeality – seems consonant with subtle resonances of desire we hear in the voice of the text throughout the narratives. She obviously wants to delineate sanctity as utterly desirable, unsullied beauty.

Hrotsvit's desire to incorporate ideal physical beauty into her depiction of sancity manifests itself clearly in *Pelagius*. She tells us that she has based *Pelagius*, unlike her other saints' lives, on an eyewitness's oral report, rather than on a written account.[18] By choosing an oral report upon which to base her story of the young martyr, Hrotsvit is once more asserting her own authority as a hagiographer rather than adhering to the orthodoxy of a Latin source. In comparing the details of Hrotsvit's version of Pelagius's martyrdom to early Spanish sources, Wiegand notes significant differences in details about the boy's familial relationship, age, term of imprisonment, and form of death.[19] In the Spanish *vita*, she tells us, Pelagius's father sent his ten-year-old son to serve as a hostage for a relative, Hermogius, bishop of Tuy, who had been taken prisoner in a battle against the Muslim forces. The handsome boy languished in a Cordoban prison for three or four years before being noticed by the Islamic ruler, Abd al-Rahman III, who attempted to win the boy's sexual favours by offering him riches. Because the boy refused and disparaged Islam, he was dismembered with a sword and his mutilated body was thrown in a river. In Hrotsvit's version, Pelagius is a noble adolescent who persuades his aged father to allow him to take his place in prison where he remains for only a short time before his beauty is noticed. After he is presented to Abd al-Rahman, Pelagius refuses al-Rahman's sexual advances, mocks Islam, and survives the bizarre execution of being catapulted to rocks outside the city's walls before being finally dispatched by a sword. The specific details of Hrotsvit's version are at least as dramatic as those in the Spanish *vita,* and they enhance Pelagius's character and build suspenseful moments in the narrative when it is unclear what will happen to the boy next. Along with presenting her young protagonist as a self-sacrificing, virginal adolescent, a perfect candidate for martyrdom, Hrotsvit is also obviously interested in constructing an engaging story for her community of readers, one full of pathos and edifying instruction.

Likewise in *Agnes*, Hrotsvit sanctifies the young woman's life. Basically, she reduces the usual pathos of Agnes's story – the young girl's humiliation through public exposure, the threat of rape, and the prospect of enforced prostitution – by changing the narrative focus from her degradation to her triumph over these dangers of violation. With the same stroke, she characterizes the beautiful, eloquent, and capable young woman as possessing a sanctity guarded by an angel and illuminated by holy light. In Hrotsvit's treatment, Agnes's story becomes a triumphant affirmation of heroic virginity rather than what Brigitte Cazelles calls 'the theatrics of female exposure' in her analysis of a thirteenth-century French version of the Agnes story.[20]

A careful reading of *Pelagius* and *Agnes* reveals several thematic concerns – agency, corporeality, alterity, and voyeurism – that are central to Hrotsvit's construction of subjectivity. The most prominent is corporeality, the physical body, the ground of one's being, the seat of the senses and appetites. For most medieval writers, the body and its physical, mortal identity oppose the spirit and its unsubstantial identity, its locus of immortality and divine nature. In the vast majority of medieval narratives, the body is thus marked unambiguously as the source of both erotic power and spiritual absence while the spirit is inscribed contrarily with spiritual power and erotic absence. This dialectical tension, as Brigitte Cazelles has observed in her introductory remarks on hagiography, makes saints' lives inherently dramatic narratives:

> In giving prominence to the heroes and heroines of Christianity, the writing of Saints' Lives runs counter to the virtues of humility and self-denial that typically characterize holiness. The end, to edify the audience, may justify the hagiographic discourse, but not without 'giving flesh' to an achievement that entails, first and foremost, a denial of the flesh. Verse

hagiography is, in this respect, a particularly contradictory discourse since it gives prominence to the corporeal embodiment of the saintly protagonist.[21]

The focal place that corporeal beauty occupies in *Pelagius* and *Agnes* certainly underscores their contradictory nature as discourses. In both, corporeality serves as the catalyst for action in the narratives' dialectic of desire. But what makes Hrotsvit's treatment of this dialectic especially striking is the way she changes the signification of the body and de-genders it to erase its patristic signification as the site of evil, especially for women. At the same time, she expunges the seeming contradiction of the saintly protagonists' embodiment of corporeal beauty by fore-grounding their spiritual alterity. Significantly, neither Pelagius nor Agnes is concerned with being physically attractive because their desires are focused on the imperishable world of Christ. Only worldly people – the dignitaries of Cordoba and the Saracen caliph's court in *Pelagius* and the Roman prefect's son and citizenry of Rome in *Agnes* – are charmed by their beauty. Yet the narrator complicates the matter further by praising the martyrs extravagantly for their physical beauty, even voicing her own attraction to Pelagius's adolescent charisma.

Pelagius opens with a lengthy exposition that recounts the pathos of Cordoba's capture and rule by evil Saracens. Although the Christians were allowed to continue their religious practices without penalty, the Saracen king did impose one restriction: 'Ne quis praefate civis prę-sumeret urbis/ Ultra blasphemare diis auro fabricatis' (56–7), 'Namely that no dweller of the aforesaid city/ Should presume to blaspheme the golden idol's name' (Wilson, *Florilegium*, 30). The thirst for martyrdom ('martiriique sitis,' 64) persuaded many of those Christians to crush with words the marble statues ('corrumpere dictis/ Marmora,' 64–5). Be-cause the Christians in far-off Galicia not only persisted in practising their faith but also 'stultos verbis reprehendere divos' (84), 'were eager to denounce the king's own foolish idols' (Wilson, *Florilegium*, 31), and 'Quę sua continuo temptaret spernere iura' (95), 'freely dared to spurn his decrees and laws,' 'simulacrorumque rebellem' (94), 'making war on idols' (Wilson, *Florilegium*, 31), the most wicked of all the Saracen rulers, Caliph Abd al-Rahman, invaded and conquered Galicia, abducted the aging duke of Galicia and twelve of his nobles, and held them for ransom. Unlike that of the twelve nobles, the old duke's ransom was set at an impossibly high figure, ensuring that he would die in prison. Fortunately, the old duke had a caring son, Pelagius, who eloquently convinced his father to allow him to take his father's place.

Although the narrator introduces Pelagius as a young man graced with good blood, good sense, and every imaginable virtue, she accentuates his exemplary beauty:

Cui fuerat natus praeclari germinis unus
Omni praenitida compostus corpore forma,
Nomine Pelagius, formę splendore decorus,
Consilio prudens, tota bonitate refulgens,
Qui vix transactis iam tunc puerilibus annis
Attigit aetatis primos flores iuvenilis.   (143–8)

The duke had an only son, of illustrious descent,
Endowed with every charm of body and of shape.
Pelagius by name, elegant and lustrous;
Prudent in council, replete with all the virtues.
He barely had completed the years of his boyhood
And had just now reached the first blossoms of youth.
(Wilson, *Florilegium*, 33)

Having finished his childhood and reached 'the first blossoms of youth,' he is depicted as a young man gifted in every imaginable way. Along with being 'omni praenitida compostus corpore forma,' he is also 'formae splendore decorus.' Hrotsvit's use of the richly connotative noun *forma* to describe his physical appearance is especially significant. Having the core meaning of 'form' or 'shape,' *forma* also connotes 'beautiful shape,' 'image,' 'likeness,' and 'a shape serving as a model.' Thus, Hrotsvit appears to be suggesting that Pelagius is the model of young male beauty. Likewise, when she refers to his having attained 'primos flores iuvenilis,' she seems to be using the noun *flores* to refer not only to Pelagius's downy beard, but also to his flower-like freshness, his flourishing youth. With this description of Pelagius's physical perfection, Hrotsvit is anticipating later vernacular hagiographers who equate physical beauty with sanctity, but her emphasis on the boy's physical beauty is unusual in that such a linkage was usually reserved for the exposure and torture of the female saint.[22] In Hrotsvit's story, pagan men admire Pelagius for his beauty, but they do not torture him for it.

When the young Pelagius speaks, the narrator tells us that he is also blessed with eloquence: 'Cumque sat inmitem patri sciret fore regem,/ Tali merentem blanditur voce parentem' (149–50), 'When he learned the king's treatment of his father:/ He coaxed his grieving sire with such caressing words' (Wilson, *Florilegium*, 33). The narrator's use of the verb *blanditur*, 'coaxes,' with the semantic range including 'to allure' and 'to please,' intimates that the young man has a captivating voice.

The first words we hear from Pelagius – his plea to take his father's place in prison – confirm this assessment of his persuasiveness:

> 'O mi care pater, mea suscipe verba libenter,
> Et, que commoneo, sensu bene percipe prompto.
> Calleo namque tuam senio decrescere vitam,
> Viribus et propriis nervos penitus vacuatos
> Nec te posse quidem levis quid ferre laboris;
> Ast ego sed validis dominabor quippe lacertis
> Ad tempusque potens dominis succumbere duris.
> Quapropter moneo precibus blandisque rogabo,
> Ut regi natum me deponas tibi carum,
> Donec sufficias precium persolvere totum,
> Nec tua canities vinclis intercidat artis.'   (151–61)

> 'O my dear father,   hear my speech with kindness,
> And, to what I implore thee,   please be well disposed.
> I am quite aware that   thy years are now declining,
> And that thy strength now lacks   its accustomed vigor.
> Thou can bear no labor,   however slight it be;
> I, on the other hand,   can cope with all demands
> And can with limbs still strong   submit me to a most cruel lord.
> Therefore I entreat thee   and with prayers beseech thee
> That as a pledge thou bring   me to the pagan king,
> Until thou can furnish   the ransom gold in full,
> Or thou may die, gray haired,   in narrow fetters snared.'
> (Wilson, *Florilegium*, 33)

Although used for a dramatic purpose, the young man's calculated, eloquent language in this passages parallels the deliberate care that Hrotsvit exercises with her language in the preface.

In Pelagius's speeches, we discover the same felicitous diction, ingratiating phrasing, and complex rhetorical structures that appear in the language of the preface. For example, at the beginning of his impassioned exhortation to his elderly father, Pelagius uses *amplificatio* to emphasize his simple request by restating it in different words: 'O mi care pater, mea suscipe verba libenter,/ Et, que commoneo, sensu bene percipe prompto.' To make his next point, he continues using *amplificatio* when he attempts to persuade his aging father that he is too frail to survive prison life, but this time Pelagius complicates his plea by developing a negative consequence of his father's weakness: 'Calleo namque tuam senio decrescere vitam,/ Viribus et propriis nervos penitus vacuatos/ Nec te posse quidem levis quid ferre laboris.' In the rest of his exhortation Pelagius uses *antithesis* to oppose his aged father's weakness to his own youthful vitality, but balancing the contrast between the two once again with *amplificatio* : 'Ast ego sed validis dominabor quippe lacertis/ Ad tempusque potens dominis succumbere duris.' To conclude his argument, Pelagius uses *amplificatio* a final time, once more bringing forth a negative consequence of his father's frailty: 'Quapropter moneo precibus blandisque rogabo,/ Ut regi natum me deponas tibi carum,/ Donec sufficias precium persolvere totum,/ Nec tua canities vinclis intercidat artis.' In speaking this well, Pelagius seems to be Hrotsvit's male alter-ego, an attractive young man possessing great facility to exhort people to accept his ideas with his eloquent speech and physical allure.

Then, when Pelagius concludes his plea, the narrator underscores the boy's eloquence by having his father comment on his son's persuasiveness, admonishing him to cease his sweet words to avoid being persuaded by its eloquence: '"Desine tanta loqui, dulcissime, desine, fili,"' '"Cease such speech, sweet son; cease such speech, my dear"' (Wilson, *Florilegium*, 33). The term 'dulcissime' that the narrator has Pelagius's father use to address his son seems to express the boy's essential innocence. At the same time, Hrotsvit obviously intends her audience to see Pelagius as a powerful force for good, someone whose compassion compels him to use his eloquence to alleviate suffering. Likewise, she clearly means to rebuke those who, like Caliph Abd al-Rahman, would profane Pelagius's innocent beauty with carnal desires.

The parallels between the martyr's beautiful body and beautiful speech start to become apparent at this point in the narrative. The powers of captivating language and physical charm are reciprocal aspects of the martyr's alterity, complementary forces that initiate and drive his fate. Significantly, Pelagius's beautiful language results in his imprisonment in Cordoba; then the caliph's response to his attractiveness propels him toward his martyrdom, in the same way that female saints' beauty contributes to their martyrdom. Depicting him in this way, Hrotsvit develops him as a charismatic being who attracts everyone he meets. But his power to focus people's attention, she carefully points out, is the working of Divine Providence. Everything that has happened – the caliph's invasion and Pelagius's imprisonment and subsequent martyrdom – is part of God's secret plan:

> Nullus pro meritis credat factum fore regis
> Hoc, quod tam pulchra vincebat denique pompa,
> Sed mage iudicio secreti iudicis aequo,
> Ut populus, tanto correptus rite flagello
> Fleret totius proprii commissa reatus,
> Vel quo Pelagius Christi pro lege necandus
> Forte locum peteret, quo se morti dare posset
> Necnon sanquineum pro Christo fundere rivum
> Inpendens animam domino bene morte piatam.   (179–87)

> No one, though, should credit   this to the king's own merit,
> That he should have succeeded   in such a splendid way,
> But rather the reason lies,   and with God the Judge resides
> Whose secret plan was either   that this tribe, so chastised,
> Should beweep the sins   of which they all stood charged,
> Or that Pelagius   be killed for faith in Christ,
> And might thus reach the spot,   where to die was his lot,
> And pour forth the waters there   of his blood for Christ,
> Giving his soul to God,   made holy by his death. (Wilson, *Florilegium*, 34)

Hrotsvit's comment that the caliph's success in invading Cordoba is a manifestation of God's providence might also be read as her way of asserting a qualified authority as a hagiographer. On the one hand, her explanation that God granted the caliph success – either to chastise the invading Saracens later or to martyr Pelagius – clearly asserts that she has an intimation of God's purpose for Pelagius's passion. But, on the other hand, her lack of certainty about God's motive for granting the caliph victory underscores her appreciation for the mystery of God's actions.

Once Pelagius is imprisoned in Cordoba, the story's narrative pace quickens. Shortly after he is imprisoned in the underground vaults of Cordoba's prison, the city's dignitaries learn of his imprisonment, visit him, and, moved by his physical beauty and 'honeyed speech,' seek his release as a consort of the pederast Abd al-Rahman. Once again, Pelagius's physical appearance is foregrounded as we learn of the dignitaries' motives for wanting Pelagius released. The narrator recounts:

Necnon praedulcis gustassent ipsius oris
Verbula rethoricę circumlita melle loquelę,
Optabant speciem vinclis absolvere talem;
Hęc et suaserunt regi iam sceptra tenenti   (200–3)

As they beheld the grace   of the captive's lovely face
And as they had tasted, each,   of the sweetness of his speech
And heard words embellished,   with the honey of rhetoric
Then they all desired   to free him from his bondage.
They wished to be kind   and change the ruler's mind.

(Wilson, *Florilegium*, 34)

Hrotsvit needs to explain how Pelagius is released from prison, but it is
hard to explain her repeated description of his beauty and eloquence –
to presumably heterosexual people, less than 100 lines later – unless she
is fascinated by the power such gifts command.

Bearing their petition for Pelagius's release to Caliph Abd al-Rahman,
the Cordoban dignitaries once more repeat the litany of praises for
Pelagius's beauty. To persuade the caliph, the intercessors say:

'Non decet ergo tuum, princeps fortissime, sceptrum,
Duriter ut puerum mandes punire decorum
Obsidis et teneros insontis stringere nervos.
Eius praenitidam velles si cernere formam
Et tam mellitam saltem gustare loquelam,
Quam cuperes iuvenem tibimet coniungere talem
Gradu milicię necnon assumere prime,
Corpore candidulo tibi quo serviret in aula!'   (210–17)

'Bravest prince, it is not proper   nor becoming for you to order
That such a handsome youth   be punished so harshly,
And that the tender arms   of this guiltless boy be fettered.
If you would ever deign   to behold his splendor
And would taste the flow   of his honeyed speech
You would then desire   to join him to yourself
And to have him take on   the rank of officer,
So in his dazzling beauty,   he might serve at court.'

(Wilson, *Florilegium*, 34–5)

Abd al-Rahman's response, predictably, is to have Pelagius released from his dungeon cell and brought to court. The caliph's orders to prepare the boy for court suggest that Pelagius is treated as a new concubine:

> His rex mollitus dictis, hac voce coactus
> Iussit Pelagium nodis evellere duris
> Omneque <cum> lavacro corpus detergere puro
> Lotaque purpureo circumdare tegmine membra
> Collum gemmatis necnon ornar metallis,
> Quo bene constructa posset fore miles in aula.   (218–23)

> The king, much mollified   and roused by this speech
> Ordered that Pelagius   be freed from his bonds
> And his body be cleansed   with pure and clean water
> And his body be decked   in rich and purple garments
> And his neck adorned   with a jeweled necklace
> So he thus be brought   to that well-wrought court.
>
> (Wilson, *Florilegium*, 35)

Although the story's narrative logic requires that Pelagius be 'feminized' to underscore his identity as the object of the caliph's desire, it is also possible to read beauty more widely in both *Pelagius* and *Agnes* as androgynous and therefore transcending sexual difference. Pelagius is, of course, a chaste virgin, but his beauty, an early adolescent composite of male and female attributes, symbolizes his spiritual alterity, his angelic otherworldliness that is not profaned by the demands of gender. The narrator repeatedly gives catalogues of the boy's various physical attributes – his 'lovely face,' 'tender arms,' 'sweet neck,' and so on – physical traits most often associated with women. Likewise, his beauty, like that of women, functions in the narrative by attracting the male gaze. But Pelagius, like many women, finds nothing positive about that unbidden attraction. An elegant, androgynous virgin, he seems oblivious to his attractiveness – at least until someone tries to force attentions upon him.

In marking Pelagius's beauty and eloquence positively and sanctifying them as part of God's secret plan, Hrotsvit also seems to be filtering out the ascetic ascription of depravity to beauty. In her construction of the subject Pelagius, beauty is not only androgynous but also morally innocent. The narrator is thus free to admire him innocently for his physical as well as his spiritual beauty. Moreover, since he is to 'pour forth the waters there of his blood for Christ' (Wilson, *Florilegium*, 34), he becomes a sacrificial victim, a liminal being who requires new terms for understanding.

Once Pelagius appears in Abd al-Rahman's court, his fate is set. Seated by the caliph, Pelagius deftly avoids a kiss the Saracen attempts to plant on his mouth and witnesses for his faith by chiding his would-be defiler about the foolishness of trying to violate an anointed Christian or expecting a Christian to entice a kiss from the lewd servant of an idol. Remarkably, Abd al-Rahman responds merely by chiding Pelagius for his rash words and behaviour. Then, when Abd al-Rahman seizes Pelagius and forcibly tries to kiss him, Pelagius assaults the caliph by punching him in the face, bloodying his nose, beard, and clothing. Significantly, the wicked caliph suffers physically while Pelagius remains unharmed. Hrotsvit seems to be suggesting that his beauty, an emblem of his spiritual perfection, is inviolate.

At this point, Abd al-Rahman sentences Pelagius to the unusual death of being catapulted onto the rocks outside the city walls, a form of execution that will leave his body intact, rather than dismembered or incinerated. Elizabeth Petroff reads this form of execution as Hrotsvit's way of evading for Pelagius the horrific death by mutilation typically suffered by saints in traditional virgin-martyr legends. As she puts it, this peculiar kind of death rids the *vita* of the usual violence found in saints' lives, especially those in early medieval martyr narratives:

> The only blood that is shed in the story is shed by the Caliph, not by the martyr. This underscores another contrast between Hrotsvit's narrative and traditional accounts of martyrdom: the sadism and voyeurism of most of the early virgin-martyr legends is completely absent in her poem. There is no interest in the vulnerability of the saint and no interest in tortures that may be inflicted.[23]

This observation is no doubt true, but it does not go far enough. Hrotsvit values Pelagius's virginal beauty too highly to include the sadistic defilements. The idealized desire we find her recounting throughout the *Pelagius* legend simply precludes the gratuitous mutilation that satisfies the sadistic interests of many male-authored legends of virgin-martyrs. The rest of the legend recounts Pelagius's translation into sainthood. When his body is not broken by the rocks, the caliph orders him beheaded, whereupon Pelagius is immediately apotheosized. Arab fishermen find the body in a river and sell it to Christians, who bury it with great honours. As miracles start to occur at Pelagius's tomb, the faithful devise a test to discover if Pelagius is indeed a saint. They place his head in a furnace and pray to God for a sign of the degree of Pelagius's sanctity by the extent to which his head is undamaged. When they remove the head an hour later, they discover, 'quod iam splendidius puro radiaverat auro/ Expers ardoris penitus tantique caloris' (404–5), 'but the head just glowed more splendidly than gold/ Unharmed and entire, in spite of the raging fire' (Wilson, *Florilegium*, 39).

Aside from testing Pelagius's worth as a true witness to his faith, the transformation of his head by the furnace symbolically suggests the highest expression of Hrotsvit's desiring subject – her corporeal imaginings about the transcendent saintly body. In Hrotsvit's imaginative interpretation of Pelagius's elevation to sainthood, she sees him spiritually transmuted from perishable flesh to an imperishable substance, radiating spiritual light brighter than gold. This otherworldly transformation is the final step in defining Pelagius as a cult figure. His beauty 'unharmed and entire,' he becomes a precious icon, a worthy relic for a cult.

In her construction of the Agnes legend, Hrotsvit replicates, in a general way, the virgin-martyr story she uses for *Pelagius*. But while *Pelagius* opens with a prayer to the martyr, asking that he lend his aid as Hrotsvit, his servant, acclaims his triumphs, *Agnes* opens with a short disquisition on the spiritual splendours of holy virginity, which connects Agnes's life and death explicitly to anyone who has chosen the life – and garb – of a nun. After this preparation, Hrotsvit introduces her heroine Agnes, emphasizing not only her virginity but also her nobility ('praenobilis incola,' 27, 'inclita nobilitas,' 29, and 'ortus atque sui respondens nobilitati' 30). Although Hrotsvit presents her as well-born, attractive, charming, and impeccably virtuous, the physical description of the young virgin is perfunctory compared to the fulsome praises she makes of Pelagius's physical beauty throughout his *vita*: 'pulchra fuit facie fideique decora nitore/ praecipuis nimium meritis mundoque celebris' (31–2), 'she was comely of form and charming in the splendor of her faith and celebrated throughout the world because of her outstanding virtues' (Wiegand, 237).

This rather abstract description seems curious, especially since it is her beauty that inspires in the son of the Roman prefect Simphronius a desire to marry her. Perhaps Hrotsvit is deemphasizing Agnes's corporeality to underscore her spiritual perfection. On the other hand, Hrotsvit simply may not have given herself permission to imagine feminine beauty or praise it in a narrative that is obviously directed to encouraging female modesty. Whatever the case may be, she is clearly transferring corporeal beauty to Christ, the handsome celestial bridegroom.

Whenever Agnes has the opportunity to speak of Christ, she always does so eloquently, emphasizing not only his heavenly power but also his erotic attractiveness. Not only has Christ bound her close to him, Agnes tells her suitor, but he has given her gifts far superior to the ones the suitor offers, and his virtue and beauty put him in a class higher than any man born of woman. Even the sun and moon are amazed by his beauty: '"Cuius praepulchram mirantur denique formam/ Solaris splendor lunę renitens quoque candor/ Laudantes radiis dominum fulgentibus orbis"' (78–80), '"His outstanding comeliness the splendor of the sun and the gleaming glory of the moon do marvel at"' (Wiegand, 241). Agnes even identifies Christ's gifts to her as the source of her own attractiveness. Furthermore, Christ's speech is fully sensual, even material: 'Ipsius certe dulcedo fluxit ab ore,/ Quę me lactavit dulci pastuque cibavit/ Ceu nectar mellis suavis vel copia lactis' (95–7), 'From His Lips hath flowed forth a sweetness that hath nourished me with milk and fed me with a sweet food like to the nectar of sweet honey and an abundance of milk' (Wiegand, 241). In describing Christ in these terms, Hrotsvit has once again complicated her construction of the saintly subject. The way she has Agnes imagine and describe her relationship with Christ suggests there is no conflict between flesh and spirit. For her, transcendental virginity paradoxically includes an erotic life.

Other details in Agnes's first speech also contribute to the idea that the virgin's love for Christ will result in a physical relationship remarkably similar to what the suitor himself has in mind but with no loss of virginity:

'Affectu quem secreto <cum> cordis amabo,
Nulla puellaris pacior detrimenta pudoris;
Ast ubi forte sui merear complexibus uti
Eius in thalamum sponsarum more coruscum
Duci, permaneo virgo sine sorde pudica.
Cui debebo fidem soli servare perennem:
Ipsi me toto cordis conamine credo.'   (104–10)

'When I love him in the inmost affection of my heart, no loss do I suffer of maidenhood; but when I merit the joy of His embrace and like a bride am led to His glorious bridal-chamber, I remain a virgin without violation of chastity.' (Wiegand, 243)

This phrasing constructs Agnes as anticipating unconstrained physical embraces and love from her heavenly lover, yet mysteriously with a consummation that leaves her still virginal; Agnes expresses a longing for Christ that is at once chaste and thoroughly corporeal. This paradoxical conception of union with her celestial bridegroom emphasizes the otherworldliness of the 'secret affection of [her] heart.' At the same time, Hrotsvit's characterization of Agnes's erotic spirituality enables her to imagine for herself and her community the great reward promised to nuns – becoming a bride of Christ.

Overwhelmed by his disappointment at rejection, Agnes's pagan suitor feigns illness. In giving the suitor this kind of passive response, Hrotsvit suggests the diseased nature of his erotic desire in contrast to the nobility and virtue of Agnes's erotic desire. After summoning physicians to heal his son, Simphronius learns from them that unrequited love is the cause of his son's malady. When he confronts Agnes with being the cause of his son's suffering, Agnes's response suggests another contrast between Christian virginity and virginity in the service of pagan Roman religion. Agnes replies:

> 'Si mihi iure tuum placuit contempnere natum,
> Qui ratione vigens cunctis quoque sensibus utens
> Corporeis anima regitur numquam moritura
> ...
> Quis te posse minis vel quis tandem suadelis
> Ad simulachrorum reris me cogere cultum,
> Artificum cura quę conformata metallo
> Membrorum falsam portant solummodo formam
> Mobilis officium complent nec corporis ullum
> Neque suum quid viventis monstrant animalis?'   (160–72)

'If it rightfully pleased me to reject thy son who, endowed with reason and having the use of all his bodily senses, is ruled by a soul destined never to die ... how then dost thou think by any threats or by any persuasions to force me to worship idols, which are formed from metal by the labor of artisans and bear only a false form of limbs, and fulfill no functions of a nimble body, and do not show anything in common with living beings?' (Wiegand, 245–7)

Her passion for Christ is as physical as the suitor's passion for her but infinitely superior; even loving the prefect's son would be superior to virginity in service of idol-worship. Thus it isn't the virginity itself that is glorified but rather the passion for Christ that is expressed through virginity.

Hrotsvit's (and Agnes's) attitudes toward sexuality are complicated further when the prefect threatens to put Agnes into a brothel where she will not only be physically violated but will also lose her good name and shame her noble parents. Threatened thus by the power and authority of a secular ruler, Agnes responds by invoking the power and authority of God:

'Ipsius dextra me defendente superna
Spero delicti numquam maculis violari,
Carnis spurcitias fragilis sed vincere cunctas.'   (203–5)

'and I hope that under the protection of the right Hand of God, I will never be defiled by sin but will conquer all the allurements of the frail flesh.' (Wiegand, 247)

From this point on, the miraculous dominates, as it so often does in saints' legends. Simphronius orders a punishment he believes to be particularly appropriate for a proud young woman:

Cẹlestis sponsam regis iussit venerandam
Vestibus exutam, toto quoque corpore nudam,
Concurrente trahi conventiculo populari
Inque lupanaris nigrum concludier antrum,
In quo lascivi iuvenes rationis egeni
Colloquio scelerosarum gaudent mulierum.   (207–12)

he commanded the esteemed spouse of the Celestial King to be deprived of her garments and with body entirely exposed to be dragged in the midst of a great concourse of people that had gathered, and to be shut up in the dark den of a brothel, in which wanton youths, maddened with passion, delighted in association with evil women. (Wiegand, 249)

Christ, however, protects Agnes from shame by causing her hair to grow until it reaches the soles of her feet and sends an angel to dress her in a gleaming robe after she enters the brothel. The minute the mob of youths see the illumination her entrance in the brothel has caused, they convert to Christianity. Significantly, this miraculous growth of hair inverts the familiar medieval prohibition against women baring their heads, revealing their hair, and thus inciting men to lust. In Hrotsvit's hands, Agnes's hair is not only resplendently visible, but the very means by which Christ protects her virginal innocence. It is hard to see how these transformations could be construed as anything less than religious passion conceived as, to use Northrop Frye's felicitous concept, 'the imaginative limit of desire.'[24] At the same time, since Agnes escapes both the humiliation and torture that usually figure in *vitae* of female virgin martyrs, Hrotsvit seems to be undoing the male gaze that follows women and, with it, Agnes's vulnerability. In doing so, Hrotsvit posits Christian faith as a miraculous agency, one that enables her saintly maiden to become erotically invisible, inviolable by earthly eyes, and at the same time allows the poet to reverse or undo some of the negative characteristics of physical existence for women. Significantly, at this point in the narrative, Hrotsvit begins to depict Agnes's own agency in the miraculous events. Each individual in the mob who hopes to rape Agnes prostrates himself at her feet and begs her to free him:

> Ut radios lucis vidit mire rutilantis
> Angelicę prefulgentem vestisque nitorem,
> Correptus signi nimio terrore stupendi
> Prostratus sacrę plantis extimplo puellę
> Postulat errorum laxari vincla suorum
> Testaturque deum verum fore iure colendum,
> Eius cultores qui consolabitur omnes;   (246–52)

> when he beheld the rays of light scintillating in a wonderful manner and saw the splendor of the angelic garb, each was so seized with extreme terror at such an extraordinary manifestation, that he forthwith prostrated himself at the feet of the holy virgin, imploring to be freed from the shackles of his errors and testifying that the true God was rightly to be worshiped, Who thus wills to console all His clients. (Wiegand, 251)

Clearly God must be the object of worship (in contrast to pagan worship of idols), but Agnes herself seems to be the agent of their conversion. Furthermore, when the prefect's son enters the brothel in hopes of raping Agnes, Hrotsvit depicts Agnes as acting in concert with Christ:

> Sed Christi pietas necnon praecelsa potestas
> Fortiter obsistens illi perversa volenti

A corruptela propriam protexit alumnam
In reprobam miserum mortem tradebat et illum.
Nam mox ut rapido cursu properaverat illo,
Quo supplex laudes domino resonaverat Agnes,
Infelix membris inprovisa resolutis
Morte ruit pronus Christi virtute peremptus.   (262–9)

But the goodness of Christ and His most high power mightily resisting this
man who was willing sin, shielded His own child from disgrace and delivered the unhappy man to an evil death. For as soon as he had with quick
steps hastened to this place where Agnes supplicatingly was singing praises
to God, the unhappy wretch, his limbs unexpectedly relaxed in death, fell
prone, laid low by the power of Christ. (Wiegand, 251)

By singing God's praises (as Hrotsvit has sung Pelagius's and Agnes's
praises), Agnes not only passively experiences God's protection but also
actively participates in God's plan for humanity. Later, taking pity on the
grief-stricken prefect, Agnes prays to Christ to raise the prefect's son
from the dead. She thus seems as much an agent of God's will as is the
angel who appears and 'In verboque dei iussit virtute potenti/ Extinctum
subito flato vixisse resumpto' (304–5), 'in the name of God commanded
that the dead man, destroyed by the power of the Most High, should
resume his breathing forthwith and live' (Wiegand, 258). In this scene,
and the subsequent account of the suitor's and the prefect's conversions,
Hrotsvit's desiring subject acquires saintly agency. The heavenly power of
virginity is fully revealed.

After reading these two highly stylized *vitae*, what, then, are we to
understand about the nature of the desiring subject expressed in the
voices of the text? How are we to accommodate the medieval otherness
of this desiring subject – with its antagonistic inflections of passivity and
agency, of self-destruction and self-creation, and its antithetical locus in
corporeality and spirituality – to our modern or post-modern sensibilities? How are we to grasp the complex subjective relationship between
Hrotsvit the hagiographer and the virgin martyrs she impersonates? The
struggles that these martyrs must wage against the profane inscriptions
that their worldly communities would write upon them? The passionate
desire for spiritual transcendence that Hrotsvit's narrator and characters
express?

Lee Patterson's summarizing formulation about the role of desire in
medieval culture provides at least a starting point for understanding

the complexities of Hrotsvit's desiring subject:

> Medieval anthropology defined the subject as desire: as the Augustinian will, with its opposed movements of *caritas* and *cupiditas*; as the Boethian *intentio naturalis* that tends ineluctably toward the *summum bonum*; as the scholastic powers of appetition, in which the intellectual appetite seeks to govern its concupiscible and irascible partners, or as *amor*, the sense of insufficiency that drives the Christian self forward on its journey through the historical world.[25]

On the one hand, Hrotsvit the narrator defines herself as being attracted to the beautiful, but enacts in the legends the potential for the beautiful to elicit both *caritas* and *cupiditas*, love and lust. She constructs Pelagius and Agnes both as naturally drawn (*intentio naturalis*) toward the highest good of virgin martyrdom (the *summum bonum*). Yet the desiring subjects of the narrator and the two martyrs express their *amor*, their sense of insufficiency or incompleteness, in various ways. The narrator repeatedly voices her desire to become the accomplished poet, a writer worthy of admiration, the consummate hagiographer. Pelagius desires to save his father from harm and to resist the evil of the Saracen caliph. Agnes yearns to keep her virginity and to overcome her fears of violation so that she might enjoy the rapturous embrace of her celestial bridegroom.

Paradoxically, then, the composite subject that emerges from the narrator's nuanced construction of the Pelagius and Agnes legends appears to embody the protean nature of Hrotsvit's desire itself. In assuming the challenging vocation of hagiographer, she has embraced a creative force that expresses itself as an opposition between charity and cupidity, as a natural inclination toward goodness, as an enduring struggle between soul and body, and as a deep desire for spiritual self-actualization. In pursuing this vocation, she transforms herself from a young canoness into a remarkable writer, a medieval Latin poet who realizes her own passionate desire for transcendence, in part at least, by constructing the desires of virgin martyrs.

NOTES

1 Dronke, *Women Writers of the Middle Ages*, 77.
2 In chapter 3 of *Jesus as Mother*, 'Did the Twelfth Century Discover the

Individual?' Caroline Walker Bynum revisits the question of when a sense of individuality arose in medieval Europe and offers a political, literary, and religious context for answering it. She concludes that 'if the twelfth century did not "discover the individual" in the modern meaning of expression of unique personality and isolation of the person from firm group membership, it did in some sense discover – or rediscover – the self, the inner mystery, the inner man, the inner landscape' (106).

3 Wilson, *Hrotsvit of Gandersheim: A Florilegium of Her Works*, 29, n. 2. Hrotsvit's six references to herself are particularly interesting considering that the entire corpus of Anglo-Saxon poetry that was written down in approximately the same historical era is anonymous, except for the four saints' lives (*Juliana, Elene, Christ II,* and *The Fates of the Apostles*) that contain Cynewulf's runic signature.

4 For the most complete, recent treatment of Hrotsvit's self-definition, see Gold, 'Hrotsvitha Writes Herself.' Her discussion of Hrotsvit's works from the theoretical perspective of medieval women's autobiographies is especially valuable.

5 A useful discussion of Gandersheim's intellectual and cultural vitality during Hrotsvit's time is Peter Dronke's chapter on 'Hrotsvitha' in his *Women Writers of the Middle Ages,* 55–6.

6 Ibid., 56.

7 Borch-Jacobensen, *The Freudian Subject,* 47.

8 Wilson, *Hrotsvit of Gandersheim: The Ethics of Authorial Stance,* 30. Wilson's analysis of Hrotsvit's use of classical Greek and Latin rhetoric throughout her works is indispensable for understanding the social, intellectual, and scholastic milieu of her art.

9 Homeyer, *Hrotsvithae Opera,* 205. In mistakenly referring to Hrotsvit as a nun, Homeyer seems to be overlooking the considerable freedom Hrotsvit had as a canoness, the wide sphere of social and intellectual acquaintances she had outside the abbey of Gandersheim.

10 Wilson, *Hrotsvit of Gandersheim: A Florilegium of Her Works,* 111.

11 Bynum, 'Did the Twelfth Century,' 85.

12 The expressions that Hrotsvit is using here, 'I offer' and 'I confess,' belong to a special class of utterances known as 'performative expressions': according to Jeffrey P. Kaplan, these are 'expressions that accomplish acts by virtue of being spoken: when you say *I resign* ... in the proper context you have resigned' *English Grammar,* 176. Hrotsvit frequently uses performative expressions to construct subjects throughout her works.

13 Petroff, *Body and Soul,* 91.

14 Heffernan, *Sacred Biography,* 35.

15 Ibid.
16 Cazelles, *The Lady as Saint*, 25.
17 Cadden, *Meanings of Sex Difference in the Middle Ages*, 260.
18 For accounts of the historical background to the Pelagius legend, see Linda McMillin's essay in this volume; Thiébaux, 'Hagiographer, Playwright, Epic Historian, Hrotswitha of Gandersheim,' in *The Writings of Medieval Women*, 172–84; Wiegand, Notes to *The Pelagius*, in 'The Non-Dramatic Works of Hrotsvitha,' 153–4; and Homeyer's prefatory notes in *Hrotsvithae Opera*, 123–6.
19 Wiegand, Notes to *The Pelagius*, 153–4.
20 Cazelles, *The Lady as Saint*, 51.
21 Ibid., 50–1.
22 Ibid. Even though Cazelles is discussing verse hagiography in thirteenth-century France, the distinction that she makes between the treatment of male and female physical beauty is still relevant to Hrotsvit's saints' lives in the tenth century. Although Pelagius and Agnes are both depicted as being beautiful, only Agnes suffers exposure and torture at the hand of pagans.
23 Petroff, *Body and Soul*, 88.
24 Northrop Frye, *Anatomy of Criticism*, 119.
25 Patterson, *Chaucer and the Subject of History*, 8.

Pulchrum Signum? Sexuality and the Politics of Religion in the Works of Hrotsvit of Gandersheim Composed between 963 and 973

ULRIKE WIETHAUS

> ... pulchrum cuius fidei fero signum
> In facie summa necnon in corpore toto,
> Quo me signavit strictimque sibi religavit,
>
> Passio Sanct Agnetis, 66–8

> ... the beautiful token of whose faith I bear upon my brow and in my whole body; that token with which He has signed me and has bound me closely to Himself,
>
> Wiegand, 240–1

Introduction

It is hard to argue that sexual politics are not at the centre of Hrotsvit's writings. In her plot lines, virginity is taken, endangered, or defended; marriage vows are broken in adultery; sexual non-conformity is explored without shying away from necrophilia, anal intercourse, and fetishism. She herself claimed that sexuality motivated her to compose the major part of her works, her dramas. In a somewhat surprising rhetorical move, Hrotsvit argues that she read and composed plays about lewd women and lecherous men to celebrate Christ's glory and strength:

> quia quanto blandicię amentium ad illiciendum promptiores · tanto et superni adiutoris gloria sublimior · et triumphantium victoria probatur gloriosior presertim cum feminea fragilitas vinceret · et virilis robur confusioni subiaceret · (*Liber Secundus, Praefatio*, 5)

because the more seductive the unlawful flatteries of those who have lost their sense,/ the greater the Heavenly Helper's munificence/ and the more glorious the victories of triumphant innocence are shown to be,/ especially/ when female weakness triumphs in conclusion./ And male strength succumbs in confusion. (Wilson, *Florilegium*, 41)

It is therefore instructive to tease out the meaning sexuality plays in her work, and to question its role in her construction of gender and authorial stance. To that end, I will begin with a brief sketch of the social, historical and cultural forces that shaped Hrotsvit's age.

With the exception of the first five of her legends, composed before 959, all of Hrotsvit's remarkable works were written in the shadow of Otto I's imperial rule.[1] During the decade of Hrotsvit's most active literary productivity, the Saxon ruler increased the centralization of royal power by subduing and unifying dukes ruling over other Germanic tribes. Otto I also reversed the ecclesiastical politics of his father Henry by expanding the rights and wealth of the church. In return for imperial favours, the ecclesiastical elite provided military and financial services. Enlisting the church's support in his struggle against the dukes culminated in Otto's coronation as Holy Roman Emperor.

As elsewhere in Europe, Germanic society before and during Ottonian rule was militaristic, characterized by fluctuating alliances among tribal leaders, who were locked in a constant need to expand their own territories and to defend them against intruders and competitors.[2] Scholars agree that in terms of gender arrangements, a war-based social order tends to devalue femininity and male effeminacy.[3] The result is a decline in the status of women and scorn for receptive (i.e., 'feminized') homosexuality.[4]

Saxony has a special status in the history of Christianity due to the ruthless violence of Charlemagne's expansionist politics, including forced conversions that began a mere century and a half before Hrotsvit's birth. Charlemagne's so-called Saxonian Wars, which lasted from 772 to 804, are marked by two especially harrowing events: the destruction of the Irminsul and the massacre of thousands of rebellious Saxons betrayed by their leaders at Verden in 782.[5] Charlemagne's *Saxonian Capitulary* made it a capital offence to refuse baptism, to cremate the dead, to participate in pagan rituals, and to eat meat during Lent.[6] Hrotsvit's stories of Christian martyrs tell a very local history indeed, albeit with inverted positions.

After Charlemagne's bloody conversion of the Saxons, Christianity was taught through the cooperation between royal families, especially their women, and the church. Following Charlemagne's lead, Ottonian rule became defined as divinely sanctioned theocracy. Thus Christianity was tightly associated with royal families and their privileges, with holiness seen as a quality of the aristocracy rather than the poor.[7] Christianity and secular law restricted sexuality only insofar as it impinged on other men's property rights. Therefore it did not attempt to control noblemen's access to concubines and prostitutes or to punish them for the rape of lower status females or female captives, as Hrotsvit's stories amply illustrate. From the ruling classes' point of view, sexuality was firmly tied to procreativity in its dual aspects of either legitimately continuing the royal lineage or wreaking havoc through dynastic politics that could lead to rival claims to power. From an aristocratic point of view, the unruliness of sexuality was more than lust; it was politically disruptive when it caused miscalculations in connection with political alliances and property distribution.[8]

Therefore, celibacy, the absence of sexual activity, offered the church a great advantage – which it often exploited astutely – in political and economic negotiations with the nobility. At least in the short run, an alliance between a noble family and the church, through a well-placed abbess, abbot, or bishop, offered a welcome alternative to the competitive dynastic politics usually employed by the nobility. Nonprocreative ecclesiastical male elites, who would not start rival dynasties, could be trustworthy allies indeed, much like eunuchs at the Byzantine courts. Furthermore, daughters, sisters, and even widowed mothers could be comfortably placed in well-endowed monasteries rather than married off to potentially aggressive male up-starts from other tribes.[9] The Christian promise of marriage to Christ, the noblest of bridegrooms, no doubt made celibacy more attractive to many young noblewomen destined by their families for a religious vocation.

As in the early spread of Christianity, noblewomen were instrumental in the support of the new faith in Saxony, possibly in part because they could thus counterbalance their inferior status in a warrior society.[10] Ottonian queens and empresses used monastic houses as trustworthy refuges and alternative seats to the male-dominated courts.[11] The female monastery of Gandersheim, for example, was founded in 852 by ancestors of the Ottonian royal house, and was governed during Hrotsvit's lifetime by Gerberga, a niece of Otto I. Gerberga's case is especially interesting, because her father Henry had staged several revolts against Otto. Otto finally forced his brother into submission in 941. Placing his niece Gerberga in a Saxon convent and making her an abbess in the mid-fifties no doubt helped Otto I prevent Henry from pursuing hostile dynastic family alliances by marrying his daughter to a rival aristocratic house. Not surprisingly, Hrotsvit's lengthy account of the fraternal conflict absolves Henry from all responsibility and depicts him as a victim of evil advisers.[12]

It is in this nexus of royal politics, religion, and sexuality that I wish to place Hrotsvit's writings and identity as a female author. Possibly of Saxon noble origins, Hrotsvit the author, like her monastery, was dependent upon the royal court and its support. Even as a canoness, with more freedom than, for instance, a Benedictine nun, she did not enjoy the relative independence in choice of topics another medieval courtly female author, the laywoman Christine de Pizan, could later exploit. Hrotsvit produced her work in a position of subalterity and unavoidable ideological identification with royal and ecclesiastical interests.[13] It should puzzle us why she repeatedly chose martyrs' legends as her source materials, given that so many other topics were available to her due to her excellent education. What *Pelagius, Gallicanus,* and other martyrs' legends share, however, is an intense preoccupation with negotiating political power. In her legends, Christian beliefs are usually challenged, defended, and/or propagated through the political scene at court, and imperial decisions are executed by military personnel at sites familiar to aristocrats. Hrotsvit's choice of stories thus mirrors her and her audience's social environment. Underneath the cover of Christian martyrdom, another world emerges: that of the Ottonian nobility.

More immediate reasons for choice of materials were events that connected a certain saint with the Ottonian house, such as the transfer of a saint's relics to Ottonian territory, the building of a new church in honour of a saint, or other recent events.[14] It is also conceivable that Hrotsvit's intense preoccupation with martyrs' legends allowed her audience to relive Charlemagne's violent conversion of Saxons with a potent narrative inversion. In a sense, Hrotsvit substitutes Christian martyrs from the more distant past for the pagans massacred in the formation of Christian empire in the recent Saxon past. Instead of a Christian emperor who brings destruction and demands submission, Hrotsvit depicts non-Christian rulers unable to impose their will on the Christians. The story of religiously inspired violence can still be told, but with an exchange of ideological labels. Religious violence permeates her writings, calling into question Hrotsvit's assertion in *Gesta Ottonis* that she cannot and should not write about war:

Sed nec hoc fragilis fas esse reor mulieris
Inter cenobii positȩ secreta quieti,
Ut bellum dictet, quod nec cognoscere debet.   (243–5)

But it is not decorous   for a fragile woman
Residing in the folds   of a cloister's quiet,
To tell the tale of warfare,   of which she does not know.

(Wilson, *Florilegium*, 107)

Clearly Hrotsvit's authorial identification with patriarchal imperial power
is complicated, perhaps involving inversions like the substitution of Christian martyrs for pagan. Readers familiar with her work know she is
capable of writing about warfare and other forms of violence and that
she has indeed penetrated the literary spaces of male privilege. However,
the claim that since so many of her main characters are female Hrotsvit
must have been writing unambiguously in support of women[15] must be
carefully modified, as I will discuss in the final section of this paper.

Idealized Sexuality: An Economic Contract

Hrotsvit's depictions of sexuality privilege interpersonal conflict and its
resolution over complex emotional motivations or psychological complications. In this, she follows her Christian source materials closely. The
last text in her legend cycle, the *Passio Sanctȩ Agnetis Virginis et Martiris*
illustrates particularly succinctly the various elements that constitute
conflicts over sexuality. The plot is based on a courtship gone awry.
Pubescent Agnes's rejection of a pagan youth's advances results in his
illness, death, and resurrection, and in Agnes's being dragged to a
brothel, where she is miraculously protected from an attempted gang
rape; later she is cast into a fire, which destroys the unbelieving bystand-
ers but cannot hurt her because the passion of carnal love had never
enkindled her body; after Agnes finally is decapitated, she is borne by
angels to heaven, where she is united with Christ, her celestial bridegroom. The suitor's father, a Roman prefect, attempts to force her into a
marriage alliance; her choice of martyrdom in preference to that political alliance is not so much to preserve her virginity as to hold out for a
more prestigious marriage alliance.

   Thus Agnes's ardently defended virginity is far from asexual; rather, it
plays a key role in ideal female sexuality. As Hrotsvit's legends and plays
make clear, virginity and chastity are forms of selective female absti-

nence: the virgin reserves the pleasures of sexual intercourse for one male only rather than sharing it with multiple partners. This distinction matters a great deal, when we ask who profits from such female restraint. Clearly, female self-imposed selective abstinence ensures first and foremost patrilinearity, a crucial element in property distribution based on Ottonian primogeniture.[16] In the legends and the plays, acts of sexual self-control are rewarded with a promise of access to royal privilege. Sexual self-control can give Agnes and other women access to the divine court of the heavenly bridegroom:

> Si velit angelicę pro virginitatis honore
> Ipsius astrigera sponsi caelestis in aula
> Addita caelicolis nitida fulgere corona   (4–6)

> ... if because of the charm of angelic purity she wills to shine in the starry court of the Celestial Bridegroom, in resplendent crown (Wiegand, 237)

Although much of the language in Hrotsvit's legend emphasizes Agnes's virginity and the pagan youth's desire for a sexual union, issues relating to the exchange of land and property and its relationships to socioeconomic status are equally or more important ultimately.

In the narrative comments on virginity with which the legend begins, Hrotsvit specifies that the nun's veil functions as 'signum laudabilis ... virginitatis' (9), 'the token of praiseworthy virginity' (Wiegand, 237), that will result in a marriage to the 'regis ... perennis' (3), 'the eternal king' (Wiegand, 237). When Agnes first speaks in the legend, she says to her unwanted noble, pagan suitor:

> 'Nec credas te posse meum pervertere purum
> Cor, quod amatoris praevenit nobilioris
> Dulcis amor, pulchrum cuius fidei fero signum
> In facie summa necnon in corpore toto'   (64–7)

> 'neither do thou trust that thou wilt be able to pervert my chaste heart, which the sweet love of a far nobler Spouse has anticipated, the beautiful token of Whose faith I bear upon my brow and in my whole body' (Wiegand, 239)

The Ottonian nobles, in the monastery and the court, would readily recognize the relationship of the sexual and the economic generally and, in particular, the way the nun's veil functions as a sign of class-consciousness in Hrotsvit's legend. This virginity is a means to a union with a spouse of the very highest rank. Furthermore, the status-integrity of the family that she will marry into, 'caelicolis' (6), is safeguarded by any nun's but particularly, in this legend, Agnes's submission to the superior bridegroom. A nun's clothing and Agnes's female body itself become the signs of exchange in place of the usual land and property exchanged through marriage, and the religiously coded intactness of the female body ensures the integrity and continuity of aristocratic men's property and hence their power over other men. In this set-up, the noble woman survives by playing by the rules. Stories such as Agnes's *Passio* signal the idealized strength of female loyalty. They reinforce socially appropriate ideals in women, and reassure doubting men of female faithfulness unto death and unshakable resistance to temptation.[17]

The material sign of this contract is Agnes's veil. Key scenes throughout the play centre on male efforts to pull away the veil – through physical action, through removal to a brothel, through fire – and the return of the veil in different manifestations: as female hair, as male blindness, as walls of fire. However, female abstinence is replaced by female sexual passion after Agnes has passed all tests and joined Christ in his royal chambers. At the end of the legend, both Agnes and her parents rejoice when her disembodied spirit tells of the joys of sex awaiting her at the celestial court: 'Et nunc in celis illi coniungor amoris/ Amplexu dulci' (451–2), 'And now in heaven I am joined in the sweet embrace of love to Him' (Wiegand, 261–2). Not so much sex as danger or pleasure but the relevance of sex to male property and blood lines surfaces as a central issue in Hrotsvit's ideals of sexual conduct for both men and women.[18]

Transgressive Sexuality: Breaking the Contract

Hrotsvit not only idealizes sexuality within the framework of economic contracts that contribute to political stability; she also explores a remarkable range of sexual transgressions in her writings.[19] As noted above, the issue of sexuality played an important role in her decision to write plays in the first place. In her preface to the dramas, Hrotsvit informs her readers,

Unde ego Clamor Validus Gandeshemensis · non recusavi illum imitari dictando · dum alii colunt legendo · quo eodem dictationis genere · quo

turpia lascivarum incesta feminarum recitabantur · laudabilis sacrarum
castimonia virginum iuxta mei facultatem ingenioli celebraretur ·

(*Liber Secundus, Praefatio,* 3)

Therefore I, the Strong Voice of Gandersheim, have not refused to imitate
him in writing/ whom others laud in reading,/ so that in that selfsame
form of composition in which the shameless acts of lascivious women were
phrased/ the laudable chastity of sacred virgins be praised, within the limits
of my little talent. (Wilson, *Florilegium,* 41)

Her source materials of course already determined to a certain degree
the sexual conflicts that found their way into her writings. Neither
Hrotsvit's texts nor early Christian stories about martyrs include examples of sexual transgressions such as masturbation, bestiality, or in-
cest, which appear frequently in later penitential literature.[20] The sexual
conflicts that are recounted in the genre of martyrs' deaths stylize and
make meaningful the nature of forced conversion to paganism as a form
of adultery or promiscuity.[21] For Hrotsvit, female sexual transgression
appears to be framed by the context of patriarchal family politics, in
which the female (or the male of female status) serves as means of
exchange between men. Female religious loyalty becomes synonymous
with sexual fidelity to one male, whether Christ or earthly spouse.

When analysed from the perspective of male rights over women as
property, all sexual transgressions and temptations recounted in Hrotsvit's
texts thus express violations of high status male privilege. Female adultery in *Gongolf* and *Calimachus* is provoked or demanded by a low status
servant or acquaintance of the husband – the unnamed cleric in *Gongolf,*
and the servant Fortunatus and the young (that is, lower status)
Calimachus in the play. It follows the logic of patriarchal ownership over
females that in both cases, the adulterer or adulterers-to-be are punished
more severely than the wives. If female adultery is understood as theft of
male property, the illicit male lovers were indeed guiltier, and the crime
committed defined primarily as having concerned the two males. The
transgression was not the sex act per se, in which both male and female
participated or might have participated, but the violation of status and
property rights of a high status male by a low status male.

The theme of class-inappropriate liaisons, albeit this time in the form
of marriage, is emphasized in *Basilius*; the pursuer is of lower social
status than the female pursued. In *Basilius,* an unnamed servant marries
a rich heiress with the help of a magician. Class differences are accentu-
ated from the beginning of the legend, when Hrotsvit underlines the

daughter's impressive inheritance: (Nec alius substantiole mansit sibi magne/ Heres) (24–5), 'No other child was there to be his riches' heir' (Wilson, *Florilegium*, 21). Moreover, the servant is aware of his social inferiority: 'indignum se coniugio meminit' (39), 'he knew himself unworthy for such an exalted union' (Wilson, *Florilegium*, 22), and Proterius, the father, admonishes his daughter twice not to pollute her family's nobility by marrying below her social group: 'ne genus omne tuum male confundas generosum' (122), 'else you will bring us shame and all your ancestors defame' (Wilson, *Florilegium*, 24), and 'tocius et nostri generis confusio turpis' (135), 'you brought foul disgrace to our ancestral race' (Wilson, *Florilegium*, 24). Not surprisingly, the social conflict is resolved in the servant's conversion to Christianity.

Prostitution, a third type of sexual transgression, is characterized not as an excess of female lust, but as the inversion of marital fidelity – indiscriminate female promiscuity. Whereas the female body becomes the sign of normative female sexuality, the act of sexual purification, religiously encoded as female conversion to Christianity, is encoded geographically, that is, site-specific. In contrast to male piety, it very concretely means enclosure, the drastic and life-threatening limitation of accessible space.[22] The prostitutes Thais and Mary allow random rather than selective access to their bodies. The sign of the veil is replaced by a geography of sexual desire. The prostitutes' sexual generosity is symbolized spatially by their ubiquitous presence in public spaces and travels across the land. Note the stark spatial contrasts in both dramatic works. The opening scenes of *Lapsus et Conversio Mariae* present the enclosure of Mary with the intention of safeguarding access to her body for the heavenly bridegroom only.[23] In contrast, Mary's life as a prostitute is highlighted as a life without specific boundaries,[24] and she is redeemed only when she willingly encloses herself in a small room more thoroughly enclosed than her original cell. Abraham instructs her, 'Ingredere in cellulam interiorem · ne vetustus serpens decipiendi · ultra inveniat occasionem'(VIII.2), 'Go into the small interior room so that the ancient serpent will not find another opportunity to deceive you' (Wilson, *Florilegium*, 78).

Pafnutius describes Thais to his disciple (and thus to the audience) as a foreigner without a claim to relatives, to land, or to roots: 'Quaedam inpudens femina moratur in hac patria' (I.23), 'A certain shameless woman dwells in this land' (Wilson, *Plays*, 102).[25] Lack of geographical boundaries equals lack of sexual boundaries. Sexual love loses its symbolic force and becomes its own exchange value. In Thais' words, 'Quicumque me amore colit · aequam vicem amore a me recipit' (III.1),

'Whoever seeks me in love/ finds me returning his love' (Wilson, *Plays*, 106). If everything is up for grabs, literally, male competitiveness loses all constraint. The prostitutes become a danger to social order, since men kill themselves for them, that is, for the land. In Pafnutius's words, the lovers engage in combat as follows: 'Deinde inito certamine nunc ora naresque pugnis frangendo · nunc armis vicissim eiciendo · decurrentis illuviȩ sanguinis madefaciunt limina lupanaris' (I.26), 'Then follows a fist fight to slam a face here, break a nose there, then weapons are drawn, and pushing out the door, they [the suitors] soak the brothel's doorstep with a filthy stream of blood' (translation mine).

War also can be defined as intentional spatial transgression, yet unlike a prostitute's excursions, it is marked by the excessive use of violence. Hrotsvit's fourth type of sexual non-conformity is typical of sexual aggression during wars, that is, the rape, mutilation and sexual torture of the enemy's women and men by military personnel. Sexual crimes symbolically represent the taking of control over another group's territory; again, women and feminized men are used as pawns in the struggle for power between groups of men. In *Sapientia*, soldiers cut off a virgin's breasts to sexually shame her. In *Dulcitius*, a city governor exercises his right over female captives by raping their effigies in a highly guarded prison. And in *Agnes* a captive woman is threatened by gang rape sanctioned by a city prefect's orders. In *Pelagius*, Hrotsvit presents a male version of the sexual abuse, when a male virgin captive is held hostage in an enemy's court during war. Both caliph and courtiers attempt to feminize Pelagius by first dressing him up and then submitting him to the king's caresses.[26] Unlike female virgins, the youth resists not only verbally, but also physically by bloodying the king's nose. It is only in this story that a sexual practice is explicitly associated with ethnic others, although penitentials tell us clearly that homosexual activity was widespread among Christians.[27] Christian steadfastness evokes divine miracles that do not prevent the killing of the martyrs but do safeguard their sexual purity. The issue is not the well-being and survival of the individual, but sexual control or ownership of inferior members of one's group (male youths, female virgins, and brides).

Hrotsvit and the Historicity of the Concepts of 'Woman' and 'Female Solidarity'

I will now return to a question posed at the beginning of my essay. Does Hrotsvit champion the cause of all women? Can she be understood as a 'foremother to think back through'? Clearly, Hrotsvit excludes large groups of women through several strategies based on both secular and religious ideologies that postulate the inferiority of woman and other outsiders. As I will demonstrate below, Hrotsvit affords no room for the voices of women of the peasant class, or for the voices of Jewish or Muslim women. Valorizing the men of her own class, she depicts the sons, brothers, spouses, and fathers of outsiders as untrustworthy if not outright despicable in *Pelagius* and *Theophilus*. She turns a silent ear to the plight of women who suffer cruelly from the acts of her fellow Saxons in *Gesta Ottonis*. She fully endorses the supremacy of religious ideology and national identity over a mother's care for her children in *Sapientia*. Indeed, her depiction of Sapientia exceeds in cruelty that of comparable saints' stories about motherhood, in which the mothers are given a modicum of maternal tenderness.[28]

It is obviously too simplistic to claim that because most of her protagonists are feminine, she writes in support of all women. What her texts demonstrate precisely through the exclusion of so many groups of women is only that 'femininity' as a positively coded abstraction did not exist for her. What Hrotsvit explores and even celebrates in her writings is only the patriarchal Christian idea of womanhood, defined as female strength in the service of male sexual ownership, female eloquence in the service of Christian ideology, female loyalty unto death to male authority figures who insist on their power over them. What Hrotsvit suggests to her audience, in short, is a model of survival of the weak, based on obedience and complete identification with the stronger. Hers is a female model in that the body and therefore procreative sexuality rather than the land become the means of exchange, the tithe to be paid, the token of submission.[29]

It is nonetheless easy to be seduced by Hrotsvit's Christian rhetoric of heroic virginity into thinking that, as numerous contemporary critics have done, the author spoke 'for' women *qua* women, extolling their virtues and worthiness. Hrotsvit drew harsh distinctions between women by turning all women outside of her small group of elite female peers into negligible others. Despised outsiders and marginalized groups are represented through their male constituents, but no attention is paid to females or to families, a typical simplification of one's enemy in militaristic rhetoric.[30] Concomitantly, Hrotsvit projects socially devalued practices of her own group onto the Other.

This triple strategy of exclusion, social fragmentation through the erasure of female presence, and projection of nonnormative behaviours is exemplified in Hrotsvit's depiction of Jews, Muslims, and peasants. Although the penitentials inform us that Christians engaged in magical practices, it is a 'vile' Jewish magician who assists Theophilus in regaining his social status.[31] Hrotsvit also emphasizes the evilness of Jews in her account of Christ's crucifixion, where images of the Jews echo in her depiction of soldiers' tortures of holy virgins.[32] Although we possess ample evidence of homosexual practices among Germanic tribes, in *Pelagius* it is a Muslim ruler who engages in sodomy.[33] Stories of betrayal and cunning are plenty among the nobility, but in the story of the well in *Gongolf*, it is peasants who are stereotypically treacherous. Although Hrotsvit expands on the suffering of individual Christian virgins held captive by hostile rulers, she mentions with approval that Gerberga's father Henry and his army abducted the wives and children (both male and female) of their Hungarian enemies: 'Uxores procerum soboles rapuit quoque dulces:/ Et sic prostratis rediit gaudens inimicis' (*Gesta Ottonis*, 393–5), 'He also abducted the sweet wives and offspring of the nobles and thus returned happily from the enemy's subjugation' (my translation). The verb chosen for his actions is 'rapere,' which may also include rape.[34] Henry's actions mirror the plot lines of Hrotsvit's martyrs' legends, but multiply the number of suffering women and their children.

Even her treatment of maternal protection for male and female children differs drastically. In both the *Historia Nativitatis* (the legend of Mary's virginal conception and birth, often called *Maria*) as well as in *Theophilus*, where the Virgin Mary functions as intercessor before her son, maternal care and love for a son are celebrated. This certainly reflects women's efforts in a patrilineal society to gain influence through close ties with their sons. Several Ottonian queens successfully employed this strategy, most notably perhaps Adelheid.[35] In contrast, however, the *Passio Fidei, Spei et Karitatis* depicts a mother who sacrifices her daughters in the name of patriarchal authority, in part surely also a sign of her own weakness.[36] It is only in Hrotsvit's evocation of imperial protection for the monastery of Gandersheim that positive maternal bonds between mother and daughters are assumed.[37]

Counterpoint: The Female Author as Abject and Other

Hrotsvit's authorial identification with patriarchal imperial power is complicated, however, by her own transgressiveness as female writer and her use of controversial sources, be they apocryphal accounts, pagan authors, or oral communications. Her self-definitions as author in the prefaces and prologues are built around inversions of the hierarchical social systems described above. Whereas the protection of proper blood-lines is the foremost concern in safeguarding virginity in her plays and legends, Hrotsvit's literary lineage is impure, polluted by bastard materials of inferior and doubtful paternity.[38] Whereas her heroes and hero-ines remain in their socially elevated place unto death, Hrotsvit's authorial stance is similar to that of a thief, 'quasi furtim' (*Liber Primus, Praefatio,* 6), writing furtively so as to avoid being noticed. She fears that like the prostitutes in her works, she is weak, 'feminea fragilitas' (*Praefatio Liber Secundus,* 5), abject or worthless, 'pro mei abiectione' (*Liber Secundus, Praefatio,* 9), and that she has strayed from her proper place and correct-ness: 'Et sic tandem ad normam rectitudinis reformatum mihi remittite · quo vestri magisterio pręmonstrante · in quibus maxime peccassem possim agnoscere' (*Liber Secundus, Epistola,* 12), 'And then, righted ac-cording to the rules of correct composition,/ send it back to me, so that, enlightened by your instruction/ I may be able to recognize where I have failed the most' (Wilson, *Florilegium,* 44). Significantly, 'peccassem' con-veys a sense of sinning as well as the less morally charged failing, or making a mistake. She portrays herself as servant to her female master Gerberga: 'famula herae' (*Liber Tertius, Praefatio,* 1), handmaid to the lady of the household. Most telling, however, is Hrotsvit's evaluation of her speech as rustic: 'rusticitas' (*Liber Primus, Praefatio,* 6); 'pro vitiosi sermonis rusticitate' (*Liber Secundus, Praefatio,* 9), 'the rusticity of my inelegant style' (Wilson, *Florilegium,* 42). Fighting against unjust label-ling, Hrotsvit takes the position of the only Jewish woman mentioned at any length in her works, Salome, who is described as a temptress: 'temptatrix' (*Maria,* 608). In order to defend herself, Salome acts ac-cording to what Hrotsvit characterizes as the Jewish custom by insisting on one's merit and achievements: 'Moreque Iudaico proprium meritum recitando' (*Maria,* 612), by reciting personal merit in the Jewish fashion (my translation).[39] This 'Jewish' stance is present in Hrotsvit's dedicatory letter preceding the dramas, where she emphasizes her own sharp mind, 'perspicax' (*Liber Secundus, Epistola,* 8), while acknowledging that her intelligence is 'donum dei,' a gift of God (*Liber Secundus, Epistola,* 9). Her own literal transgression into literary spaces of male privilege, that is, choosing to write herself, is coded as a supreme act of literary adultery, promiscuity, and prostitution by a peasant, a Jew, a servant.

Thus in her dual roles as female author and noblewoman, Hrotsvit simultaneously occupies subject and object positions. Given the generally high educational level of noblewomen during the Ottonian rule, however, Hrotsvit's self-depreciation is more posture and play with conventions than an actual experience of the religiously sanctioned social marginalization that real Jews, prostitutes, and peasants had to endure. Hrotsvit had the luxury of playing these roles rather than the misfortune of living them.

Two women in her writings exemplify Hrotsvit's dual persona as female noble/writer and link it to issues of sexuality, gender, and procreativity. Her positive foil is Sapientia, whose speech is seen as a threat to the state, since she tellingly lures wives away from their husbands and thus destroys patrilineal family arrangements. Through her activities, Sapientia risks and loses the lives of her female children and in the end dies on their graves. Underneath a patriarchal Christian plot of the lack of maternal care for daughters, this play contains glimpses of women's lives outside of patriarchal rule through acts of solidarity and support that lack any counterpart in male group behaviour, which is structured within the group as an inflexible hierarchy of power and influence.[40] Sapientia and her daughters form strong bonds of affection; women flock around Sapientia, their religious leader; and finally, Sapientia and a group of women mourn for the slaughtered daughters and express care for each other.

Hrotsvit's negative counterfoil risks not only transgressive speech like Sapientia, but also sexual nonconformity by bonding with a lower class lover. Like Sapientia, Gongolf's unnamed wife is of noble descent and well educated. Her character manifests utopian visions much like Sapientia's female support networks. Gongolf's unnamed wife, however, is far more radical than Sapientia. Instead of a pagan emperor, Gongolf's wife challenges male divine authority and potency and courageously posits her own female embodiment as equal to patriarchal might.[41] This must not go unpunished: her body becomes a sign of her transgression much as Agnes's veil signifies conformity. Having bravely engaged in what Pelagius refused – anal intercourse – her anus and mouth become interchangeable: whenever she opens her mouth, she makes farting noises. Female words of transgression are like breaking wind. Hrotsvit's lesson: to be able to speak as a woman, one must abide by patriarchal law. To describe patriarchal law, however, one must name its transgressions, the eternal return of the repressed, the abject, and the marginalized. Feminized transgression as perverted and grotesque thus invokes the core of patriarchal rule as well, indeed, its very limitation: the deadly monotony of homogeneity.

NOTES

1 This is the decade between the momentous coronation of Otto I as emperor in Rome and his death in 973, which also marks the beginning of the rule of his eighteen-year-old son Otto II. See Nagel, *Hrotsvit von Gandersheim. Sämtliche Dichtungen*, especially 6–7. On the Ottonian empire, see Leyser's classic study, *Rule and Conflict in an Early Medieval Society*. For a list of editions and translations of Hrotsvit's oeuvre, see Kadel, *Matrology*, 81–4.

2 For a survey of these issues in medieval Europe, with special emphasis on France, see Bouchard, *Strong of Body, Brave and Noble*. See also Airlie, 'Review Article: After Empire.'

3 See Lerner, *The Creation of Patriarchy*.

4 See Greenberg, *The Construction of Homosexuality*, chapter 6, esp. 249 ff.; and Richard Trexler's introduction to *Sex and Conquest*.

5 The cutting down of the Irminsul, a stone or wooden altar representing sacred trees (possibly the Yggdrasil), and the sacred nature of groves are mirrored in several settings in Hrotsvit's works, such as in Gongolf's miracle of the well enclosed by heavy brushwork, and the founding of the Gandersheim monastery.

6 Boretius, *Capitularia Regnum Francorum*. For Charlemagne's expansionist politics, see Richard Fletcher's lively discussion 'Campaigning Sceptres.' On the negative aspect of Carolingian politics on religious women, see McNamara, *Sisters in Arms*, 152 ff. For theological repercussions of Charlemagne's Christianity, see Herrin, *The Formation of Christendom*, chapters 10 and 11. For Germanic religious practices, see Baetke, *Das Heilige im Germanischen*.

7 On the emerging cult of saints, see Brown, *The Cult of the Saints*. On the image of Christ in the tenth century, see Pelikan, 'Christ Crucified.' For the Ottonians, see Warner, 'Henry II at Magdeburg.'

8 The church adjusted as best as it could. See Bishop, 'Bishops as Marital Advisors in the Ninth Century.'

9 For a similar reading of Ottonian politics, see McNamara, *Sisters in Arms*, 184 ff.

10 See, for example, Fox, *Pagans and Christians*, 309 ff. On Ottonian aristocratic women, see Leyser, *Rule and Conflict in an Early Medieval Society*. On Theophano and women of the Ottonian royalty, see Davids, *The Empress Theophano*.

11 For primary sources see Kuhn, *Frauen in Mittelalter*.

12 Hrotsvit, *Gesta Ottonis*, 25–154. Helena Homeyer comments, 'Der Historiker wird es bedauern, dass die Dichterin sich Zwang auferlegen musste; es

kann aber kein Zweifel darüber bestehen, dass sie über die jahrelangen Zwistigkeiten im Herrscherhaus und über die Urheber der Streitigkeiten unterrichtet war ... Sie hat auch keineswegs, wie gelegentlich behauptet worden ist, den Teufel zum Alleinschuldigen gemacht' ('Einleitung Gesta Ottonis' in *Hrotsvithae Opera*, 393–4). See also Jay Lees's essay in this volume.

13 On the intricate relationships between royal monasteries and the Ottonians, see Bernhardt, *Itinerant Kingship and Royal Monasteries*. On Gandersheim, see especially 149–62.

14 See Homeyer's introductions to individual works for excellent references to immediate historical circumstances that might have motivated Hrotsvit. It is clear that Hrotsvit did not choose her subject matter randomly, but it is certainly difficult to account for all the factors that might have influenced her choice of subject material.

15 So, for example, Pätzold in 'Hrotsvit of Gandersheim: Lebensnormen und Wertvorstellungen,' 27, noting as the only exception the nameless wife of St Gongolf. See also McNamara, *Sisters in Arms*, 200–1, especially, 'In the plays and poems she made the case for religious women as worthy objects of respect and, by extension, investment' (200).

16 This practice differs from Carolingian practice, the equal distribution of inherited wealth, which led to the fragmentation of the Carolingian rule. Perhaps the main reason for Henry's challenge of Otto's primacy lies in the newness of the practice of primogeniture.

17 After summarizing Ottonian views on women expressed in the chronicles of the late tenth and early eleventh centuries, Bange writes, 'The final judgement of these authors concerning the women they described might be rendered in one single sentence: a woman has to know her place, and what this place is is clear from the beginning' ('Women of the Nobility in the German Chronicles,' 165).

18 This view is mirrored in Jane Bishop's reading of aristocratic concerns in 'Bishops as Marital Advisors in the Ninth Century.' She also observes the frankness with which sexual matters were discussed in public.

19 Homeyer notes, 'Mit Ausnahme der Sapientia enthalten alle Dramen Szenen, in denen das Begehren nach Liebeserfüllung mit dem ernsten Verlangen nach einem vollkommenen Tugendleben in Konflikt gerät' (*Hrotsvithae Opera*, 22).

20 See Payer, *Sex and the Penitentials*.

21 The paradigm for such sexual coding of religious allegiance is to be found in Hos. 1:2; 2:2–13. He codes Israel's worship of foreign divinities as prostitution or bridal infidelity.

22 On medieval prostitution, see Karras, *Common Women*; and Kettle, 'Ruined Maids.'

23 Mary comes closer to medieval reality in that she lives in a brothel and is dependent upon a brothel keeper. The dramatically more independent Thais lives rather atypically, but follows closely the model of the independent Thais depicted in Terence's play *The Eunuch*. For accounts of other female saints who formerly were prostitutes, see the 'Life of St. Mary of Egypt' and the 'Life of St. Thomaïs of Lesbos,' in which two unknown prostitutes ask St Thomaïs for healing, in Talbot, *Holy Women of Byzantium*. In the 'Life of St. Mary of Egypt,' Mary's issue is excessive lust, which causes her to be excluded from sacred space. While a sinner, Mary of Egypt miraculously cannot pass the threshold of a church; directed by the Virgin Mary, her healing happens not by enclosure but by free roaming in the desert. Female illnesses (hemorrhaging and breast cancer) rather than space mark the spiritual and social outlaw condition of the two unknown prostitutes in the 'Life of St. Thomaïs.' See also Ward, *Harlots of the Desert*, for a theological discussion of St Mary of Egypt, Thais, and Mary, the niece of Abraham.

24 Abraham tells Effrem his friend is searching for Mary 'civitates villasque peragrans' (III.16), 'travelling through villages and towns' (Wilson, *Florilegium*, 72).

25 See Phyllis R. Brown's essay on Sapientia as a foreign woman in this volume.

26 See Linda A. McMillin's and Ron Stottlemyer's essays in this volume and Mark D. Jordan's discussion of *Pelagius* in his study, *The Invention of Sodomy in Christian Theology*, 10–29.

27 See Payer, *Sex and the Penitentials*.

28 See Talbot, *Holy Women of Byzantium*.

29 This raises the question of the impact of Christianity on the status of Germanic women. As noted above, aristocratic women did benefit from its new regulations, but had to pay a price for their new alliance. On Germanic women, see Bruder, *Die germanische Frau im Lichte der Runenschriften und der antiken Historiographie*.

30 For the relationship between military rhetoric and religion, especially in the Middle Ages, see Peter Partner, *God of Battles*.

31 The magician is 'Quendam perversum petiit festinus Hebreum,/ qui magica plures decepit fraude fideles' (83–4), 'a certain wicked Jew who had deceived many of the faithful by his magic fraud' (Wiegand, 163), and 'magus maledictus' (97), an 'accursed magician' (Wiegand, 163). That Judaism could prove dangerously seductive to Christians was made perfectly clear in the scandal of an imperial chaplain's conversion to Judaism

during the reign of Charlemagne's son, Louis the Pious (814–40). For the story of Bodo's conversion, see Marcus, *The Jew in the Medieval World*, chapter 72.

32 For example:

> Iudęi spurcis hanc sed petiere salivis
> Maxillisque meis alapas tribuere malignas
> Atque manus clavis ligno fixere cruentis,
> De limo pulchrum quis plasmavi protoplastum,
> Cum quibus et caelos extendi denique celsos
> (Nam si respicio terram, pavitat tremefacta,
> Nec mis terroris potis est vim ferre potentis);
> Et precedentes acriter caput atque moventes
> Me male Iudaei deridebant scelerosi. *(Ascensio, 42–50)*

But the Jews attacked this face with filthy spittle; they distributed malign blows on my jaws, and transfixed my hands on the wood with a bloody nail; I, who made the first man beautiful from the clay, with the same hands I also stretched out the high heavens. (Indeed when I look upon the earth, shaken, it trembles, nor is it able to bear the power of my potent terror.) And the Jews, preceding violently and shaking their head[s], criminally derided me evilly. (my translation)

33 For another example of associating sodomy with military aggressiveness in medieval literature, see Lankewisch, 'Assault from Behind.'

34 On the rhetoric of rape, see Woods, 'Rape and the Pedagogical Rhetoric of Sexual Violence.'

35 On Adelheid, see Beyreuther, 'Kaiserin Adelheid.' This pattern was also typical of other royal houses during the Middle Ages.

36 Most of Hrotsvit's stories lack a description of the complete set of family members and depict fragmented familial subsets and broken lineages: mothers and daughters without fathers, children without parents, sons and fathers without mothers, and so on. The major exceptions are her historical works, which present elaborate aristocratic genealogies.

37 This appeal to the empress as 'mother' is of course highly tendentious. It would be fascinating to explore more deeply the problematics of mother-daughter relationships in Hrotsvit's works. For example, Anne's love for her daughter, the Virgin Mary, is conditional in so far as Mary will be mother of Christ. The one unambiguously positive maternal presence throughout Hrotsvit's works is Mother Earth. But even she was seen as dependent upon male power. See Power, 'Bodo, A Frankish Peasant in the Time of Charlemagne.' For mother-daughter relationships in German literature of the later Middle Ages, see Rasmussen, *Mothers and Daughters in*

Medieval German Literature. For a sophisticated reading of the figure of
Sapientia, see Jeffrey, 'Virginal Allegories of Self-Knowledge in Hrotsvit's
Sapientia.'

38 She is aware of the criticism of the authenticity of apocryphal material, as
she notes in her preface to the legends. She warns of unreliable informants
in the introduction to her historical accounts of Otto I's rule, and spends
much time describing the authentication process of Pelagius's sanctity
through the elaborate ceremonial manipulation of his corpse (366–405),
which in turn serves to legitimize her own authorial reliability.

39 Homeyer notes that Hrotsvit highlighted the perceived Jewishness of
Salome's defence, and wonders if Salome might represent Synagoga
(*Hrotsvithae Opera*, 70, note to lines 612–14).

40 For an analysis of male hierarchical group behaviour, see Schwarz, *Die
Heilige Ordnung der Männer.*

41 She resembles another subversive Other, Anne's pouting female servant in
Maria.

SECTION 3

Creating Affinities

Hrotsvit's Dramas: Is There a Roman in These Texts?

ROBERT TALBOT

'Clearly there is little in these six plays which, from our point of view, can justly be called Terentian,' writes Cornelia Coulter about Hrotsvit's drama in a 1929 article.[1] Thus she restates with slight qualifications an earlier assessment that the only similarity between Terence and Hrotsvit is that they both wrote drama.[2] Today it is still widely accepted that Hrotsvit refers primarily to matters of form and style when she claims to write in a Terentian mode.[3] On the contrary, I will argue that Hrotsvit's plays also make use of the subject matter of Terence's work in a systematic and persistent way. A close affinity between Hrotsvit and Terence is suggested by each author's habit of returning, almost obsessively, to the same plot elements in play after play. Indeed, I contend that there is a stark correspondence between the repeated elements in each corpus.

Once gathered from various sources, the accumulation of contentual correspondences between the two dramatists seems something more than slight. The prevalence of love conflict in each corpus has been noted more than once.[4] The motifs of scheming and disguise have also not gone without notice.[5] Peter Dronke has offered the following similarities:

> For Terence, like Hrotsvitha, had presented with imaginative sympathy a number of young women who were innocent victims. The girls in the *Andria, Eunuchus,* or *Adelphoi* do not speak, yet in each case they are the focal point of the play's plot. Always the victimized girl triumphs at the close: she wins her freedom, wins her love-match. In the *Andria* and *Eunuchus* the girls, like Hrotsvitha's heroines, are even hedged by 'miracles' – won-

drous revelations that lead to the discovery of their true identity and their distinguished birth ... As in Hrotsvitha's scenes of confrontation and martyrdom, there are continual threats of whipping and torture, which hardly ever have any effect: in Terence as in Hrotsvitha, there is a hair's breadth between the comic and the horrible. Terence's emotional gamut – the spheres of tenderness, of trickery, and of blustering force nimbly defeated – is (if we leave the specifically Christian motifs out of account) humanly close to Hrotsvitha's.[6]

Sometimes these similarities are discounted by detractors because of the anti-Terentian way they appear in Hrotsvit. As for the theme of love, for instance, Coulter has noted that 'Hrotsvitha has deliberately set herself to supplant Terence, by showing the inferiority of earthly to heavenly love.'[7] But this is precisely the point. The key to the recognition of Terentian elements within Hrotsvit is to notice the way she transposes them.

Hrotsvit expresses both the allure and the inadequacy of her literary antecedent in the preface to her dramas where she notes,

Plures inveniuntur catholici cuius nos penitus expurgare nequimus facti · qui pro cultioris facundia sermonis · gentilium vanitatem librorum utilitati praeferunt sacrarum scripturarum · Sunt etiam alii sacris inherentes paginis · qui licet alia gentilium spernant · Terentii tamen fingmenta frequentius lectitant · et dum dulcedine sermonis delectantur · nefandarum notitia rerum maculantur · (*Liber Secundus, Praefatio,* 1)

Many Catholics one may find,/ and we are also guilty of charges of this kind,/ who for the beauty of their eloquent style,/ prefer the uselessness of pagan guile/ to the usefulness of Sacred Scripture. There are also others, who, devoted to sacred reading and scorning the works of other pagans, yet frequently read Terence's fiction,/ and as they delight in the sweetness of his style and diction, they are stained by learning of wicked things in his depiction. (Wilson, *Florilegium,* 41)

Hrotsvit thus faces the dilemma also experienced by later Christian writers such as Dante and Spenser, who desired to reconcile their admiration of classical culture with their Christian belief. Their solution was to find in classical literature and myth the expression of Christian truth, veiled to the pagan mind but discernible through Christian exegesis. I contend that Hrotsvit anticipates these writers with a similar solution when she exploits in her plays the secular patterns of Terentian drama for their Christian meanings. Her plays become, in effect, an allegorical rereading of Terence.

That Hrotsvit would adapt Terence's form of style for Christian purposes while leaving the content of his plays untouched at first seems unlikely given her view of learning elucidated by Katharina Wilson:

> Learning, and for that matter intellectual simplicity, then, are not 'goods' by themselves but terms empty of connotation (i.e., morally neutral); they are tools capable of both use and abuse. If used rightly – i.e., for the glorification of God and his saints or for the enhancement of man's moral character – they become values; if used perversely – i.e., in a manner opposed to God's will or for selfish gain and empty arrogance – they are anti-values.[8]

In this view, if the reading of Terence brings familiarity with an eloquent style that allows one to write elegant Christian literature, then it follows that the reading of Terence is acceptable because it is done for a moral purpose. But if in the process of reading Terence for his style one is 'stained by learning of wicked things' that moral purpose is undermined. From a Christian perspective, one cannot both value reading Terence for his style and remain unstained by 'wicked things in his depiction,' so long as Terence's content is left unredeemed. As Hrotvsit tells us at the end of her preface, she reworked Terence, 'in hoc dramatica vinctam serie colo · perniciosas gentilium delicias abstinendo devito' (*Praefatio Liber Secundus*, 9), 'always trying to avoid the perilous fetter/ and the dangerous allurement of pagan subject matter' (Wilson, *Florilegium*, 42). Does this statement mean that she sought to avoid the incorporation of inappropriate subject matter in her plays or to avoid the corruption of her mind by involvement with Terence? In either case, she would be free from the danger by reading Terence as a Christian exegete. If, as I argue, Hrotsvit rereads Terence allegorically through her plays, then she and her readers need not read Terence in the same way again; their minds will be diverted from the sinful content toward a higher Christian meaning.

Hrotsvit is not alone, of course, in the late antique and early medieval use of pagan texts for moral and Christian purposes. Writing from the late antique period by Christians such as Ambrose and Augustine is replete with quotations from pagan writers, usually with the purpose of interpreting them in a Christian sense.[9] Macrobius unveiled philosophical and didactic meaning in Homer, Plato, Cicero, and Virgil by allegorizing them, and henceforth allegory became a standard method of exegesis.[10] In the Middle Ages, the stories of Ovid particularly were interpreted allegorically for their moral meanings. What is more, classical figures provided *exempla* of human virtue (Diana's chastity, etc.) for authors such as Baudri of Bourgueil, writing about a century later than Hrotsvit.[11] In the extensive library of Gandersheim, or in the libraries of nearby cloisters, or in contact with the many scholars brought to Gandersheim by Archbishop Bruno of Cologne,[12] Hrotsvit could hardly escape exposure to this tradition of purification of pagan texts.

One early example of Christian rereading of pagan writing exemplifies what I see as Hrotsvit's Christian allegorization of Terence. In the first section of Book 7 in her mid-eighth-century *Liber Manualis*, written for her sixteen-year-old son, Dhuoda quotes a phrase from Ovid's *Amores* expressing a lover's dilemma over the impossibility of living with or without a beloved who both draws him by her beauty and repels him by her behaviour: 'aliquis dicit: "Cum quibus et sine quibus vivere non possumus." Et licet aliter hoc in loco volvatur sensus, pro certis differentium causis, ego volo ut ita teneas sicut fateor' ('someone says: "With them and without them we cannot live." While the meaning of this passage may vary from my own – and there are certain reasons for the difference – I want you to take it in the sense that I declare it).'[13] Although she is aware of the erotic import of the words, the passage nevertheless expresses for Dhuoda her lesson about being reborn in Christ and about the coexistence of the spiritual and the physical in one human being: 'Nunc vero deinceps militiam animae tuae qualiter, auxiliante Deo, ad summum usque perducas, velut genitrix secunda mente et corpore ut in Christo cotidie renascaris ammonere non cesso' ('From now on I will not cease to teach you how with God's help you may guide your soul's service to perfection, so that you may be reborn each day in Christ. In this I am twice a mother to you, both in soul and in body').[14] Dhuoda's allegorization of Ovid here cogently suggests the habit of mind of an educated woman in Frankish society, one surely shared by Hrotsvit.

Also in common with contemporary authors, Hrotsvit shared a lively interest in typology expressed in all of the genres in which she wrote. She thus applies to extrabiblical texts a patristic method of biblical exegesis, in which Old Testament characters and events are interpreted as prefiguring New Testament ones. Katharina Wilson has demonstrated, for instance, that her legends and dramas are interconnected by a series of figural relationships in which the central characters of her legends have thematic and structural connections to characters in her dramas.[15] Similar figural representations are found in individual dramas: Sandro Sticca has shown that Dulcitius is a figure of Satan,[16] and demonstrates in his articles on *Abraham* and *Pafnutius* that the title character of each play is a type of Christ.[17] Likewise, Dennis Kratz has argued that a consistent theme of Hrotsvit's first epic, the *Gesta Ottonis*, is the representation of Otto I as a new biblical David.[18] Indeed I believe all of the major characters and situations of Hrotsvit's dramas are prefigured in her first drama, *Gallicanus*. With the same figural patterning that interrelates the material of her various works, Hrotsvit weaves together the characters and events of her corpus with that of Terence.

In Hrotsvit's dramas, a major figural pattern stems from the central recurring element of Terence's plays – the dispute between an overbearing father and a wayward son over the future course of the son's life. We should not imagine, however, because her plays with one exception contain no fathers and sons, that this pattern is not present in Hrotsvitian drama. In the place of fathers in her plays are father-like figures ranging from the avuncular Pafnutius to the oppressive emperor Diocletian to would-be husbands such as Gallicanus. In their diversity, these father figures thus express the attitudinal range of each Terentian father. Furthermore, Hrotsvit's young virgins are invariably figures of Terence's sons.[19] All are at odds with a father figure in their respective plays regarding their choice of a spouse, lover, or, in the case of *Abraham* and *Pafnutius*, multiple lovers. Just as Terence's sons wind up with the most appropriate wife, personally and socially, after much conflict, so do Hrotsvit's heroines ultimately embrace their truest lover, the heavenly bridegroom, after being tempted or threatened by substitutes.[20] These heroines vary widely, as do Hrotsvit's father figures, since some are prostitutes and some are virgin martyrs. These modulations of a basic pattern correspond to different emphases in Terence's plays, so that certain of Terence's plays serve as better models for certain of Hrotsvit's, although all of the plays (Hrotsvit's and Terence's) adhere to a single basic pattern.

Terence's *Andria* serves as a good model for *Dulcitius* and *Sapientia*. It is not difficult to see Simo's desire for absolute authority over the life of his son Pamphilus mirrored in the ultimatums of Hrotsvit's emperors to young virgins. Diocletian, particularly, is an apt figure of Simo, since he attempts to incorporate Agape, Chionia, and Hirena into Roman society by marrying them to prominent men of his court, just as Simo seeks to incorporate his son into respectable society through a proper marriage. In addition to being imperious, Hadrian also acts fatherly in *Sapientia* when he offers to adopt Spes if she will worship Diana: 'Depone callum pectoris · et conquinisce turificando magnę Dianę · et ego te proprię prolis vice excolo · atque extollo omni dilectione' (V.17), 'Lay aside this callousness of heart and relent; bring incense to the great Diana. Then I will adopt you as my own child and cherish you with all my heart' (Wilson, *Florilegium*, 90). Spes's reply is unequivocal: 'Paternitatem tuam repudio · tua benefitia minime desidero' (V.17), 'I don't want you for my father; I have no desire for your favors' (Wilson, *Florilegium*, 90). Unlike Diocletian, Hadrian does not try to marry off Fides, Spes, and Karitas, but he and Antiochus both specifically condemn Sapientia's religious dissent because it results in social disruption. Citizens have been persuaded by this Christian family to abandon ancient rites and, as Antiochus complains, newly converted wives have refused to eat and sleep with their husbands. The female characters of *Sapientia* thus provide a fitting rewriting of Pamphilus, and, for that matter, of all of Terence's sons, who likewise threaten social mores. Indeed, the family dynamic of Terentian drama provides Hrotsvit with a fitting image of the radical incommensurability of Christian and worldly desire, as Terence's sons are no more likely to find common ground with their fathers than are Christian virgins with their pagan persecutors. What is more, the radical devotion of Hrotsvit's virgins to Christ, even to the point of longing for martyrdom, echoes the unswerving devotion of each of Terence's sons to his beloved in the face of his father's displeasure. Pamphilus's expression of his ardour serves to illustrate the point. 'To hell with those who want to part us! Nothing shall take me from her but death!'[21]

Much of the *Andria* involves the machinations of the slave, Davos, as he attempts, out of loyalty and love for Pamphilus, to counter Simo's attempts to catch his son in a punishable offence. A similar thwarting of the antagonists of the faithful is found in *Dulcitius* when the divine plotter not only deludes the would-be rapist Dulcitius into believing that dirty kitchen pots are his intended victims, but arranges that Agape and Chionia feel no pain when they are burned to death, and sends two agents falsely claiming to represent Sissinus to keep Hirena from a brothel. Similarly, in *Sapientia*, the virgins are protected from suffering any pain under gruesome torture. Hrotsvit's plot elements that confound the plans of the wicked emphasize the superior wisdom of the Christian God, who not only is always successful in protecting the faithful but also undoes the tensions of moral uncertainty that are central to the comedy in Terence's plays. The profundity of the divine mind is also expressed in Sapientia's God-inspired mathematical lesson, which is beyond the understanding of the pagan Hadrian.

These and other echos in Hrotsvit's plays of the attempts of one Terentian character to outwit another are examples of Hrotsvit's transposition of a Terentian motif into an enactment of divine grace. Often this grace involves a miracle that can be understood as a reconstruction of the crowning revelation in Terence's plays, when new knowledge about the disreputable lovers of the sons paves the way for the play's comic resolution and restoration of social order.[22] Furthermore, the wedding that is part of that resolution in Terence's comedies is rewritten as a union of the faithful Christian with Christ and God. Thus, for instance, Hirena's final words in *Dulcitius*, closing the speech that ends the play, are 'intrabo aethereum aeterni regis thalamum · Cui est honor et gloria in saecula' (XIV.1), 'I will enter the heavenly bridal chamber of the Eternal King, to whom are all honor and glory in all eternity' (Wilson, *Florilegium*, 53). Similarly, Sapientia tells her daughters, 'Ad hoc vos materno lacte affluenter alui · ad hoc delicate nutrivi · ut vox cęlesti non terreno sponso traderem · quo vestri causa socrus aeterni regis dici meruissem' (IV.3), 'It was for this that I nursed you with my milk flowing free;/ it was for this that I carefully reared you three;/ that I may espouse you to a heavenly, not an earthly bridegroom and may deserve to be called the mother-in-law of the Eternal King thereby' (Wilson, *Florilegium*, 87). Certainly the espousal imagery in these passages cites and transforms Terence. However, not all plot elements in Hrotsvit's plays can be explained by links to the plots or quotation of figural patterns in Terence. The variety and extent of divine trickery in *Dulcitius*, for instance, has no precise correlative in Terence's plays. Likewise, the rich evocation of female community in *Sapientia* (found in a mother's affection for her daughters, sisterly support in a time of trial, and the consolation Sapientia receives from the matrons) certainly cannot be explained by recourse to Terence. Rather they indicate Hrotsvit's talent for producing dramatic individuation within the confines of a recurrent structure.

Another indication of Hrotsvit's adaptability is her exploration of alternative figural significations for Terentian family drama in her two conversion plays *Abraham* and *Pafnutius*. In these plays, the demands of the father figures are not associated with the pull of the carnal world on the life of the Christian, as they are in *Dulcitius* and *Sapientia*. Rather, in these plays, Hrotsvit extracts from the solicitousness of Terence's fathers for their sons an image of the divine guidance of a loving Heavenly

Father. In their conscientious upbringing of their charges, in their salvific hopes for the prostitutes, Mary and Thais, in the lengths to which they go to bring their charges into a life of Christian practice and belief, and in Abraham's familial status as Mary's compassionate uncle, Abraham and Pafnutius express positive fatherly attributes unlike Hrotsvit's Roman emperors.[23] Likewise, the figural meaning of Terence's sons is also inverted in these plays. When Mary and Thais pursue lives of prostitution, Hrotsvit transforms the passion of Terence's sons into the actions and feelings of wayward sinners in the grip of illicit desire. By doing so, she glorifies God's grace, since both plays conclude with the women in a state of grace. Thus Thais says toward the end of *Pafnutius,*

> Unde laudet illum cęli concentus · omnisque terrę surculus · necnon universę animalis species atque confusę aquarum gurgites · quia non solum peccantes patitur · sed etiam pęnitentibus pręmia gratis largitur · (XII.6)

> Therefore praise Him all the company of Heaven, and on Earth the least little sprout or bush,/ not only all living creatures but even the waterfall's rush,/ because He not only suffers men to live in sinful ways/ but rewards the penitent with the gift of grace. (Wilson, *Plays,* 121)

This grace corresponds to the 'salvation' of Terence's sons from the ignominy of parental rejection.

Such inversions may have been suggested by the specific plot elements of the *Eunuchus* which serves as the closest, if not only, corollary of Hrotsvit's conversion plays. In the *Eunuchus* the role of the father is greatly attenuated as Demea is given only a few lines toward the end of the play. Hence, Demea's objection to the relationship of his son Chaerea with the supposed slave girl, Pamphila, is implied rather than stated, and his role as the typical Terentian father is somewhat usurped in this play by, of all people, Thais. After all, it is Thais who works tirelessly (whatever motives we may construct for her) to restore Pamphila to her family just as the typical Terentian father exerts his efforts to install his son in a new family. Thais's lack of coerciveness in pursuing Pamphila's interests suggests the more benign father figures of the conversion plays. On the other hand, Chaerea serves as a likely model for Hrotsvit's Thais and Mary since his sexual assault of Pamphila suggests the association of these characters with carnal desire. *Abraham* and *Pafnutius* are also distinguished by the absence of salvific miracles. This is perhaps explained by the nature of 'the wondrous revelation' in the *Eunuchus*, which is somewhat less wondrous by virtue of its being known to the audience and some characters at the outset of the play. It nevertheless remains a cogent expression of shifting identity, the correlative of Hrotsvit's conversions. The theme of trickery is also developed somewhat differently in the conversion plays. The employments of disguise by Abraham and Pafnutius are further illustrations of scheming as an instrument of God's grace as these deceptions will ultimately lead to the salvation of Mary and Thais. However, in contrast to the passion plays, grace is manifest in the conversion plays through human agency. The disguise motif also seems derived from the *Eunuchus* in that it allows the hermits to bring about their longing for the conversion of their charges, just as Chaerea's disguise allows him to fulfil his longing. Hrotsvit's technique here is aptly stated by de Luca who finds the disguise theme to represent a 'deliberate "reverse imitation" of Terence,' as a salacious plot element is reworked by Hrotsvit to glorify chastity.[24]

In conclusion I would also note Hrotsvit's transformation of Terence's theme of marriage in the conversion plays. As in *Dulcitius* and, more tacitly, in *Sapientia,* the social and economic advantages of the good marriages that end Terence's plays are exploited in *Pafnutius* as figures of a believer's heavenly reward. This link between earthly marriage and heavenly reward is cogently realized in the material elements of Paul's vision of Thais's spiritual inheritance: 'Videbam in visione lectulum candidulis paliolis in cęlo magnifice stratum · cui quattuor splendidę virgines pręerant · et quasi custodiendo astabant' (XI.2), 'In my vision of Heaven, I saw a bed/ with white linen beautifully spread/ surrounded by four resplendent maidens who stood as if guarding the bed' (Wilson, *Plays,* 119). Moreover, the plot detail that both Paul and Antonius expected Paul's vision to anticipate Antonius's reward in heaven, when in fact it concerns Thais's salvation, emphasizes the power of God's forgiveness and grace.

In *Gallicanus* and *Calimachus,* Hrotsvit combines the plot elements (and the attendant figural significations) of her conversion and passion plays. Each play presents benign father figures (Constantinus, and John) as well as oppressive masculine authority in the form of unwanted suitors. Thus Calimachus's attempt to force Drusiana to violate her faith suggests a parallel to the father figures, Hadrian and Diocletion. Similarly, Gallicanus attempts to convince Constantius to be an oppressive father figure by betrothing Constantius's daughter Constantia to him (which would involve breaking her Christian vow of chastity) as a reward for his military service to the empire. The heroines of *Gallicanus* and

Calimachus manifest both the steely resolve of the virgins in the passion plays and an alternative to the wavering weakness of Mary and Thais. Drusiana rejects the advances of Calimachus in the strongest of terms, but her prayer for death in order to evade 'that charming young man' may indicate her doubts about her own resolve. Constantia is firmly against marriage to Gallicanus; rather than reject him outright, however, she advises her father that they agree to marriage and trust God to resolve their dilemma by the time Gallicanus returns from the war.[25] *Gallicanus* and *Calimachus* also conflate the elements of human and divine plotting found in the other plays. Constantia conspires with her father to put off her marriage, but her virginity is ultimately spared by the miracle of heavenly aid that brings about the victory in battle and Gallicanus's resultant conversion. In *Calimachus* villains are thwarted by divine intervention, as when Drusiana's body is protected from violation by the miracle of the avenging snake and God's direct intervention, but human beings are also participants in divine plans. Constantia sends her servants John and Paul to war with Gallicanus to prepare the way for his conversion, and she initiates the education and conversion of Gallicanus's sisters. Drusiana prays for saving death and she and John resurrect others. Moreover, the plots of both *Gallicanus* and *Calimachus* turn on both salvific miracle and conversion.

In addition to the doubling of plot variations discussed above, *Gallicanus* prefigures the major elements of all of the other plays in a number of other ways. A few more examples will suffice to make the point. John and Paul, who follow Gallicanus in the hope of converting him, are figures of Abraham and Pafnutius. Constantinus, the solicitous (biological) father prefigures the solicitous mother Sapientia. In this way a harmonious symmetry is achieved between the first and the last plays. My examples thus far have concerned the first part of the play, but many can also be drawn from the latter part of *Gallicanus*. John and Paul are martyred by Constantinus's successor, Julianus the Apostate, as the virgin women in *Dulcitius* and *Sapientia* are martyred by pagan Roman emperors. In all three cases, the emperor proffers blandishments and rewards in order to persuade the Christians to revert to paganism, and they are given time to reconsider their faith before their execution. The emperor Julianus, as an apostate, prefigures Mary in *Abraham*. Terrentianus converts to Christianity after he realizes his son has been driven mad as punishment for his sins and thus prefigures Calimachus and Thais.

Terrentianus is a particularly notable choice for the name of the character who speaks last in a play that introduces and is a microcosm of

Hrotsvit's entire dramatic corpus. Evoking the name of Hrotsvit's literary antecedent, his fate becomes a statement of Hrotsvit's literary relationship to Terence: his conversion at the end of the play mirrors the rehabilitation undergone by Terence's plays at the hand of Hrotsvit. Placed at a position of rhetorical emphasis in a play that inaugurates her dramatic production by both its position and content, his conversion may be read as a kind of manifesto of Hrotsvit's dramatic intent.

Hrotsvit's rehabilitation of Latin classics is thus in line with a contemporary interest in a renewed Christian Rome. For this reason, my reading of Hrotsvit is one encouraged by the shared cultural desire and expectation of renewal of Hrotsvit's contemporaries. As Wallace-Hadrill has shown, there remained a continuing interest in the Roman past in the centuries following the demise of the Roman Empire, which in the Carolingian and Ottonian renaissances, particularly, took the form of its reestablishment. For Hrotsvit, Otto I is, in her dedication to her epic, 'Pollens imperii regnator cęsariani' (*Prologus ad Ottonem [I] Imperatorem*, 1), the powerful ruler of the Caesars' empire, and Otto II is 'Romani pręfulgens gemmula regni' (*Prologus ad Ottonem [II] Imperatorem*, 1) the sparkling jewel of the Roman Empire. The reestablishment of Rome, hence, had a textual, as well as a political (empire building) dimension. Textually, classical models were reworked to provide laudatory representations of monarchs. Liutpold Wallach points out, 'As Einhard modeled his *Life of Charlemagne* on Suetonius' *Lives of the Caesars*, so Widukind of Corvey described Otto the Great after the model of Sallust.'[26] Hrotsvit's dramas should perhaps be classed with these works. To be sure, they are not written in overt praise of Otto, but their themes surely had implications for the emperor. Gandersheim was founded by Otto I and remained an imperial abbey (directly responsible to the king rather than a bishop) until 947 when its rule devolved to the abbess. The close association of the abbey with the royal family continued throughout the century, however, as its abbesses continued to be drawn from the royal family. Thus, its literary production would naturally reflect upon the royal family and serve to buttress imperial prestige by demonstrating that Otto's reign could deliver a new Christian Rome culturally and spiritually as well as politically.

Hrotsvit's involvement in the dissemination of political ideology in her dramas should come as no surprise, considering the seamless nexus between church and imperial ideology in the *Gesta Ottonis*. Nor does she manifest strictly religious concerns in the *Primordia* which Wilson describes as follows:

Hrotsvit's paramount concern, thus, appears to be twofold: first to link the Gandersheim community to the power of earthly patrons and to the protectorate of celestial patrons through miracles and by presenting divine agents involved in the foundation of the Abbey; second, to establish legal and historical precedent for the Abbey's rights to independence.[27]

What might be discovered if we were to look for a similar admixture of spiritual and mundane involvements in her other works? Such a course need not discount Hrotsvit's religious zeal, nor gainsay the relevance of religious knowledge to interpretation, but merely acknowledge the crucial role of class alignments in the literary production of a canoness who, after all, hailed from noble stock, as did her spiritual sisters at Gandersheim. Nor are we to imagine Hrotsvit to have lived in cloistered detachment from political life.[28] Peter Dronke has suggested that similarities between Hrotsvit's rhymed prose and the literary style of Rather, who visited Otto I's court in 952, may be evidence that Hrotsvit spent her early years at court.[29] What is more, great assemblies convened at Gandershiem, and the abbey often provided hospitality for the court.[30] Given this milieu, it is unlikely that the literary imagination of Hrotsvit remained unaffected by court politics and ideology. Long concerned with Hrotsvit's religious intent, Hrotsvit scholarship would surely benefit from more attention to the political meanings, intended or not, of not only Hrotsvit's epics but also her dramas and legends.

NOTES

1 Coulter, 'The "Terentian" Comedies,' 526.
2 Roberts, 'Did Hrotswitha Imitate Terence?' 480.
3 Judith Tarr, for example, argues that Hrotsvit's relationship to Terence is one of *aemulatio* rather than of *imitatio*, 'of rivalry, of "one-upmanship" as it were. This is Hrotsvit's own avowed purpose, to provide an "antidote" to the seductions of the pagan poet: a series of dramatic works centering upon Christian themes and characters' 'Terentian Elements in Hrotsvit,' 56. See also Wilson, *Hrotsvit of Gandersheim: The Ethics of Authorial Stance*, especially chapters 2 and 3, and Sticca, 'Sacred Drama and Comic Realism in the Plays of Hrotswitha of Gandersheim,' 124–5.
4 See Coulter, 'The "Terentian" Comedies,' 526–7, and de Luca, 'Hrotsvit's "Imitation" of Terence,' 91.
5 See de Luca, 'Hrotsvit's "Imitation" of Terence,' 100–1.

6 Dronke, 'Hrotsvita,' in *Women Writers of the Middle Ages*, 72.
7 Coulter, 'The "Terentian" Comedies,' 527.
8 Wilson, 'Hrotsvit and the *Artes*,' 6.
9 See, for example, Hagendahl, *Augustine and the Latin Classics*, 386–8.
10 Curtius, *European Literature and the Latin Middle Ages*, 443–5.
11 Ibid., 362–3.
12 Haight, *Hrotswitha of Gandersheim*, 9.
13 Dhuoda, *Handbook for Her Warrior Son*, trans. Marcelle Thiebaux, 190–1. Peter Dronke discusses this example in 'Dhuoda,' in *Women Writers of the Middle Ages*, 45–6.
14 Dhuoda, *Handbook for Her Warrior Son*, 190–1.
15 Wilson, *Hrotsvit of Gandersheim: The Ethics of Authorial Stance*, 25–6.
16 Sticca, 'Hroswitha's *Dulcitius* and Christian Symbolism.' See also Patricia Silber's essay in this volume.
17 Sticca, 'Hroswitha's *Abraham* and Exegetical Tradition,' and 'Sacred Drama and Tragic Realism in Hroswitha's *Pafnutius*.'
18 Kratz, 'The Nun's Epic,' 132–8.
19 Terence's sons' prefiguration of female characters thus parallels the prefiguration of female characters in the dramas by the males of the legends.
20 *Sapientia* is the one play that does not offer a substitute lover/husband. However, the conflict between an earthly and heavenly lover is none the less present since Sapientia's goal in raising her children is that she 'may espouse [them] to a heavenly, not an earthly bridgroom' (Wilson, *Florilegium*, 87).
21 Terence, *The Comedies [of] Terence*, 72–3.
22 See Peter Dronke's discussion of parallels between Terence's and Hrotsvit's plots, 'Hrotsvitha,' 72.
23 See Michael Zampelli's essay in this volume for an alternative reading of Abraham's relationship to Mary.
24 de Luca, 'Hrotsvit's "Imitation" of Terence,' 100–1.
25 See Jane Chance's discussion of *Gallicanus* in this volume.
26 Wallach, 'Education and Culture in the Tenth Century,' 21.
27 Wilson, *Hrotsvit of Gandersheim: The Ethics of Authorial Stance*, 131.
28 See essays by Linda McMillin and Jay Lees in this volume for discussion of the political context in which Hrotsvit wrote.
29 Dronke, *Women Writers of the Middle Ages*, 56–7.
30 See, for example, Nelson, 'Rulers and Government,' 105.

Hrotsvit's Sapientia as a Foreign Woman

PHYLLIS R. BROWN

Until fairly recently the Catholic Church celebrated on 1 August the martyrdom of Faith, Hope, and Charity, daughters of St Wisdom. Evidence of two separate legends survives: that Pistis, Elpis, Agape, and their mother, Sophia, were martyred under the emperor Hadrian and buried on the Aurelian Way, and that another group, Fides, Spes, Karitas, and their mother, Sapientia, at some later time were martyred and interred in the cemetery of St Callistus on the Appian Way. As late as 1909, John F.X. Murphy wrote for the *Catholic Encyclopedia*, 'the extent and antiquity of their cult and the universality with which their names are found not only in the various early martyrologies of the Western Church, but also in the Menaia and Menologies of the Greeks, render the fact of their existence and martyrdom unquestionable.'[1] Although the names of the first group are usually given in Greek and the second group in Latin, scholars have frequently conflated the two, as Hrotsvit seems to have done in her dramatic version of the legend, *Passio Sanctarum Virginum Fidei, Spei, et Karitatis*, often referred to as *Sapientia*. Probably more significant than using the Latin names for the family martyred by Hadrian, Hrotsvit has introduced the idea that the mother, Sapientia, an Italian noblewoman is *advena* (foreign or coming from outside) rather than a Roman widow, as is usually the case in the legends using the Latin names. Biblical sources for the idea that Wisdom might be characterized as a foreign woman, in particular a foreign woman with no fixed abode, help elucidate some of the richness and complexity of theme in Hrotsvit of Gandersheim's longest play, the one she chose to close her sequence of plays.

At the beginning of Hrotsvit's *Sapientia,* when Antiochus first tells Hadrian about Sapientia's arrival in Rome with her children Fides, Spes, and Karitas, specifying that their arrival poses a danger to the state, Antiochus labels Sapientia as 'advena mulier,' a foreign woman, one who has come in from outside. He repeats this phrase, with word order reversed, when a few lines later he first addresses Sapientia, asking her what her name is: 'Quid vocaris o mulier advena?' (II.1), 'Foreign woman, what's your name?' (Wilson, *Florilegium,* 82). Later, when Hadrian observes that Sapientia appears to be of noble birth, Sapientia replies that she comes from a line of prominent Italian leaders. After acknowledging the nobility of her ancestors, Hadrian asks why she has entered his territory: 'Dic cur advenires · vel quare nostrates adires' (III.7), 'Tell me why you came here, and why you incite our people, subverting our reign' (Wilson, *Florilegium,* 84). The first verb, 'advenires,' etymologically related to the adjective and noun 'advena,' underscores the idea of her foreignness; the second verb, 'adires,' returns to the idea that her coming is at least a potential threat to Hadrian's rule, as Antiochus had said in the opening scene.

The implicit contrast and enmity between Hadrian's native country and Sapientia's contributes to the contrast established a few lines earlier between the threatening face of Hadrian ('minacem imperatoris vultum,' II.1) – ruler of Rome – and the Ruler of the Universe, who not only cannot be conquered, threatened, or subverted but also protects his people rather than menacing them: 'Princeps universitatis qui nescit vinci · non patitur suos ab hoste superari' (II.1–2), 'The Ruler of the Universe, who never can be conquered, will not permit the fiend to overcome His people' (Wilson, *Florilegium,* 82). Thus the beginning of the play establishes Sapientia as both Italian and Christian, from a noble Italian family of rulers but ruled by God, 'Ruler of the Universe.' Sapientia, as Italian and Christian, threatens Hadrian's rule specifically, Antiochus says, because teachings of the Christians lead to abandonment of ancestral and ancient rites and estrangement of Roman wives from their husbands: Antiochus tells Hadrian, 'dedignantur nobiscum comedere · quanto minus dormire' (I.5), 'our wives despise us so that they refuse to eat with us, or even more to sleep with us' (Wilson, *Florilegium,* 82). The conflict between Hadrian and his followers and the outsider Sapientia and her daughters, which occupies the rest of the play, thus is at the same time between the pagan ruler Hadrian and the Christian God.

An understanding of the probable biblical basis of Sapientia's characterization as a foreign woman adds to the thematic richness of the antagonism between Sapientia and Hadrian in Hrotsvit's play. Roland Murphy identifies Lady Wisdom as 'the most striking personification in the entire Bible' and a significant element in the 'wisdom literature' of the Hebrew Bible and the Apocrypha.[2] Evidence in Proverbs, The Book of Wisdom, and Ecclesiasticus (in current parlance more usually called Ben Sirach or The Book of Jesus the Son of Sirach) clarifies the implications of Sapientia's being foreign, while examples from a variety of biblical texts contribute to an understanding of Hrotsvit's choice of the word *advena* (as opposed to *alienigena*, *alienus*, or *extraneus*). The later association of Old Testament Wisdom with Christ's wisdom in the New Testament and some contemporary feminist criticism further contribute to an understanding of character and theme in Hrotsvit's *Sapientia*.

One element of Sapientia's characterization as a foreign woman is suggested by qualities of Wisdom developed in the Old Testament. For example, midway through a speech in Proverbs 8, Wisdom says:

> The Lord possessed me in the beginning of his ways, before he made any thing from the beginning./ I was set up from eternity, and of old before the earth was made./ The depths were not as yet, and I was already conceived: neither had the fountains of waters as yet sprung out./ The mountains with their huge bulk had not as yet been established: before the hills I was brought forth./ He had not yet made the earth, nor the rivers, nor the poles of the world./ When he prepared the heavens, I was present: when with a certain law and compass he enclosed the depths:/ When he established the sky above, and poised the fountains of waters:/ When he compassed the sea with its bounds, and set a law to the waters that they should not pass their limits: when he balanced the foundations of the earth:/ I was with him forming all things: and was delighted every day, playing before him at all times:/ Playing in the world. And my delights were to be with the children of men.[3]

Since Wisdom existed before time and before the creation, even participated with God in the creation, she is an outsider joining men in their world, with them but not one of them, and thus in a sense a foreign woman. Similarly, in the apocryphal Book of Wisdom, Solomon asks God to send wisdom – which was present at the creation – to him:

> Thou has chosen me to be king of thy people and a judge of the sons and daughters./ And hast commanded me to build a temple on thy holy mount, and an altar in the city of thy dwelling place, a resemblance of thy holy tabernacle, which thou hast prepared from the beginning./And thy

wisdom with thee, which knoweth thy works, *which then also was present when thou madest the world, and knew what was agreeable to thy eyes, and what was right in thy commandments*:/ Send her out of thy holy heaven, and from the throne of thy majesty, that she may be with me, and may labour with me, that I may know what is acceptable with thee./ For she knoweth and understandeth all things, and shall lead me soberly in my works, and shall preserve me by her power. [my emphasis][4]

Wisdom's personification in Ecclesiasticus confirms this characterization of Wisdom as being with men, accessible to men, but different from them because of her special association with God. Chapter 1 opens, 'All wisdom is from the Lord God, and hath been always with him, and is before all time' and continues in verse 4, 'Wisdom hath been created before all things, and the understanding of prudence from everlasting.'[5] In Ecclesiasticus 24:5–11, Wisdom speaks, saying:

I came out of the mouth of the most High, the firstborn before all creatures./ I made that in the heavens there should rise light that never faileth, and as a cloud I covered all the earth./ I dwelt in the highest places, and my throne is in a pillar of a cloud./ I alone have compassed the circuit of heaven, and have penetrated into the bottom of the deep, and have walked in the waves of the sea, And have stood in all the earth./ And in every people,/ And in every nation I have had the chief rule./ And by my power I have trodden under my feet the hearts of all the high and low: and in all these I sought rest, and I shall abide in the inheritance of the Lord.[6]

Since Wisdom's dwelling place and rule are with God, Sapientia can be understood to be a foreign woman entering pagan Rome, bringing with her knowledge of the true God's revealed truth.

This last passage from Ecclesiasticus also seems relevant to Sapientia's role of bringing a new rule to the Roman people and to the power her daughters exercise when Hadrian's men attempt to torture them. Though Sapientia dies before Christianity accomplishes 'the chief rule' in Rome, the play provides the larger context of Christian history for its viewers, creating a dramatic irony in Hadrian's seeming victory in accomplishing the martyrdom of Faith, Hope, and Charity. Just as Christ initiated the *new* 'chief rule' with his death and resurrection, Sapientia and her daughters effectively 'have trodden under [their] feet the hearts of all the high and low,' in a New Testament mode, through their devotion to Christ even in the face of torture and death.

Ecclesiasticus's characterization of Wisdom not only identifies her as being from and with God, existing before the creation, it also specifically links Lady Wisdom with Israel. Thus in chapter 24:14–16, Wisdom says:

> From the beginning, and before the world, was I created, and unto the world to come I shall not cease to be: and in the holy dwelling place I have ministered before him./ And so was I established in Sion, and in the holy city likewise I rested: and my power *was* in Jerusalem./ And I took root in an honourable people, and in the portion of my God his inheritance: and my abode is in the full assembly of saints.[7]

Though existing before the created world, she has entered the world to dwell in Sion, with the Israelites. Significantly, the Old Testament books of laws include frequent reminders to the Jews that they must receive strangers with kindness, always remembering the times when they themselves were strangers, both in Canaan and in Egypt. Yet Hrotsvit has Sapientia identify herself not with Israel but rather with Italy: she is from a noble Italian family, a stranger in Rome.

Hrotsvit's relationship to the court of the Holy Roman Emperor adds to the dramatic irony. An early sixteenth-century woodcut attributed to Albrecht Dürer depicts Hrotsvit presenting her book to Otto the Great. Otto is crowned and holding the orb signifying his consecration as Holy Roman Emperor; behind Hrotsvit, who kneels, and Otto, who is enthroned, stands the abbess Gerberga, herself crowned, holding the staff signifying her authority, with her hands in the gesture of a blessing.[8] In sharp contrast to Sapientia's role as an outsider in Hadrian's court, Otto's court, Christian rather than pagan, welcomes and values not only Christian and Old Testament Wisdom but also the wisdom in Hrotsvit's writings. The main difference suggested by Hrotsvit's play is that while Hadrian's Rome has not accepted the wisdom of Christianity and therefore perceives Sapientia as a stranger, by Hrotsvit's own day, Rome and the Roman Empire have been transformed by Christianity[9] into something comparable to the Israel of Ecclesiasticus. While in Hrotsvit's play a double allegiance to Hadrian and the Christian God is impossible, the Holy Roman Empire, initiated by Charlemagne and renewed and perpetuated by Otto the Great, undoes that conflict.[10]

Many details in Old Testament wisdom literature emphasize an opposition between Wisdom, whether personified or not, and folly, which is occasionally personified. Proverbs 9 sets up the contrast by having Wisdom (Sapientia) invite both the wise and the foolish to come to the house she has built, with its seven pillars, and eat and drink with her while a foolish woman (mulier stulta) sits by her house and calls to those who are passing by, saying to the fools among them, 'Stolen waters are sweeter, and hidden bread is more pleasant' (9:17). Complicating our understanding of Hrotsvit's construction of Sapientia as a foreign woman is the antithesis elsewhere in Proverbs between associating with Wisdom and keeping company with strange or foreign women. Significantly, however, these biblical texts use the words *extranea* and *aliena* to denote the foreignness of the stranger, not *advena*. So Proverbs 7:4–5 instructs, 'Dic sapientiae soror mea es et prudentiam voca amicam tuam/ ut custodiat te a muliere extranea et ab aliena quae verba sua dulcia facit,' 'Say to wisdom: Thou are my sister. And call prudence thy friend:/ That she may keep thee from the woman that is not thine, and from the stranger who sweeteneth her words.' A few verses later, this stranger, 'in harlot's attire, prepared to deceive souls; talkative and wandering;/ Not bearing to be quiet, not able to abide still at home,' kisses, flatters, and then addresses a foolish young man saying:

> I have woven my bed with cords; I have covered it with painted tapestry, brought from Egypt./ I have perfumed my bed with myrrh, aloes, and cinnamon./ Come, let us be inebriated with the breasts, and let us enjoy the desired embraces, till the day appear./ For my husband is not at home: he is gone a very long journey./ He took with him a bag of money: he will return home the day of the full moon./ She entangled him with many words, and drew him away with the flattery of her lips. (Proverbs 7:16–21)

Biblical scholars have long debated the connotative value of the Hebrew words creating the figure of the Strange Woman.[11] Claudia Camp writes:

> Scholars have reached a certain level of agreement in the past few years that the figure is the product of a postexilic Judean setting, her 'strange-ness' alluding in some way to the tensions of that period. These tensions resulted from the return of some of the descendants of the exiled Judean leadership group (the *golah*, 'exile') from Babylon ... At stake behind the more material concerns was the fundamental matter of Jewish identity – who would be regarded as inside and outside the congregation, and who would decide.[12]

Some critics see in the figure of the Strange Woman more specifically an exploration of the threat of intermarriage between Israelites and foreigners and 'the anxiety of this elite to preserve its social status and economic assets' as 'an important factor in generating the language in which the Outsider Woman is described and her activities denounced.'[13] Others have argued that the Strange Woman in Proverbs gives the commonplace stereotype of the dangers of women and sexuality an archetypal dimension, in which she embodies a *via negativa*. To this end, Camp argues:

> Sexual misconduct both induces and represents social disorder. The strange woman thus becomes a metaphorical vehicle for the disruptive and chaotic forces that threaten the shalom of individual and society. The chaos and death embodied in the *mala fide* sexuality of the strange woman stand in direct antithesis to the affirmation of life present in Wisdom's allusions to the covenant of love between woman and man.[14]

The young man addressed throughout Proverbs in either view is depicted as a potential victim of a danger characterized as a Strange Woman whom he must avoid to maintain his own safety and the safety of his family and his society.

In the early Middle Ages, the foreign woman in Proverbs was understood to be an allegorical representation of heresy. Bede (673–735) writes, 'Potest autem per mulierem extraneam hereticorum prauitas intellegi a Christi et ecclesiae membris aliena quae mollitia dissertitudinis et linguae blandimentis corda decipere innocentium solet,' 'One can understand by the foreign woman the perversity of heretics estranged from the members of Christ and the Church, [a perversity] which is accustomed to deceive the hearts of the innocent by softness of speech and blandishments of the tongue.'[15] Rabanus Maurus (780–856) repeats this interpretation in *Expositio in Proverbia Salomonis*,[16] which, in turn, is repeated in the Glossa Ordinaria, which reached its definitive form by mid-twelfth century. In all of these interpretations, the foreign woman is understood to be a danger that contrasts with Wisdom.

Hrotsvit, on the other hand, seems to have complicated and inverted this pattern in her depiction of Sapientia as a foreign woman and her use of the word *advena*. Folly and sexuality are associated with Hadrian rather than with the foreign woman Sapientia or her daughters. Not only does Sapientia make a fool of Hadrian through her disquisition on numbers, first having asked her daughters, 'Placetne vobis o filię · ut hunc stultum aritmetica · fatigem disputatione?' (III.8), Would it please you, children, if I fatigued this fool/ with a lesson in arithmetical rule?' (Wilson, *Florilegium*, 84); Fides also derides Hadrian's foolishness, perhaps echoing the doxology (As it was in the beginning, it is now and ever shall be) by saying, 'Dixi · et dico · dicamque, quamdiu vixero' (V.5), 'I have called him a fool,/ I now call him a fool,/ and I shall call him a fool/ as long as I live' (Wilson, *Florilegium*, 89). Even Karitas, Sapientia's youngest daughter, says, 'Licet tenella sim aetate · tamen gnara sum te argumentose confundere' (V.34), 'I may be young in years, yet I am expert enough to confound you in argument' (Wilson, *Florilegium*, 93). Hadrian's embodiment of folly suggests that to set one's rule in opposition to God's rule is as disruptive to God's order as the foolish and strange women of Proverbs are to Israel.

Though *advena* is in effect synonymous with *aliena* and *extranea*, all of which signify that the person or item described or denoted has come into one region from another, an examination of where and how these words were used in Latin translations of the Bible reveals another layer of complexity in Hrotsvit's construction of Sapientia as a foreign woman. Although there are instances of *aliena* and *advena* used side by side in ways that suggest similarity of meaning,[17] other instances suggest a more positive register to the meaning of *advena* than of *aliena*. For example, Psalm 38, which is concerned with 'a just man's peace and patience in his sufferings from considering the vanity of the world and the providence of God,' concludes:

Exaudi orationem meam Domine
et deprecationem meam
auribus percipe lacrimas meas
ne sileas quoniam *advena* sum apud te et peregrinus
sicut omnes patres mei
remitte mihi ut refrigerer
priusquam abeam et amplius non ero (Ps. 38:13–14)

Hear my prayer, O Lord, and my supplication: give ear to my tears. Be not silent: for I am a *stranger* with thee, and a sojourner as all my fathers were./ O forgive me, that I may be refreshed, before I go hence, and be no more.[18]

Even more significantly, in the First Epistle of St Peter the Apostle, which 'contains much doctrine concerning Faith, Hope, and Charity, with divers instructions to all persons of what state or condition soever,' and which was believed to have been written in Rome about fifteen years after Christ's ascension,[19] opens by addressing the readers as 'electis advenis dispersionis Ponti Galatiae Cappadociae Asiae et Bithyniae,' 'the strangers dispersed through Pontus, Galatia, Cappadocia, Asia and Bithynia, elect,' and later exhorts the reader, 'carissimi obsecro tamquam advenas et peregrinos/ abstinere vos a carnalibus desideriis quae militant adversus animam' (I Pt. 2:11), 'Dearly beloved, I beseech you, as strangers and pilgrims, to refrain yourselves from carnal desires which war against the soul.' These texts emphasize the identity of stranger, *advena* or *peregrinus*, adumbrated by the Israelites' experiences as strangers during the Egyptian captivity, before entering the Promised Land, an identity very different from that of the foreign woman who is *aliena* and *extranea* in the passage from Proverbs cited above.

Parallels between the sexuality of the foreign women in biblical wisdom literature and sexuality in Hrotsvit's play highlight the differences between them. When Hadrian draws attention to Fides's breasts by ordering Antiochus to have her nipples cut off, thus attempting to sexualize Sapientia's oldest daughter, the effect is to highlight the contrast between Fides's breasts, which are chaste and gush forth milk rather than blood when the nipples are cut off, and the overt and dangerous sexuality of the strange woman in Proverbs. Sapientia herself draws attention to the difference between her daughters' virgin martyrdom and her own chastity at the end of the play when she asks Karitas to remember her mother and be her patron after Karitas is with Christ in heaven. While virgins, especially virgin martyrs, have precedence, salvation is also available to Sapientia, a mother, and the Roman matrons who are with her at the end of the play.

Furthermore, the virginity of Sapientia's daughters and the chastity which is often associated with Christian converts during the period of the persecutions are central to the problem Sapientia and Christianity pose to Antiochus and Hadrian. Antiochus specified at the beginning of the play that Sapientia's teachings threaten to disrupt pagan Roman society because she 'hortatur nostrates avitos ritus deserere · et christianę religioni se dedere' (I.5), 'exhorts our citizens and clients/ to abandon the ancestral and ancient rites/ and to convert to Christianity' (Wilson, *Florilegium*, 82). Furthermore, Hrotsvit disrupts not only civic peace but also familial harmony. Antiochus says, 'nam nostrę coniuges fastidiendo nos contempnunt · adeo · ut dedignantur nobiscum comedere · quanto minus dormire' (I.5), 'Our wives despise us so that they refuse to eat with us,/ or even more to sleep with us' (Wilson, *Florilegium*, 82). In a sense, then, Sapientia is a reversal of the strange woman of Proverbs. While the strange woman of Proverbs disrupts Israeli society through her adultery, Sapientia disrupts Roman society, making space for a chaste Christian society, available to the wise and the foolish alike, and coming between married women and their husbands.

Sapientia's disruption of Roman society can also be read in light of Peter's First Epistle. When Peter focuses in chapter 3 on the need for women to be subject to their husbands, giving Sara, wife of Abraham, as a positive example, his concern seems to parallel (to some extent) Antiochus's concern that Christianity has alienated husbands from wives. But he opens, 'In like manner also, let wives be subject to their husbands: that, if any believe not the word, they may be won without the word, by the conversation of the wives' (I Peter 3:1). The history of early Christianity affords many examples of kings and noblemen coming to Christianity through the influence of their wives.[20] Moreover, Sapientia and her daughters are, in fact, enacting what Peter urges on the early Christians: 'Christ therefore having suffered in the flesh, be you also armed with the same thought, for he that hath suffered in the flesh hath ceased from sins: That now he may live the rest of his time in the flesh, not after the desires of men but according to the will of God' (I Peter 4:1–2) and 'Dearly beloved, think not strange the burning heat which is to try you: as if some new thing happened to you. But if you partake of the sufferings of Christ, rejoice that, when his glory shall be revealed, you may also be glad with exceeding joy' (I Peter 4:12–13). Though the eagerness for torture and death that Hrotsvit's Christian martyrs enact may seem excessive to twenty-first century readers, the Epistle of St Peter urges precisely that attitude to the earliest Christians. By the time Hrotsvit is writing, martyrdom was a less real option. Virginity and chastity may have become ascetic substitutes for martyrdom; they certainly were politically significant in light of the Ottonian policy of endowing monastic houses for the noblewomen who might otherwise confuse dynastic plans by their childbearing.[21]

Hrotsvit's choice of the adjectival noun *advena* to identify Sapientia as a foreign woman not only sets up an association between the mother of Faith, Hope, and Charity, and Old Testament personifications of Wisdom, it also points to a parallel with Christ, who in his advent as Word made flesh is an embodiment of God's wisdom. Patristic writings suggest that for medieval theologians parallels between the hypostatic qualities of Lady Wisdom in Proverbs and Ecclesiasticus and hypostasis in Christ were significant. Both Wisdom and Christ existed before and participated in the creation of the world, both embody God the Creator's superior and inscrutable wisdom, and both dwelled among humans functioning as a link between God the Creator and his creation.[22]

According to Jesuit scholar H. Jaeger,

> The quasi-identification of Christ and Wisdom and the new interpretation
> of Wisdom as a way of Christian salvation in the New Testament appears in
> the two currents of the patristic conception of Wisdom. One is the homi-
> letic current, which is based on the Christ-experience of early Judeo-
> Christianity. The other is the more theologically systematical current.[23]

Jaeger goes on to identify passages in the writings of Clement of Rome,
Pseudo-Barnabas, second-century Apologists (he names Theophilus and
Irenaeus), Origen, Gregory of Nyssa, St Basil, Maximus Confessor, St
Hilary, St Augustine, and even St Thomas Aquinas to support his argu-
ment that more than the Gnostic tradition contributed to the New
Testament conception of Christ's wisdom.

    Thus by calling Sapientia an 'advena mulier,' Hrotsvit may be suggest-
ing a parallel between Sapientia's advent in Hadrian's Rome and Christ's
advent in Roman Judea. This parallel may help further make sense of
Hrotsvit's inversion of Wisdom's role in Old Testament wisdom literature, for in Christ's coming, especially as described in 1 Corinthians 1
and 2, the relationship of wisdom and folly becomes more complicated
than it is in Proverbs. In his first letter, Paul says:

> For Christ sent me not to baptize, but to preach the gospel not in wisdom of
> speech, lest the cross of Christ should be made void./ For the word of the
> cross, to them indeed that perish, is foolishness: but to them that are saved,
> that is, to us, it is the power of God./ For it is written: *I will destroy the wisdom
> of the wise: and the prudence of the prudent I will reject. Where is the wise? Where is
> the scribe? Where is the disputer of this world?* (Citing Isaiah 24:14 and 33:18)
> Hath not God made foolish the wisdom of this world?/ For, seeing that in
> the wisdom of God, the world, by wisdom, knew not God, it pleased God, by
> the foolishness of *our* preaching, to save them that believe. (I Cor. 1:17–21)

Just as Christ's New Law resulted in the wise fool for Christ, so Sapientia,
according to the Roman pagan point of view enacted by Hadrian, is a
weak and foolish woman while from a Christian point of view it is
Hadrian and Antiochus who are fools, whose wisdom will be destroyed
and whose prudence will be rejected. Paul goes on to say a few verses
later, 'For the foolishness of God is wiser than men: and the weakness of
God is stronger than men.' Not only Sapientia herself but the martyrdom of her three daughters enacts a similar inversion. Pheme Perkins
writes in *Jesus as Teacher*:

Jesus wants people to see that it is time for a new experience of God's presence in human life. This new vision challenges old ways of thinking and acting. In order to show people how radical the challenge is, he often uses images that are extreme or even paradoxical. Unlike the commonplaces of much wisdom tradition, which says the world will always go on as a place in which the fools repeat the same mistakes, Jesus sees the coming of the Reign of God as an opportunity for radical change.[24]

Similarly, Hrotsvit has Sapientia present to Antiochus, Hadrian, the pagan Romans, and her Christian readers the existence of the Reign of God as an opportunity for radical change. The martyrdom of her daughters not only offers an example of the right way to transcend the folly of paganism but also enacts the foolishness of God, which Paul says is wiser than men. While her Christian readers may be able to see that Sapientia's foreignness has a positive valence, Hadrian and Antiochus are incapable of understanding the difference between being a dangerous foreign woman ('mulier aliena') and being a foreign woman ('advena mulier') offering, with God and Christ, an opportunity for new life.

Sapientia's characterization as a foreign woman may also be illuminated by Ben Witherington's reading of Matthew 8:20 and Luke 9:58 as relevant to Jesus as an embodiment of Wisdom. In both gospels Jesus says, 'The foxes have holes, and the birds of the air nests; but the Son of man hath not where to lay his head.' Witherington suggests in this statement that Jesus is interpreting 'his mission in the light of the earlier Wisdom poems/hymns,' particularly in Ecclesiasticus 24:7ff and 14–16, cited earlier in this essay. Witherington writes:

> In that text Wisdom is *seeking*, but not finding, a resting place *until* she comes to rest in Jerusalem having been commanded by God to go there (vv 8–11). In the hymn in Sirach [Ecclesiasticus] this amounts to cosmic and international Wisdom taking up residence amongst a particular people in their chief religious center. Is it not possible that Jesus heard the call of God for him to go up to Jerusalem through a careful meditation on Sirach 24 and a realization that he was experiencing rejection and no *shalom* elsewhere. Could this life orientation of Jesus not be behind the journeying up to Jerusalem motif so important to all the Gospels?[25]

Christ goes to Jerusalem, where his death and resurrection will result in his return home to God. Jerusalem, then, is his home and is not his home. Sapientia journeys to Rome, where her teachings lead to the martyrdom of her daughters and thus their reunion with God. So the final words Fides speaks, just before inviting the executioner to perform his office, are directed to her sisters: 'O uterinę sorores · libate mihi osculum pacis · et parate vos ad tolerantiam futuri certaminis' (V.14) 'O my sisters, born of the same mother, give me a kiss of peace, and prepare yourselves to bear the impending strife' (Wilson, *Florilegium*, 90). Similarly, Spes says to Karitas after the order is given to behead her, 'ne formides tyranni minas · ne trepides ad poenas · nitere · constanti fide imitari sorores · ad cęli palatium precedentes' (V.26), 'Do not fear the tyrant's threat,/ and do not dread his punishments./ Follow in firm faith the example of your sisters, who precede you to Heaven's palace' (Wilson, *Florilegium*, 92). These details contribute to the interpretation that Sapientia is a foreigner because her true home is with God in heaven.

Karitas's response to Hadrian's admonition that she worship the Great Diana also underscores the motif that Sapientia and her daughters are foreigners. She says she will not do as Hadrian orders

> Quia mentiri nolo · Ego quidem et sorores meae · eisdem parentibus genitae · eisdem sacramentis imbutae · sumus una eademque fidei constantia roboratę · quapropter scito nostrum velle · nostrum sentire · nostrum sapere · unum idemque esse · nec me in ullo umquam illis dissidere (V.33)

> Because I don't wish to lie./ I am born of the same parents as my sisters, imbued by the same sacraments, strengthened by the same firmness of faith. Know, therefore, that we are one and the same in what we want, what we feel and what we think. In nothing will I differ from them. (Wilson, *Florilegium*, 93)

All three are foreign to the ways of Hadrian and his pagan rites. Their identity as citizens of the Kingdom of God makes it impossible for them to obey the laws of pagan Rome. This impossibility makes them enact the statements in Matthew 11.19 and Luke 7.35: 'Wisdom is justified by all her children.'

In 'Hrotsvit von Gandersheim: Madwoman in the Abbey,' Charles Nelson suggests that the feminist idea that 'women live simultaneously in two cultures, their own and the dominant male culture' can help readers understand Hrotsvit's world and thus her writings.[26] Nelson draws on Eleanor McLaughlin's 'Equality of Souls, Inequality of Sexes: Women in Medieval Theology' to argue an association between a 'general and continuing cultural duality for women' and 'another duality rooted in the conflict engendered by two parallel traditions: a "creation theology of subordination" and a "salvation theology of equivalence.'"[27] Hrotsvit's achievement of what Peter Dronke calls her 'vast and elaborate internal symmetries' and 'the boldest most elaborate compositional design in Carolingian or Ottonian literature and art' within and among the several individual works sets up a contrast between the discordant, unbalanced man-made world of her woman's experience and the 'thematically, structurally, dramatically, and virtually geometrically ... harmonious, perfect symmetry ... [of] her created world.'[28] Nelson's argument about Hrotsvit's dual existence may also help explain the characterization of Sapientia as a foreign woman, if Sapientia, like Hrotsvit and many other women, perceives herself as an outsider struggling to get along in a man's world. However, one important result of understanding Christ to be a new embodiment of Wisdom is to note the differences between Old Testament and gospel attitudes toward women. Ben Witherington, points out:

> Comments about strange or foreign women being morally dangerous or temptresses are notably lacking in the Jesus tradition. Indeed ... Jesus seems to locate the source of sexual danger for men in their own lust and desires.[29]

In *Sapientia*, Hrotsvit may simultaneously depict not only the present reality of Sapientia herself and women more generally as foreigners finding their way in a man's world but also the promise of a better world made possible by Christ's incarnation, a final victory, through Wisdom and Christ, of a 'salvation theology of equivalence' over a 'creation theology of subordination.'

NOTES

1 Murphy's entry, however, was no doubt influenced by papal policies of Pius X (1903–14), during a conservative period of church history. In particular, concern about the dangers of modernism seems to have resulted, in that period, in an insistence on 'facts' with dubious historical verity in many ecclesiastically sanctioned writings.

2 Roland Murphy, *Tree of Life*, 133. Manuscripts surviving from the early Middle Ages suggest biblical wisdom literature was highly valued then also. Richard Marsden reports that a large number of the surviving biblical manuscripts containing a limited number of biblical books (as opposed to pandects, or complete Bibles) are collections of the wisdom books. Of

about forty early-medieval continental part-Bibles, fourteen consist of or include wisdom literature. One nearly complete eighth-century Anglo-Saxon manuscript (BL Egerton 1046) is a volume of five wisdom books. One mid-tenth century Anglo-Saxon manuscript fragment (BL Add. 34652) 'contains the end of the text of Song of Songs and the beginning of a capitula list for Wisdom'; another complete mid-tenth-century Anglo-Saxon manuscript (BL Cotton Vespasian D.vi) contains a copy of Proverbs along with patristic and devotional texts. See Marsden, 'The Old Testament in late Anglo-Saxon England,' 102–7.

3   Dominus possedit me initium viarum suarum antequam quicquam
          faceret a principio
      ab aeterno ordita sum et ex antiquis antequam terra fieret
      necdum erant abyssi et ego iam concepta eram necdum fontes aquarum
          eruperant
      necdum montes gravi mole constiterant ante colles ego parturiebar
      adhuc terram non fecerat et flumina et cardines orbis terrae
      quando praeparabat caelos aderam quando certa lege et gyro vallabat
          abyssos
      quando aethera firmabat sursum et librabat fontes aquarum
      quando circumdabat mari terminum suum et legem ponebat aquis ne
          transirent fines suos
      quando adpendebat fundamenta terrae cum eo eram cuncta conponens
      et delectabar per singulos dies ludens coram eo omni tempore
      ludens in orbe terrarum et deliciae meae esse cum filiis hominum
                                                              (Prov. 8:22–31)
The Latin texts are from *Biblia Sacra Iuxta Vulgatam Versionem*; the translations are from *The Holy Bible translated from the Latin Vulgate*.

4   tu me elegisti regem populo tuo
      et iudicem filiorum tuorum et filiarum
      dixisti aedificare templum in monte sancto tuo
      et in civitate habitationis tuae aram similitudinem tabernaculi sancti tui
          quod praeparasti ab initio
      et tecum sapientia quae novit opera tua
      quae et adfuit tunc cum orbem terrarum faceres
      et sciebat quid placitum esset oculis tuis
      et quid directum in praeceptis tuis
      mitte illam de sanctis caelis tuis
      et mitte illam a sede magnitudinis tuae
      ut mecum sit et mecum laboret

et sciam quid acceptum sit apud te
scit enim illa omnia et intellegit
et deducet me in operibus meis sobrie
et custodiet me in sua potentia   (Sapientia 9:7–11)
5   Omnis sapientia a Deo Domino est
et cum illo fuit semper et est ante aevum   (Ecclesiasticus 1:1)
6   ego ex ore Altissimi prodivi primogenita ante omnem creaturam
ego in caelis feci ut oriretur lumen indeficiens
et sicut nebula texi omnem terram
ego in altis habitavi
et thronus meus in columna nubis
gyrum caeli circuivi sola
et in profundum abyssi penetravi
et in fluctibus maris ambulavi
et in omni terra steti
et in omni populo et in omni gente primatum habui
et omnium excellentium et humilium corda virtute calcavi
et in his omnibus requiem quaesivi
et in hereditate eius morabor   (Ecclesiasticus 24:5–11)
7   ab initio ante saeculum creata sum
et usque ad futurum saeculum non desinam
et in habitatione sancta coram ipso ministravi
et sic in Sion firmata sum
et in civitate sanctificata similiter requievi
et in Hierusalem potestas mea
et radicavi in populo honorificato
et in parte Dei mei hereditas illius
et in plenitudine sanctorum detentio mea   (Ecclesiasticus 24:14–16)

8 Two woodcuts in the first printed edition of Hrotsvit's *Opera*, ed. Conrad
   Celtis (Nuremberg, 1501), have been attributed to Dürer. Wilson, *The Plays
   of Hrotsvit of Gandersheim*, reproduces the illustrations from the *editio princeps*, including the woodcut of Hrotsvit presenting her works to Emperor
   Otto I (2), and discusses the attribution to Dürer (xxix).

9 Otto the Great's marriage to the Italian heiress Adelheid and Otto II's
   marriage to the Theophano also contributed.

10 See Ulrike Wiethaus's essay in this volume for a different way of understanding how the values of the Ottonian Empire contribute to meaning in
   Sapientia.

11 See Camp, 'The Strange Woman of Proverbs,' for an overview.

12 Ibid., 41–2.

13 See, for example, Blenkinsopp, 'The Social Context of the "Outsider Woman" in Proverbs 1–9,' 473.

14 Camp, *Wisdom and the Feminine in the Book of Proverbs*, 118–20.

15 Bede, *In Proverbia Salomonis*, I.106–9 [on Proverbs 2,16]; translated by George Brown.

16 Rabanus Maurus, *Expositio in Proverbia Salomonis*, lib. I, *PL* 111.690B [see also 690C].

17 In the Vulgate text of Exodus 2:22, for instance, Moses's wife Sephora says, after naming a son Gersam (meaning 'a stranger there'), 'advena fui in terra aliena,' 'I have been a stranger in a foreign country.'

18 And the parallel text in I Paralipomenon (I Chronicles) 29:15: 'Peregrini enim sumus coram te et advenae sicut omnes patres nostri/ dies nostri quasi umbra super terram et nulla est mora,' 'For we are sojourners before thee, and strangers, as were all our fathers. Our days upon earth are as a shadow: and there is no stay.'

19 These details are provided in the headnote to the translation.

20 The conversions of Clovis, king of the Franks, in 496, of Ethelbert of Kent in 597 or 598, and Edwin of Northumbria on Easter Day in 627 are described by Gregory of Tours and the Venerable Bede as occurring in part, at least, through the efforts of their Christian wives. Richard Fletcher discusses these examples of Christian queens converting their pagan husbands in 'The New Constantines,' in *The Barbarian Conversion from Paganism to Christianity*, 104 ff.

21 See, for instance, Leyser, 'The Women of the Saxon Aristocracy,' in *Rule and Conflict in an Early Medieval Society: Ottonian Saxony*, 49–73, and Ulrike Wiethaus's essay in this volume.

22 Lang, *Wisdom and the Book of Proverbs*, 6, and Witherington, *Jesus the Sage*, 202 et passim.

23 Jaeger, 'The Patristic Conception of Wisdom,' 101.

24 Perkins, *Jesus as Teacher*, 44.

25 Witherington, *Jesus the Sage*, 202–3.

26 Nelson, 'Hrotsvit von Gandersheim: Madwoman in the Abbey,' 43.

27 Ibid., 47.

28 Dronke, *Women Writers of the Middle Ages*, 60, 64, 51.

29 Witherington, *Jesus the Sage*, 161.

Hrotsvit and the Devil

PATRICIA SILBER

Hrotsvit is indisputably deeply concerned with confrontation between good and evil. Her preface to the plays makes this clear:

> Unde ego Clamor Validus Gandeshemensis · non recusavi illum imitari dictando · dum alii colunt legendo · quo eodem dictationis genere · quo turpia lascivarum incesta feminarum recitabantur · laudabilis sacrarum castimonia virginum iuxta mei facultatem ingenioli celebraretur ·
>
> (*Liber Secundus, Praefatio*, 3)

> Therefore I, the strong voice of Gandersheim, have not refused to imitate him [Terence] in writing/ whom others laud in reading,/ so that in that selfsame form of composition in which the shameless acts of lascivious women were phrased/ the laudable chastity of sacred virgins may be praised/ within the limits of my little talent. (Wilson, *Florilegium*, 41)

Although the shameless acts of lascivious women and the lustful acts of lecherous men may not really drive Terence's plots,[1] Hrotsvit's focus on them contributes to her emphasis in the preface, plays, and legends on the theme of a modest but determined foe taking a stand against the powers of evil. Since in Western tradition the ultimate power of evil is the devil, variously referred to in literature as Satan and Lucifer among other names, and since he figures as a character in so many literary forms, it might be expected that Hrotsvit would follow the diabolic conventions of plays and legends that pit holiness against wickedness. In fact, while Hrotsvit's plays include this convention to some extent, her legends offer a greater contribution to devil-lore; perhaps most significant is her use of a motif that was to become a major literary device, the pact with the devil.

I began this study with the belief that Hrotsvit, whose plays are centred to such a degree on contests between good and evil, would have drawn, in some fashion, on the view of the devil as a threatening but essentially comic figure made familiar by the mystery plays. This comic devil derived from patristic writings and from the Apocrypha and is marked by his boastful aspiration to God's throne and his ignorance of God's plan for Redemption. An ambivalence in these devils makes them comic-grotesque at the same time as they prefigure Machiavellian pragmatics. They tempt people, but are frequently confused and inept as they go about it. They speak in rants couched in low or vulgar language. In some versions of the Harrowing of Hell we find devils pleading their legal claim to humankind before God, often in quite elaborate suits.[2]

Since Hrotsvit was clearly familiar with the apocryphal gospels and the writings of the Fathers, it might be expected that her characterizations of the devil would be in line with this established tradition.[3] In fact, her allusions to the forces of evil in the plays and most of the legends are completely conventional, even though the Prince of Darkness seldom plays an active role; it is his human deputies who carry on his work. Only in the legends *Theophilus* and *Basilius* do we have active participation of a character named Satan (*Theophilus*, 146; *Basilius*, 138), who is characterized as 'demon sevus' (*Theophilus*, 93, 111), a brutal or barbaric demon, and 'auctor sed scelerum, qui decepit protoplastum' (*Basilius*, 33), 'the author of all evil, seducer of man primeval' (Wilson, *Florilegium*, 21), and 'princeps inferni' (*Basilius*, 50), 'Prince of infernal hell' (Wilson, *Florilegium*, 22). On the whole, Hrotsvit treats her demons with a lighter, if not actually comic, touch. Her naming of the devil seems to highlight the contrast between good and evil while at the same time undermining any sense of real power in the hands of the devil. Her purpose diverges dramatically in *Theophilus* and *Basilius* to address the working of grace in weak humanity. She achieves this through subtle means by using parallel plots, strategic location among the legends, and sources that are distinctly unTerentian.

Her contention that she is using the plays of Terence as a model is not supported by a search for figures who might be translated by their behaviour into devils in Hrotsvit's works. While Terence certainly builds conflict from deceit and devious plots, the attitudes toward sin and evil and therefore the tone of his plays is quite different from hers. The 'nefandarum ... rerum' (*Liber Secundus, Praefatio* 2), 'wicked things' (Wilson, *Florilegium*, 41), in Terence's plays that 'hoc tamen facit non raro verecundari · gravique rubore perfundi' (*Liber Secundus, Praefatio* 3), 'not infrequently caused me to blush/ and brought to my cheeks a scarlet flush' (Wilson, *Florilegium*, 41) seem to have little or nothing to do with her depictions of evil or the devil. Robert Talbot makes a strong case for Hrotsvit's plays as an allegorical Christian rereading of pagan writing:

> [The solution of Christian writers] was to find in classical literature and myth the expression of Christian truth, veiled to the pagan mind but discernible through Christian exegesis. I contend that Hrotsvit anticipates these writers with a similar solution when she exploits in her plays the secular patterns of Terentian drama for their Christian meanings. Her plays become, in effect, an allegorical rereading of Terence.[4]

While both Terence and Hrotsvit employ characters associated with the devil in their plots, Terence's characters are manipulative rather than evil; wit and mischief take the place of genuine wickedness.[5] Consider *The Eunuch*, of interest here because one of its central characters is the courtesan Thaïs, who figures so importantly in Hrotsvit's *Pafnutius*. In this play as well as others, disguise leads to seduction. While *The Eunuch* and other of Terence's plays may lead Hrotsvit to insist in her preface on her aim of substituting the 'laudable chastity of sacred virgins' for 'the shameless acts of lascivious women,' the 'shameless acts' more often are those of men rather than women.[6] Nonetheless, however unsavoury the behaviour of Terence's characters, it is difficult to find in them any genuine points of comparison with the devil and the devil's power or lack of power in Hrotsvit's writings.

In Hrotsvit's plays, on the other hand, we find the workings of the devil, if not his persona, throughout. Drusiana accuses Calimachus of being 'plenum diabolica deceptione' (III.3), 'full of diabolical guile' (Wilson, *Florilegium*, 56), and prays to Christ for help avoiding 'insidiis diabolicis' (IV), 'these devilish snares' (Wilson, *Florilegium*, 57), while at the end of *Calimachus* John laments Fortunatus's rejection of grace saying, 'O admiranda invidia diaboli' (X.9), 'O wondrous envy of Satan' (Wilson, *Florilegium*, 64), and attributes Fortunatus's malice to his being 'diabolic amaritudinis felle plenissimus' (X.9), 'full of Satan's bitter fall' (Wilson, *Florilegium*, 64). Similarly, Effrem prays when Mary first enters the cell adjacent to Abraham's hermitage that Mary will be protected 'ab omni fraude diabolica' (II.8), 'from all the guiles of Satan' (Wilson,

Florilegium, 69), and Abraham later asks him, 'me precibus adiuvare ne inpediar diabolica fraude' (III.19), 'assist me with prayer so that I will not be impeded by the Devil's guiles' (Wilson, *Florilegium*, 72). When Pafnutius asks his disciples for prayers to protect him from 'insidiis vitiosi serpentis' (I.28), 'the vicious serpent's guile' (Wilson, *Plays* 103), they respond, 'Qui regem prostravit tenebricolarum · largiatur tibi contra hostem triumphum' (I.28), 'He who overcame the Prince of the Dark, may He grant you triumph over the fiend' (Wilson, *Plays*, 103). In *Sapientia*, Sapientia warns her daughters to beware of 'serpentinis huius satan lenociniis [Adrianus]' (III.5), 'the tricks of this devilish snake [Hadrian]' (Wilson, *Florilegium*, 83). Thus even though the devil himself does not appear, his traits are attributed to those characters in the plays who do perpetrate evil. In addition to the epithets, attributes of the devil are freely applied to characters in the plays. The apostate Julianus in *Gallicanus* is called 'Diaboli capellanus' (II.V.4), 'the Devil's chaplain' (Wilson, *Plays*, 31) while the son of his henchman Terrentianus is possessed by a demon as punishment for Terrentianus's role in the torture and death of John and Paul.

Of all the characters in the plays associated with the devil, the most striking is, of course, Dulcitius. However evil his aims and achievements, he must be recognized as essentially a comic figure, recalling those devils of the mystery plays who are clowns as well as demons. He begins, like other of Diocletian's lieutenants, as the conventional tormentor, exulting in his evil. But as he cavorts among the pots and pans his intended victims find him 'stultus mente alienatus' (IV.2), 'the fool, the madman base' (Wilson, *Florilegium*, 48), and 'ridiculum' (IV.3), 'ridiculous' (Wilson, *Florilegium*, 48). Agape then says, 'Decet ut talis appareat corpore · qualis a diabolo possidetur in mente' (IV.3), 'It is only right that he should appear in body the way he is in his mind: possessed by the Devil' (Wilson, *Florilegium*, 48), but his intended victims do not identify him with any really dangerous diabolical powers. When the soldiers respond, 'Quis hic egreditur? demoniacus · Vel magis ipse diabolus? Fugiamus' (V), 'Who is coming out?/ A demon without doubt./ Or rather, the Devil himself is he;/ let us flee!' (Wilson, *Florilegium*, 48), they clearly are frightened, but the audience would see even greater humour in the intensity of their fear rather than cause for fear themselves.

Although most of the legends, like the plays, are peopled by such stock figures, their uses of the devil theme are far more intriguing than those in the plays. Once again the familiar epithets appear. In *Gongalfus* the 'vaffer deceptor hominum' (433), 'wily deceiver of men' (Wiegand, 113) shares characteristics with the devils of the cycle plays. For example, the devil inspires in Gongolfus's wife a passion for their scribe and then spreads word of the infidelity:

Ei mihi, sed coluber cupidus, versutus, amarus
  Ingenium nupte illicit indocile:
Scilicet infelix Gongolfi clericus audax
  Ardebat propriam plus licito dominam.
Pro dolor, haec male victa dolo serpentis amaro
  Infelix cicius aestuat in facinus,
Inherens servo cordisque calore secreto
  Legalem dominum respuit ob famulum.
Crimina tunc hostis scalpsit nudare feralis,
  Quę caluit proprio structa fuisse dolo,
Inpaciensque morae vacuas iaculabat in auras
  Divulgando suam denique leticiam.   (353–64)

But alas! The ravening serpent, wily and hateful, beguiled the intractable heart of the wife. It chanced that a bold and wretched scribe of Gongolf was inflamed by a more than lawful affection for his mistress. And woe! This woman, overcome by the bitter wiles of the evil one, speedily was aflame with sinful passion, and clinging to the scribe she, in the secret infatuation of her heart, rejected her lawful lord for the servant. The fierce enemy now itched to expose the crime which he knew had been formed by his own cunning, and therefore, impatient of delay, he kept proclaiming it from the house-tops, making many sharers in his malicious joy. (Wiegand, 107–9)

As in the plays, however, his malicious joy is short-lived but he is persistent. Thus after the wife and scribe are punished for their crime, the narrator relates, 'Tempore tunc longo sudavit fraude maligna/ Ledere famosum' (439–40), 'Then for a long time he strove with malicious guile to injure the famous general' (Wiegand, 113). The depiction of the devil's futile persistence in contrast to Gongolfus's and God's patient steadfastness is heightened by Hrotsvit's emphasis on the different effects of their uses of language. Although the devil's speech is not foul, as it often is in the later cycle plays, it instigates disordered behaviour, while Gongolfus's speech brings about a merciful justice:

Sed tristis meritam mentis mitigaverat iram
  Princeps Gongolfus, arbiter egregious,

Mandans, ut propria damnandus clericus ergo
   Expulsus subito pergeret e patria,
Quo sua finetenus mala defleret scelerosus
   Seclusus patria et datus exilio,
Et donat miseram veniae miseratus honore,
   Ultra sed proprio non locat in thalamo.   (423–30)

But restraining the just wrath of his sad heart, Gongolf, the general, that excellent peacemaker, demanded that the profligate scribe be at once expelled and go from his own country, in order that the criminal might to the end of his days bewail his evil life, shut out from his fatherland and driven into exile; and pitying the wretched woman, he bestowed upon her the distinction of pardon, but suffered her to dwell no more in his abode. (Wiegand, 111)

Similarly, in *Pelagius*, the Saracen Abd al-Rahman contrasts with the Christians who have been set on fire by Christ's love: 'Quo rex comperto fervebat demonis ira/ Corde gerens veterem serpentis denique bilem' (97–8), 'Hearing this, set afire, the king burned with demonic ire./ And in his heart, awake, was the bile of the ancient snake' (Wilson, *Florilegium*, 31). Abd al-Rahman also adopts in his speech the boastful posture of devils in the cycle plays, 'talia pestifero latrando verbula rostro' (103), 'barking such evil words from his pestiferous maw' (Wilson, *Florilegium*, 32).

   The presence and force of the devil and his wiles take on a much more central role in *Theophilus* and *Basilius*. Here Hrotsvit departs dramatically from other early literary demons, and, by adapting a folkloric motif to the pact with the devil, adds her own spiritual dimension to a convention that later became the subject of some of the world's great drama and music; her treatment is the first in verse, and the first written in Germany.

   Hrotsvit's sources for the legends of both Theophilus and Basilius are pious stories from the fifth and sixth centuries with even earlier roots.[7] According to Maximilian Rudwin, the devil compact has origins deep in antiquity. Of Hrotsvit's version Rudwin says:

The first poetical treatment given the Theophilus legend was the play [*sic*] in Latin hexameters *Lapsus et conversia Theophili vice-domini* written in the tenth century by the first original German woman poet and dramatist, Hroswitha or Roswitha, the learned abbess of the Benedictine convent of Gandersheim.[8]

Hrotsvit's contribution was more than a poetical treatment, however. Originally cautionary tales about dealings with the devil, *Theophilus* and *Basilius* become in her hands explorations of the Christian response to evil.

According to M. Gonsalva Wiegand, the version of the life of the apocryphal saint Theophilus that Hrotsvit used is the translation from the Greek by Paul the Deacon, *Miraculum S. Marie de Theophilo Poenitente, interprete Paulo Diacono Neapoleos, Ex. III Codicibus Mes,* and her probable source for *Basilius* is a ninth-century *Vita* by the subdeacon Ursus.[9] The basic story in both legends is a simple one: a protagonist who desires a seemingly unattainable prize, agrees to deny Christ and give his soul to the devil in return for help achieving that prize. Eventually overcome by remorse – or fear – he calls on a holy figure who outwits the devil and cancels the agreement. To this story Hrotsvit adds not just metrical form but also a wealth of psychological insight and a good deal of perceptive detail. In *Theophilus* complexity of character and scriptural allusions enrich the story. We learn that from his baptism Theophilus was marked out for divine service by his intellect as well as his virtue; he is 'puer pius' (14) whose parents, recognizing these qualities, entrust his education to a certain bishop.

As he advances to the office of vicar, he earns the love of the people. The narrator concludes the second verse paragraph of the poem by saying that because of his humility and limitless generosity to widows, orphans, and wandering indigents, 'ipsum ceu dulcem venerantur amando parentem' (28), 'in love they cherished him as a dear father' (Wiegand, 159). It is no wonder that his flock urge his appointment to succeed the bishop he had served so admirably. Continuing in his unassuming persona he eschews the office, claiming to be 'Infectum viciis sese dicens fore multis/ Non aptum sancto Christi populo dominari' (50–1), 'infected with many vices and...not fit to rule the holy people of Christ' (Wiegand, 161). When the new bishop strips him of his role as vicar this paragon even rejoices:

> Istec sed fragilis tolerans patienter honoris
> Damnum tristiciam pellit de pectore cunctam
> Gaudebatque satis sese iam posse vacare
> Tanto liberius studio Christi famulatus,
> Quanto curarum securus erat variarum.   (62–6)

But Theophilus, patiently bearing the loss of that precarious dignity, expelled from his heart all sadness and even rejoiced that, just as he had been relieved of manifold duties, so he could now be proportionately more free to labor in the service of Christ. (Wiegand, 161)

His humble posture is short-lived, however, for in the next sentence the narrator reports:

Cuius mox mentem detestatur pacientem
Tocius humani generis sevissimus hostis
Et, qua primates decepit fraude parentes,
Hac huiusce viri pulsat penetralia iusti
Adducens eius fragili sepissime menti
Blanda potestatis delectamenta prioris
Despectusque gravem facti nuperrime sortem.
Nec laqueos harum retraxerat insidiarum,
Donec captivum Christi duxit sibi servum;
Nec mora, vir fortis, vita meritisque celebris,
Mentis virtutem demens abiecerat omnem
Nec temptamentis studuit restare nefandis,
Sed victus cessit mentisque dolore tabescit;
Quique prius plebi sprevit princeps dominari,
Affectat iuris pompas nunc inferioris.   (67–81)

But the savage enemy of all humankind soon came to loathe this patient soul, and with that same cunning with which he had erstwhile deceived our first parents, he assailed the inmost heart of this just man, bringing before his frail mind very often the quiet delights of his former position of influence and the heavy lot of the loss of prestige he had lately sustained. Neither did he take away these traps of treachery until finally he had made the servant of Christ his captive. And without delay that excellent man, renowned for a life of virtue, in mad folly had rejected all virtue and made no effort to resist abominable temptation; but vanquished he withdrew from the conflict and languished in grief of soul. And he, who had heretofore spurned to rule the people as a prince, now affected the parade of a lesser power. (Wiegand, 163)

The very saintliness that has marked the story thus far makes the shock of his fall more devastating; at the same time, the rhetoric and syntax, especially the *nec* clauses in the account of his fall to the treachery of the devil, emphasize his human frailty and the devil's cunning. He becomes a 'seductus misellus' (82), 'perverted wretch' (Wiegand, 163) who grovels as he pleads with a 'perversum Hebreum' (84), 'wicked Jew' (Wiegand, 163) to restore his rank. Then, the assignation with the devil carried out and the contract signed, Theophilus is returned to office.

But just as Satan prompted the envy that nets him a willing captive, God wills that the soul be saved:

> Tandem caelestis pietas inmensa parentis,
> Qui numquam cupit interitum mortemque reorum,
> Sed mage conversis lętam concedere vitam,
> Condoluit facti meritum periisse benigni,
> Quo quondam stabili fulsit celeberrimus orbi
> Istec sollicitans omnes clementer egentes;
> Moreque divino pietas eadem veneranda
> Concutit errantem digna formidine mentem.   (149–56)

At length, the inexhaustible Goodness of the Heavenly Father, Who never desires the destruction and death of the wicked but rather to grant a happy life to them upon their conversion, was grieved that the merit of so charitable a life had been lost, wherewith that man had once shone so brightly in the stable earth, being so mercifully solicitous for all the wretched; and thus in manner divine that Adorable Goodness touched this erring soul with a just fear. (Wiegand, 167)

Prompted by this fear Theophilus petitions the Virgin, who, after gentle scolding and making confession a condition of forgiveness, responds that he will be restored to grace. The Virgin reminds him:

> 'Quamvis sis gravibus viciis nimium maculatus,
> Attamen, ut monui, dominum non sperne fateri,
> Est quia factus homo nostri solummodo causa,
> Ut spem conversis venię praeberet habende.'   (292–5)

'Although thou art stained with exceedingly grievous sins, nevertheless, as I have admonished, do not spurn to confess the Lord, because He was made Man solely for our sakes, that He might afford a hope of winning pardon to such as were converted.' (Wiegand, 175)

Her intercession wins him release from his contract and a holy death and at the same time recalls for the reader the source of all salvation.

In addition to the hyperbolic descriptions of the vicar's sanctity and of his encounters with both diabolic and heavenly figures, *Theophilus* contains a number of scriptural and liturgical allusions, suggesting that it is to be read on more than one level. Like the Child Jesus in the Temple, he shows uncommon wisdom and virtue in infancy (Luke 2:41–52). Further, on his repentance, Theophilus spends forty days in fasting and prayer as did Jesus in the desert (Matt. 4:1–11, Mark 1:12–13, Luke 4:1–13). In pleading with the Virgin for pardon, he cites the forgiveness of the Ninevites and of David, and the denial of Christ for which Peter was forgiven (Matt. 26:69–75, Mark 14:66–72, Luke 22:31–4, 54–62, John 18:15–27). And finally, Mary appears to him in a dream, the traditional vehicle of divine messages.

At the dramatic conclusion of the scene, upon the destruction of the contract, he makes a public confession at which moment, in transfiguration,

> ... miro splendore refulsit
> Instar surgentis Phębi facies vicedomni,
> Quo mentis splendor lucens anime quoque candor
> Eius per faciem monstraretur rutilantem.   (423–6)

> the features of the vicar shone with a wondrous splendor as of the rising sun, so that the radiant beauty of his soul and the purity of his heart were made manifest through his beaming countenance. (Wiegand, 183)

This view of a transformed Theophilus echoes the description of Jesus' transfigured face in Matt. 17.2 (Vulgate): 'Et transfiguratus est ante eos; et resplenduit facies eius sicut sol, vestimenta autem eius facta sunt alba sicut lux.' By thus manifesting 'the beauty of his soul and the purity of his heart,' the changed appearance suggests that he has returned to the Christlike state of grace he had deserted by dealing with the devil.

Basilius at first blush is so like *Theophilus* in plot that the two might almost be taken as the same story with names and places changed. A servant of the noble Proterius is so maddened by love for his master's daughter that he seeks out the devil's aid, enters into a pact, and is ultimately released from it through the intercession of St Basilius. Even this brief summary, however, makes obvious some key differences: the social status of the signers, the disparate nature of their requests, and the intercession by a heavenly figure in *Theophilus* and by earthly figures in *Basilius*. Character development in *Basilius* is sketchy and the scriptural allusions that mark *Theophilus* are missing here. On the other hand, in

Basilius Hrotsvit examines the questionable legality of the devil pact at some length as David Day has so convincingly shown in his essay in this volume. Even more marked in *Basilius* is its concentration on the physical. While *Theophilus* is concerned with spiritual offences, *Basilius* deals with sins of the flesh.

Both legends share the assistance of a magician/intermediary who leads the petitioners through dark passages to the devil's council, and in both Satan insists on a written document. There is some irony in the requirement of such a written contract since, according to the devil, Christians have a record of failing to keep their promises to him. When the devil in *Basilius* – 'inventor sceleris cunctę quoque fraudis' (74), 'author of all fraud and of all crime and feud' (Wilson, *Florilegium*, 23) – reads the message from the magician interceding for the servant, he says:

'Numquam christicole permansistis mihi fidi,
Sed, mox ut vestrum complevi velle iocundum
Protinus ad vestrum fugistis denique Christum
Me detestando penitus post munera tanta
Credentes talis certe Christum pietatis,
Ut veniam nulli vellet tardare petenti
Reddere conversum mihimet nec post scelus ullum.'   (83–9)

'Never do you stay faithful to me, you Christians,
But as soon as I ordain your desire to obtain,
Then promptly you flee and to Christ take your plea.
Me you desire and scorn after the gifts I had borne,
And full trust you embrace in Christ's mercy and grace,
Because He's willing to grant to those who repent
His forgiveness sublime regardless of the crime.'   (Wilson, *Florilegium*, 23)

Yet he seems to believe a written contract will protect him from the Christians' inconstancy: '"Hincque tuis manibus scriptam mihi porrige caram:/ Ostendamque citus, quantum possit mea virtus"' (94–5), '"Give me then a note by your own hand wrought/ And I shall quickly act to show my might's effect"' (Wilson, *Florilegium*, 23).

Further, not only does *Basilius* lack the detailed character analysis of *Theophilis*, but the central figure is nameless and, except for the pact, does little to advance the action. It is the noble daughter he has married who insists, on hearing the story, that her husband seek the aid of St Basil to revoke the contract that he had 'scribebat ... ridenti pectore' (97), 'signed with happy heart' (Wilson, *Florilegium*, 23). He has none of the strength of spirit that propels Theophilus through his rise, fall, and return to grace. He is 'nimis infelix' (37), a 'miserable swain' (Wilson, *Florilegium*, 22), a 'lascivious servant,' distinguished only by the lust, the 'mad desire,' that leads him to seek the devil. In spite of a forty-day period of torment by demons, analogous to the forty days of penance imposed on Theophilus as well as the forty days of Jesus' fast in the desert, the servant is not required to make a public confession and St Basil regains the written agreement handily.

Key elements in both legends are the frustration of characters seeking a prize and their turning in desperation to the devil to achieve it. Yet, the signatories of the two pacts are distinctly different. In fact we have two characters representing opposite ends of the scale both socially and morally: the holy and revered vicar and the lustful servant. And what of the nature of their sins? Are they to be equated or are they similarly distinct? Wilson says, 'In the legends men sell their immortal souls to the devil for earthly gain.'[10] But is the nature of that gain the same for both, and is it related to their essential characters as defined above?

When all of Theophilus's honour and respectability are reversed after the death of his teacher, the bishop, he is consumed by envious anger inspired by the fiend. But in *Basilius*, the devil's malice is not directed at the impassioned but ineffectual servant; it is aimed at thwarting Proterius's plan to enclose his daughter in the cloister. The suitor is a hapless dupe who is selected by the devil as his pawn and therefore 'dementer amore puelle' (36), is caused 'to burn in mad desire' (Wilson, *Florilegium*, 21). The exact nature of the sin is more difficult to pin down – attempted seduction or signing the pact – but it certainly has a great deal to do with lust.

The major difference between the two sinners – Theophilus and the nameless servant – and their relative importance in the two stories is best defined, then, in terms of the nature of their sins. That of Theophilus is a sin of the intellect and of the spirit, motivated by pride and anger, while the servant's is solely one of the flesh. We must ask whether Hrotsvit is making a statement here about degrees of culpability. Wiegand, who believes this to be the case, writes, 'Theophilus is not only a philosopher but a servant of God, who has apparently mounted high the ladder of perfection; his fall is therefore more lamentable and his conversion more delightful.'[11]

We know that Hrotsvit is making a significant choice in positioning these two legends dealing with the nature of sin in the centre of the sequence. Dronke, comparing the tales with the plays *Mary the Niece of Abraham* and *The Conversion of Thaïs*, notes that the theme of an individual who 'sinks to the depths by renouncing God, and rises again at last, through repentance, to win heavenly bliss...meant so much to Hrotsvitha that she illustrated it, with the help of deliberate echoes and analogies, in four different ways.'[12]

If the theme's central position underscores its importance, the legends of martyrdom that precede and follow *Theophilus* and *Basilius* are worth examining for the light they shed on the relative seriousness of the sins. The first of this series of four is the story of Pelagius, the telling of which shows Hrotsvit playing with 'certain conventions of a martyrdom tale.'[13] The pure virgin in this case is a male whose virtue is assailed by a homosexual tyrant. And the sin on which the tale is centred is, of course, the lust of the tyrant, not the sin of pride that marks the tale of Theophilus that follows. This contrast is reversed in the next pair; at the other end of the four, after *Basilius* and its 'burning passion,' is the legend of the saintly Dionysius, who suffers for his learning from those who envy his intellect. Rather than throwing light on the tales that precede and follow, these four legends seem to demonstrate the destructive – and demonic – nature of all sin.

We find a curious pattern here of *fleshly sin – spiritual sin/fleshly sin – spiritual sin*. If, as seems highly probable from Hrotsvit's ordering of the plays and legends, these juxtapositions are intentional, both kinds of sin are not only of equal importance but are in some way related. These four legends thus demonstrate the interconnected nature of all sin, and ways in which it, and its diabolic source, can be overcome through repentance.

The dramatic reversals also suggest a further dimension of Hrotsvit's understanding of God's grace for those who show true repentance. In later versions of the devil pact, notably Marlowe's *Dr. Faustus*, the maker of the pact seems unable to achieve penitence once his soul has been consigned to the devil because despair is a consequence of entering into the pact. But in Hrotsvit's two legends repentance can be and is achieved after the fulfilment of certain requirements. The first of these is the presence of an intercessor. In *Basilius* Christ himself begins the chain of events that ultimately results in the servant's redemption. Hrotsvit writes:

Tali coniugio Satane cum fraude peracto
Condoluit Christus mundi salvator amandus,
Quos pius effusa salvavit sanguinis unda,

Hostis sub diri vinclis captos retineri;
Et placet auxilium lapsis praestare benignum.   (138–42)

When the marriage vows were taken, so fraught by the fraud of Satan,
Then it pained Christ the King who salvation to us did bring,
That those whom He had saved and with His precious blood redeemed
Should in the enemy's chain as captives still remain.
It pleases Christ to aid even those renegade.   (Wilson, *Florilegium*, 24)

Although Hrotsvit specifies that it pleases Christ to aid the fallen, it is the wife who seeks aid for her husband from the saintly Basilius, after she learns that her husband is not behaving like a good Christian. Thus the legend sets the fraud of Satan up in opposition to Christ's mercy but within that context requires and allows humans who have fallen to participate actively in their salvation. Therefore, the offender must undergo soul-searching contrition followed by confession. Given the gravity of the offences in these stories, this is a relatively easy escape from the jaws of hell. Again, we have a commentary on the nature of sin: it is neither the degree of depravity nor of penitence that determines the fate of the soul, but, as Hrotsvit specifies in the prologue that precedes *Basilius*, introducing the second set of legends:

Qui velit exemplum veniae comprendere certum
Necnon larga dei pietatis munera magni,
Pectore versiculos submisso perlegat istos
...
Sed mage cęlestem Christi laudet pietatem,
Qui non vult digna peccantes perdere poena,
Sed plus perpetuę conversos reddere vitę: (*Primus Pars, Prologus II*, 7–14)

He who wants to learn and by sure proof discern
God's mercy and the Lord's many and great rewards,
With humble heart and meek, these small verses should read.
...
But, rather should he praise the Lord's celestial grace
Who wants not that in due pain sinners their punishment gain,
But eternal life He grants to the sinner who repents.
                                        (Wilson, *Florilegium*, 21)

It is clear that Hrotsvit sees God's redemptive mercy as boundless for those who repent. She also appears to draw little distinction between sins of the flesh and those of the spirit in terms of severity as the framing stories suggest. Above all, she does not place much value on the legality of the pact itself, which can be invalidated without serious opposition from the devil. Rather she is intent on extolling God's gift of redemption promised freely to all sinners.

It turns out that, after all, Hrotsvit is little concerned with characterizing the devil, although she accepts implicitly his role as source of all evil and draws freely on the conventional epithets. Neither is she much concerned with the misuses of power that Marlowe and Goethe will later dramatize in their work.[14] Her real purpose is to demonstrate the workings of divine mercy through the theme of the fallen restored to grace. Her devil is a plotter – he enlists the servant to confute Proterius's plan for his daughter. He is a sceptic – he refuses to believe a human soul will keep a promise that is not in writing. He is a tempter – he kindles rage and envy in Theophilus and lust in Proterius's servant. But in all these he remains an abstraction, a useful device through which Hrotsvit can pursue her genuine object: to show that humanity has been redeemed and that there is always hope for a sinner.

NOTES

1 See Dronke, 'Hrotsvitha,' in *Women Writers of the Middle Ages*, 68–73.
2 Critics agree that the earliest treatment of the Harrowing of Hell appears in the *Gospel of Nicodemus*, dating from the second or third century. See Hennecke and Schneemelcher, 'Christ's Descent into Hell,' and Marx, *The Devil's Rights*. One important example is the *Processus Satanae*, the origin of which can be traced to the fifth-century Armenian bishop Eznik, whose 'Against the Sects' is a refutation of Marcionism. An English translation of Eznik's account is found in the entry for 'Marcionism' in the *Encyclopaedia of Religion and Ethics*. R. von Stintzing, *Geschichte der popularen Literatur der romischkanonischen Rechts in Deutschlan*, lists sixteen German and Latin manuscripts and editions of the *Processus*, but others exist in several languages. Elsewhere in this volume David Day discusses Hrotsvit's probable knowledge of the law.
3 Among the many patristic characterizations of the devil as a liar and beguiler are those in Gregory the Great's commentary on the Book of Job, *Moralium Lib.* IV, 2 (*PL* 76, 646), Tertullian (*PL* 1, 1256–7), Gregory of Nyssa (*PG* 44, 1192), and Cassian (*PL* 125, 767–70). The latter two refer to the devil as 'the father of lies.' The inability of the devil to comprehend God's plan for salvation, cited by Bede among many of the Fathers, be-

comes the basis for a number of comic literary portrayals. See, for example, *Matthei Evangelium Expositio* 4.2.1 (*PL* 94.192).

4 See Robert Talbot's paper, 'Hrotsvit's Dramas: Is There a Roman in These Texts?' in this volume, 148–9.

5 Although lacking the malice of most devils, the manipulators of Terence's plays share such characteristics as tempting, lying, and deceits that involve disguise, a form of shape-shifting. Among them are Phormio (*Phormio* 1.2), who plots to outwit Demipho; Syrus, who lies to Demea (*Adelphoi* 3.3, 4.2), and Parmeno, who in *The Eunuch* instigates Chaerea to disguise himself (2.3). The Theophilus story, widely circulated after Hrostvit's treatment, originated in Greece. Two Greek manuscripts are known, one of which purports to be an eyewitness account: Coislin 283 in the Bibliothéque Nationale, possibly eleventh century, and an earlier, undated version, Palat. Gr. 3 in the Nationalbibliothek, Vienna. Less well known, the story of St Basil was circulated by Jerome in the sixth century.

6 Dronke, *Women Writers of the Middle Ages*, points out that Terence, in fact, 'presented with imaginative sympathy a number of young women who were innocent victims' (72).

7 Russell, *Lucifer: The Devil in the Middle Ages*, 80.

8 Rudwin, *The Devil in Legend and Literature*, 182.

9 Wiegand, 'The Non-Dramatic Works of Hrosvitha,' 185, 209.

10 Wilson, *Hrotsvit of Gandersheim: The Ethics of Authorial Stance*, 19.

11 Wiegand, 'The Non-Dramatic Works of Hrosvitha,' 187.

12 Dronke, *Women Writers of the Middle Ages*, 60.

13 Petroff, *Medieval Women's Visionary Literature*, 89.

14 Although no direct connection between Hrotsvit's treatment of devil pacts and the later Faust stories has been determined, at least two later versions of Theophilus circulated: that of the monk Marbodus and that of the trouvére Rutebeuf. Wiegand calls Hrotsvit's legend 'a precursor' of the Faust tales ('Non-Dramatic Works of Hrotsvitha,' 186). The theme of the Virgin Mary as intercessor was common throughout the Middle Ages, as Beverly Boyd demonstrates in her translation of Middle English Marian legends. She says the '*Libri miraculorum* of Gregory of Tours (ca. 538–ca. 594) are the earliest writings in the West which contain miracles of the Virgin' (*The Middle English Miracles of the Virgin*, 3). Hrostvit's are among early versions of legends in which the Virgin outwits the devil.

Hrotsvit's Latin Drama *Gallicanus* and the Old English Epic *Elene*: Intercultural Founding Narratives of a Feminized Church

JANE CHANCE

According to Bede's *Historia ecclesiastica* (731), women played a crucial role in the founding of the English church by means of their endowment of women's houses and their conversion of pagan Germanic husbands.[1] Recent scholarship on Anglo-Saxon women, particularly by Clare A. Lees and Gillian R. Overing in *Double Agents: Women and Clerical Culture in Anglo-Saxon England* (2001), has demonstrated the 'patriarchal maternity' of the early church, a church nurtured through the religious faith of women leaders and educators as agents, but with their voices recorded by male clerics.[2] For example, Hild, as abbess or mother, oversaw at Streonaeshalch or Whitby what early scholar Frank Stenton termed a 'nursery of bishops' from which five bishops emerged, but Bede's account of her tenure keeps her in the background while foregrounding the story of the illiterate shepherd Caedmon. Lees and Overing's discussion of Hild in Bede, along with Ælfflæd and Æðelþryþ, reveals that 'The female agent is a double agent: she moves in this 'real' world of Anglo-Saxon society, but we can only perceive her in that penumbral, nether world to which she is relegated by clerical culture.'[3] That the female agent did have power in the 'real' Anglo-Saxon world is the position taken by Mary Dockray-Miller, in *Motherhood and Mothering in Anglo-Saxon England* (2000), in which she singles out networks of maternal genealogies of historical women and their daughters, including eighth-century Kentish abbess Mildrið and Mercian Æðelflæd.[4]

In Saxon Germany in the tenth century, unlike Anglo-Saxon England, one female agent, at least, writes her own chronicles and testaments: the plays and other writings of the female canon Hrotsvit of Gandersheim (ca. 935–ca. 1000) demonstrate the importance of women in the founding of the early church. But even so, Hrotsvit masks this importance with her celebration of what looks like patriarchal convention, that is, the founding of the early church through apostolic genealogy – most specifically, the conversion to Christianity of the Roman emperor's general, Gallicanus, through Saints Paul and John and their subsequent martyrdom, in a play entitled *Gallicanus*. And – deferring once more to patristic culture – she writes in the father tongue of Latin, rather than in the mother tongue of the vernacular.

Familiar with Latin traditions and genres,[5] including the medieval monastic, historiographic, and hagiographic,[6] Hrotsvit is equally familiar with the classical Latin drama in its style, vocabulary, and mode.[7] The Latin tradition offers examples of monks and male martyrs upon whom Hrotsvit draws, according to early Hrotsvit critics like Sandro Sticca: the life of the martyr was understood as the perfect example of the life of Christ, often written in martial terms to express the role of the *miles Christi* and, therefore, focused upon monastic and hermetic contexts as the site in which such examples are most likely to occur.[8] This tradition is mirrored in the titles of Hrotsvit's plays as provided by her first editor, focused as they are upon male *reclusi*, holy apostles, and martyrs, in particular, *Abraham, Paphnutius* (or *Pafnutius*), *Gallicanus,* and *Callimachus*.[9] Accordingly, as sources and backgrounds for her own legends but also, to a lesser extent, for her plays, especially *Gallicanus*, Hrotsvit scholars – chiefly, Elizabeth Petroff writing on holy virginity – have appropriately focused on Latin saints' lives and legends.[10] The Latin legends of Gallicanus, John, and Paul relay the story of the conversions to Christianity of all three pagans, Constantia, daughter of the Roman emperor Constantine, and his general, Gallicanus, and were said to have been written by the Roman Terentianus (Terence?).[11]

What has received relatively little notice among Hrotsvit scholars is what appears to be the intertextuality of works in the vernacular with her Latin works, specifically some significant narrative, thematic, structural, and symbolic parallels found in her plays. This idea of vernacular intertextuality in Hrotsvit's works was introduced as long ago as 1939 by Fritz Preissl, who compared the concept of the *miles Christianus* in both Hrotsvit's Latin works and the Saxon *Ruodlieb*.[12] But there also exist correlations between Hrotsvit's plays, particularly the little-read or performed *Gallicanus*, or, as the title appears in full, *Conversio Gallicani principis militię*, and the ninth-to-tenth-century Old English saint's life and religious epic *Elene*, thought to have been written by Cynewulf.[13]

This similarity has been noted in passing recently by Joan M. Ferrante, a clue I would like to develop in this essay: she declares, speaking about one of the male characters in *Gallicanus*, 'Constantine is not only the father of the heroine, he is also the son of a major figure in religious lore, Helena, who found the cross' – and (I would add to Ferrante's statement) hero of the Anglo-Saxon *Elene*.[14]

While both *Elene* and *Gallicanus*, as founding narratives, appear to focus on the conversion of men – one is situated in early England and one in Rome – in each case such conversion takes place through and depends upon female agency, mastery, and leadership. The putative subject of *Elene*, Constantine the Great, the Roman emperor of the West (306–37), receives the vision of the True Cross (*epiphania*) and thereafter converts (*conversio*) from paganism to Christianity during the night in 312 before a famous battle; his mother, Elene, or Helena, is responsible for later finding the True Cross in Jerusalem (*epiphania*) and converting Judas Quiriacus from Judaism to Christianity (*conversio*) through what she has learned about Christianity. And in *Gallicanus*, as Ferrante declares, 'Daughters precede their fathers in religion in this play, Gallicanus's daughters in their conversion, Constantina [*sic*] in her devotion.'[15] These two roughly contemporary literary works, one Anglo-Saxon and one Saxon, form a complementary whole to illustrate the feminization of the early church, that is, reliance upon female rather than male agency (monastic and saintly) and upon process as essentially spiritual rather than martial.

Although *Gallicanus* has been neglected in recent scholarship, it is the first to appear in the manuscript in which Hrotsvit's plays are contained, as if to focus attention on its significance as an introduction to the remaining plays. The drama represents a founding narrative both for the church and for the dramatist's own developing interest in sacred historiography as a working out of Providence. Founding narratives generally create stories in which the identity of a personified concept, abstraction, or institution is constructed as if a character. Founding narratives were especially popular in early Anglo-Saxon culture – just as Bede's *Historia ecclesiastica* established the English church as a monolithic and powerful agent by disseminating its founding principles and its mission as a builder of monastic communities, so also the *Anglo-Saxon Chronicle* established the nation as an entity by means of the adversaries it confronted in battles. Founding narratives are also an important part of Hrotsvit's corpus – *Primordia Coenobii Gandeshemensis* and *Gesta Ottonis* celebrate the founding of a monastery (Gandersheim Abbey up to 918 and the death of Abbess Christina) and of a nation (the epic of the Ottonian Empire in the tenth century as ruled by a Christian ruler). About the Saxon dynasty Katharina Wilson notes, 'The two epics, *Gesta Ottonis Imperatori* and *Primordia,* concern members of the Saxon dynasty in their roles as secular rulers (*Gesta*) and religious rulers/benefactors (*Primordia*).'[16]

Though less often thought of as founding narratives, both the Old English *Elene* and Hrotsvit's *Gallicanus,* like Bede's eighth-century *Historia ecclesiastica,* also focus on the founding of the early Christian church, whether it takes place in Anglo-Saxon England or in Europe. They all do so through central epiphanic and historical events, specifically, *conversio* (conversion to Christianity) and *epiphania* (manifestation of Christ). Overall, as if compressing the whole of Bede's early history into the symbolic etiology of the Anglo-Saxon church, the poem *Elene* celebrates the founding of a specifically *English* church: in this religious epic Constantine has been crowned emperor at York in the year 306, and his mother, Elene (Helena), who finds the True Cross, is British-born.[17] *Gallicanus,* the only Hrotsvit play named for a male character both by modern editors and by Hrotsvit, is connected to *Elene* because the central character Gallicanus, a Roman general of Constantine the Great, seeks the hand in marriage of the emperor's daughter Constantia. Through the intervention of Constantia's advisors John and Paul, Gallicanus converts to Christianity in a scene that directly parallels Constantine's legendary conversion on the battlefield. As in *Elene,* both *conversio* and *epiphania* are significant elements in the first part of Hrotsvit's play. The eventual martyrdom of Gallicanus, John, and Paul in part two of the play, in *imitatio* of Christ's Crucifixion, results from their resistance to the pagan emperor Julian the Apostate and his emissaries.

In addition, *Gallicanus* demonstrates what Monique Wittig, writing on gender, defines as 'crabbed' moments in which gender difference marks the intrusion of the feminine.[18] Almost all of Hrotsvit's plays centre on decision-making, either by pagan male military and government leaders or by Christian monks or hermits, about threats to the nation or to the national religion. And in almost all the plays the characters who threaten to subvert the authority of such male leaders and advisers[19] or the hegemony of a pagan state or religion are wise holy women or allegorical personifications. Through this subversion and resistance, the wise Christian women or female figures succeed in appropriating the position of spiritual leader and therefore in displacing the hegemony of the putative male authority. As virgins like Constantia or chaste married women like

Drusiana, by means of their Christian faith (which correlates with the fact of their virginity or chastity) they succeed in resisting either marriage or seduction.[20] Their success depends upon the conversion of their male antagonists to Christianity, a victory preceded – not by marriage to these men (like the queens in Bede's *Historia ecclesiastica* or in the *Anglo-Saxon Chronicle*) – but by the men's willingness to be instructed by these women. When Constantia discusses Gallicanus's marriage proposal with her father, paradoxically, her Christian faith is so firm that she agrees to a betrothal, relying on God to preserve her chastity through the conversion of Gallicanus. Thus she replies to her father's question without anxiety about what he is to do when Gallicanus returns from war to marry Constantia: 'Reor omnipatrem prius esse invocandum · quo ab huiusmodi intentione Gallicani revocet animum' (I.II.5), 'I believe that we must pray as is meet/ and God the Father of all entreat/ that He change Gallicanus's mind' (Wilson, *Plays*, 13). In other words, Constantia is reminding Constantine to have faith that, with God's help, the problem will cease to be irresoluble. Furthermore, Constantia's advice seems closely related to her statement immediately before, 'Nunc autem nullus relinquitur locus mesticię pręsumenti de domini pietate' (I.II.4), 'But in the hearts of those who rely on God's grace,/ despair and sadness have no valid place' (Wilson, *Plays*, 13). Significantly, motivated by her faith in God, she creates a situation in which education can and does lead to conversion and in doing so creates the means for God's grace to do its work.

Gender difference marks Hrotsvit's own authority as playwright, engaged as she is in redefining the mode of the founding Christian narrative in the parallel literary text of *Elene*. Such feminization takes place by means of Hrotsvit's emphasis upon conversion and education as apostolic and epiphanic – both superficially patriarchal in nature, but deployed in *Gallicanus* against masculine martial cunning and trickery. Constantia advises pretence as a way to resolve Constantine's dilemma, the conflict between his responsibilities as an emperor (to reward his military leaders appropriately) and as a Christian (to honour his daughter's vow of chastity). She says:

Simula prudenter peracta expedicione · ipsius votis te satisfacturum esse ·
Et ut meum concordari credat velle · suade · quo suas interim filias ·
Atticam · ac Artemiam · velut pro solidandi pignore amoris mecum mansum
ire · meosque primicerios · Iohannem et Paulum · secum faciat iter arreptum
ire · (I.II.5)

Pretend prudently that you will fulfill his wish after he wins the war, and, so that he believes that I agreed to his plea,/ suggest to him that as pledges of his love, he let his two daughters Attica and Artemia live at court with me,/ while he accepts my chamberlains, John and Paul, in his retinue. (Wilson, *Plays*, 13)

The main function of the pretence is to gain time and to use that time to educate/convert Gallicanus's daughters and Gallicanus himself.[21]

In addition to having Constantia send her advisors to educate and convert Gallicanus, Hrotsvit also introduces details to the battlefield conversion of Gallicanus to highlight the parallel conversion of Constantine – and thus of the Roman Empire – in *Elene* and that at the same time rewrite that foundation story in subtle ways. Gallicanus, caught as Constantine had been before his conversion, in the middle of a seemingly hopeless battle (with the Scythians), and seeing his outnumbered forces abandon him in flight, converts to Christianity as instructed by the humble Christians Paul and John. The moment Gallicanus promises to convert, his enemies lose all their strength and courage and have no choice but to surrender:

Johannes   Fac votum deo cęli · te christianum fieri ·et vinces ·
Gallicanus   Voveo · et opere implebo ·
Hostes   Heus rex Bradan · sperande fortuna victorię alludit nos · en
   dextrę languescunt · vires fatiscunt · sed et inconstantia pectoris · cogit
   nos discedere ab armis ·   (I.IX.2)

John   Promise to God to become a Christian and you shall win victory's
   splendor.
Gallicanus: I promise and I shall put my promise into action.
Enemy   Alas, King Bradan, the good fortune of hoped-for victory eludes
   us; our arms grow lame, our strength tires,/ our courage expires/ and
   we are forced to lay down our weapons.   (Wilson, *Plays*, 20)

Later, describing the outcome of the war, Gallicanus adds details about his conversion and its accompanying epiphany not included in the battle scene enacted on stage. In this account, the conversion of Gallicanus, like that of Constantine, is associated with a vision of the Cross, but the Cross is carried by Christ himself, armed for battle. Christ proceeds to lead a 'cęlestis milicia' (I.XII.7), 'heavenly brigade' (Wilson, *Plays*, 24), now including Gallicanus, as if in anticipation of the later

Franciscan mission. After relaying the utter failure of sacrifices to pagan gods, Gallicanus recounts the vision of divine grace after he vowed to convert to Christianity:

> *Gallicanus*   ... · ut os ad vovendum aperui · cęleste iuvamen sensi ·
> *Constantinus* Quo pacto?
> *Gallicanus*   Apparuit mihi iuvenis procerę magnitudinis · crucem ferens
>   in humeris et praecepit · ut stricto mucrone illum sequerer ·
> *Constantinus* Quisquis ille erat · cęlitus missus fuerat ·
> *Gallicanus*   Comprobavi · nec mora astiterunt mihi a dextra levaque
>   milites armati · quorum vultum minime agnovi promittentes auxilium
>   sui ·   (I.XII.6–7)

> *Gallicanus*   ... I saw heavenly aid approach as soon as I opened my mouth
>   to take the vow./
> *Constantinus* How?/
> *Gallicanus*   A tall youth appeared bearing a cross on His shoulders and
>   ordered me to follow Him with my drawn sword.
> *Constantinus* Whoever He was, Heaven must have sent Him.
> *Gallicanus*   I am sure of that. Without any delay,/ there appeared an
>   armed military array,/ soldiers whose faces I didn't know, but who
>   promised me their aid./   (Wilson, *Plays*, 24)

Unlike Constantine, Gallicanus converts because of the apostolic mission of Ecclesia, as enacted by Constantia and her servants. The community of the church draws him in – educates and converts him – and in doing so allows him to have the immediate and visionary spiritual experience.

In the Anglo-Saxon epic *Elene*, the conversion of Constantine provides the pretext for the real drama, his mother Elene's finding of the True Cross and her own teaching and subsequent conversion of Judas, who becomes 'Cyriacus' (Saint Judas Quiriacus, a character referred to in the Anglo-Saxon as *ae haelendes*, 'the Savior's faith').[22] So also, in Hrosvit's play *Gallicanus*, the conversion of Constantine provides the pretext for the real drama, Constantia and her servants' teaching and the conversion of Gallicanus and his pagan daughters, followed by his life of chastity and eventual martyrdom as a kind of reward. The remarkably similar narrative frames of the double conversion in each work bracket the epiphanic moment. This moment is the finding of the True Cross in *Elene* (a memorialization of the historical fact of Christ's Crucifixion and thus his signal Resurrection and Redemption of humankind) and in *Gallicanus* the vision of an armed and insistent Christ (a symbolic re-enactment of the mission of Christ's disciples and the spiritual ministry of the church, Ecclesia). In both cases the seeming threat of physical annihilation in battle spurs the general or commander, in a gesture of real humility, to call upon a higher power for help, which results in a double victory, military and spiritual. In both cases, the real threat is spiritual annihilation by a diabolic and vicious adversary, whether Jew or pagan (Judas; Julian the Apostate), whose power is subverted by the Christian virtue of constancy (Constancia), personified in the mother, Elene, in the one work, and in the daughter, Constantia, in the other.[23]

In each work, however, it is not military operations but dialogue and debate with a female agent and her education of a convert to encourage faith and virtue that undermine the foe. In each work, the female agent – whether mother or daughter of Constantine – as ancillary to a male leader – whether Constantine or Gallicanus – accomplishes her mission successfully in both the spiritual and military spheres. In the one, Elene questions Judas and in the process educates (converts) him to Christianity, so that he might lead her to the True Cross, perform the miracle of the raising to life of a lifeless corpse upon the True Cross, successfully battle with the devil, earn his renaming as Cyriacus and his bishopric, and discover the nails of the True Cross:

> Hæfde Ciriacus
> eall gefylled,   swa him seo æðele bebead,
> wifes willan ...
>   ... wuldres gefylled
> cwene willa.[24]

Cyriacus had wholly accomplished the woman's will, as the noble one had commanded him ... The queen's desire was gloriously fulfilled.[25]

Her military strategy emerges in her navigational skill on sea and land: 'Ne hyrde ic sið ne ær/ on egstreame idese lædan,/ on merestræte, mægen fægerre,'[26] 'I have not heard before or since of a woman leading a fairer company on the ocean stream, on the sea road';[27] as 'sio guðcwen,' 'the warlike queen,' Elene searches for 'Iudeas/ ofer herefeldas heape gecoste/ lindwigendra land gesohte,/ secga þreate,' 'the land of the Jews across fields of battle with a trusty band of shield-warriors, with a troop of heroes.'[28] In Jerusalem, in order to evoke knowledge of the place of

Calvary, Elene spars verbally with the Jews, with the wisest men, and, finally, with Judas, in a battle that becomes physical – in his imprisonment and starvation – but ends in the victory of his spiritual conversion to Christianity. Marking his conversion by a change in name (Judas to Cyriacus), like Saul to Paul, *Elene* also shows him taking up an apostolic mission, first as priest and then as bishop of the city of Jerusalem – modelling his behaviour on Christ's disciples but led to this decision by a *magistra*, Elene herself.

The conversion and education of Judas/Cyriacus by a female links *Elene* to the view of Christianity as a theologically feminized religion, with which late twentieth- and twenty-first century scholars have become increasingly familiar.[29] The imperialism and masculinization of culture – associated with the warfare and destruction waged by the Roman Empire in late antiquity and in the later Middle Ages with church inquisitions and punishment of heresy, bolstered by orthodox doctrine – have dominated thinking about Christianity for centuries, although the historical advent of Christianity was characterized by a radical break from traditional masculine power and authority. Luce Irigaray, among others, has argued that it was precisely Christ's radical message of peace and forgiveness, along with his validation of women and others marginalized by society, which appealed to women. The importance of Constantine's conversion (and later those of Clovis and the Anglo-Saxon kings) on the battlefield exists in the substitution of Christian education/conversion for military prowess as the means to political and military success.

Similarly, Hrotsvit's play *Gallicanus* emphasizes a spiritual order radically opposed to the societal norms of the pagan Roman Empire and, less overtly, to the masculine imperialism of the Holy Roman Empire. After conversion the central male figure leads a life of chastity, poverty, exile, and finally martyrdom, like Christ himself and like Gallicanus's teachers Paul and John, who also are martyred in the second part of the play. Thus Gallicanus's career as a soldier is profoundly changed by his conversion. He says to Constantine, 'Ecce habes quadruplicatum exercitum Christo favente · et me laborante · Patere ut nunc militem imperatori · cuius iuvamine vici · et cui debeo quicquid feliciter vixi' (I.XIV.1), 'By Christ's aid and through my own labors, you have an army four times larger than before./ So allow that I now fight for the Emperor by whose aid I won the war/ and to whom I owe all my good fortunes' (Wilson, *Plays*, 27). These new 'military' labours, shared equally by Christian men and women, are those of Ecclesia. Constantia, like

Elene, educates Gallicanus's daughters in (converts them to) Christianity, while her confessors at her behest advise and educate Gallicanus in obedience to God. For this reason it is no accident that much of the play takes place in the women's quarters and the cloister to which Constantia and Gallicanus's daughters retire; the masculine sites for Gallicanus that are parallel in their isolation, the hermitage at Ostia in part 1 and exile in Alexandria in part 2, are attained only after he has emasculated himself of all secular power and property by giving what he owns to his daughters, pilgrims, freed slaves, and the poor (I.XIII.6; Wilson, *Plays*, 27).

In the second part of the play, the dialogue between Julian the Apostate and Constantia's servants John and Paul further undermines the traditional masculine imperial authority of the Roman Empire. When Julian invites them to return to service in the imperial palace, John and Paul refuse; Paul says, 'Postquam enim mundus eis non erat dignus habendis · suscepti sunt inter angelos · tibique infelix res publica relinquebatur regenda' (II.V.5), 'After the earth was no longer worthy of housing these men [the Emperors Constantine, Constans, and Constantinus], they were received among the angels and left you to rule this miserable state' (Wilson, *Plays*, 31). The Roman Empire is a 'miserable state' without Christian leadership; Christian apostolic activity and martyrdom are the main characteristics of the alternative empire Hrotsvit's play celebrates. At the end of the play, the tomb of the martyrs John and Paul is the location of the final conversions, the final drama within a drama, indeed, a family drama. The son is first possessed by demons because of the command of the emperor Julian to lay hands on the saints John and Paul and then reclaimed by his newly converted father Terrentianus through the saints' intercession.

Further feminization is seen in Hrotsvit's domestication of the Roman concept of the *familia*, both imperial and personal, headed by a *paterfamilias*, Constantine, and extended to include members of the household not related by blood, such as servants and confessors. The community of which Gallicanus and Saints Paul and John are a part is initially Constantine's imperial house, or 'family,' and then his own family (including his daughter Constantia). At the end of the first part of the play, Constantine invites Gallicanus to be a closer part of the family: 'Cum vinculum Christi amoris · in unius nos societate coniungat religionis · decet ut quasi gener augustorum · honorifice nobiscum habites · intra palatium' (I.XIV.1) 'Since the tie of Christ's love unites us in the fellowship of one religion, it is proper that you, the Emperor's son-in-law so to say, live honorably in the palace with us' (Wilson, *Plays*, 27). Gallicanus recognizes, however, that Constantine's *familia* is subsumed by the 'family' of the church, with Christ as father and emperor.

Instead of Jerusalem and the Anglo-Saxon site of York as founding sites for the church, in her play Hrotsvit (as it were) situates her European church on the Roman and Mediterranean sites where Gallicanus's battle takes place against the pagan Scythians and where, by analogy, the more figurative rhetorical 'battles' of strategy, education, and conversion also take place among Constantine, Constantia, Gallicanus, his daughters, Paul and John, and Julian the Apostate. Perhaps for Hrotsvit the Roman (or Scythian) threat to Christianity more aptly or interestingly dramatizes the conversion of Gallicanus, especially given the reactionary bias of Julian the Apostate and the subsequent martyrdom of the apostles. If genre dictates the nature of the drama of spiritual conversion in *Gallicanus*, then the epic genre of *Elene* may also format the poem's literal and spiritual martial contests. In *Elene*, as in *Gallicanus*, the agenda is education, in particular Elene's education of Judas, but also as part of Alfred's precedent-setting ninth-century program of education through the translation of Latin works into a more readily accessible vernacular suitable to the Anglo-Saxon audience.

The marks of gender difference in the two founding narratives are similar and related, whatever specific differences may exist between them. As founding narratives of the early church, then, these two works are themselves feminized. First, female choice and decision making are crucial to the narratives: whatever their own plans, Gallicanus and Constantine both desire and depend upon Constantia's own consent for marriage – as if women at that time had some choice and were not bestowed by their fathers upon their suitors.[30] In *Elene*, although it may seem that the choices are masculine and belong, first, to Constantine and, then, to Judas, it is mother and battle-queen Elene who orchestrates the conversion of both men and also the journey-quest that results in the miracles of the resurrection of a corpse by a Jew and the uncovering of the nails and site of the True Cross.

Second, the exemplary woman Constantia, like her grandmother Elene in the Old English epic, is not only an educator, Christian theologian, and wise woman but also a model of Christian faith. Constantia in her perfect faith differs from all men in the play except for her subordinate and eventually martyred saintly confessors, just as Elene resembles only her converted son, the emperor, and her own convert, Cyriacus. As an educator Constantia easily convinces her father to stage a choice for

Gallicanus: let him have what he wants after the campaign is won. As is appropriate for conversion associated with education, Constantia articulates her faith and strategy eloquently: her father exclaims, 'Quam bene dicis mea Constantia' (I.II.4), 'My Constantia, you speak very well' (Wilson, *Plays*, 13). She knows that Constantine's promise to Gallicanus will be guaranteed by the presence in her company of Gallicanus's pagan daughters Artemia and Attica, exchanged for her own advisors John and Paul as spiritual guides for the general. This literal exchange will foster spiritual transformation, that is, conversion, *conversio*. Because of her Christian faith, she believes that, in response to their prayers and appropriately guided by Paul and John, Gallicanus will freely choose a life of chastity for himself that will allow her to keep her own vow of chastity. She is, accordingly, a better military strategist than the Roman general, who fails to lead his fleeing officers, and a better political leader than her imperial father; additionally, she has faith that God will help them achieve a happy resolution of the problem. Exchange and change signal the shifting (or upended) gender roles that have been reversed through Christian empowerment.

In both works, Christianity is manifested as a feminized religious faith, one also catalysed through women leaders and educators. In Hrotsvit's Gandersheim, if we imagine her nuns reading (if not playing) these roles,[31] women educators then also can be seen as promoted through their literacy and their 'performance' (in the theoretical sense) into political positions of power, if not translated (like the bones of a martyr moved to a holy site) into sanctity. Women thus also come to occupy the roles of a Holy Roman Emperor, two priests, and the general known for his military acumen, as well as the role of the wise woman whose faith, intelligence, and eloquence contribute to the transformation of the Roman Empire into the Holy Roman Empire. By this means, therefore, they enjoy the delicious sensation of masculine power humbled before female authority.

Indeed, Hrotsvit herself reads female preaching at the end of her preface to the dramas as a gesture of humility that she is obliged to pursue: 'Ideoque non sum adeo amatrix mei · ut pro vitanda reprehensione Christi qui in sanctis operatur, virtutem quocumque ipse dabit posse cessem praedicare' (*Liber Secundus, Praefatio*, 8), 'For I am not such a lover of myself nor so vain/ that in order to avoid censure I would refrain/ from preaching Christ's glory and strength as it works through His saints to the extent He grants me the ability to do so' (Wilson, *Florilegium*, 42). Through this gift she understands the concept of gender difference, despite the fact that she is 'nesciola nullaque probitate,' 'of little learning and worth' (according to her dedicatory letter in Book II, 'Epistola eiusdem ad quosdam sapientes huius libri fautores,' 'Her Letter to the Learned Patrons of This Book,' Wilson, *Florilegium*, 43). She has therefore constantly tried hard to make her work more philosophical so that God, who has given her talent, will be the more justly praised, 'quanto muliebris sensus tardior esse creditur' (*Liber Secundus, Epistola,* 9), 'the more limited the female intellect is believed to be' (Wilson, *Florilegium*, 44). Insisting that 'tantum scio quod nescio' (*Liber Secundus, Epistola,* 10), 'the only thing I know is that I know naught' (Wilson, *Florilegium*, 44), she tries to quilt Philosophia's robe into her text: 'si qua forte fila vel etiam floccos de panniculis a veste Philosophię abruptis evellere quivi · praefato opusculo inserere curavi · quo vilitas meę inscientię intermixtione nobilioris materiae illustraretur' (*Liber Secundus, Epistola,* 9), 'I have tried whenever I could probe,/ to rip small patches from Philosophy's robe/ and weave them into this little work of mine,/ so that the worthlessness of my own ignorance may be ennobled by their interweaving of this nobler material's shine' (Wilson, *Florilegium*, 44).

In *Gallicanus,* Hrotsvit's program is to legitimize female presence and authority within the Latin tradition and to rewrite the history of the early church in order to emphasize the contribution of founding mothers (who can be virgins) as well as founding fathers. Because she embodies strength and virtue in the service of *Ecclesia,* Constantia is another version of Peter as the rock on which Christ will found his church. Like many other female characters of Hrotsvit, Constantia sums up the qualities of the *miles Christi* through sharp contrasts with the male generals and emperors Hrotsvit delights in satirizing, and thus Constantine's daughter feminizes the internal strengths of every Christian. Because Constantia also is a historical daughter (or at least plays the role of one, whether or not 'Constantia' actually existed), she participates in a rewriting of Christian history, in which she overshadows or displaces Constantine's role in the apostolic work of the early church and in the Christianization of the Roman Empire. So also Elene, who finds the True Cross, can be seen as a founder through recovery of the central symbolism on which the church is founded. Founding daughters and founding mothers: indeed, the daughter and the mother in both of these works, *Elene* and *Gallicanus,* shape the nature of *Ecclesia* as a feminized institution accessible to and necessary for the empowerment of male and female leaders. In rewriting spiritual and ecclesiastical history to include

the indelible imprint of women, Hrotsvit performs a function very like
that of Christine de Pizan in her *Livre de la Cité des Dames* and that of the
author of *Elene*.

NOTES

A small portion of this paper was delivered initially as part of a 1998 Rice
University Alumni College Lecture entitled 'Looking for Shakespeare's Sister:
Medieval Women Writers,' Houston, Texas, 27 March 1998. It was also read, in
shortened form, at a session, Hrotsvit and Literary Traditions, Hrotsvit 2000
Symposium (organized by Phyllis Brown and Jane Chance), Santa Clara Univer-
sity, Santa Clara, California, 11 February 2000. Portions also appear in a paper,
'The Legend of the Roman Virgin-Saint Agnes as Physician: Healing the
Disease of Paganism in Hrotsvit of Gandersheim's *Gallicanus*,' presented at the
International Interdisciplinary Conference on Medieval Medicine: Texts,
Practices, Institutions, Rila Monastery, Sofia, Bulgaria, 30 August 2000. I am
grateful to Theresa Munisteri of the English department at Rice University for
helpful suggestions in regard to the styling of this essay and to Ronit Berger,
my research assistant for the spring of 2000, for her help in obtaining secondary materials.

1 See *Bede's Ecclesiastical History of the English People* and *The Old English Version
   of Bede's Ecclesiastical History of the English People*. For women as agents in the
   building of the English church, see Fell, Clark, and Williams, *Women in
   Anglo-Saxon England*, and my discussion of women in Bede's *Ecclesiastical
   History*, in 'The Saint, the Abbess, the Chaste Queen: Wise, Holy, and
   Heroic,' in *Woman as Hero*, 58–60.
2 See Lees and Overing, *Double Agents*. Their chapter on Bede was published
   earlier as 'Birthing Bishops and Fathering Poets.' See also, by the same
   authors, 'Before History, Before Difference.'
3 Lees and Overing, *Double Agents*, 2.
4 See Dockray-Miller, 'Matrilineal Genealogy and Mildrið's Maternal Legacy,'
   for the eighth-century Kentish abbess Mildrið, and 'The Maternal Genealogy of Æðelflæd, Lady of the Mercians,' in *Motherhood and Mothering in
   Anglo-Saxon England*, 9–76.
5 For Hrotsvit's indebtedness to other Latin traditions in her own legends
   and epics, in addition to comments made in the articles cited below, see,
   for example, Head, 'Hrotsvit's *Primordia* and the Historical Traditions of
   Monastic Communities,' and, in the same collection, Black, 'The Use of

Liturgical Texts in Hrotsvit's Works'; Vynckier, 'Arms-Talks in the Middle Ages: Hrotsvit'; and Kratz, 'The *Gesta Ottonis* in Its Contexts.' Although such intertextuality is not wholly forgotten in examinations of her plays, scholars interested in the sources on which Hrotsvit drew in constructing her plays seldom veer from the Latin classical, philosophical (that is, scholastic, also including the astronomical, mathematical, and musical), ecclesiastical, or liturgical traditions, even when her legends and lives are the subject. See, for example, Hughes, 'Augustinian Elements in Hrotsvit's Plays'; Provost, 'The Boethian Voice in the Dramas of Hrotsvit'; Chamberlain, 'Musical Imagery and Musical Learning in Hrotsvit'; Wilson, 'Mathematical Learning and Structural Composition in Hrotsvit's Works.'

6 In regard to the hagiographical and monastic context of Hrotsvit's plays, Sandro Sticca has argued that Hrotsvit depends on the *Vitae Patrum*, in so far as she is drawing on religious historiography, for which the touchstone was the Bible itself. Sticca states, 'In the Middle Ages, the term *historia* was indiscriminately applied not only to saints' lives, segments of the Bible, the literal sense of scriptural texts, parts of the Divine Office, epics, poems, school books such as Peter Comestor's *Historia scolastica* but also to biographies and to other narratives that in modern times might be designated as history. The conceiving of *history* under these broad headings can be attributed to the consideration that medieval church historians usually thought everything to be in some sense *res ecclesiastica*; since history appeared to be a providential process, every *factum* was inseparable from *intelligentia spiritualis* ... In other words, the Bible was considered to be the touchstone of medieval historiography, together with its inseparable associates hagiography, exegesis and the liturgy' (5). See his 'The Hagiographical and Monastic Context of Hrotswitha's Plays.' As Sticca points out, histories of the church were compiled incorporating the two canons of the Bible (Old and New), beginning with the fourth-century *Chronographia* and *Historica ecclesiastica* of Eusebius, bishop of Caesarea; Augustine's *De civitate Dei*; the sixth-century *Historia ecclesiastica* of Cassiodorus and the *Historia francorum* of Gregory of Tours; and Bede's eighth-century *Historia ecclesiastica gentis Anglorum* (Ecclesiastical History of the English People). Sacred history was supplemented by the *Vitae patrum* and *Acta sanctorum* as exemplary texts.

7 The style, vocabulary, and mode in *Dulcitius*, probably Hrotsvit's best-known play, as in many of Hrotsvit's plays, derive from her classical models, the sexually explicit burlesque and slapstick comedies of Terence, whose licentious misogyny she reappropriates within a Christian and feminized context. For example, in *Dulcitius*, the pagan seducer is magically tricked

into believing he is kissing and fondling Christian virgins in the kitchen, whereas in fact he is fingering blackened pots and pans. The double symbol of the pots and pans represents female sexuality and the domestic quotidian roles women play according to superficial misogynistic stereotypes. His pagan idolatry and literalism render him a buffoon, in contrast to the admirable Christian faith and figurative empowerment of the Christian virgins themselves. In her preface to the dramas, Hrotsvit purports to exchange for the 'turpia lascivarum incesta feminarum' (*Liber Secundus, Praefatio*, 3), 'shameless acts of licentious women' (Wilson, *Florilegium*, 41), of Terence the praiseworthy virtue of virginity. See, for recent treatments of her indebtedness to Terence, Burgess, 'Hroswitha and Terence'; de Luca, 'Hrotsvit's "Imitation" of Terence'; Tarr, 'Terentian Elements in Hrotsvit'; and, on *Pafnutius* as a moralized *Eunuchus*, Thompson, '*Paphnutius* and the Cultural Vision.' See also Tarr, 'Holy Virgins and Wanton Women.' A feminist analysis of Hrotsvit's 'anti-Terence' plays appears in Case, 'Re-Viewing Hrotsvit.'

8 Sticca, 'The Hagiographical and Monastic Context of Hrotswitha's Plays,' 20.

9 The five men for whom the plays are named, these four plus *Dulcitius*, derive from the 1501 *editio princeps* of Conrad Celtis; the original titles provided by Hrotsvit for all of them except *Gallicanus* stress the female and not the male characters, namely, *Passio Sanctarum Virginum Agapus Chioniae et Hirenae* (= *Dulcitius*), *Resuscitatio Drusianae et Calimachi* (= *Calimachus*); *Lapsus et conversio Mariae Neptis Habrahae Heremicolae* (= *Abraham*); *Conversio Thaidis Meretricis* (= *Pafnutius*). See the discussion by Gold, 'Hrotswitha Writes Herself,' 62 n. 9.

10 See Petroff, 'Eloquence and Heroic Virginity in Hrotsvit's Verse Legends'; on virginity as a unifying link in the plays, see Demers, '*In virginea forma.*'

11 Legendary sources for *Gallicanus* include the *Magnum legendarium Austriacum*, a *Passionale* (*Conversio Gallicani*), and the *Acta sanctorum* for 7 June. See Jefferis, 'Hrotsvit and the *Magnum Legendarium Austriacum*'; Sticca, 'The Hagiographical and Monastic Context of Hrotswitha's Plays,' 11; and, for the sources of the two parts of *Gallicanus*, taken from the different legends of the saints, specifically, the conversion of Gallicanus and the martyrdom of John and Paul, in the *Acta sanctorum*, 1868, for 7 June, see Schütze-Pflugk, *Herrscher- und Märtyrerauffassung bei Hrotsvit von Gandersheim*, 38–53. The *Acta sanctorum* includes as the source for the first part, on the price of the ascetic life that Gallicanus will choose, *De sancto Gallicano duce et consule Romano martyre in Aegypto*; for the second part, on the martyrdom of the two confessors, the *Passio SS. Joannis et Pauli, De sancti fratribus martyribus Joanne et Paulo Romae in propria domo nunc ecclesia, item Terentiano et filio ejus ibidem.*

12 See Preissl, *Hrotsvit von Gandersheim und die Entstehung des mittelalterlichen Heldenbilds.*

13 Although a precise date for Cynewulf or the Cynewulfian School poet remains a vexed issue, Patrick Conner argues for the tenth century, in 'On Dating Cynewulf.'

14 Ferrante, *To the Glory of Her Sex,* 181.

15 Ibid.

16 Wilson, ed. *Hrotsvit of Gandersheim: A Florilegium of Her Works,* 13.

17 See Chance, *Woman as Hero,* 31–52, esp. 37–8.

18 Wittig, 'The Mark of Gender.'

19 On the issue of Hrotsvit's dramatic response to cultural and literary misogyny, see Frankforter, 'Sexism and the Search for the Thematic Structure of the Plays of Hroswitha of Gandersheim'; and Sperberg-McQueen, 'Whose Body Is It?'

20 See, for example, Jeffrey, 'Virginal Allegories of Self Knowledge in Hrotsvit's *Sapientia.*'

21 The situation Hrotsvit creates in this play has striking parallels to her exploration of legal issues involved in vows in *Basilius.* See David Day's essay in this volume.

22 *Elene,* in *The Vercelli Book,* line 1062; *Elene,* in Gordon, *Anglo-Saxon Poetry,* 230.

23 Elene appears briefly in *Gallicanus* when the women greet the returning general and the emperor as they pass into the women's abode in the palace; Constantine cries out, 'Ecce occurrunt · cum augusta Helena · mei genitrice gloriosa · omnibusque lacrimę fluunt prae gaudio' (I.XII.11), 'Look, here they come with my noble mother, Empress Helena, and they are shedding tears of joy' (Wilson, *Plays,* 26).

24 *Elene,* in *The Vercelli Book,* 1129–35.

25 *Elene,* trans. Gordon, 231.

26 *Elene,* in *The Vercelli Book,* 240–2.

27 *Elene,* trans. Gordon, 215.

28 *Elene,* in *The Vercelli Book,* 254, 268–70; *Elene,* trans. Gordon, 216.

29 See, for example, works such as Elm, *Virgins of God;* Salisbury, *Church Fathers, Independent Virgins;* and Reid, *Choosing the Better Part? Women in the Gospel of Luke.*

30 On the feminization of Constantine, see also the brief discussion in Schroeder, 'Hroswitha and the Feminization of Drama,' 56–7.

31 See Wilson, trans., *The Plays of Hrotsvit of Gandersheim,* 95–101, for a discussion of the likely reading rather than performance of these plays within the convent. However, David Wiles has also argued that these plays are records

of actual performances: see his 'Hrosvitha of Gandersheim: The Performance of Her Plays in the Tenth Century.' See also, for embedded stage directions in the plays that suggest they were performed, Snyder, '"Bring me a soldier's garb and a good horse": Embedded Stage Directions in the Dramas of Hrotsvit of Gandersheim,' in this collection. Also telling is the observation of Michael A. Zampelli (shared by those of us who have asked students to perform her plays) that Hrotsvit's plays change in the performance from pious and conventional nods to the patriarchal to the comic – despite their emphasis on torture, death, and martyrdom. See his 'Playing with Hrotsvit: Adventures in Contemporary Performance,' also in this volume.

SECTION 4

Conducting Performances

Hrotsvit's Literary Legacy

DEBRA L. STOUDT

The literary oeuvre of Hrotsvit of Gandersheim lay in relative obscurity until the end of the fifteenth century. There are occasional references in twelfth- and thirteenth-century chronicles and biographies to some of her works, namely the *Gesta Ottonis*, the *Primordia*, the legend *Maria*, and the dramas *Sapientia* and *Gallicanus*.[1] However, it was the discovery of the Emmeram-Munich manuscript in the last decade of the fifteenth century and the publication of the first edition of Hrotsvit's dramatic works by the 'archhumanist' Conrad Celtis (1459–1508) in 1501 that reintroduced the Benedictine canoness to the literary world.[2]

The German humanists immediately embraced Hrotsvit as the initiator of the German dramatic tradition; her accomplishments afforded them the longed-for opportunity to boast of a Latin literary history in the German-speaking territories. In the preface of his edition, Celtis included epigrams written by members of the Rhenish Sodalitas Litteraris, which accorded the newly discovered playwright inordinate praise. Johannes Tritheim (1462–1516), abbot of Sponheim, wrote, 'Why should we not praise the writings of the German maid, who, were she Greek, would long be a goddess without doubt.'[3] Johannes Stabius, a pupil of Celtis, stated, 'Although our native land is called barbarous, unversed in Greek teaching and in Latium, nevertheless a German virgin could do this with her pen – Hrotsvitha – what men of Latium could scarcely do.'[4] Based on their comments, the humanists were interested primarily in Hrotsvit's dramatic technique and less in her choice of themes. The humble, ascetic lifestyle espoused by Hrotsvit's heroines – if not throughout their life, then at least as their life came to an end – undoubtedly found little resonance with the worldly Celtis, who died of syphilis.[5]

During the first half of the sixteenth century a number of Latin comedies modelled on those of Hrotsvit were produced, and her reputation spread to England, Italy, and Hungary. Some scholars offered praise, but others cast doubt on Hrotsvit's identity, suggesting that she had been a seventh-century English nun or a Greek princess.[6] Such qualms concerning her personal history caused the decline of her fame toward the end of the century.

However, the publication of editions of Hrotsvit's other works, such as the *Gesta Ottonis,* and the preparation of new editions of her dramas fostered a revival of interest.[7] With the development of dramatic theory in the eighteenth century by German literary scholars like Johann Christoph Gottsched (1700–66), Hrotsvit's contribution to the genre was thrust into the limelight once again, although still regarded askance. In his study of theater history Gottsched offered a summary of each of Hrotsvit's six plays along with a tempered endorsement of her artistic abilities: 'One knows full well that the writing style of the good Hrotsvit is not of Terentian beauty, nor are her poetic works composed according to the rules of art. But who would expect such in the midst of her age? The most learned men of her time did not write better than she: and how much more leniency cannot her sex demand of us, especially [since she wrote] in a learned and foreign language.'[8]

This sceptical stance toward Hrotsvit obtained until the third decade of the nineteenth century, when the German dramatist Gustav Freytag (1816–95) wrote his dissertation on Hrotsvit's works, and three French scholars, the literary historian Charles Villemain and the translators Charles Magnin and Vignon Rétif de la Bretonne, published studies and translations of Hrotsvit's works from the 1830s to the 1850s.[9] It is therefore perhaps surprising that in the subsequent decades there was a backlash in Germany against the native daughter. In 1867 the historian Joseph Aschbach posited that Hrotsvit was a fabrication of Celtis and that Celtis's fellow humanist Johannes Reuchlin was the true author of the works attributed to her.[10] In his review of Aschbach's study, published the same year, Georg Waitz dismissed the arguments as lacking in evidence,[11] but the controversy did not subside until the mid-twentieth century, when the discovery of additional manuscript evidence offered compelling corroboration of the authenticity of Hrotsvit's works. In 1922 Goswin Frenken published a description of a twelfth-century Cologne manuscript containing the four plays *Gallicanus, Dulcitius, Calimachus,* and *Abraham* by Hrotsvit.[12] Three years later Hermann Menhardt described the fragments of Hrotsvit's work he found in an eleventh-century manuscript in Klagenfurt.[13]

The debates throughout the centuries regarding Hrotsvit's identity and writing ability may account in part for the limited impact her works have had on subsequent generations of writers.[14] Nonetheless, several lyric, epic, and dramatic pieces by nineteenth- and twentieth-century authors owe a debt to the Gandersheim canoness. Some writers have been influenced by motifs found in Hrotsvit's works, and others have been inspired by her life. Several American authors are indebted to her literary legacy,[15] and the influence of her legends on Spanish and Portuguese authors has been demonstrated as well;[16] here, however, the focus is her influence on the French and German literary traditions.

Among the writings of the nineteenth-century Swiss author Conrad Ferdinand Meyer (1825–98) are a number of historical novels, verse epics, and ballads. His poem 'Der gleitende Purpur' (The Flowing Purple Robe)[17] has much in common with the scene in Hrotsvit's *Gesta Ottonis*,[18] verses 336–71, in which the sovereign Otto reconciles with his brother Henry. Although there is no evidence that Meyer knew Hrotsvit's epic version, scholars of the Benedictine canoness by and large assert that her work served as Meyer's inspiration.[19] In contrast Meyer scholars tend to seek the Swiss poet's stimulus elsewhere, namely in the poem 'Kaiser Otto I' by Heinrich von Mühler (1813–74), published in 1842, which treats the same incident, or the account of the brothers' reconciliation by the historian Wilhelm von Giesebrecht (1814–89).[20]

Otto the Great (Otto I), often considered the founder of the Holy Roman Empire, succeeded his father Henry I as German king in 936; it was only in 962 that he finally became emperor. Almost immediately after Otto was crowned king, his younger brother Henry of Bavaria, along with several other nobles, led a series of insurrections against him, all of which were thwarted. The final reconciliation between the brothers came on Christmas day in 941.[21]

Both Hrotsvit and Meyer emphasize the significance of the liturgical season in their descriptions of the meeting between Otto and Henry.[22] For Hrotsvit it serves as the impetus for Otto's compassion toward his brother:

Instantisque memor festi cunctis venerandi,
In quo cęlicole pacem mundo cecinere,
Lęti rege suo tenera de virgine nato,

Ut pie salvaret mundum merito periturum,
Pro diei tantę pacem portantis honore
Condoluit miserans fratri commissa fatenti   (364–9)

and mindful of the approach of the feast of universal veneration on which
the heavenly hosts sang peace to the world in their joy at the birth of their
King, from a tender Virgin, He might generously save the world which
deserved to perish, Otto, in deference to the greatness of that peace-
bringing day, pitied his repentant brother[23] (Bergman, 63)

In celebration of the season, Meyer begins and concludes his poem with
the cry 'Oh, Christmas, oh, Christmas' (Eia Weihnacht! Eia Weihnacht!),[24]
framing his piece with the liturgical reference.[25]

Similar as well is the characterization of Otto in the two works. For
Hrotsvit and Meyer the leader of the Holy Roman Empire and defender
of Christianity is a Christlike figure whose inherent benevolence leads
him to magnanimously pardon his brother, who assumes the role of
penitent.[26] Hrotsvit alludes to Henry's humble attire as he prostrates
himself before his older brother:

Depositisque suis ornamentis preciosis
Simplicis et tenuis fruitur velamine vestis
Inter sacratos noctis venerabilis hymnos
Intrans nudatis templi sacra limina plantis;
...
Sed prono sacram vultu prostratus ad aram
Corpus frigoreę sociavit nobile terrę.   (354–60)

There, laying aside his costly jewels, [Henry] donned a garment of simple
and thin texture, and amid the venerable hymns of the Holy Night he
entered the sacred threshold of the church with bare feet ... with downcast
countenance prostrating himself at the sacred altar and throwing his princely
form upon the icy earth. (Bergman, 61–3)

Whereas Hrotsvit draws attention to Henry's modest clothing, Meyer
counters with Otto's royal robe as the focus of attention and as the title of
his poem. He extrapolates from Hrotsvit's brief recounting of the episode to create a dramatic encounter between the brothers in 941.[27]
Meyer portrays Henry as one of a hundred beggars gathered around
Emperor Otto, beleaguering him with requests for clothes and alms. As

Otto makes his way through the throng of poor, whose limbs have been rubbed raw by the chains of their imprisonment,[28] Henry grasps the purple robe of the sovereign. Otto tries to extricate himself from the beggar's grasp, admonishing him not to tear the royal robe from him – at this point an unwitting reference by Otto to Henry's earlier attempts at wresting the crown from him. Otto rebukes the beggar, 'Do you know me to be a stingy man?' The beggar responds, 'Do you know me, the wicked one? ... You, anointed and illustrious one? Do you know me?'[29] It is at this point that the beggar begins to make known his identity. He reveals that he and Otto came from the same womb; as children they had their clothes made from the same woolen cloth and sang from the same psalter. He even refers to Otto's use of his nickname, Heinz, to invoke images of their childhood together: how Otto called out to him in the great chambers, hallways, and on the spiral staircases to come and play. With a great sigh Henry confesses how envy led to his downfall: 'Alas! When you had yourself crowned, the snake of envy bit me. In consort with the lying spirit I tore apart this German empire. You imagined me to be an untrue brother and a traitor. You were angered and had me cast, bound, into the depths of prison ... In the depths of my prison I have frozen today without a cloak.'[30]

Here Henry breaks off his reminiscences and reminds himself and those listening that it is Christmas: 'Today the Saviour is born to the world.'[31] The hundred beggars take up the cry: 'Oh, Christmas,' and plead to the sovereign for cloaks, alms, and his mercy. Otto loosens the clasp and covers his 'sinning' brother with the purple robe, the symbol of royal power. This act, the ultimate gesture of the munificence of the Christian king, gives rise to cries of 'Glory,' 'Peace,' and 'Joy' in earth and heaven and calls to mind the humility and beneficence of Christ himself, whose birth is celebrated on this day.

Although Otto is the focus of attention in the works of both Hrotsvit and Meyer, the emperor must share the scene with the church in Hrotsvit's work. She prefaces her description by noting that Henry had been 'Christi gratiola tactus sub corde secreto' (337), 'touched in his inmost heart with the grace of Christ' (Bergman 61), and thus moved to reconsider his behaviour toward his brother. As Henry is about to seek forgiveness, Hrotsvit makes reference to hymns, the sacred threshold of the church, and the altar. She presents Otto working in tandem with the church to bring about a peaceful conclusion to internal strife and thus to strengthen the Christian nation. Meyer focuses solely on the fraternal relationship as the two men confront each other. Christian virtues still are paramount, but Meyer replaces the religious trappings so significant for the Benedictine canoness with references to the secular world: the chambers and spiral staircase of the palace and the chains of the dungeon.[32]

More than half a century later Hrotsvit's *Gesta Ottonis* inspired a historical account of the life of Adelheid, Otto's second wife, by Gertrud Bäumer (1873–1954). Although the novel itself has been forgotten, the name of its author is remembered because of her pivotal role in the German women's movement of the first decades of the twentieth century. An advocate of education for women and a supporter of the role of women in professional arenas and in politics, Bäumer was the co-founder of the German Democratic Party (Deutsche Demokratische Partei) and served as its representative to the National Assembly and the Parliament from 1919–33. Active in politics throughout the 1920s, she also worked in the Ministry of the Interior on Cultural Affairs until the National Socialists removed her from the position in 1933. By this time she had turned her literary attention from social and political criticism to the genre of historical novel – and by 1938 found herself being supported by the National Socialists, who considered her historical novels sympathetic to Nazi ideology.

Of particular interest to Bäumer were the tenth-century rulers of the Holy Roman Empire, especially Otto I and Adelheid. In 1934 Bäumer published *Männer und Frauen im geistigen Werden des deutschen Volkes*, which included chapters about the sovereigns Otto and Adelheid and their contemporaries Hrotsvit of Gandersheim and Widukind of Corvey,[33] both of whose extant writings provided insights into the Ottonian period.[34] This work served as the basis for Bäumer's historical novel *Adelheid, Mutter der Königreiche* published two years later.[35] The fictionalized account of Adelheid's life not only alludes to passages in the *Gesta* but also describes the Gandersheim community and a meeting between Adelheid and Hrotsvit. Bäumer grew up near Magdeburg, located about 100 miles from Gandersheim and Quedlinburg. In her work she frequently praises the communities for religious women established and administered by the Saxon royal family in these two towns. When Adelheid laments her limited writing ability in Latin, the margrave Gero responds with an encomium of the Gandersheim community and its sister institution in Quedlinburg, where female members of the Saxon nobility were trained in the sciences and in a lifestyle pleasing to God.[36] Later in the novel Adelheid, now empress, visits her husband's niece, the abbess Gerberga, in Gandersheim, where she is introduced to the petite, blond-haired, blue-eyed Hrotsvit. Gerberga explains that Hrotsvit is writing a poem about the deeds of the emperor and invites Adelheid to tell her life story to Hrotsvit.[37] Occasionally in the course of the 600-page novel Bäumer offers details concerning political and religious controversies of Hrotsvit's time. When King Henry of Bavaria, Otto's brother, dies, his widow Mathilde becomes a canoness. Her lifestyle causes the clerics much consternation since she does not wear a veil nor does she refrain from wearing the royal purple and gold jewels. However, her chamber is outfitted like a cell: it contains a loom, a distaff, and a psalter on her desk.

In the course of her career Bäumer penned volumes in which she portrayed the lives of important women in cultural history from medieval times to the twentieth century;[38] surprisingly, she seldom mentions Hrotsvit's name in these works. Perhaps Hrotsvit's cloistered existence makes the Benedictine a less appealing heroine to the social-action-minded Bäumer, whose essays on historical female figures focus on politically engaged women and women whose relationships with men of authority inspire or facilitate their own accomplishments. Like so many scholars of previous generations, Bäumer characterizes remarkable medieval women from a male perspective: 'Their importance lay more in the fact that they fulfilled relatively well and in any case for their contemporaries surprisingly well the male positions to which they had been called by fate and circumstance.'[39] Bäumer chooses Adelheid, the mother of kingdoms, as a Germanic heroine, a woman equal to the tasks thrust upon her by political exigency. In contrast, Hrotsvit confines her heroines to the narrow stage proscribed by their religious calling. However, as portrayed by both women authors, Adelheid is not only a sympathetic figure but also a woman of action.[40]

Like Meyer, Bäumer uses Hrotsvit's epic poem as an inspiration for her own depiction of the glory days of the Holy Roman Empire. Just as Meyer touts Otto's Christian virtuousness, Bäumer's novel lauds the Ottonians as the new founders of Christendom.[41] However, both Meyer and Bäumer substitute the chauvinistic or patriotic for the tenth-century German playwright's religious-ascetic tone. Meyer's poem may be viewed as a product of the German romantic movement of the early and mid-nineteenth century. Although Bäumer's novel coincides chronologically with the National Socialist glorification of the Germanic past, it is best understood as an exemplar of women's intellectual and political history.[42]

The poem and novel discussed above establish the influence of Hrotsvit's epic work on subsequent generations. Also of note is the fact that the Benedictine canoness herself and her life at Gandersheim serve as the theme for several novels in the twentieth century: Maurus Carnot's *Roswitha: Eine Klostergeschichte* (1919), Dörthe Ulmer-Stichel's *Roswitha von Gandersheim* (1957), and Hanna Klose-Greger's *Roswitha von Gandersheim* (1961). These three fictionalized accounts focus on Hrotsvit's calling to a religious vocation, her inspiration to write, the reaction of other women in her community to the writings, the performance of her works, and her own reaction to her fame – all issues that still intrigue today.

Of equal significance is the impact of Hrotsvit's dramatic works. The most notable use of a Hrotsvit drama is in the 1890 novel *Thaïs* by the French writer and critic Anatole France (1844–1924), who was awarded the Nobel Prize for Literature in 1921.[43] Although classified as a novel, France's tripartite work employs a great deal of dialogue; indeed, the second part consists of extensive dialogue and monologues by the guests at the banquet the actress Thaïs and the hermit monk Paphnutius attend. France was familiar with Hrotsvit's work; in 1888 and 1889 he published two essays about her and her plays, noting that he had seen marionette performances of *Abraham*, *Pafnutius*, and *Calimachus*.[44] The relationship between Hrotsvit's play *Pafnutius* and France's novel has been recognized and studied in detail by a few scholars.[45] The discussion here will be limited to remarks concerning the protagonists and the final scene of each work.

Whereas Hrotsvit's play is commonly known as *Pafnutius* and France's novel is named for the harlot converted by the holy man, in each work the opposite character is actually the protagonist. Hrotsvit's hermit monk takes centre stage more frequently than Thais, but it is the harlot's conversion that is identified as the crux of the drama, as acknowledged in the first line of the prologue: 'The conversion of Thais the courtesan.' Diane Van Hoof relates the titles France chose for the three parts of his novel, 'The Lotus,' 'The Papyrus,' and 'The Euphorium,' to Thaïs's sensuality, her 'poisoning' of Pafnutius's spirit, and her temptation of him respectively,[46] yet the titles have more to do with the monk's reaction to the actress. The opening line of France's novel – 'The desert, in those days, was settled by anchorites'[47] – has a legendary quality and sets the stage for the description of the trials and tribulations of Pafnutius that are recounted in the first part. At the onset the actress Thaïs appears only in Pafnutius's dreams and thoughts; she first becomes flesh and blood in the second part, which focuses on Pafnutius's conversion of her. This section ends as Pafnutius leaves the actress in a house of refuge and continues on into the desert. In the third part the monk is again haunted by the memory of Thaïs, with whom he believes he is in love. For twenty years he struggles against his feelings, and upon hearing that Thaïs is dying, journeys to Alexandria to see her. When Papfutius arrives at the place where Thaïs has been living, the abbess Albina tells of the life the penitent actress has been leading among the religious. In addition to working and praying with the other women, Thaïs has acted out 'scenes from the lives of brave women and wise virgins of the scriptures.'[48] Karl A. Zaenker suggests that France provides a composite of the fictional Thaïs and the historical Hrotsvit with this reference.[49]

In the final scene of Hrotsvit's play Pafnutius urges Thais to pray and offers supplications of his own on her behalf. In contrast France's Paphnutius inveighs against Thaïs's impending death; he declares, 'God and heaven, all are nothing. The only truth is in life on earth and human love.'[50] He implores Thaïs to stave off death and come with him. As Hrotsvit's Thais dies, Pafnutius makes the sign of the cross over her and himself; he offers up a prayer on behalf of his spiritual daughter, entreating God that Thais's 'anima cęlitus indita · cęlestibus gaudiis intermisceatur · et corpus in molli gremio terrę suę materię pacifice foveatur quoadusque pulverea favilla coeunte' (XIII.3), 'that the soul, divinely imparted, live on in heavenly bliss,/ and that the body may rest in peace/ in the soft lap of Earth, from which it came,/ until ashes and dirt combine again/ and breath animates the revived members' (Wilson, *Plays*,122). Although France's Thaïs dies with a 'sigh of delight,' at this point Pafnutius gives in to his base instincts, and 'in a desperate embrace, devour[s] her with desire, rage, and love.'[51] The virgins chanting over the dead woman's body brand him a vampire and flee in fear as they look upon Pafnutius's face: 'he had become so hideous that, passing his hand across his face, he could feel its ugliness.'[52] Given France's knowledge of the canoness's oeuvre through the Magnin edition of her works,[53] it is possible that he drew his inspiration for the final scene of his novel from another of Hrotsvit's dramas: Paphnutius's lust for the deceased Thaïs and his sudden change in demeanour in the final scene are reminiscent of the ninth scene in Hrotsvit's *Calimachus*, in which John rebukes the title character: 'Quę dementia · quę insania te decepit · ut castis praesumeres fragmentis alicuius iniuriam conferre dehonestatis?' (IX.11), 'What madness, what craze held you in chains/ that you would presume to inflict the injury of dishonor upon these chaste remains [of Drusiana]' (Wilson, *Florilegium*, 60).[54] Whatever France's stimulus, the grotesqueness of his monk offers a stark contrast to Hrotsvit's Pafnutius, who is on his knees at prayer in the final scene of the drama.

Hrotsvit's play ends on a positive note for both characters, whose salvation is assured. France allows Paphnutius to save Thaïs's soul but to lose in the end not only his spiritual way but also his humanity, reducing the abbot to a less-than-human figure, a vampire. In his second essay about Hrotsvit, France states, 'Hrotswitha was a simple creature; restricted by her surroundings, and conceiving nothing more beautiful than the religious life, she had no other object in writing her comedies than the praise of Chastity.'[55] The final scene demonstrates France's reaction to the Benedictine canoness's approach. In *Pafnutius* the tenth-century German playwright presents an optimistic world view in which the Christian faith, once attained, is unwavering (although in other works such as the legend *Theophilus* and the play *Abraham* she does portray a faith that wavers, especially when the devil intervenes). The world of the nineteenth-century Frenchman is fraught with obstacles and temptations that can mislead even the most devout.[56]

In the second and third decades of the twentieth century there was renewed interest in Hrotsvit's dramas, especially among women. English suffragettes produced *Pafnutius* in London in 1914, and there were other English and U.S. productions in the early 1920s.[57] Christabel Marshall, under the pseudonym Christopher St. John, translated Hrotsvit's plays into English in 1923.

More recently Hrotsvit's dramatic work has again been the source of inspiration. The German essayist and playwright Peter Hacks (1928–2003) transforms Hrotsvit herself into one of the dramatic figures in his play *Rosie träumt.* Hacks was born in Breslau and studied in Munich; he immigrated to the German Democratic Republic in 1955 and remained in the East until the fall of the wall and the annexation of the GDR in 1991. Known for his adaptations of selected works from antiquity to the present laden with social criticism,[58] he became a provocative literary figure in the 1960s and 1970s, but his popularity declined after the collapse of the East German state. *Rosie träumt: Legende in fünf Aufzügen nach Hrosvith von Gandersheim* (Rosie Dreams: A Legend in Five Acts According to Hrosvith of Gandersheim) was inspired by the commemoration of the anniversary year of the canoness's death in 1973.[59] Written in 1974, the play was first performed in East Berlin in 1975;[60] it was published in 1976.[61] The drama is a fantastic mélange of Hrotsvit's dramas *Gallicanus, Dulcitius, Pafnutius,* and *Sapientia,*[62] with social critique as its underlying message. Hacks's move to East Germany serves as unambiguous evidence of the playwright's preference for the socialist system over the socio-political establishment of the West. However, the reality of GDR life falls short of Hacks's expectations, and he gives voice to his disappointment in several of his works, of which *Rosie träumt* is one.[63]

A female figure with the name Rosvitha – Rosie for short – appears in the first act, but she is not part of any religious community for women. Rosie is the youngest daughter of the emperor Diocletian and the intended bride of Gallikan, who rules with Diocletian and whom the senior leader treats like a son. In crafting the first act, Hacks borrows the names of several characters from Hrotsvit's *Sapientia* and *Dulcitius*, namely Spes, Fides, and Diocletian, as well as a motif from the latter drama, that is, the desire of a Roman leader to have a Christian virgin deny Christ and marry a pagan noble. When Spes and Fides vow that they will not marry Gallikan, they are sentenced to death. In the farcical scene that follows, the executioner twice falls down on the job – literally – in his attempt to carry out the sentence, but with his third attempt he beheads both girls with one blow.

As Diocletian laments the fact that there are no more royal daughters whom Gallikan might wed, Rosvitha suddenly appears. Her entrance in place of Hrotsvit's Karitas is jarring, not only because of her incongruous Germanic name but also because of the anachronistic bag of candy she carries with her, a symbol of the sensual temptations that entice the otherwise devout Christian girl. The audience may expect Rosvitha to be of the same mould as her sisters, but it is immediately apparent that this is not the case. Rosie has arrived late – and thus been spared the fate of Spes and Fides – because she has been primping herself and attending to household chores. In the course of her first conversation with Gallikan, she occasionally makes statements that are misunderstood by the young coregent and intimate that she is flirting with him.

Hacks's stance toward religion also is apparent in the first act. When questioned about the bag of candy, Rosie explains that she constantly eats sweets because 'it takes a lot of energy to be pious.'[64] Except for the name, the flippant young woman has little in common with Hrotsvit or with any of the dramatic heroines of the tenth-century Benedictine. Hacks continues his satire of legendary motifs as Rosie performs her first miracle. When she raises her sisters from the dead, the executioner proclaims, 'I won't take the blame for this ... but believe me, emperors, as soon as you get involved with Christians, then the mishaps start.'[65] Both the language used and the sentiments expressed mock Rosie's wondrous deed. The act concludes in a more traditional manner: Rosie agrees to become Gallikan's slave, believing that in this role God will help her convert her new master.

As the second act begins, Rosie is expecting to be put to death and is disappointed to hear that she will not even be tortured. When she learns that the executioner has been sent to disrobe her before Gallikan violates her, she forbids him to do so. Try as he may, the executioner is unable to cut or tear the clothes from Rosie's body, despite his use of ever-larger cutting instruments: first scissors, then tongs, and finally a crowbar. Rosie remains unperturbed; she proclaims, 'Jesus will stand by me.'[66] The miraculous events that constitute the high points of Hrotsvit's dramas become slapstick in Hacks's work. The comedic shifts to the vulgar when the executioner loses his patience and decides on another course of action. As he is about to unzip his trousers, Gallikan arrives at the door. The executioner departs and the emperor enters to rape Rosie. In a scene reminiscent of the pots and pans episode in Hrotsvit's *Dulcitius*, the young sovereign mistakes the oven for the girl, caressing it and knocking it onto the floor. As Gallikan opens the oven door, the trumpets sound and he is called to battle.

During the battle scene of the third act Rosie repeatedly offers Gallikan divine assistance so that the Romans can be victorious over the Karpen, but the coregent demurs. Nevertheless, in the eleventh hour the Romans unexpectedly prevail. Rosie attempts to explain the victory in terms of holy signs, but the Roman general offers more rational explanations; for example, what Rosie sees as a reliquary carried into battle is identified as a little chest full of lice that attack the enemy soldiers.

Tiring of Rosie's unwanted interference, Gallikan sends her off to learn the arts of the courtesan Thais, and in the fourth act Rosie regales the courtesan and the monk Pafnutius with tales of her own life. By the time Gallikan arrives, Rosie has converted Thais, who throws her jewels and finery into the fire. Once again subverting the intent of his sources, Hacks has Pafnutius introduce himself to Gallikan as a procurer (*Kuppler*), and in a jealous rage the coregent questions Rosie as to the identity of her lover, whom she reveals to be Jesus.

The plot comes full circle in the final act, with Diokletian again demanding of his daughter that she renounce her belief in God. This time Gallikan comes to her defence and proclaims that he himself is now a Christian. Once he and Rosie are alone, he denies the conversion and laments that if God were almighty, he would save them from death. Rosie glibly replies that God has indeed come to their rescue because as

Christians they will enjoy eternal life. Rosie and Gallikan are parted; the executioner beheads Gallikan, whereupon he is struck by lightning and reduced to a pile of ashes. Disconcerted by these events, Diocletian relinquishes the crown.

The final scene takes place in heaven, where Gallikan is soon reunited with Rosie.[67] Both appear in stereotypical martyr poses: Gallikan carries a lance on which his head is stuck and Hrotsvit, like St Barbara, holds a tower in her arms. They encounter a virgin, who identifies herself as an abbess as well as Jesus' mother.[68] When Rosie is startled to see the executioner in heaven, the Virgin explains that everyone ascends to heaven since 'there are so many heavens, certainly not fewer than seven.'[69] Confused, Rosie asks the Virgin if she believes in God, to which the Virgin responds: 'You have to believe, if you still can.'[70]

Hacks's afterword, 'Ten Lines about *Rosie Dreams*,' provides some insight into the playwright's intent. He describes the drama as 'a love story between a man with most resolute propensities toward things that are practical and a girl from the Apo.'[71] 'Apo' is a term that Hacks equates in the afterword with the 'apostolic movement';[72] however, in contemporaneous East German parlance APO stood for Außerparlamentarische Opposition, a reference to young revolutionaries.[73] Elsewhere in his commentary on the play Hacks asserts that because love stories engage an audience so easily, playwrights often frame political struggles within a romantic framework,[74] and thus *Rosie träumt* has been interpreted as a commentary on the socialist East German state, as noted above. Critics have branded Rosie a disillusioned socialist, a malcontent in the less-than-perfect East German state – like Hacks himself.[75] But as the few plot details described here attest, the religious satire is overwhelming and the social satire is relegated to too small a role to achieve Hacks's purposes; as Michael Mitchell notes, Hacks plays the plot too much for laughs.[76] Rosie's Christian idealism convinces neither Gallikan nor the audience, but the Romans' pagan rationalism is also uninspiring, as Gallikan's conversion and Diocletian's renunciation of the crown attest. Hacks ends his play with the Virgin's query to the new arrivals: 'Don't you want to follow me?'[77] Although both Rosie and Gallikan now have attained heavenly paradise, neither is satisfied. Hacks's equivocal ending provides a stark contrast to the unambiguous moral of each of Hrotsvit's plays that serves as a source for *Rosie träumt*. Rosie's dream is heavenly paradise; Hacks reveals to the audience that, upon reaching her goal, the girl has no sense of fulfilment.[78] The virgin martyrs in Hrotsvit's plays also yearn and strive for an existence beyond that accorded them on earth. Although there are no scenes in which the audience sees the Benedictine's female characters in heaven, there is never any doubt that they remain resolute in the end. Hrotsvit leaves the viewers with the inspiring image of Irena holding up her arms to heaven as she faces martyrdom and of Pafnutius praying that Thais, now lying on her deathbed, 'resurgat perfecta ut fuit homo · inter candidulas oves collocanda · et in gaudium aeternitatis inducenda' (XIII.4), 'be resurrected exactly as she was,/ a human being, and joining the white lambs may enter eternal joys' (Wilson, *Plays*, 122). The doubt and disappointment experienced by Hacks's characters, both secular and religious, never undermine Hrotsvit's heroes and heroines.

Since the first modern editions of Hrotsvit's works were published in the nineteenth century, a number of German women authors have identified her as their literary model and progenitor, but it is two modern European male authors who have chosen to draw on Hrotsvit's works directly and parody her themes in their writings.[79] Whereas Hrotsvit's life and her epic works inspired Meyer, Bäumer, and others to dramatize the canoness's life and scenes from the *Gesta Ottonis* as part of a glorification of the Germanic past, her dramas motivated France and Hacks to transform the Benedictine playwright's intentions into a critique of the turbulence and perplexity of modern society.

NOTES

1 Zeydel, 'Knowledge of Hrotsvitha's Works Prior to 1500,' discusses these references.
2 It has been debated whether Celtis or Johannes Tritheim actually discovered the manuscript. See Zeydel, 'The Reception of Hrotsvitha by the German Humanists after 1493,' 239–41. Zaenker, 'Homage to Roswitha,' outlines the rediscovery of Hrotsvit's writings beginning with the humanists and discusses several literary works mentioned in this essay that were influenced by her epics and dramas.
3 The English translation is from Zeydel, 'The Reception of Hrotsvitha by the German Humanists after 1493,' 244, who includes the Latin original: 'Cur non laudemus germanae scripta puellae,/ Quae si graeca esset iam dea certa foret.'
4 Zeydel, 'The Reception of Hrotsvitha by the German Humanists after 1493,' 246: 'Barbara nostra licet dicatur patria tellus,/ Expers et gray dog-

matis et lacii,/ Attamen hoc calamo potuit germana virago,/ Hrosuitha, quod lacii vix potuere viri.' Zeydel also notes that, despite their chauvinistic tone, the humanists touted Hrotsvit more as a 'continuator of the traditions of Sappho, Terence, and Vergil,' than as a fellow German (249). See also Wall, 'Hrotsvit and the German Humanists.'

5 Wall, 'Hrotsvit and the German Humanists,' discusses this point, 257–8.

6 Zeydel, 'The Reception of Hrotsvitha by the German Humanists after 1493,' 247–8.

7 Three editions of the *Gesta Ottonis* and one of fragments of the *Primordia* appeared in Germany between 1584 and 1693. In 1707 Heinrich Leonhard Schurzfleisch published a new edition of the 1501 version by Celtis. This was followed by several fresh editions of Hrotsvit's nondramatic works in the first half of the eighteenth century. Haight, *Hrotsvitha of Gandersheim: Her Life, Times, and Works, and a Comprehensive Bibliography*, 58–67, describes these editions.

8 Gottsched, *Nöthiger Vorrath zur Geschichte der deutschen Dramatischen Dichtkunst*, 9–10: 'Man weis es wohl, daß weder die Schreibart der guten Rhoswita von terenzianischer Schönheit ist; noch ihre Fabeln, recht nach den Regeln der Kunst abgefasset sind. Allein wer will das, mitten in der Finsterniß ihres Weltalters, begehren? Die allergelehrtesten Männer ihrer Zeit schrieben nicht besser als Sie: und wieviel Nachsicht kann nicht ihr Geschlecht, zumal in einer gelehrten und fremden Sprache, von uns fodern?' All translations of German are mine unless otherwise stated.

   Gottsched already had made brief reference to Hrotsvit as author of the *Gesta Ottonis* in his *Versuch einer Critischen Dichtkunst* (1730). Wagner, 'Johann Christoph Gottsched und Hrotsvit von Gandersheim,' offers details on Gottsched's commentary on Hrotsvit.

9 In 'Homage to Roswitha,' 124–5, and again in 'The Metamorphosis of Roswitha von Gandersheim in Works by Anatole France and Peter Hacks,' 79, Karl A. Zaenker provides details about the critical edition prepared by the theatre historian Charles Magnin. He notes that in the introduction to his edition Magnin suggests that the detailed descriptions of passions found in the canoness's plays could only have been written by a woman who had had such experiences before taking the veil – once again casting doubt on Hrotsvit's identity and background.

10 Aschbach, *Roswitha und Conrad Celtes*. At the beginning of the twentieth century Aschbach's assertion still found favour with some scholars; see, for example, Hart, 'Allotria 2,5,' 232. Recently, Alfred Tamerl, *Hrotsvith von Gandersheim: Eine Entmystifizierung* has resurrected Aschbach's ideas and

formulated several arguments of his own to refute Hrotsvit's identity and the authenticity of the writings attributed to her. Tamerl claims that the true author is Caritas Pirckheimer (1467–1532), a Nuremberg abbess active in Humanist circles.

11 The review was published in *Göttingische Gelehrte Anzeigen*, 2 (1867): 1261–70. Waitz took issue in particular with three of Aschbach's key ideas: the orthography was different from what one would expect in an eleventh-century manuscript; the Latin expressions resembled those of the fifteenth-century humanists; and references in the letters of the humanists provided evidence of their contribution to the counterfeit edition. For a summary of the controversy, see Zeydel, 'The Reception of Hrotsvitha by the German Humanists after 1493,' 249, n. 56, and Tamerl, *Hrotsvith von Gandersheim*, 103–18.

12 Frenken, 'Eine neue Hrotsvithandschrift.'

13 Menhardt, 'Eine unbekannte Hrotsvitha-Handschrift.' Tamerl, *Hrotsvit von Gandersheim*, comments on this and other manuscript evidence, 119–30.

14 Zaenker, 'Homage to Roswitha,' examines this issue from slightly different perspectives.

15 The works of two American authors, the play *J.B.* by Archibald MacLeish (1892–1982) and the Pulitzer-Prize-winning novel *A Confederacy of Dunces* by John Kennedy Toole (1937–69) are frequently mentioned as works with a Hrotsvit connection. Reference to MacLeish's drama is found in Nagel, *Hrotsvit von Gandersheim*, 79. The relationship between Toole's work and that of Hrotsvit is discussed in Zaenker, 'Hrotsvit and the Moderns: Her Impact on John Kennedy Toole and Peter Hacks,' 275–9.

16 Walz, 'Die Rezeption von Hrotsvits "Paraiso Sancti Pelagii" im iberischen Raum.'

17 Zaenker, 'Hrotsvit and the Moderns,' 276, translates the poem's title as 'The Gliding Scarlet Robe' and comments briefly on the political significance of the work.

18 For a more detailed study of the relationship of Hrotsvit's *Gesta Ottonis* to its contemporaneous sources, see Köpke, *Hrotsvit von Gandersheim: Zur Litteraturgeschichte des zehnten Jahrhunderts*, 86–117. In his essay in this volume, 'Hrotsvit of Gandersheim and the Problem of Royal Succession in the East Frankish Kingdom,' Jay T. Lees discusses Hrotsvit's intentions in writing the *Gesta Ottonis* and the political circumstances prevalent at the time.

19 Nagel, *Hrotsvit von Gandersheim* (1965), 83; Zaenker 'Hrotsvit and the Moderns,' 276; and Kronenberg, *Roswitha von Gandersheim: Leben und Werk*, 65–7, assert Meyer's indebtedness to Hrotsvit. Kronenberg offers a detailed comparison of the Hrotsvit scene and the Meyer poem.

20 Mühler, 'Kaiser Otto I,' and Giesebrecht, 'Geschichte der deutschen Kaiserzeit.' 276–7. Nentwig, 'Conrad Ferdinand Meyer,' 414–15 and 422–4, and Henel, *The Poetry of Conrad Ferdinand Meyer*, 322, mention both sources. Osterholz, '"Der gleitende Purpur": Versuch einer Deutung des C.F. Meyerschen Gedichtes,' 255, draws attention only to the Giesebrecht account. Nentwig is the only one to mention Hrotsvit in connection with 'Der gleitende Purpur,' maintaining, however, that there is no proof of Meyer's familiarity with the canoness's writings.

21 Both Mühler and Meyer incorrectly refer to Otto as 'emperor' in their poems about this incident.

22 See also the commentary by Kronenberg, *Roswitha von Gandersheim: Leben und Werk*, 65–7.

23 Bergman, *Hrosvithae Liber Tertius*. Sister Mary's work remains the sole published translation in English of all extant verses of the *Gesta* to date. Giesebrecht, 'Geschichte der deutschen Kaiserzeit,' 277, makes specific reference to the phrase 'Peace on Earth' (Friede auf Erden), sung by heavenly voices and echoing in Otto's heart as he makes the decision to pardon his brother.

24 Schöffler, *Conrad Ferdinand Meyer: Werke*, 193–4.

25 Mühler also mentions Christmas at the beginning (line 4) and the end (line 44) of 'Kaiser Otto I' but does not otherwise develop the motif.

26 Mühler likens Otto to a lion and portrays him as a man who shows mercy only when prompted to do so by others (see note 32 below). When Henry begs forgiveness, Otto coldly responds that he has already forgiven his brother twice and this time Henry will be put to death: '"Zweimal hab' ich vergeben, nicht fürder mehr fortan;/ Die Acht ist ausgesprochen, das Leben dir geraubt,/ Nach dreier Tage Wechsel, da fällt dein schuldig Haupt,"' ('Kaiser Otto I,' 314).

27 Meyer rewrote the poem in the 1860s; its original title was 'Kaiser Ottos Weihnachten.' He shortened the work from 21 to 13 stanzas, narrowing the literary focus to the moment when the brothers encounter each other in Frankfurt Cathedral. Nentwig, 'Conrad Ferdinand Meyer: Der gleitende Purpur,' 415–21, offers a worthwhile comparison of the two versions. Kraeger, *Conrad Ferdinand Meyer*, 87–93, provides a somewhat briefer commentary on the two versions. Henel, *The Poetry of Conrad Ferdinand Meyer*, 323, notes several theories regarding how and why the original text was modified.

28 In the *Gesta Ottonis* Hrotsvit alludes to Heinrich's captivity several years earlier by Duke Eberhard of Franconia, who bound 'with cruel chains [Heinrich's] white hands.' See Bergman, *Hrosvithae Liber Tertius*, 53, lines 179–85.

29 Schöffler, *Conrad Ferdinand Meyer: Werke*, 193: 'Kennst du mich als Kargen?' –

'Kennst du mich, den Argen? ... Du Gesalbter und Erlauchter!/ Kennst du mich?'

30 Ibid., 194: 'Wehe mir! Da du dich kröntest,/ Hat des Neides Natter mich gebissen!/ Mit dem Lügengeist im Bunde/ Hab ich dieses deutsche Reich zerrissen!/ Als den ungetreuen Bruder/ Und Verräter hast du mich erfunden!/ Du ergrimmtest und du warfest/ In die Kerkertiefe mich gebunden ... / In der Tiefe meines Kerkers /Hab ich ohne Mantel heut gefroren.'

31 Ibid. 'Heute wird der Welt das Heil geboren!'

32 Mühler presents a third scenario. Adamant about punishing Heinrich, Otto is moved to reconcile with his brother only when the abbot present in the cathedral reads Matthew 18:21–2, in which Christ admonishes Peter to forgive his brother seventy times seven times ('Kaiser Otto I' lines 37–40, p. 315). The sovereign's harshness gives way to tears, he embraces his brother, and a cry of joy stirs among those present – never had there been a more blessed Christmas celebration: 'Da schmilzt des Kaisers Strenge in Thränen, unbewußt,/ Er hebt ihn auf, den Bruder, er drückt ihn an die Brust,/ Ein lauter Ruf der Freude ist jubelnd rings erwacht –/ Nie schöner ward begangen die heil'ge Weihenacht' ('Kaiser Otto I' lines 41–4, p. 315). According to Giesebrecht, 'Geschichte der deutschen Kaiserzeit,' 277, it is Otto's recollection of the phrase 'Peace on earth' from the heavenly song that moves him to offer forgiveness.

33 Bäumer, *Männer und Frauen im geistigen Werden des deutschen Volkes*, 180–235 and 350–96 respectively.

34 Waitz, 'Über das Verhältnis von Hrotsuits *Gesta Oddonis* zu Widukind,' examines the relationship between the texts about Otto I authored by the canoness and the monk.

35 Bäumer, *Adelheid, Mutter der Königreiche*.

36 Ibid., 142.

37 Ibid., 513–14.

38 Among these are *Die Frau und das geistige Leben* (1911), *Studien über Frauen* (1920), *Die Frauengestalt der deutschen Frühe* (1928), and *Gestalt und Wandel: Frauenbildnisse* (1939).

39 Bäumer, *Die Frau und das geistige Leben*, 37: 'Ihre Bedeutung lag mehr darin, daß sie, auf männliche Posten durch Schicksal und Umstände berufen, sie relativ und jedenfalls für ihre Zeitgenossen überraschend gut ausfüllten.'

40 Although Adelheid's involvement in the politics of her day is well known, after Otto's death her attention shifted to religion. In her later years Adelheid devoted much time and effort to fostering the Cluniac movement, founding a number of religious houses, and aiding the poor. Canon-

ized in 1097, she is not included in the Roman martyrology, but she is venerated in some German dioceses today.

41 Bäumer, *Adelheid, Mutter der Königreiche*, 219.

42 Of interest as well from this time period is the essay on Hrotsvit by the poet and translator Rudolf Alexander Schröder. As a champion of Christian poetry and of his fellow citizens of Lower Saxony, Schröder recounts Hrotsvit reception, summarizes a number of her works, and offers words of praise for her accomplishments. His 1938 text is not the product of the prevailing political hierarchy but rather the work of a devout Christian who was a member of the 'Bekennende Kirche,' the 'confessing church' in Germany that opposed the Nazi regime. See Schröder, 'Roswitha von Gandersheim.'

43 Zaenker, 'Hrotsvit and the Moderns,' 276, and Zeydel, 'Hrotsvit von Gandersheim and the Eternal Womanly,' 10, note that Jules Massenet's opera *Thaïs* (1894) was inspired by France's novel, and Zeydel at least alleges the indirect influence of Hrotsvit on Massenet's work.

No Hrotsvit influence has been claimed for *Thais: The Story of a Sinner Who Became a Saint and a Saint Who Sinned* (1911) by the American playwright Paul Wilstach or the 1918 motion picture *Thais*. See Kuehne, *A Study of the Thais Legend*, 106–15, for descriptions of these productions.

44 The two essays first appeared in *Le Temps* and were included in France's oeuvre: Anatole France, 'Les marionnettes de M. Signoret,' and 'Hrotswitha aux marionnettes.' Kuehne, *A Study of the Thais Legend*, 90–2, is among the first to make reference to these essays. Gout, 'Anatole France et le théâtre de Hrotsvitha,' 598–603, discusses them and quotes from them more extensively.

45 See Kuehne, *A Study of the Thais Legend*, 90–2 and 99–100; Gout, 'Anatole France et le théâtre de Hrotsvitha'; Zaenker, 'Homage to Roswitha,' 125–8, and 'The Metamorphosis of Roswitha von Gandersheim in Works by Anatole France and Peter Hacks,' 79–80; Wilson, 'Two Notes on Anatole France's Debt to Hrotsvit,' 18–19, 22; and Van Hoof, 'The Saint and the Sinner.' Among the aspects that have been examined are the verbatim borrowings from Hrotsvit's *Pafnutius* as well as *Abraham* and *Sapientia*; the significance of the abbess figure; Thais's burning of her possessions; and animal imagery that depicts Thais as a kid and a gazelle in the clutches of the manly wolves. Kuehne, 99–101, and Gout, 609, identify other works that influenced France's novel.

46 Van Hoof, 'The Saint and the Sinner,' writes, '"The Lotus," the white flower of the Nile which is associated with sensuality, purity and oblivion, refers to Thais ... The second part, "The Papyrus," tells us about Thais's childhood

and includes the very important banquet-scene ... Additionally, the word "Papyrus" also denotes poison. The author hints at the similarity between Thais poisoning Pafnutius's emotions and the philosophical discussion corrupting his spirit ... In the third part, "The Euphorbium," meaning a crown of thorns, France displays his ironical skills ... [T]he saintly hermit ... has turned into a caricature of Christ' (266).

47 France, *Thaïs*, trans. Gulati, 27. The French original, Anatole France, *Œuvres*, 721, states: 'En ce temps-là le désert était peuplé d'anachorètes.'

48 *Thaïs*, trans. Gulati, 181; *Œuvres*, 861: 'Je l'invitais à représenter devant nous les actions des femmes fortes et des vierges sages de l'Écriture.'

49 Zaenker, 'The Metamorphosis of Roswitha von Gandersheim in Works by Anatole France and Peter Hacks,' 80.

50 *Thaïs*, trans. Gulati, 182; *Œuvres*, 861: 'Dieu, le ciel, tout cela n'est rien. Il n'y a de vrai que la vie de la terre et l'amour des êtres.'

51 *Thaïs*, trans. Gulati, 182; *Œuvres*, 863: 'Elle poussa un soupir d'allégresse ... Paphnuce ... la dévorait de désir, de rage et d'amour.'

52 *Thaïs*, trans. Gulati, 183; *Œuvres*, 863: 'Il était devenu si hideux qu'en passant la main sur son visage il sentit sa laideur.'

53 Zaenker, 'The Metamorphosis of Roswitha von Gandersheim in Works by Anatole France and Peter Hacks,' 79.

54 I would like to thank Phyllis Brown for this reference. Gout, 'Anatole France et le théatre de Hrotsvitha,' 607, also suggests that France is borrowing from *Calimachus* in this scene.

55 Stewart, *On Life and Letters by Anatole France*, 14; France, 'Hrotswitha aux marionettes,' 13: 'C'était une honnête créature, que Hrotswitha; attachée à son état, ne concevant rien de plus beau que la vie religieuse, elle n'eut d'autre objet, en écrivant des comédies, que de célébrer les louanges de la chasteté.'

56 Bertini, *Il 'Teatro' di Rosvita*, 72–3, notes the contradictory nature of France's world as opposed to that of Hrotsvit in his brief comparison of the two works.

57 Case, *Feminism and Theatre*, 35.

58 Bosker, *Sechs Stücke nach Stücken*, 8–9, provides a list of Hacks's dramas and the works from which they were adapted.

59 Zaenker, 'The Metamorphosis of Roswitha von Gandersheim in Works by Anatole France and Peter Hacks,' 79.

60 Zaenker, 'Hrotsvit and the Moderns,' 276 and 279.

61 Hacks, *Das Jahrmarktsfest*.

62 Zaenker describes each scene of Hacks's play and identifies the source of it from among Hrotsvit's plays in 'Hrotsvit and the Moderns,' 279–80.

Lenschen, 'Du drame religieux au théâtre socialiste: Hrotsvit de Gandersheim et Peter Hacks,' provides additional commentary, especially on Hrotsvit's *Dulcitius*, as well as the socialist aspects of Hacks's work, as the title indicates. Franco, 'I drammi di Rosvita e *Rosie träumt* di Peter Hacks,' offers the most detailed description of the relationship between Hacks's work and Hrotsvit's various plays.

63 Zaenker, 'Hrotsvit and the Moderns,' 280, makes this point, as does Glew, 'From Brecht to "Socialist Classicism": The Aesthetic Theory of Peter Hacks,' 533. Glew's extensive (unpublished) study – almost 600 pages – characterizes the change in Hacks's attitude toward socialism during his career up to 1980. In his recent commentary on the final scene of *Rosie träumt*, Volker Riedel offers a more general critique in terms of disillusionment with 'a teaching that had promised final freedom and salvation in the near future and [with] a practice that delayed this goal ever further' (... Desillusionierung über eine Lehre, die für die nächste Zukunft eine endgültige Befreiung und Erlösung versprochen hatte, und über eine Praxis, die dieses Ziel immer weiter hinausschob), 'Utopien und Wirklichkeit,' 64.

64 Hacks, *Das Jahrmarktfest*, 73: 'Aber es kostet Kräfte, fromm zu sein.'

65 Ibid., 72: 'Hiervon nehme ich keine Schuld auf mich ... aber glaubt mir, Kaisers, sobald man es irgend mit Christen zu tun hat, gehen die Pannen los.'

66 Ibid., 81: 'Jesus wird mir bestehen.'

67 Zaenker, 'Hrotsvit and the Moderns,' 282–3, suggests a different source for the final scene, namely the novella *Légende Poldéve* by Marcel Aymé (1902–67); however, he notes, 283, that Hacks has not abandoned Hrotsvit, citing references to her as well. Glew, 'From Brecht to "Socialist Classicism": The Aesthetic Theory of Peter Hacks,' 532, describes this scene as 'almost Kafkaesque.'

68 Zaenker, 'Hrotsvit and the Moderns,' 283, comments on the significance of this identification.

69 Hacks, *Das Jahrmarktfest*, 120: 'Es gibt so viele Himmel, doch kaum weniger als sieben ...'

70 Ibid., 121: '... man muß glauben, wenn man noch kann.'

71 Hacks, 'Zehn Zeilen über *Rosie träumt*,' 122: '[Dies ist] die Liebesgeschichte zwischen einem Mann von dem entschlossensten Hange zum Durchführbaren und einem Mädchen von der Apo ...'

72 Ibid., 129.

73 Zaenker, 'The Metamorphosis of Roswitha von Gandersheim in Works by Anatole France and Peter Hacks,' 81.

74 Hacks, 'Zehn Zeilen über *Rosie traümt*,' 122–3.

75 Zaenker, 'Hrotsvit and the Moderns,' 281–2.

76 Mitchell, *Peter Hacks: Theatre for a Socialist Society*, 138. Trilse, *Peter Hacks: Leben und Werk*, 246–54, also is of the opinion that Hacks falls short of his mark with *Rosie träumt*.

77 Hacks, *Das Jahrmarktfest*, 121: 'Wollt ihr mir nicht folgen?'

78 Trilse, *Peter Hacks: Leben und Werk*, 253.

79 Zaenker, 'Homage to Roswitha,' 131, and 'The Metamorphosis of Roswitha von Gandersheim in Works by Anatole France and Peter Hacks,' 81, notes the dramatists' use of parody.

'Bring me a soldier's garb and a good horse': Embedded Stage Directions in the Dramas of Hrotsvit of Gandersheim

JANET SNYDER

Much has been made of the reading as opposed to the performance of the plays of Hrotsvit of Gandersheim during the tenth century.[1] Participants in the recent debate must contend with three difficulties: defining performance, whether it is a staged reading, mime, or fully staged drama; allowing the short plays to exist as a different kind of drama rather than requiring them to conform to guidelines of alien (classical) forms; and accepting that women might have participated in some sort of presentation within the confines of Gandersheim. In the preface to her plays, words suggest the dramas were meant to be read (or read aloud) rather than acted.[2] For example, Hrotsvit writes:

> Sunt etiam alii sacris inherentes paginis · qui licet alia gentilium spernant · Terentii tamen fingmenta frequentius lectitant · et dum dulcedine sermonis delectantur · nefandarum notitia rerum maculantur · Unde ego Clamor Validus Gandeshemensis · non recusavi illum imitari dictando · dum alii colunt legendo (*Liber Secundus, Praefatio*, 2)

> There are also others, who, devoted to sacred reading and scorning the works of other pagans, yet frequently read Terence's fiction,/ and as they delight in the sweetness of his style and diction,/ they are stained by learning of wicked things in his depiction./ Therefore I, the strong voice of Gandersheim, have not refused to imitate him in writing/ whom others laud in reading (Wilson, *Florilegium*, 41)

Despite words like these, the plays themselves provide evidence for their performability and perhaps even of performance, because the necessary actions of characters are so clearly embedded in the text that amateurs can easily decipher the requirements of staging. The six plays Hrotsvit wrote also contain textual evidence suggesting her role as writer-director. She was so skilful in weaving this staging information into the dialogue that one familiar with subsequent theatre work might assume that the text records a script created collaboratively with readers or performers. This essay will investigate these internal cues, which are strong and constant throughout Hrotsvit's plays. The focus will be on the manner in which the characters' words direct the plot and the mise en scène in the plays.

The range of possible performances that were taking place in various venues during Hrotsvit's lifetime was tremendous and had been since the fall of the Roman Empire.[3] Although in recent years one group of scholars concluded that 'these texts were not written for the stage,'[4] others propose a reevaluation of the plays as pigeon-holed into classical dramatic genres of literature (and more precisely, theatre literature) as social institution, and the notion of 'the stage' during this period.[5] However, absence of evidence that these plays were intended for public performance on a conventional theatrical stage does not mean they were not performed, since this is a period when the conventions of classical theatrical staging were rare or perhaps absent. Nevertheless, classical works were read in monasteries and schools,[6] women were known to have sung parts in liturgical presentations,[7] and gestural accompaniment to Christian ritual was promoted.[8] Thus even though the boundaries between closet drama, playlets read aloud, and fully-staged theatre remain elusive, there is evidence that Hrotsvit wrote like a director, in a manner similar to that of twentieth-century playwright Samuel Beckett, stipulating gestures and actions within the text.[9] In fact, the equivalent of stage directions are so much a part of the unfolding of the plot that some critics now argue that Hrotsvit's manuscripts are records of performances that actually took place in the tenth century. For example, David Wiles writes, 'These texts are the encoding of a dramatic event ... the texts were performed first and then processed by the scriptorium in order that they could be read by scholars and incorporated in a manuscript.'[10]

In the plays, Hrotsvit provides sufficient information not only for the thread of the story and the actions of the characters to be understood but also for the details of setting and costume to be clear.[11] For example, at the very end of *Calimachus* John says to Andronicus, 'Recedamus · suumque diabolo filium relinquamus' (X.13), 'Let us return and not stay any further, let us leave the Devil's son to his father' (Wilson, *Florilegium*,

65), suggesting action to accompany the words. In a more complex example early in *Sapientia*, Sapientia says to Antiochus, 'Monstra viam pręeundo · nos subsequimur accelerando' (II.2), 'Go ahead, and show the way; we shall follow without delay' (Wilson, *Florilegium*, 83); Antiochus's next words to Sapientia and her daughters, 'Hic ipse est imperator quem in solio residentem conspicis · pręcogita quid loquaris' (III.1), 'Behold the Emperor seated on his throne; be careful of what you say' (Wilson, *Florilegium*, 83), specify that movement to a new place has occurred.

Detailed analysis of two plays, *Lapsus et Conversio Marię Neptis Habrahę Heremicolę* (The Fall and Repentance of Mary, the Hermit Abraham's Niece) and *Dulcitius*, provides further evidence that textual cues function as stage directions. In *Lapsus et Conversio Marię*, after Abraham learns that Mary has become a prostitute, the dialogue specifies costume and action:

> *Abraham* Affer mihi sonipedem delicatum · et militarem habitum · quo
>   deposito tegmine religionis · ipsam adeam sub specie amatoris ·
> *Amicus* Ecce omnia ·
> *Abraham* Affer obsecro et pilleum · quo coronam velem capitis
> *Amicus* Hoc maxime opus est ne agnoscaris ·   (IV.5)

> *Abraham* Bring me a soldier's garb and a good horse so that, after I lay
>   aside my religious habit, I may go to her, disguised as a lover, with all
>   speed./
> *Friend* Here is all you need./
> *Abraham* Give me a hat also to hide my tonsure.
> *Friend* This, too, is very necessary/ so as not to reveal your identity.
>   (Wilson, *Florilegium*, 73)

Another scene in *Lapsus et Conversio Marię* is particularly notable for the way in which Hrotsvit develops the plot and specifies what action should take place on stage through the lines spoken by the characters. After Abraham has arrived at the inn, disguised as a traveling soldier, he arranges with the Innkeeper for a place to stay, dinner, and 'praepulchra quam tecum observari experiebar puella · nostro intersit convivio' (V.2), 'the most beautiful girl who, as I hear, stays with you, to share our meal' (Wilson, *Florilegium*, 74). The Innkeeper announces Mary's arrival by speaking directly to her, 'Procede · procede Maria · tuique pulchritudinem nostro neophitae ostende' (VI.1), 'Come Mary, come along. Show your beauty to our newcomer' (Wilson, *Florilegium*, 74). Mary replies, 'Ecce venio' (VI.1), 'Here I am' (Wilson, *Florilegium*, 74).

Abraham's aside – allowing a reader or audience but not other characters in the play to know his thoughts – specifies that he will play his part in disguise with aplomb, even when, as in contemporary conventional visual representations, Mary's clothing signals the state of her soul:

> (Secum dicit ·) Quę fiducia · quę constantia mentis mihi post hęc · cum hanc quam nutrivi in heremi latibulis meretricio cultu ornatam conspicio? Sed non est tempus ut praefiguretur in facie · quod tenetur in corde · erumpentes lacrimas viriliter stringo · et simulata vultus hilaritate internę amaritudinem mestitudinis contego · (VI.1)

> What boldness, what constancy of mind I must muster as I see her whom I raised in my hidden hermitage decked out in a harlot's garb./ But this is not the time to show in my face what is in my heart;/ I must be on guard:/ I will bravely suppress my tears gushing forth, like a man. With feigned cheerfulness of countenance I will veil the bitterness of my internal grief. (Wilson, *Florilegium*, 74)

This opportunity to present one character's thoughts while other performers participate in the scene is one of the tools of a playwright not available to the author of a legend or romance. The narrator or storyteller might explain a character's feelings or describe the scene, but in drama, only words, actions, and gestures can reveal a character's interior condition. Hrotsvit's use of the aside supports the modern contention that these dramas were meant to be heard. Theatre historians have generally accepted that Shakespeare's published texts record the staging of performances by his company, the Chamberlain's Men, including the theatrical conventions employed to convey ideas.[12] In much the same way, Hrotsvit's use of such conventions suggests her written texts at once dictate action and record performance.

Soon after Mary directs her attention to Abraham, her words mark a change in the tone of the drama. Her aside, followed by another from Abraham, gives the play an operatic quality:

> *Maria*   Quid sentio? quid stupendę novitatis gustando haurio? Ecce odor istius flagrantię praetendit flagrantiam mihi quondam usitate abstinentię
> *Abraham*   Nunc nunc est · simulandum · nunc lascivientis more pueri iocis instandum · ne et ego agnoscar prae gravitate · et ipsa se reddat latibulis prae pudore   (VI.3)

Mary What is it I feel? What is this spell?/ What is this rare and wonderful odor I smell?/ Oh the smell of this fragrance reminds me of the fragrance of chastity I once practiced!

Abraham Now, now I must pretend, now I must persist, now I must be lustful in the manner of lewd young men and play the game/ so that I am not recognized by my seriousness or else she might leave and hide for shame. (Wilson, *Florilegium*, 75)

Mary's words, full of remorse, befit her true, pure self, which still recognizes Abraham's odour of sanctity,[13] and invite the viewer or reader to contrast her earlier condition with her present employment. Abraham's words remind the viewer or reader, but not other characters on stage, play-acting is fundamental to his goal of bringing Mary back to her true self.

Both the Innkeeper and Abraham respond to Mary's next words ('Ve mihi infelici · unde cecidi · et in quam perdicionis foveam corrui,' 'Woe is me, wretched woman! How I sank, how I fell into perdition's pit!'), setting the action of the play back in motion, including action in a lapse of time specified by the dialogue:

Maria Levi compunctione permovebar · ideo talia fabar · sed epulemur · et letemur · quia ut monuisti · hic non est tempus peccata plangendi

Abraham Affatim refecti affatim sumus inebriati · tua largitate administrante · o bone stabularie · da licentiam a cena surgendi · quo lassum corpus in stratu componam · dulcique quiete recreem (VI.6)

Mary I was moved by a slight regret to utter such words; but let us now dine and be merry/ because, as you admonished me,/ this is certainly not the time to bewail one's sins.

Abraham Abundantly we have wined,/ abundantly we have dined,/ and are now tipsy, good host, with generous portions you served. Give us now leave to rise from the table/ so that I might be able/ to lay down and refresh my weary body by sweet rest. (Wilson, *Florilegium*, 75)

In the space between these two statements, they must have luxuriated in extravagant feasting and carousing. The theatrical opportunity is tremendous: if this were nineteenth-century opera, the ballet corps would burst onto the stage for a wild and decadent dance. Although such improvisation is unlikely under Hrotsvit's direction and for her audience, nevertheless the playwright's choice of silence leaves open infinite possibilities for the imagination. While the fragrance of chastity invites readers and viewers to compare the scene with other scenes characterized by sanctity, the space between Mary's statement and Abraham's statement invites enactment of the sensual activities in the inn that contrast with the (presumed) sanctity of Abraham's ordinary life.

After the Innkeeper grants Abraham's request, Mary says, 'Surge domine mi · surge · tecum pariter tendam ad cubile' (VI.6), 'Rise, my lord, rise up. I shall accompany you to your bedroom' (Wilson, *Florilegium*, 75). In the dramatic scene that follows, Hrotsvit is at her best in the description and narration specifying mise en scène. On entering the bedroom, Mary behaves like a tour guide, chatting about the luxurious furnishings before asking if she can take off his shoes: 'Ecce triclinium ad inhabitandum nobis aptum · ecce lectus haut vilibus stramentis compositus · Sede ut tibi detraham calciamenta · ne tu ipse fatigeris discalciando' (VII.1), 'Here is a bedroom for us to stay in. Here is the bed, decked with rich and lovely coverlets. Sit down, so that I may take off your shoes and then you won't have to tire yourself removing them' (Wilson, *Florilegium*, 75). At his request, they lock the door and in the scene's denouement Mary's repentance is achieved via repartee which compares well with the best nineteenth-century plays.

Although a very different play, details in *Dulcitius* are similar in their specifications for staging. For example, as Dulcitius comes on stage from the pantry where his prisoners Agape, Chionia, and Hirena had observed his fondling of the pots and pans, Hirena says, 'Nam facies · manus · ac vestimenta · adeo sordidata · coinquinata · ut nigredo quę inhęsit · similitudinem Aethiopis exprimat' (IV.3), 'His face, his hands, his clothes, are so soiled, so filthy, that with all the soot that clings to him, he looks like an Ethiopian' (Wilson, *Florilegium*, 48); then some soldiers announce his entrance before running away, confirming Hirena's description of his appearance:

> *Milites*   Quis hic egreditur? dęmoniacus · Vel magis ipse diabolus?
> Fugiamus ·
> *Dulcitius*   Milites · quo fugitis? state · expectate · dulcite me cum lucernis
> ad cubile ·
> *Milites*   Vox senioris nostri · sed imago diaboli · Non subsistamus · sed
> fugam maturemus · fantasma vult nos pessumdare ·
> *Dulcitius*   Ad palatium ibo · et quam abiectionem patiar · principibus
> vulgabo ·   (V.1)

Soldiers   Who is coming out?/ A demon without doubt./ Or rather, the
   Devil himself is he;/ let us flee!
Dulcitius   Soldiers, where are you taking yourself in flight?/ Stay! Wait!
   Escort me home with your light!/
Soldiers   The voice is our master's tone/ but the look the Devil's own./
   Let us not stay!/ Let us run away; the apparition will slay us!/
Dulcitius   I will go to the palace and complain,/ and reveal to the
   whole court the insults I had to sustain.   (Wilson, *Florilegium*, 48)

Since Dulcitius demands light as well as an escort, the scene must be
dark. After Dulcitius arrives at the palace, the dialogue makes explicit
that the scene has changed and a group of guards is beating Dulcitius,
denying him an audience with Diocletian:

Dulcitius   Hostiarii introducite me in palatium · quia ad imperatorem
   habeo secretum ·
Hostiarii   Quid hoc vile ac detestabile monstrum · scissis et nigellis
   panniculis obsitum? pugnis tundamus · de gradu praecipitemus · nec
   ultra huc detur liber accessus ·   (VI.1)

Dulcitius   Guards, let me into the palace;/ I must have a private audience.
Soldiers   Who is this vile and detestable monster/ covered in torn and
   despicable rags?/ Let us beat him,/ from the steps let us sweep him;/ he
   must not be allowed to enter.   (Wilson, *Florilegium*, 48)

These details not only contribute to the reader's or viewer's understanding of the central action and characterization of the play, they also
suggest opportunities for improvised stage business, including the rough-
handling of Dulcitius by the palace guards.

   Like asides, soliloquies can provide information otherwise presented
in stage directions. Shakespeare's actors really had no need for stage
directions when, in the first scene of the third act of *Hamlet*, Polonious
says, 'I hear him coming. Let's withdraw, my Lord'; and in the next line
Hamlet's third soliloquy, 'To be or not to be,' begins. The words specify
Hamlet's arrival and his solitude for the soliloquy. While not marked by
the moral ambiguities of *Hamlet* or by other characters' observations
from onstage, the emperor Diocletian's soliloquy in *Dulcitius* nevertheless anticipates later developments in drama. First the soldiers announce their failure to carry out Dulcitius's command that they strip
the girls of their clothing; then they note the fact that Dulcitius has

242 Janet Snyder

fallen asleep, and voice their intention to report these things to the emperor:

> Frustra sudamus · in vanum laboramus · ecce vestimenta virgineis corporibus inherent velut coria · sed et ipse qui nos ad exspoliandum urgebat preses stertit sedendo · nec ullatenus excitari potest a somno · Ad imperatorem adeamus · ipsique rerum quę geruntur propalemus · (VIII)

> We labor in vain;/ we sweat without gain./ Behold, their garments stick to their virginal bodies like skin,/ and he who urged us to strip them snores in his seat,/ and he cannot be awakened from his sleep./ Let us go to the Emperor and report what has happened. (Wilson, *Florilegium*, 49)

Then, in the next speech of the play, Diocletian says,

> Dolet nimium quod presidem Dulcitium audio · adeo illusum · adeo exprobratum · adeo calumniatum · Sed ne viles mulierculę iactent se impune nostris diis · deorumque cultoribus illudere · Sisinnium comitem dirigam ad ultionem exercendam (IX)

> It grieves me very much/ to hear that Governor Dulcitius has been so greatly deluded,/ so greatly insulted,/ so utterly humiliated./ But these vile young women shall not boast with impunity of having made a mockery of our gods and those who worship them. I shall direct Count Sissinus to take due vengeance. (Wilson, *Florilegium*, 49)

If this speech is performed as a soliloquy, [14] it emphasizes the contrast between the sinister emperor, standing alone, and the buffoon Dulcitius, who not only made a fool of himself by making love to the pots and pans, thinking they were lovely virgins, but also fell asleep as his soldiers struggled to carry out his commands. Significantly, that contrast ultimately serves to suggest that the dramatic parallel between the emperor and Dulcitius extends to Sissinus, who predictably is no more successful than Dulcitius had been in carrying out the vengeance on the girls. In a sense, the emperor's speech emphasizes the fact that no Roman power, not even that of the emperor himself, is equal to that of Christian martyrs. This comic-serious / religious-secular combination would not appear incongruous for the medieval audience, who would perceive it, in Alan Knight's words, 'as an association rendered dramatically necessary by the nature of the world.' [15]

Hrotsvit's plays vary in the extent to which they seem dramatic. In some scenes, the dramatic elements are fully developed, and the action is advanced through dialogue; more often, the characters narrate what has happened in a more static fashion. In both instances, though, the specification of blocking (the large movements of the actors) and gestures through the dialogue suggests that Hrotsvit may have written down the dialogues after she had witnessed one or more of them performed. In *Conversio Thaidis Meretricis*, often referred to as *Pafnutius*, disguises, joyous greetings, and named recognitions shape interactions between characters; and in *The Fall and Repentance of Mary, Gallicanus, Calimachus*, and *Pafnutius*, large movements are spelled out by characters' remarks. As early as the fifth century BCE in Greece, Western playwrights employed script-centred information to structure dramatic action. Moreover, the habits of mind practised during the Middle Ages[16] – that is, habits of thought, memory, and imagination – would contribute to listeners' abilities to understand spoken stage directions. As in the classical Latin plays Hrotsvit identifies as her models and as in the Elizabethan plays which followed, it was a dramatic convention to have the characters make direct statements concerning entrances and exits, recognitions, disguises, and actions to be undertaken – in other words, to have the words convey the substance of the action produced on the stage. Like her predecessors and successors, Hrostvit interwove spoken stage directions into the dramatic dialogues, soliloquies, and asides to direct the action and to shape the gestures of the performance – whether fully staged, declaimed, presented with mimed action accompanying a public reading of the script, or read silently and privately. Therefore, although the manuscripts contain no stage directions in the modern sense, the embedded stage directions answer many of the questions modern scholars have posed concerning the logistics of scene changes and internal consistency in the physical arrangement of entrances, exits, and stage space. These cues for action and gesture in Hrotsvit's plays are strong and frequent.

Hrotsvit's plays function best for audiences prepared to receive the multivalent messages conveyed through the performance of the texts. Although one of the intended audiences was certainly readers – the group of literate patrons to whom Hrotsvit sent the manuscript, soliciting advice and approval – performances probably addressed a broader community. Who might have participated in that audience? The techniques employed in Hrotsvit's crafting of the plays suggest that both readers and audiences who might have been present for performances of her plays would have shared acquaintance with common works of literature and conventions of visual expression. Lynette Muir avers, 'We can be sure that the plays had a well-behaved audience since they would be under the authority of the convent's superior.'[17] They probably were also conversant with the oral traditions of narrative storytelling and the visual structures of narrative in representation. Members of courtly communities were accustomed to listening to stories. These were active listeners: they could retain complex stories in the mind and they could comprehend relationships between characters in different genres.[18] Further, Hrotsvit could depend on the use of the trained memory; intellectuals among her audience would easily understand the abbreviation of episodes into small scenes, tableaux, and gestures, appreciate emphasis through ornamentation, and be able to recall information even when it was presented in seemingly random order.[19]

The sophisticated ability of Hrotsvit's audience to process various modes of information delivery is suggested by the visual arts of her contemporaries.[20] A successive narrative style of wall painting and the use of simultaneous images in Ottonian miniatures illustrates potential staging of miraculous and violent events. In the tenth-century plays of Hrotsvit as in ancient Greek drama, some gruesome tortures or miraculous events which occur offstage are graphically described by witnesses. Hrotsvit's descriptions of tortures may function much like descriptions in Greek tragedies. In *Oedipus the King*, the second messenger reports the actions of Oedipus and then his words direct audience attention to the entrance of the blind king.[21] In *Medea*, audience empathy and sympathetic experience soar when the Nurse describes the agonizing death Medea caused Jason's bride. Catharsis might be experienced through the words declaimed/sung in the vast space of the Greek theatre. In the plays of Hrotsvit, the words of the martyrs conjure up scenes in the mind with such force that minimal dramatization of action would be appropriate, given the expectations of her possible audience. However horrific each episode of martyrdom seems to be, these are conventional rather than unique episodes of martyrdom.[22] The precise details with which those tortures are described in Hrotsvit's dramas suggest parallels with classical declamation rather than the literal performance of tortures. The characters' words articulate plot and mise en scène: when the tortured martyrs describe their experiences, their lines conjure up the scenes in the imagination so that minimal dramatization of that action would be necessary, given the expectations of the contemporary audience. As a result of experiencing a performance, the believing audience might feel transported through a kind of spiritual contact with personified holy characters.

Miraculous events occurring offstage also benefit from Hrotsvit's sensitive descriptions in the dialogue. Courtly auditors could appreciate Gallicanus's description of divine intervention in battle: 'Apparuit mihi iuvenis procerę magnitudinis · crucem ferens in humeris et praecepit · ut stricto mucrone illum sequerer' (I.XII.7), 'A tall youth appeared bearing a cross on His shoulders and ordered me to follow Him with my drawn sword' (Wilson, *Plays*, 24). They would not only note the parallel to the conversion of the emperor Constantine in a similar battle; they would also be aware of the differences between Gallicanus's description of the event and the version presented earlier in *Gallicanus*, in which the surrender of the enemy was an immediate response to Gallicanus's conversion.[23]

A similar double report of a miraculous event involving a handsome youth occurs in *Calimachus*. In this instance the first witnesses are Andronicus and Saint John, who reports the vision in real time: 'Ecce invisibilis deus nobis apparet visibilis · in pulcherrimi similitudine iuvenis' (VIII.2), 'Behold the invisible God appears visible in the likeness of a handsome young man' (Wilson, *Florilegium*, 59). Though he recognizes God in the likeness of the handsome young man, John nevertheless is unable to understand God's explanation for his appearance. Therefore, it remains to Andronicus, recovered from the trembling he announced at the Divine appearance, to speak reasonably, like an ancient Greek chorus, and to advise action: 'Maturemus gressum · forte re experieris in perventione · quod asseris te minus intellegere' (VIII.3), 'Let us hurry. Perhaps you will understand when we arrive there what you don't understand now' (Wilson, *Florilegium*, 59). The second report comes from the recovered Calimachus, after confessing his intended sin:

Mihi autem apparuit iuvenis aspectu terribilis · qui detectum corpus honorifice texit · ex cuius flammea facie candentes in bustum scintillę transiliebant · quarum una resiliens mihi in faciem ferebatur · simulque vox facta est dicens · 'Calimache morere ut vivas' · His dictis exspiravi · (IX.13)

But to me a youth appeared, of terrifying sight/ who respectfully covered the naked corpse as He did alight./ From His flaming countenance sparks rained on the place/ and one of them, rebounding, hit my face./ At the same time I heard a voice that cried:/ 'Calimachus, die so that you may live.' Then I died. (Wilson, *Florilegium*, 61)

In none of these examples is it absolutely explicit whether God would be impersonated. In *Gallicanus* it seems likely that he would not appear, though the second narrated version of Gallicanus's conversion could determine the staging of the earlier scene. In *Calimachus*, God could speak to John and Andronicus from off stage and not appear in the enactment of Calimachus's death, but in both plays it is also possible for the words to encourage particular details in the staging of the scenes. Hrotsvit so skillfully weaves information about the visual arrangements and gestural action into the dialogue that one might accept David Wiles's hypothesis that the text records a script developed through a workshop with readers or performers. A director/playwright's vision of performed language contained in the dramatic script would enable subsequent performers to impersonate the characters. The words of the play guide actors in their performance and readers or listeners in their interpretation.

Concerns about the appropriateness of members of the religious community, known to all the audience, assuming fictional roles in performances can be assuaged in light of medieval visual conventions. The aesthetic in which extended narrative is represented by a series of static scenes provides the visual vocabulary: in sculpture, carved panels, manuscript illuminations, and fresco paintings throughout Europe, miraculous moments and episodes of torture were recorded in excruciating detail. In manuscripts like the Moutier-Grandval Bible of Tours, ca. 840, illuminations include distinctively costumed central characters of narratives who reappear in sequence on the page, as if in tableaux vivants.[24] In the ninth century, incidents arranged as units in registers or loosely gathered in scenic fields symbolically stood for whole narratives as opposed to the single static central figure of earlier manuscripts. Members of the Ottonian court and persons in Hrotsvit's social stratum were well travelled and acquainted with visual representations similar to those of the martyrs in *Sapientia*. The wealth of detail and narration in the wall frescoes in the little monastery church of Müstair in Graubünden, ca. 800, demonstrates the conventions of representation in Carolingian monumental painting.[25]

Though most early Ottonian manuscripts were copies of Carolingian codices, during the tenth and eleventh centuries the empire experienced a cultural upswing. Under Otto III the passion for books reached a high point.[26] In this period the production of precious manuscripts was sponsored by lay noblemen, bishops, and abbots as well as the king. The royal court made a free exchange of artistic ideas possible.[27] In these luxury manuscripts, simultaneous images of known personages, usually recognizable from costume details, populate the full-page illustrations. For example, in The Gospel Book of Otto III (ca. 1000), the dramatic Christ Washing of the Feet of the Disciples shows all participants frozen in the moment of confrontation when Jesus overrules Peter's objections to his humble task.[28] A successive narrative style of wall painting employed in the picture cycles at St Georg, Oberzell/Reichenau, ca. 980, illustrates a potential staging of miracles and a violent storm through its 'dramaturgical construction of the narrative.'[29] Other examples of the conventional presentation of narrative in individual tableaux appear on the bronze doors of Bishop Bernward for Saint Michael's, Hildesheim (ca. 1015), and on the painted wooden reliefs representing the Life of Christ on the doors of St Maria im Kapitol, Cologne (ca. 1065).

Medieval performances like the early tenth-century trope *Quem Queritis* may have functioned as a liturgical elaboration on the Easter Mass, but lacking the attempt at impersonation, they were not truly drama.[30] The actions and gestures specified in the stage directions embedded in the dialogue of Hrotsvit's plays bring the characters to life. In writing this impersonation through action, Hrotsvit conceived a drama which did not have to be but could be enacted. The substance of the theatre – plot, character, gesture, action, dialogue – is contained in the scripts of her plays, and the words of the plays demand imaginative involvement, whether or not they were staged in a way recognizable to modern critics. Just as the liturgical elaborations of holy events collapsed past, present, and future, so that events in the life of Christ could be experienced in real time, Hrotsvit's plays allow her readers and the audiences of her plays to experience in real time something of the laudable excellence of her heroes and heroines. As Katharina Wilson explains, she grafted elements of the sacred *vita*, 'which not only intended to manifest the continuing nature of divine grace or Church dogma but also mandated – by insistence on author-reader interaction – an adherence to and emulation of the ideal promoted,' onto the form provided to her by Terentian comedy.[31]

Hrotsvit worked self-consciously as the creator of the performed word, like the modern director/playwright. For her dramatic works she devised ways to communicate experiences by employing ancient theatrical conventions adapted to her needs, including embedded stage directions. She put actions into the text in order to communicate with her sisters and others who might perform the plays, in whatever venue they might find an audience. Her characters make direct statements concerning entrances and exits, recognitions, disguises, and actions to be undertaken. She took care to keep most gruesome tortures and miraculous events out of sight but allowed them to be graphically described by witnesses. Evidence from other periods suggest these practical issues were worked out through practice reading or performance before a script was committed to the written page. The text is, then, the shadow of performed action, especially since gesture has often been considered 'truer' than language.[32] The habits of mind practised among intellectuals of the tenth century and the formulas of illustration practised in contemporary visual arts meant that her audience was endowed with a vivid imagination and a spiritual readiness for her plays. Neither the scripts that have survived nor performances suggested by the scripts would have disappointed them.

NOTES

1 The debate concerning the performance of Hrotsvit's plays has been raging for at least two centuries: see Wiles, 'Hrosvitha of Gandersheim: The Performance of Her Plays in the Tenth Century,' and, for a summary and analysis of earlier debate, see Zeydel, 'Were Hrotsvitha's Dramas Performed during Her Lifetime?' For a summary of the analysis by Italian scholars, see Sticca, 'Italy: Liturgy and Christocentric Spirituality,' 176–7.
2 For a discussion of the tenth-century reading of ancient authors see Dronke, *Women Writers of the Middle Ages*, 69–70.
3 See Harris, *Medieval Theatre in Context*, 11–22.
4 Simon, Preface, *The Theatre of Medieval Europe*, xiii.
5 For example, Alan E. Knight writes, 'The attempt to classify medieval plays in terms of religious and profane genres forces them into the structural categories of an alien mentality, distorting their meaning in the process' (*Aspects of Genre in Late Medieval French Drama*, 14). Although his focus is on plays written much later than Hrotsvit's, his comment nevertheless seems germane. See also, Case, 'Re-Viewing Hrotsvit,' 534, and Harris, *Medieval Theatre in Context*, 32.
6 Richardson and Johnston, *Medieval Drama*, 3.
7 Muir, *The Biblical Drama of Medieval Europe*, 54–5.
8 Harris, *Medieval Theatre in Context*, 23.

9 Gesture is an important part of dramatic storytelling as well as of dramatization of plays. Jody Enders writes, 'Early theorists consistently held that gesture was no mere "accompaniment." It was itself a language – and a universal one at that' ('Of Miming and Signing,' 2).

10 Wiles, 'Hrotsvit of Gandersheim: The Performance of Her Plays in the Tenth Century,' 135.

11 Edwin Zeydel lists didascalia that some critics have cited as evidence that the plays were written to be performed, 'Were Hrotsvit's Dramas Performed during Her Lifetime' 452, n. 1. This essay examines very different examples.

12 Gurr, *The Shakespearean Stage*, 34.

13 During the Middle Ages 'the odour of sanctity' characteristically enveloped the holy. For example, with the invention of the coffin of the fifth-century protomartyr Stephen, 'the earth trembled and a smell of sweet perfume came from the place such as no man had ever known of, so much that we thought that we were standing in the sweet garden of Paradise' (*Épistula Luciani 2, Patrologia Latina*, 41, 809), quoted in Brown, *The Cult of the Saints*, 92. The invention near Amiens of the lost relics of Saint Firmin, the evangelist of the North, was accompanied by a similar fragrance. That miracle is represented by tableaux on three sculpted registers of the northwest portal of Amiens Cathedral, as the Life of Christ is depicted on the capital frieze at Chartres Cathedral.

   In *Sapientia*, when Hadrian has Spes torn to pieces, he asks, 'What new fragrance do I smell?/ What amazing sweetness do I sense?' Spes responds, 'The pieces of my lacerated flesh give off this fragrant heavenly scent' (92) With such a description, it seems unlikely that the literal laceration of Spes would need to be graphically presented in performance, since contemporary illustrations demonstrate how audiences were habituated to imaginatively completing narratives. Similarly, Mary's statement about the odour of sanctity that she detects when she enters the scene would allow Hrotsvit's audience to complete the situation, filling in information about both Abraham and Mary.

14 The words of the play do not specify that Diocletian is alone on stage when he speaks these lines, though the soldiers' words must have been spoken before going to report to him. Similarly, Sissinus's words, which follow Diocletian's speech, specify that Diocletian has carried out his plan to order Sissinus to take over where Dulcitius has failed. Rather than present dialogue between the emperor and his soldiers' minions, the play provides one speech that suggests the dialogues that take place off stage.

15 Knight, *Aspects of Genre*, 13. Although Knight is discussing late medieval French plays, his comment is appropriate to Hrotsvit's plays as well.

16 See Carruthers, *The Book of Memory*.

17 Muir, *The Biblical Drama of Medieval Europe*, 55.

18 See Bossuat, Pichard, and Raynaud de Lage, *Dictionnaire des lettres françaises: Le Moyen Age*, 'Chanson de geste,' 238–43, and 'Troubadours,' 1456–8.

19 Hugh of Saint-Victor talks about the value of being able to recite Scripture forward or backward, on demand. See Jaeger, *The Envy of Angels*, 11–13.

20 See Ericksen, 'Offering the Forbidden Fruit in MS. Junius 11.'

21 See *The Oedipus Rex of Sophocles*, in *Four Greek Plays*, ed. Dudley Fitts and trans., Dudley Fitts and Robert Fitzgerald (New York: Harcourt, Brace and Co., 1960).

22 The martyrdom of Sapientia's daughters recalls the martyrdom of Saint Zenobius depicted in a fresco cycle in the Church of San Zeno.

23 See Jane Chance's essay in this volume for a fuller discussion of this scene.

24 London, British Museum. Add. MS 10546, fol. 5v. See a similar use of repeated figures in narrative illustrations in The Gospel Book of Otto III, ca. 1000, Munich, Bayeriche Staatsbibliotek. Clm 4453, fols 103v and 244v. These illustrations are reproduced in Toman and Bednorz, *Romanesque: Architecture, Sculpture, Painting*, 456–7.

25 For photographs, see Toman and Bednorz, *Romanesque: Architecture, Sculpture, Painting*, 407.

26 See de Hamel, *A History of Illuminated Manuscripts*, 60.

27 Kluckert, 'Romanesque Painting,' 404. For a discussion of Carolingian and Ottonian illustration, see 400–5 and 422–5.

28 Munich, Bayerische Staatsbibliotek. Clm 4453, fol. 237r, illustrated in Toman and Bednorz, *Romanesque, Architecture, Sculpture, Painting*, 424.

29 Kluckert, 'Romanesque Painting,' 450.

30 From the monastery of St-Martial in Limoges, ca. 923–34; see Harris, *Medieval Theatre in Context*, 28.

31 Wilson, 'Interpretive Essay,' in *Hrotsvit of Gandersheim: A Florilegium of Her Works*, 112.

32 Enders notes Quintilian's observation: 'This is a perception of gesture as "truer" than language, truer than words, truer than writing in that it could agree holistically not with language but with such internal motivations as thought and character' (Enders, *The Medieval Theater of Cruelty*, 8).

Dramatic Convergence in Times Square: Hrotsvit's *Sapientia* and Collapsable Giraffe's *3 Virgins*

JANE E. JEFFREY

> But there should be no misunderstanding: men and women are caught up
> in a network of millennial cultural determinations of a complexity that is
> practically unanalyzable: we can no more talk about 'woman' than about
> 'man' without getting caught up in an ideological theater where the multi-
> plication of representations, images, reflections, myths, identifications con-
> stantly transforms, deforms, alters each person's imaginary order and in
> advance, renders all conceptualization null and void.
>
> Hélène Cixous[1]

Hrotsvit of Gandersheim wrote *Sapientia* close to the millennial year
1000, thereby creating an eerie association with American culture during the years preceding its own millennial 2000. One connection began
in 1993, when Rudolph Giuliani was elected mayor of New York City
largely on the strength of his promise to clean up festering areas of
urban blight that were contributing to the image of New York City as a
place of menacing drug and gang activity, of large numbers of panhan-
dlers harassing tourists for money, and, in particular, of a Times Square
that had sunk into the officially perceived filth of a vibrant and successful
sex industry. Once elected, Mayor Giuliani rallied social service agencies
to find adequate shelters for the homeless and ordered the police and
the courts to enforce strictly the city's drug laws. Mayor Giuliani, mean-
while, focused his own energy and business connections on restoring
Times Square to its former glory as the business, theatre, arts, and
entertainment crossroads of the world. To that end, Giuliani established

the 42nd Street Redevelopment Plan and elicited laudable civic contributions from wealthy corporate conglomerates to underwrite the Plan's
'quality of life reforms,' a hollow, yet genially agreeable do-good phi-
lanthropy that might make Times Square a seriously profitable tourist
attraction.

Giuliani appointed Disney, Condé Nast, Morgan Stanley, and Virgin
(echoing yet another disturbing millennial connection) to direct the
42nd Street Redevelopment Plan because of their advertised commitment to family values. The Plan's first action was an all-out assault on the
sex clubs, peep shows, X-rated movie theatres, and adult bookstores
prospering in Times Square. Even though the Plan succeeded in closing
most of the adult entertainment establishments, many of them relocated
to the outskirts of Manhattan, creating the same problems (drugs, gang
activity, uncollected trash) for nearby communities as they had for Times
Square. Nonetheless, the Plan's officially loathed Times Square sex shows,
which, predictably, played for audiences of well-to-do male business
clientele, were replaced by the Plan's idea of what wholesome families
with values were thought to want, such as food emporiums, retail
megastores, and a twenty-six screen cinemaplex seating 5,000 movie-
goers. In 1999, the Plan's urban renewal reforms were complete, and, in
a peculiar correspondence with a familiar medieval dichotomy, Times
Square had gone from a profitable whore to a domesticated Madonna.

Establishing Times Square as a global crossroads for real estate interests, transnational corporations, and multinational conglomerates, many
of which have large subsidiary interests in the tourist industry, was not
without its own moral and ethical problems. For example, the 42nd
Street Redevelopment Plan agreed to finance the restoration of the 107-
year-old Gospel Tabernacle Church, a church predating the original
theatre district by more than a decade. The Gospel Tabernacle Church
was restored, not as a church, but as John's Pizzeria, which with its ability
to seat over 400 people became New York City's largest pizzeria. This
exchange of spiritual for corporate presence underscored the importance of corporate influence on urban public space; by the late 1990s
Times Square had become a profitable place for food emporiums, retail
megastores, and corporate real estate interests, a capitalist utopia where
the hands that exchanged money did so under the rubric of 'family
values.'

In his 1998 article, 'New York's Facelift,' Mark Sussman asks:

In what sense will the body be affected in the new Times Square? The
obvious case is the drastic reduction of sex venues where the (carefully

circumscribed) observer's body can be admitted into the performance of sexual arousal. Anaesthetized from Times Square, a regulated and stable sex industry is in the process of being closed, or scattered across the city's manufacturing districts.[2]

In place of the once profitable male desire for the female body, Sussman predicts, will be substituted another kind of desire, consumer lust:

> The Arquitechtonica design of the Disney hotel gives us a building that performs, that explodes with light and becomes an attraction worthy of Las Vegas. It will not be a building to be lit or a surface to be covered. It will be a light show. The Times Square signage refers less than ever to anything: it is the attraction. A familiar formula, the sign slipping into thinghood, out of its poor role in early modernity as the mere bearer of a message.[3]

Sussman's foreboding becomes realized when, with the backing of the 42nd Redevelopment Plan, Toys R Us built the world's largest toy store on the site of two former movie palaces, the Empire and Loews. Rising through the middle of all three levels of the store is a sixty-foot-tall, neon flashing Ferris wheel on which customers can ride and become hypnotized by the store's panorama of consumer must-haves, such as a huge smiling and waving Mr Potato Head, a Toys R Us Amusement Park construction set, a life-size Barbie® Dollhouse or, if Barbie® would prefer, a Townhouse, and, with whisperings of the imminent deterioration of women's rights, a Barbie® Make-Me-Pretty Styling (not talking) Head, any or all of which parents with cash – or plastic – can buy. This interactive retail experience provides the type of ideological theatre Cixous cautions against, 'where the multiplication of representations, images, reflections, myths, identifications constantly transforms, deforms, alters each person's imaginary order and in advance, renders all conceptualization null and void.'[4] Among the reasons Giuliani (Julian the Apostate?) and the underwriters of the 42nd Redevelopment Plan gave for closing down the sex industry in Times Square was to show an official respect for, and protection of, women and children, the most vulnerable victims of adult entertainment establishments. Many commentators have since criticized Giuliani's reforms – and the 'woman reason' in particular – as misguided, duplicitous, and ethically empty as the sex industry itself because the new Disney and Virgin inspired Times Square also exploits women's bodies as deliberately and with as much profit in mind as had the shuttered sex clubs.

An incisive commentary on the problems associated with the Times

Square reforms came from an unlikely source in a July 1999 performance of Hrotsvit's *Sapientia* by the theatre company Collapsable Giraffe. The performance troupe chose one of the still functioning sex clubs, Show World, to stage *3 Virgins*, its adaptation of *Sapientia*. During the 1970s and 1980s, Show World was one of New York City's most popular and infamous sex entertainment centres. In his book *Down 42nd Street: Sex, Money, Culture, and Politics at the Crossroads of the World*, Marc Eliot describes Show World as the

> raunchiest sex show on the street. Not long after it opened it became 42nd Street's (and America's) first supermarket of porn. Every conceivable adult toy was for sale there, every category of porn magazine on display, every sex act imaginable available on film, even the newest craze – $250-a-pop videos. On the second floor were cages surrounded by small rooms that reeked of Lysol and Clorox. Inside them, windows were covered with wooden panels that for twenty-five cents would lift up to reveal a minute's worth of a live show of naked women playing with themselves and each other; the customer was then supposed to show his appreciation by slipping a tip through a one-way slot. Often, the glass was missing, and for the right price direct contact was available.[5]

Setting *Sapientia*, a convent play, in a former brothel, specifically in the Big Top Lounge, and substituting the title *3 Virgins* for *Sapientia*, the director, Amy Huggans, aligned the medieval cult of the Virgin with the lures and come-ons used by sex clubs to attract male customers: look, desire, spend money, light a candle, pray, but do not touch or even think about acting out. Moreover, by leaving Show World's staging pretty much intact, Huggans could bring out the dramatic-voyeuristic connection that makes *Sapientia* such a disturbing play. Signs on Show World's walls issue firm warnings to male customers: 'No Tipping,' 'Touching Girls Is Not Allowed!' and 'All Exits Are Final.' Other signs direct male clients to popular peep-shows, such as 'Lusty Ladies,' 'Exotic Beauties,' and 'Bitch Booth.' In ways similar to the Toys R Us's marketing strategy of full immersion into consumer fantasyland, Show World's hyperkinetic venue had the cumulative effect of first eroticizing, then protecting, and finally profiting from an imaginary virginity.

As a canoness at the royal abbey of Gandersheim, Hrotsvit belonged to the class of nobly born Christian women who received a classical Latin and Christian education, an education that elevated abstract conceptualization, or, for Hrotsvit, wisdom, to a spiritual connection with God. In the Terentian plays, Christian saints' lives, and church fathers' commentaries on Scripture that Hrotsvit studied, virginity was a major, sometimes the only, redeeming possibility a woman could depend on to transcend the Christian-defined evil unleashed into the physical world by Eve's reckless sexuality. According to early medieval ecclesiastical interpretation, Eve was an ignorant whore redeemed by Christ's mother, Mary, who offered medieval Christian women a possibility for transcendent and eternal virginity.

In *Sapientia*, Hrotsvit dramatizes what happens when Mater Sapientia and her three virgin daughters bring Christianity, the new female religion, to pagan Rome.[6] The emperor Hadrian and his advisor Antiochus perceive Sapientia and her daughters as a threat to civic and domestic order, because they fear the Roman women will follow Sapientia and her daughters into a life of virginity and no longer have sex with their husbands:

> *Antiochus*   Haec igitur femina cuius mentionem facio hortatur nostrates avitos ritus deserere · et christianę religioni se dedere ·
> *Adrianus*   Num pręvalet hortamentum?
> *Antiochus*   Nimium · nam nostrę coniuges fastidiendo nos contempnunt · adeo · ut dedignantur nobiscum comedere · quanto minus dormire.
> *Adrianus*   Fateor periculum   (I.5)

> *Antiochus*   This woman whom I just mentioned exhorts our citizens and clients/ to abandon the ancestral and ancient rites/ and to convert to Christianity.
> *Hadrian*   Do her exhortations succeed?/
> *Antiochus*   They do so indeed!/ Our wives despise us so that they refuse to eat with us, or even more to sleep with us./
> *Hadrian*   I admit that poses a danger./   (Wilson, *Florilegium*, 82)

This brief exchange emphasizes that the conflict in the play is set both in a real-world context and in a world of ideas. Sapientia's presence with her virgin daughters in Rome asserts a physical threat to the patriarchal polity ruling Rome, and Sapientia's wisdom, symbolically and allegorically associated with spiritual enlightenment, is not only in conflict but also contrasts sharply with the pagans' foolish ignorance.

One example of real-world knowledge becoming allegorical wisdom is seen in the mathematical lesson Sapientia uses to ridicule Hadrian. When Hadrian asks the ages of the daughters, Sapientia answers in her characteristically tortuous way:

> *Sapientia*   O imperator si ętatem inquiris parvularum · Karitas inminutum · pariter parem mansurnorum complevit numerum · Spes autem aeque inminutum sed pariter imparem · Fides vero superfluum · impariter parem · (III.9)

> *Sapientia*   O, Emperor, you wish to know my children's ages; Karitas has completed a diminished, evenly even number of years;/ Spes, on the other hand, a diminished evenly uneven number; and Fides an augmented unevenly even number of years. (Wilson, *Florilegium*, 84)

While Sapientia goes on about diminished, augmented, and principal numbers, those that are perfect, evenly even, or evenly uneven, Hadrian becomes further and further confounded. He says, 'O quam scrupulosa et plexilis questio ex istarum etate infantularum est orta' (III.22), 'What a thorough, perplexing lecture has arisen from my simple question concerning the children's ages!' (Wilson, *Florilegium*, 86). Sapientia replies:

> In hoc laudanda est supereminens factoris sapientia · et mira mundi artificis scientia · qui non solum in principio mundum creans ex nihilo omnia in numero · et mensura et pondere posuit · sed etiam in succedentium serie temporum et in aetatibus hominum miram dedit inveniri posse scientiam artium · (III.22)

> Praise be thereof to the supreme wisdom of the Creator/ and to the marvelous science of this world's Maker,/ who not only created the world in the beginning out of nothing and ordered everything according to number, measure and weight,/ but also in the seasons and in the ages of men gave us the ability to grasp the wondrous science of the arts. (Wilson, *Florilegium*, 86)

As Katharina Wilson notes, the historical Hadrian was 'particularly reputed to have been well educated, especially in mathematics.'[7] Significantly, Hrotsvit has adapted Sapientia's lesson from Boethius's *De Institutio Arithmetica, I*, written in 138 CE, 400 years after Hadrian's death. Hrotsvit's borrowing from Boethius suggests the inferiority of

Hadrian's real-world secular knowledge to the allegorical wisdom offered by Christianity.

3 Virgins not only enacts the dramatic narrative of *Sapientia* on a stage; it also uses video monitors and a tape recorder to provide simultaneous scenes and language from the proceedings of a woman on trial, a seance in which a psychic reads excerpts from sessions in which hypnotized subjects talk with their dead loved ones, and images from the play being enacted. All three 'plays' – the enactment of *Sapientia*, the woman's trial, and the psychic's voice – are performed simultaneously by means of video monitors, overlapping dialogue, and tape loops, assembling and structuring its parts based on the principles of Sapientian mathematics. Just as Sapientia's discourse on mathematics invites viewers and readers of *Sapientia* to question the value of Hadrian's wisdom, the set design and costumes of *3 Virgins* provoke viewers to question the surface drama. Two of Sapientia's daughters wear little-girl beauty pageant dresses, while the third daughter is represented by a doll, the type longed for by little girls in Toys R Us, yet also a popular sexual fetish for men in places like Show World.

What at first appear to be fractured and fragmentary narrative and dramatic pieces of the composite *3 Virgins* ultimately suggest that the European Middle Ages is implicated in the performance of violence against women in contemporary Western culture, whether that performance is in venues like Show World or in conventionally reserved places for plays such as medieval convents or Broadway stages. The portrayal of medieval women with their modern counterparts furthers *3 Virgins*'s political critique that despite the 1000 years since the composition of *Sapientia* women are still experiencing defilement in public places, not only in strip clubs but also in all sorts of publicly sanctioned activities, from beauty contests to seances to judicial hearings. Also from the disquisition on numbers come links, connections, and recurring patterns of corporeal instability, especially as Sapientia's daughters grow older, 8-10-12, and their bodies become entertainment fodder for the Roman soldiers.

Two particular scenes in *3 Virgins* help elucidate the similarities in, and reasons for, the connection between dramatic and customary social violence against women. While Sapientia goes on about diminished evenly even numbers, a diminished evenly uneven number, and an augmented and unevenly even number on stage, one video monitor presents the 1997 trial testimony of a woman accusing local officials of forcing her to have sex with minors. It does not take long to realize that even though the woman thinks what has happened to her is God's honest truth, her testimony comes across as the ramblings of a deranged manic or schizophrenic brain as she delineates the number of police, sheriff, D.A., and judge-ordered kidnappings, beatings, assaults, rapes, and gang rapes of her while she was in police custody on 'some trumpery involving my little boy.' In juxtaposition with the tape is Sapientia explaining to Hadrian's court the connections between her daughters' ages and 'the supreme wisdom of the Creator.' The performances of *3 Virgins* make Sapientia's testimony before Hadrian's court about the connections between her daughters' ages and 'the supreme wisdom of the Creator' appear less as wisdom than as a mind that is dangerously off-balanced.

In another scene in *3 Virgins*, the audience listens to a tape of a modern seance, in which a spirit channeller reads reports from hypnotized subjects about their out-of-body experiences, while the audience also sees the tortures and executions of Sapientia's daughters on stage. When, for example, Fides is flogged, her nipples cut off, her mutilated body thrown on a fiery hot grill, and then immersed in a pot of wax and pitch, just before she is beheaded, she goads the executioner to kill her: 'Percussor accede · et iniunctum tibi offitium me necando imple ·' (V.14), 'Come then, executioner, kill me! Perform your office; don't be remiss' (Wilson, *Florilegium*, 90). Sapientia then embraces the severed head of her daughter, kisses her lips, and thanks Christ 'qui tantillulę victoriam prestitisti puellulę ·' (V.15), 'for granting victory/ to a little girl still in infancy' (Wilson, *Florilegium*, 90). As Spes is being flogged, she cries out, 'O mater · mater · quem efficaces · quam exaudibiles experior esse tui preces · Ecce te orante · anheli tortores · levatis dextris librant ictum · et ego nullum doloris sentio tactum ·' (V.21), 'O mother, mother, how efficacious, how useful are the prayers you say!/ Behold, even while you pray,/ my torturers are breathless; they flog me again and again,/ yet I feel not the slightest pain' (Wilson, *Florilegium*, 91). After Spes's death, Sapientia says, 'Nunc quidem gaudeo · sed tunc tandem perfecte exultans gaudebo · quando tui sororculam · pari conditione extinctam · cęlo pręmisero · et ego subsequar postrema ·' (V.27), 'Now I am happy, but later I will exalt in perfect joy when I have sent your little sister to Heaven, martyred like you,/ and when I myself follow you there too' (Wilson, *Florilegium*, 92).

Similarly, as Karitas dies, Sapientia's final words to her are 'Vale proles dulcissima · et cum Christo iungaris in cęlo · memento matris · iam patrona effecta te parientis ·' (VII.2), 'Farewell, my dearest daughter, and when you are united with Christ in heaven, remember your mother, having been made patron of her who bore you' (Wilson, *Florilegium*, 95). At the same time, the seance tape reveals the ghostly longing of hypnotized people trying to contact their dead loved ones through a spirit channeller, providing a dramatic complement to the ghostly transcendent experiences the three girls experience during their scenes of torture at Hadrian's court.

Allegorical epistemology provides one way of understanding Sapientia's relationship to her daughters' martyrdom in that an immediate effect of dramatic allegory is to blur distinctions among characters. In *Sapientia*, the daughters are allegorized as the virtues Faith, Hope, and Charity, each generated out of the body of Sapientia, or Wisdom, who desires transcendence into a place where distinctions of body and gender do not exist. Read as fragments of Sapientia's existence in a disordered, violent world, the deaths of Fides, Spes, and Karitas allegorize Sapientia as a woman splitting off into transcendent beings whose spiritual embodiments are solid, stable, and free from social judgments of appearance and desire. Sapientia's happiness in her daughters' tortures and deaths may seem perverse, but Sapientia's pleasure may also be read as an abject ambivalence over her own physicality, especially her own lack of virginal purity.

Then, again, Sapientia's performance is tied to her voice, and perhaps it is through her voice that Wisdom incarnates the virginal measurements and dimensions of Sapientia's physical presence. Sapientia, as do all of Hrotsvit's characters, speaks the Latin language of Christian religion. Although Hrotsvit sets *Sapientia* in pagan Rome, the first reading or performance by the tenth-century Saxon nuns was in a language that represented a distinct division between the educationally privileged royal nuns and uneducated women. Educated women, then as now, are rarely listened to, except by other educated women. Yet while Hrotsvit's use of Latin empowers her characters, their martyrdoms represent a devaluation of the female body consistent with the thematic content of Hrotsvit's other plays in which tortured female bodies are absorbed into a cleansing transcendence and saintly renewal. For example, when in *Dulcitius* the soldiers throw Chionia and Agape into the fire, the soldiers witnessing the virgins' deaths exclaim:

O novum · o stupendum miraculum · Ecce anime egressę sunt coprora · ut nulla · laesionis repperiuntur vestigia · sed nec capilli · nec vestimenta · ab igne sunt ambusta · quo minus corpora · (XI.5)

Oh, marvel, oh stupendous miracle! Behold their souls are no longer bound to their bodies,/ yet no traces of injury can be found; neither their hair, nor their clothes are burnt by the fire,/ and their bodies are not at all harmed by the pyre. (Wilson, *Florilegium*, 50)

Similarly, in the final scene of *Pafnutius*, Thais describes her three years of enclosure as a battleground between her body and soul:

Si tamen quid fecerim vis scire · numerositatem meorum scelerum intra conscientiam quasi in fasciculum collegi · et pertractando mente semper inspexi · quo sicut naribus numquam molestia foetoris · ita formido gehennę non abesset visibus cordis · (XII.3)

But if you wish to know how I spent my time, I will tell you: in my conscience I enumerated my manifold sins and wickedness and gathered them as in a bundle of crime. Then I continuously went over them in my mind, so that just as the nauseating smell here never left my nostrils, so the fear of Hell never departed from my heart's eyes. (Wilson, *Plays*, 120)

In *Sapientia*, after the torture and execution of each of the daughters, Sapientia responds with joy. As Fides prepares to die, Sapientia says, 'O filia · filia · non confundor · non contristor · sed valedico tibi exultando · et osculor os · oculosque prę guadio lacrimando · orans ut sub ictu percussoris ·inviolatum serves misterium tui nominis' (V.13), 'O my child, my child, I am not disturbed. I feel no sadness, but I say farewell exulting in you and I kiss your mouth and eyes with tears of joy praying that you preserve the holy mystery of your name, even as you fall under the executioner's blow' (Wilson, *Florilegium*, 90). Similarly, as the swordsman approaches Spes 'evaginato gladio' (V.28), 'with his naked blade' (Wilson, *Florilegium* 93), Sapientia rejoices, 'Nunc quidem gaudeo · sed tunc tandem perfecte exultans gaudebo · quando tui sororculam · pari conditione extinctam · cęlo pręmisero · et ego subsequar postrema' (V.27), 'Now I am happy, but later I will exalt in perfect joy when I have sent your little sister to Heaven, martyred like you,/ and when I myself follow you there too' (Wilson, *Florilegium*, 92). Finally, Sapientia comes close to rapture when Karitas is decapitated: 'Nunc nunc filia gratulandum nunc in Christo est gaudendum · nec est quę me mordeat cura· quia secura sum de tua victoria' (VII.1), 'Now, my child, I must exult, now I must rejoice in Christ's glory;/ no more care and no more worry,/ for I am sure of your victory' (Wilson, *Florilegium*, 94). Recent work in French philosophy on cruelty, work by Clement Rosset and Camille Dumoulie, among others, claims that abstract argument fails to accommodate the traumatic reverberations at the core of cruelty. Indeed, abstract argument can be cruel in its own right as it distances and avoids the reality of violence.[8]

In contrast, in *3 Virgins* the sexual harassment and seance narratives make real the violence entrenched in institutional controls over women's bodies, be they ecclesiastical, legal, economic, familial, or artistic, which Hrotsvit has embedded in allegorical abstraction. During the scene in which Hadrian orders the tortures of the girls, two adult actors read the daughters' parts. On the video monitors are seen three young girls also reading the parts, but with a girly, giggly innocence that underscores the dissonant reverberations evoked by the punishments that Hrostvit intended as comic allegory. Discussing the use of black humour in *King Lear*, Camille Dumoulié observes, 'Sous couvert d'humour noir, à travers son ressentiment, ce père, dont ses filles disent qu'il a mené une vie de luxure, énonce le fantasme dernier du tyran, la volonté la plus folle du pouvoir: posséder la puissance féminine de reproduction pour nourrir réellement, à l'infini, ses rêves d'hécatombe'[9] (Under the cover of black humour, through his resentment, the father, whose daughters said he lived a life of vulgar luxury, states the tyrant's final fantasy, the maddest will of power: to possess the feminine power of reproduction in order to really nurture, through eternity, his dreams of slaughter) (my translation). In *Sapientia*, a thin line separates the tyrant Hadrian from the martyr-making machine, or 'the feminine power of reproduction,' that is Sapientia. While the math lesson shows Sapientia's command of the knowledge of certainty, her response to her daughters' real and concrete executions reveals a more passionate and crazed certainty driven by Wisdom's intolerance for uncertainty. Rosset's discussion of cruelty seems relevant. He writes about

> an intolerance such that it leads many people to suffer the worst and the most real of evils in exchange for the hope, vague as it may be, for the slightest certainty. Thus martyrs, uncertain as they are of establishing or even of defining the truth of whose certainty they are persuaded, are resigned to being *witnesses* to it – as the etymology of the word *martyr* indicates – by exhibiting their suffering: 'I suffer, therefore I am right.' As if the ordeal of suffering were sufficient to validate the thought, or rather the absence of thought, in whose name the martyrs/witnesses say they are ready to suffer and to die. This confusion about the cause for which they

sacrifice themselves explains, moreover, the ever insatiable character of the expert in suffering.[10]

In *3 Virgins* the conflation of time, space, and theatricality functions to undermine any sense of certainty. The woman seen on the video monitor reiterating to a male judge her accusation that officials had forced her to have sex could be Sapientia supporting her daughters in their challenge to and denial of Roman power and authority. The comfort that Sapientia's daughters provide their mother at their moments of death can be heard in the words of the seance spirit channeller invoking the lives of the dead in language that reassures the living and absolves them from guilt and regret. The ease with which *3 Virgins* brings together a tenth-century play intended for a convent, a twentieth-century testimony meant for a court room, and a contemporary seance reuniting live and dead loved ones eradicates any illusion that by shutting down Show World and other sex clubs, long-held cultural attitudes about women and their bodies may have changed. Instead, the correspondences between *3 Virgins* and *Sapientia* indicate that in the 1000 years between the tenth and twentieth centuries, there may be little to distinguish the medieval characters in *Sapientia* from the contemporary women in *3 Virgins* and, by extension, the women working in places like Show World.

The performance of *3 Virgins* in Show World emphasizes the sexual objectification of women's bodies that Mayor Giuliani thought he was expunging from Times Square. True, the performers and audience of *3 Virgins* understood that *3 Virgins* was staged, as did the owners, workers, and customers of the original Show World, who profited from their 'dramatic' manipulation of their customers' sexual desire. However different in meaning, the three stories that make up *3 Virgins* raise the possibility that there is a common matrix shared by theatricality, sexuality, violence, and 'quality of life' politics. In her book *The Medieval Theater of Cruelty: Rhetoric, Memory, Violence,* Jody Enders argues that the

> commingled histories of torture, theater, rhetoric, and aesthetics ... suggest that the violent linguistic foundations of aesthetics offer no safe haven for spectators who seek release or sublimation in the arts. Seen from this perspective, theater does not purge violent emotions at all, but rather funnels them right back into the violent ideological structures that presumably inspired such impossible purgations and catharses.[11]

And from the perspective of the medieval playwright, the safe haven is patriarchal language.[12] Hence, Hrotsvit speaks from the masculine rather than the feminine other, praising in Latin the mother who values public self-assertion over the domestic maternal care of, and connection with, her daughters. Hrotsvit's participation in religious practices that silence women's voices as a way of saving their souls aligns her with the medieval church fathers who taught that virginity was a woman's only recourse to everlasting life, or, if not everlasting life, then at least an earthly life approved by ecclesiastical authority.

In *Theatre Semiotics*, Marvin Carlson argues, 'No other art seeks to absorb and convert into interpretive structures so much of the total human experience as the theatre does, its potential resources and meanings bounded only by the resources and meanings of humanity itself.'[13] If the medieval-inspired contemporary play *3 Virgins* is a sign of such absorption and conversion, then one may conclude, sadly, that for women, violence and cruelty determine much of 'the total human experience.' All six plays by Hrotsvit focus on physical punishments women undergo either for expressing sexual desire or for renouncing it. If a female character expresses desire, as do Mary in *Abraham* and Thais in *Pafnutius*, she must brutally discipline herself through fasting and constant vigils in a dark, isolated cell. If a character refuses male desire, as do Agape, Chionia, and Hirena in *Dulcitius*, and Drusiana in *Calimachus*, she is threatened with sexual assault. The heroine can be a virgin, such as Constantia in *Gallicanus*, resisting marriage through prayer, or a prostitute, such as Thais, whose conversion to Christianity involves obliterating her body through a regimen of extreme deprivation as penance for sexual transgression. Taken as a whole, the plays show that even if pagan and Christian expectations of women originate from different literary traditions – from Terentian comedy or from patristic treatises on virginity and Christian saints' lives – when they intersect, as they do in Hrotsvit's plays, such expectations simultaneously punish a woman when she does not behave according to convention and punish her when she does. Even in *Sapientia*, Hrotsvit seems to reject maternal desire and longing as a component of Sapientia's wisdom.

One conclusion concerning the inheritance that *Sapientia* provides for *3 Virgins* is that in acquiring the wisdom needed for understanding contemporary forms of sexual violence, deviant desires, and forms of social and personal resistance, it is helpful to understand medieval ones. After all, Sapientia's wisdom is complicit in a gender system that values public self-assertion over familial love and care of children and so, assuming the masculine voice, her wisdom delivers her daughters to the church fathers' promise of transcendence to an everlasting life, where they are never heard from again. In short, *Sapientia* teaches that conformity to the male-defined Christian culture of the tenth century is a woman's only recourse for achieving social respect and spiritual redemption. *3 Virgins*'s lesson, though similar, is challenged by its damning political perspective on the patriarchal culture of the twentieth century. Although *3 Virgins* does not intend to evoke historical authenticity, it does move the goals of the 42nd Street Redevelopment Plan into a larger historical context by dramatizing the repetitive use of the female body as a source of legal, political, commercial, and adult-entertainment profit.

NOTES

1 Cixous, 'Sorties,' 96.
2 Sussman, 'New York's Facelift,' 37.
3 Ibid., 41.
4 Cixous, 'Sorties,' 96.
5 Eliot, *Down 42nd Street*, 140.
6 Jo Ann Kay McNamara writes that early 'Christianity was widely viewed as a religion of women and slaves, a denigrating caricature but one it shared with the imperial government itself' (*Sisters In Arms*, 22).
7 Wilson, *Florilegium*, 84, n. 3.
8 In *Joyful Cruelty*, Clément Rosset argues that such joy, 'suspended in thin air and deprived of all ground, is in fact the extraordinary privilege of joy, the aptitude to persevere even though its cause is lost and condemned. It possesses the quasi-feminine art of surrendering to no argument, of blithely ignoring the most obvious adversity as well as the most flagrant contradictions. Joy has in common with femininity the fact that it remains indifferent to every objection. An incomprehensible faculty of persistence permits joy to survive its own death, to continue to strut about as if nothing had happened' (4).
9 Dumoulié, 'Formes théâtrales du délire.'
10 Rosset, *Joyful Cruelty*, 93
11 Enders, *The Medieval Theater of Cruelty*, 235.
12 See Ulrike Wiethaus's essay 'Pulchrum Signum?' in this collection for a more sympathetic discussion of *Sapientia*.
13 Carlson, *Theatre Semiotics*, xviii.

Playing with Hrotsvit: Adventures in Contemporary Performance

MICHAEL A. ZAMPELLI

In the fall of 1998, the chairperson of the Department of Theatre and Dance at Santa Clara University informed the faculty that a millennial symposium on Hrotsvit of Gandersheim would take place on our campus in February 2000. She asked if any of us would be willing to direct one of Hrotsvit's six plays in conjunction with this singular academic event. As a junior faculty member who had just arrived at the university and whose area of academic interest lay in premodern theatrical performance, I offered to undertake the project. As with much theatrical phenomena, the 'adventure' of production begins with necessities and practicalities just as often as it does with more theoretical desires.

The first step on this pilgrimage involved my devising and teaching a course in medieval theatre, not only to prepare myself for the directing project but also to introduce Hrotsvit and her plays to the students who would be potential performers. The students' reactions to the medieval theatre in general and Hrotsvit in particular helped in naming the challenges that would shape this attempt at contemporary performance.

Most generally and perhaps most importantly, the students experienced the medieval theatre as almost completely 'other.' According to David Bevington, however, this striking otherness remains 'the most important reason for teaching medieval drama.' Bevington asserts:

No subject more genuinely satisfies the demands of a liberal education: that we attempt to free the mind by enabling students to go well beyond their previous experiences into realms that offer a new perspective on most of the values they have previously encountered. The values I have in mind include the obtaining of some perspective on one's own assumptions, biases, beliefs, together with a growing awareness of and appreciation for the assumptions of those who occupy an essentially different world from one's own.[1]

The difficulty, however, came with building sturdy enough bridges that would allow for extended traffic between this 'essentially different world' and our own. Though at times frustrating for me as an instructor, their unfamiliarity with the European and theatrical scene between 500 and 1500 CE at least compelled the students to venture into this territory with a healthy humility.

In some cases the bridge building did succeed in facilitating the students' engagement with what one evaluation termed 'such a foreign form of theatre.' In others the labour failed to effect such an interaction. For example, in response to a question that asked students to comment on the course's relevance, one student wrote, 'Please ... this has nothing to do with my life.' Herein, then, lies the first challenge: Is the medieval theatre at all accessible? Does it communicate – not only to students of theatre in a liberal arts university but also to a contemporary audience? Is it possible to play these plays within a cultural context not unified by any particular religious/political world view or shared certainty about the meaning of life? The challenge is a real one, especially in performance, for if a piece has *absolutely* nothing to do with the lives of its audience then there is no compelling reason to stage it.

The second challenge, a kind of specification of the first, emerged in relationship to Hrotsvit. Within the first few weeks of the quarter, the class read two of Hrotsvit's plays, *The Martyrdom of the Holy Virgins Agape, Chionia and Hirena* (also known as *Dulcitius*) and *The Resurrection of Drusiana and Calimachus* (also known simply as *Calimachus*). Because of my interest in eventually staging Hrotsvit, the class performed the plays aloud. Steeped though we were in things medieval, the students had a very difficult time reading Hrotsvit's plays with a straight face. When, for example, the young Christian woman Drusiana successfully repels the advances of a sex-crazed and power-hungry Calimachus and actually prays for her *own* death, the actor speaking the following speech seemed to be acting in a *Saturday Night Live* skit.

Alas, my Lord Jesus Christ, what is the good of the vow of chastity I swore/ if this madman is crazed on my beauty's score?/ Oh, Lord, look upon my fear,/ look upon the pain I bear!/ I don't know what to do; if I denounce him, there will be public scandal on my account, I'm afraid;/ if I keep it secret, I cannot avoid falling into these devilish snares without Thy aid./ Help me, O Christ, therefore, with my plan,/ and permit me to die so that I won't become the ruin of that charming young man. (Wilson, *Florilegium*, 57)

At Drusiana's subsequent death, the class let loose its pent up laughter. Still less were the students able to play convincingly (whatever that might mean in this context) the martyrdom of the young virgins who speak lines like, 'The more cruelly I'll be tortured, the more gloriously I'll be exalted' (Wilson, *Florilegium*, 51). For the final exam, one group of students worked on *The Fall and Repentance of Mary*; the presentation had a decidedly 'keystone cops' flavour.

The students' reaction to Hrotsvit specified the second challenge: Could we actually perform these plays without 'winking' at the audience? Could we speak the speeches without undermining them with farce, without suggesting that Hrotsvit's playworld can no longer be taken seriously? Theatrical performance that attempts only to reconstruct a theatrical style can be terribly boring. On the other hand, theatre that does not believe in itself, that constantly distances itself *from* itself spends its energy all too quickly.[2] The first fruits of these challenges proved to be the clarification of my own directorial desires. Most simply, I wanted the audience present at Hrotsvit 2000 to be engaged by the plays *in performance*. That engagement would require acknowledging and then negotiating distances in terms of both content and performance style.[3]

After returning to Katharina Wilson's translation of the dramas, I chose to stage two of Hrotsvit's six plays: *The Resurrection of Drusiana and Calimachus* and *The Fall and Repentance of Mary*. The first engaged me because of its variety of bizarre yet wonderfully theatrical details: instantaneous deaths and resurrections, a poisonous serpent, attempted necrophilia, an appearance of the risen Christ. *The Resurrection of Drusiana and Calimachus* would provide, if nothing else, striking evidence of Hrotsvit's sense of the spectacular. The second attracted me for precisely the opposite reason; *The Fall and Repentance of Mary* seemed painfully predictable. For a long time I thought that the play did little more than retell the familiar story of a 'fallen woman' rescued by her 'spiritual father.' In the end, however, I felt sure that Hrotsvit was doing more in this play than initially meets the eye. What better way to discover what lay beneath the surface of this story than to stand it on its feet?

After choosing the plays I began thinking about their production in explicitly theatrical terms. The performance venue was to be Mission Santa Clara de Asís at Santa Clara University, a 1928 reconstruction of the 1825 Mission Church. Initially, I had thought to stage only one of the plays in the Mission and the other in a more conventionally theatrical space so as to play with the differences in medieval and contemporary staging techniques. But because of the real limitations on space in the performing arts facilities, the Mission became the *platea* of choice for both productions (demonstrating once again that necessity often provides the impetus for theatrical invention).

Situated in the centre of the university campus, Mission Santa Clara de Asís is a liturgical space; its 'sacredness' hangs in the air like traces of old incense and melted beeswax. Many different images decorate the high altar, the ceiling, the walls of the nave, the side chapels. Like Hrotsvit and her plays, these images and the stories they conjure are separated from today's visitors to the Mission by many years, many miles, and many different, often contrary, ways of seeing reality. The Mission is still a space wherein only celibate men preside at the Eucharist. Yet Clare of Assisi stands in the central niche above the high altar holding a monstrance in one hand and a crosier in the other. Depending upon one's perspective, the Mission can be a place of safety, peace, and connectedness, or it can be a place of hostility, anxiety, and exclusion. Most often, I suspect, it is both of these things at the same time; potent symbols function through complexity, ambiguity, multivalence.

As a director, I found that my contemplation of the designated playing space significantly informed my attempts at finding a point of engagement with Hrotsvit's plays. Like the Mission, Gandersheim sat within a culture of learning and sophistication; it provided a hospitable environment for art, letters, diplomacy; it underscored the centrality of spiritual experience even as it remained acutely aware of the more complicated political and ecclesiastical issues of the day. Presided over by the abbess Gerberga II, the Benedictine abbey at Gandersheim minted its own coin, conducted its own business, exercised its own religious authority.[4] Rather than being simply a religiously sanctioned place of female confinement, Gandersheim was, as Sue-Ellen Case reminds us, a place of liberation for the aristocratic Saxon women who lived there as nuns or canonesses.[5] Nine hundred years before Virginia Woolf, Hrotsvit had a room of her own. She had the space, the time, the support to create. As a result of these reflections occasioned by the theatrical space, I decided that the point of engagement with Hrotsvit would be liberation: physical, spiritual, and creative.

The location of the production in the Mission Church proved critical for at least one audience member, who reported that the venue helped her bridge the historical distance between the present and a past 'so far from ... reality.' Other members of the audience reported that the location contributed significantly to making their experience of the plays 'very moving' because it physicalized the 'strangeness,' the 'difference.' I sought to incorporate the part of the church where the audience was seated as well as the sanctuary, where the cast performed their parts in the play, to achieve the liberation that was my goal. Thus the entrance of the audience into the liminal space of the historic Mission Santa Clara, to my mind, served as the first movement toward the liberation I sought to explore.[6]

After some consideration I decided to construct a prologue that would provide the audience with an interpretive frame for seeing and hearing Hrotsvit's plays. Dressed in liturgical/medieval costume and carrying the emblematic properties to be used in the production, the company of actors entered from the front doors of the Mission Church. They walked slowly up the main aisle toward the playing space as the director of music chanted *Corde Natus Ex Parentis* (Of Creator's Love Begotten).[7] When the actors nearly reached the front of the church, the chant concluded; in the silence they surveyed their playing space and their audience. To the sound of a festive piano accompaniment they walked energetically into the sanctuary, readied their space, and took their positions.

In addition to affirming that the plays exist *as plays* only by virtue of the actor's craft, the prologue was designed to encourage the audience to play freely in the field of complexity. The Catholic tradition in which Hrotsvit wrote was no more monolithic than the Catholic tradition with which a contemporary audience would be familiar. If these plays were to focus us on liberation, then the prologue first needed to free the audience to acknowledge ambiguity. Each of the actors was assigned a 'voice' that represented parts of the 'tradition' within which Hrotsvit wrote. The 'voices' spoke texts drawn from Jewish and Christian scriptures as well as from the Fathers of the church. Treating the relationship between the sexes as well as the nature of theatrical representation, the prologue began playfully but grew hostile and chaotic.[8] At the height of the exchange, the actor portraying Hrotsvit appeared in the high pulpit overlooking the sanctuary. With a book and pen in hand, she began speaking her famous preface to the dramas. In this way, the context for Hrotsvit's writing and the audience's seeing was established performatively. Within a tradition genuinely conflicted in its attitudes toward women *and* the theatre, Hrotsvit writes *plays* about how God's greatness is actually magnified 'when female weakness triumphs in conclusion/ And male strength succumbs in confusion' (Wilson, *Florilegium*, 41).

The cast and audience reactions to the prologue were uniformly positive. Though some students found this introduction 'too long,' most agreed that it 'did something very important.' One audience member, for example, noted that the prologue was a particularly 'favorite part' because it provided a definite social and religious frame within which to experience Hrotsvit's plays. 'Shap[ing] the world that the plays lived in,' the prologue even proved enjoyable for the student actors who found in 'the back and forth bantering between the sexes' an entertainingly 'intelligent' engagement with primary source materials that highlighted Hrotsvit's own theatrical and theological ingenuity.

I employed cross-gender casting for the plays, less because I was attempting to reconstruct what might have been the original production values of Gandersheim (if, indeed, the plays were ever performed there)[9] and more because I wanted to liberate the performers and the audience from their confinement by 'realistic' or 'representational' performance models. Further, more women than men auditioned for the production; hence, despite my directorial conceits, women needed to play men's roles in order for the plays to be cast properly. *The Resurrection of Drusiana and Calimachus*, the piece staged in an explicitly medieval/liturgical idiom, found women playing most of the major characters (Calimachus, Drusiana, and St John the Apostle) and men playing the remaining roles (Fortunatus, Andronicus, Friend, and Christ). In *The Fall and Repentance of Mary*, staged in a more contemporary style, the roles remained, for the most part, gender-specific.

In *The Resurrection of Drusiana and Calimachus*, Hrotsvit plays with the legend of Drusiana, a young Christian woman whose husband had once attempted 'to prevent her from adopting the ascetic life ... [by] shut[ting] her up in a sepulchre for fourteen days when she refused to accede to his sexual requests,' according to her source, the apocryphal Acts of John.[10] Eventually, however, Drusiana's strength, endurance, and active faith succeeded in converting her husband Andronicus to Christian asceticism. Hrotsvit dramatizes a subsequent moment in Drusiana's story when Calimachus, a young pagan in Ephesus, becomes obsessed with her beauty and schemes to engage her in an adulterous affair. Rather than submit either to sexual seduction or to threats of violence, Drusiana 'depart[s] from life, not at all happy, but indeed grieving because of the spiritual shattering of that man.'[11] After her burial, Calimachus, still raging with desire, pays Fortunatus, the overseer of Drusiana's tomb, to allow him access to the tomb and Drusiana's still-fresh body. Before Drusiana's body can be violated, however, Fortunatus dies, bitten by a poisonous serpent, and Calimachus dies out of fear. Through the mediation of St John the Apostle, Calimachus is raised from the dead as if from a nightmare. His obsession has left him and he confesses his sins; Calimachus is baptized and received into the community of faith. Next John the Apostle raises Drusiana who asks that, in a true expression of God's own magnanimity and mercy, he also raise the oily Fortunatus. Ordained by John to effect this resurrection, Drusiana herself raises Fortunatus in the name of Christ. Fortunatus, however, rejects the gift of new life as he cannot abide witnessing the power of divine grace working in the likes of Drusiana and Calimachus; as quickly as he was raised, Fortunatus dies a second time.

Interestingly, Hrotsvit chooses a story in which a woman is the agent of resurrection. As Elizabeth Clark observes, 'Nowhere in the New Testament itself is a woman the agent of such a miracle.'[12] In the same way that Drusiana effects Fortunatus's liberation from the chains of death, so does Hrotsvit effect the Christian woman's liberation from the restrictions of the scriptural canon. Like the apocryphal *Acts*, *The Resurrection of Drusiana and Calimachus* creates a liminal space situated between tradition and innovation that allows its audience the freedom to play with not only the meaning of gender roles but also the meaning of true life and true death.

Because of the foreignness of the subject matter and style, I presumed that this liminal space would be best suggested to the audience through the use of medieval staging and quasi-liturgical costuming. Clearly not a representational performance, *The Resurrection of Drusiana and Calimachus* would liberate a contemporary audience from its own canonical beliefs, assumptions, perspectives – at least for the space of forty or so minutes – and give it permission to 'play.' The stylized staging employed the symbolic geography for which the medieval theatre is well known: the left side of the church as 'sinister' and the right as 'righteous,' the great doors as 'worldly' and the sanctuary as 'heavenly.' The initial dialogue, then, between Calimachus and his Friend in which Calimachus reveals his 'painful affliction' and resolves 'to seduce [Drusiana] with flattery' (Wilson, *Florilegium*, 54–5) took place on the down-stage left section of the sanctuary. In the very next 'scene,' when Calimachus approaches Drusiana in her home in what was staged as an 'anti-Annunciation,' Calimachus entered from down left and crossed to a praying Drusiana on stage right.

Further, the stylization helped in staging potentially problematic dramatic moments. The deaths and resurrections are cases in point. Drusiana's immediate death after her prayer to Christ for deliverance could be inappropriately comical were it treated at all realistically.[13] Hence, Drusiana held a lit candle and knelt in the centre of the sanctuary. She prayed directly to the actor playing Christ standing in the high pulpit above the sanctuary floor. After her prayer, Christ's hand was raised in a gesture resembling a benediction; Drusiana herself blew out her candle and knelt with her head bowed as chimes were rung in aural announcement of her death. The appearance of the poisonous snake was likewise effected by the action of Christ in the pulpit. As Christ drew his hand across the scene, one of the actors entered with a very long piece of iridescent black and gold cloth fastened to the end of a dowel. Accompanied by music, the actor dressed in liturgical garb wove the 'serpent' in and around the actors playing Fortunatus and Calimachus, at which point they also 'died.' The candles associated with these two characters were summarily extinguished and the death chimes rang once again.[14]

Arguably, the challenge of characterization proved the most substantial given the youthfulness of the performers. In particular the actors playing Drusiana, Calimachus, and St John the Apostle needed to work consistently at discovering and pursuing the goals of their characters. The initial difficulties with Hrotsvit's stylized language slowly gave way to a deeper understanding of what was 'at stake' for the characters. The actor playing Drusiana came to understand that Drusiana had a transforming encounter with Christ, an encounter that liberated her to live outside the ordinary patterns governing married life. Fidelity to this freedom gave her the power and strength to ridicule the unwanted attentions offered by a self-centred seducer. The actor playing Calimachus explored the driving obsession to possess, to use others for one's own satisfaction, to exert power – realities all too familiar to students studying in the shadow of the 'dot.com.' She found in Calimachus the ancestor of those young men for whom 'no' does not mean no.[15] Despite the initially foreign sound of the play's language, the actors playing Drusiana and Calimachus discovered that the apparent distance between themselves and the text actually provided the conditions of possibility for a deeper appropriation of that text.

Developing the character of St John the Apostle proved more difficult for the young woman playing the role. John remains the moral centre of the play; he is the preacher and teacher functioning as the link with

Christ. John's speeches are theologically dense *and* emotionally passionate. Predictably, whenever the actor spoke lines that she did not understand, the energy that had been generated during the rehearsal dissipated. The character work with John often consisted of first explaining Hrotsvit's theology and spirituality and then encouraging the actor to preach that theology and spirituality to the other characters and to the audience. This necessitated the actor's finding her own 'strong voice.' Within a contemporary Catholic frame, the tasks set for the young actor – to move as a presider within the sanctuary of a Catholic church and to preach therein with the authority of Christ – created some unease, some dissonance. Dressed in a red Roman chasuble, the liturgical vestment worn at the celebration of the Eucharist, and carrying a bishop's crosier, the actor had to discover a liturgically resonant voice and physicality in order to render John an effective presence. That these discoveries chafed against contemporary Catholic church 'order' rendered the process slow. At the same time, that the characterization was *possible* and *credible* within the liminal space of the theatre proved supremely exciting for performer and audience. Several of the audience members noted how striking it was to see a woman 'dressed as a Catholic priest in a Catholic church,' an observation pointing toward the potential of these plays – showcasing spiritually heroic women – to engage contemporary concerns *particularly* when they are staged.

Essentially the Santa Clara production of *The Resurrection of Drusiana and Calimachus* aimed at highlighting Hrotsvit's work of liberation. Drusiana, for example, is freed by Hrotsvit's pen to speak clearly against the unwanted advances of Calimachus; she names in a strong voice of her own the evil she sees in her violent suitor. Further, Drusiana is freed by God's own hand from male aggression; her death is neither punitive nor permanent but a privileged rite of passage. She is liberated from death that she might act *in persona Christi*, offering life to the sinful Fortunatus. Calimachus, through his complicated association with Drusiana, is eventually freed from his 'painful affliction' by another temporary death engineered by God. Calimachus's death is ritualized in his baptism at the hands of John wherein he claims his need for mercy, leaves behind his isolation, and is raised into a community of life. The opportunist Fortunatus, however comically, takes advantage of Calimachus' obsession and seeks to keep him trapped within the tomb of unfulfilled desires. Fortunatus's unwillingness to accept resurrection at the hands of a woman and his insistence on isolation, on being 'superior' to others constitute his rejection of life. In this context lasting death consists in the choice to remain imprisoned, apart from the community and, hence, from God.

After the stylized production of *The Resurrection of Drusiana and Calimachus*, Hrotsvit's *Fall and Repentance of Mary* called for a more 'realistic' presentation – at least for the sake of dramatic contrast. As the first play helped in naming the distance between Hrotsvit's world and our own, the second aimed at appropriating that world through the process of critical reinterpretation. Hrotsvit writes the play about a young woman nurtured in the spiritual life by the hermits Abraham and Effrem against the backdrop of a tenth-century revival of eremitic spirituality.[16] Sandro Sticca's explanation of the hermit's role in early Christianity helps also in clarifying the attitudes toward the hermit prevalent in Hrotsvit's day:

> The martyr is confessor to Christ. With the end of persecutions, however, it is the life of the ascetic, hermetic and monastic, that becomes the most widely disseminated hagiographical *exemplum* as the perfect *imitatio Christi*. When the possibility no longer existed of achieving, through martyrdom, the supreme witness and imitation of Christ's physical martyrdom, the monks took the place of the martyrs in achieving, through a bloodless martyrdom – based on ascetic discipline, renunciation of the world and the mortification of the flesh – the highest plateaus of Christian living.[17]

Within this scheme, of course, the hermit Abraham and his mentor Effrem function as models of heroic Christian living. They help the nearly eight-year-old Mary desire that same pattern of life whereby 'the unimpaired wholeness of [her] body and the pure holiness of [her] mind' will eventually lead her to 'great delight/ in the arms of the virgin's Son' (Wilson, *Florilegium*, 68–9). Despite Effrem's benediction and Abraham's regular instruction over the course of 'twice ten years,' Mary falls from spiritual heights to fleshly depths. After having been seduced by a man 'disguised as a monk' and 'despair[ing] of ever attaining forgiveness,' Mary leaves the hermit's cell and pursues a life of prostitution (Wilson, *Florilegium*, 69–70). Her uncle Abraham undertakes to rescue her by also leaving his cell and disguising himself as a young lover; in this Abraham functions as Christ, seeking out the lost with mercy and compassion. Through Abraham's agency Mary eventually returns to the spiritual life; as is evidenced by her own constant and harsh penitence, 'she works with all her strength to become an example of conversion/ to those for whom she was the cause of perdition' (Wilson, *Florilegium*, 79). Mary, then, achieves a level of Christian heroism through asceticism and mortification of the flesh.

Read in this way *The Fall and Repentance of Mary* seems all too predictable; I wondered whether Hrotsvit or the audience would be served by yet another representation of a 'fallen woman' raised up by a spiritually superior man. More seemed to be at stake in this play, and after reading David Wiles's very engaging article on the performance of Hrotsvit's plays in the tenth century, I was able to consolidate my thoughts.[18] With Wiles I chose to pursue a seemingly obvious though certainly noncanonical interpretation of the hermit Abraham's role in the drama; consequently, this interpretation opened up another possibility for appropriating the play's meaning.

At the end of the play's second scene, in which Abraham and Effrem have convinced Mary to pursue the virginal life, Abraham observes that 'it would not be prudent to leave such a young child to her own counsel.' He continues:

> Therefore, I shall build her a little cell, narrow of entrance and adjacent to my own dwelling. I will visit her often through the window [and] instruct her in the Psalms and other pages of God's law. (Wilson, *Florilegium*, 69)

In the very next scene, after the passage of many years, a distraught Abraham confesses to Effrem that Mary has been lost. When Effrem asks Abraham to reveal how 'the ancient serpent beset her,' Abraham responds thus:

> Through the forbidden passion of a certain deceiver/ who, disguised as a monk, often came to see her/ under the pretense of instructive visits, until with his devilish art/ he ignited the undisciplined instincts of her youthful heart/ to burn in love for him, so much so that she jumped from her window to perform that awful deed. (Wilson, *Florilegium*, 70)

The proximity of these lines makes it difficult for me to leave aside the possibility that the seducer is indeed Abraham himself.[19] In this reading, not only Mary but also Abraham experience the depths of sinfulness and the temptation to despair. The play becomes more about the abuse of power, gender inequalities, psychological and spiritual pain, the road to forgiveness – realities that audience and cast members alike acknowl-

edged as all too familiar in the present day and age. Mary becomes
heroic, then, not in executing the penances prescribed for her by men,
but in her physical and spiritual survival.

I chose to set *The Fall and Repentance of Mary* in the 1950s, a time in the
not-too-distant past when the West stood on the edge of profound social
and religious changes, when gender roles and spiritual sensibilities began shifting. In this setting Effrem and Abraham are not hermits, but
clerics who would have represented to the majority of Catholic faithful
the pinnacle of Christian vocation. They are deeply sincere in what they
profess about God, the church, salvation; yet the formulae, the pieties,
the ecclesiastical disciplines that comprise the edifice of their faith are
cracking under their own weight. From what could be stifling certainties
about the nature of holiness, purity, goodness, Hrotsvit liberates a group
of characters to discover a deeper holiness, purity, and godliness rooted
not only (or even primarily) in official religion but in the crucible of
human experience.

As a result some pivotal moments in the play become more resonant
for a contemporary audience. The scene in which Effrem and Abraham
convince Mary to pursue a life of virginity recalls those moments in
Catholic life when roles for women in the church have been constructed
by men, when the parameters for encountering God have emerged not
from women themselves but from male authority. In the Santa Clara
production, Mary was dressed in a parochial school uniform; when
Effrem and Abraham came upon her, she was writing in a book. As
Effrem explained to her the etymology of her most excellent name, he
took the book and pen away from her and gave her instead a rosary with
beads of clear blue glass. Mary's 'decision' to 'renounce the world and
deny [her]self' was less hers and more her mentors.'

After the passage of several years, the action continued with Abraham's
visit to Effrem, now a cardinal. Abraham's pain – emotional, psychological, spiritual – was heightened because it stemmed from both his
own sinfulness and Mary's departure. The scene became thick with
subtext and challenged the actor to reveal information about Mary's
fall and, at the same time, to conceal information about his own.
Abraham's anguish increased precisely because he understood his responsibility for Mary's situation; however, he suffered from the lack of
an adequate spiritual framework to deal with such a seemingly unfor-
givable transgression.

The discovery scene in the brothel became less a scene where Abraham
preaches to Mary about the need for repentance and more a scene

where Mary forces Abraham to confront the truth about their past. 'I take your sins upon myself,' Abraham says to Mary (Wilson, *Florilegium*, 77); in this Abraham took responsibility for the pain he caused. Mary, then, was free to begin her own journey back to God – this time on her own terms: 'Out of my own free will I shall remain contrite' (Wilson, *Florilegium*, 78).

In the last scene of the play, Abraham reveals to Effrem that Mary has confined herself in a cell and performs penance 'according to his governance' (Wilson, *Florilegium*, 79). Abraham, however, was still unable to reveal the truth to his 'superior' and revealed to Effrem only what Effrem would expect to hear. Troubled and tormented, Abraham could not muster the energy for genuine triumphalism. While Abraham and Effrem spoke, Mary retreated to her cell, the high pulpit over the sanctuary. Therein she carried out no extreme penances, but rather met the 'handsome young man' of *Drusiana and Calimachus*. Her genuine encounter with Christ – in a place free from the domination of male religious authority – found her experiencing spiritual forgiveness and creative liberation. Christ clothed her not in a hairshirt, but a warm cloak; he gave her not a *flagellum* but the book and pen taken from her at the beginning of the play. Thus Mary became the Hrotsvit of the prologue. When Abraham completed his scene with Effrem, he walked to his cell; unable to enter it, he stopped centre and collapsed under the burden of his own despair. Urged on by the Christ figure, Mary/Hrotsvit encouraged Abraham to hope by addressing him with the words he first spoke to her:

> Your sins are grave, I admit,/ but heavenly pity is greater than any sin we may commit./ Therefore cast off your despair and beware of leaving unused this short time given to you for penitence. Know that Divine Grace abounds even where the abomination of sin prevails. (Wilson, *Florilegium*, 77)

In her 'fall and repentance,' Mary is an example of who we all are and what we can choose to become. She leads Abraham to a deeper piety rooted in the complex and painful realities of human living – the arena of Incarnation.

I began this essay with reference to David Bevington's observation regarding the educational value of the medieval theatre. The exercise of preparing and producing Hrotsvit's plays confirms for me Bevington's insight that the strangeness of style and subject challenges the audience and actors 'to be led out of' themselves. In the weeks and months following the Santa Clara production, students continued to comment on the intellectual, theatrical, and in some cases spiritual distance they had travelled from first reading to performance. In fact, the foreignness of the plays proved a help rather than a hindrance in making the rehearsal process 'more and more intriguing.' More than one student involved in the project suggested that the production process was ultimately so satisfying because they themselves were charged with the responsibility of making 'three-dimensional' a world and characters too often presented in 'flat,' 'purely academic' terms. Inevitably, cast members also noted that living for a while in such a different world sharpened their observations regarding their own world. For example, students were very much aware that 'God' and 'faith' remain troubled categories in this postmodern era, that religious discourse is complicated by very many other issues. At the same time, they also acknowledged that the spiritual struggles represented by Hrotsvit continued to resonate in the contemporary world: 'What is moral?' 'What sways a person from goodness to evil?' 'Why do people become obsessed?' 'What is the intersection between sexuality and spirituality?' 'Where does redemption lie and how do we finally experience it?'

Playing with Hrotsvit is important, not only because it involves us in the project of reclaiming for the stage important texts of the Western theatrical past but also because it frees us to become more adventuresome in our ways of knowing. Unquestionably, the exciting scholarship that has emerged in recent years and has focused on Hrotsvit's literary, historical, political, and theological talents, throws wide the doors into the tenth century. Theatrical performance of Hrotsvit's plays, however, also opens those doors in particularly physical and concrete ways. Complementing the study of Hrotsvit's dramas with actual attempts to stage them, with genuine efforts to experience them *theatrically* results in a deeper understanding of Hrotsvit's craft and context. The prospect of performance forces us to make choices, to determine what is 'at stake' in these odd plays, to pursue the characters' goals vigorously, to commit to a particular reading of the dramatic situation. Performance requires us to take seriously both the tenth century and our own; to wrestle with the dissonance and to recognize the consonance. The adventure occasioned by theatrical illusion provides students the opportunity to meet Hrotsvit in their minds *and bodies*, to discover their own *clamor validus*, to negotiate ambiguity. In the end, whether the performance is a success or failure, students playing with Hrotsvit are students honestly engaging the challenges of liberal education.

NOTES

1 Bevington, 'Why Teach Medieval Drama?' 153.
2 I do not mean to suggest that contemporary performance should cultivate an *uncritical* acceptance of the world view seemingly endorsed by the playwright, the play, or the original audience. In fact, to my mind, some of the more exciting performances highlight the affinities and the dissonances between and among these world views. I *do* mean to suggest, however, that the original world view must be approached respectfully, as worthy of serious consideration.
3 Thanks to Professor Phyllis Brown, I became aware of a recent staging of Hrotsvit's *Sapientia* in New York City. Peter Marks's review appeared in *The New York Times* on 19 July 1999 ('Girls in Deep Trouble, Not Just from Hadrian'). The production entitled *3 Virgins* was mounted by the Collapsable Giraffe, a young SoHo Theatre Company, and took place in a former Times Square sex superstore. According to Marks, 'One of the conceits of Amy Huggans and her five member cast is that a full millennium [after Hrotsvit], women are still experiencing defilement in public rituals, in everything from strip joints to children's beauty contests.' This site-specific performance found two of the sisters dressed in 'little-girl pageant dresses' and the third 'portrayed by a doll.' Rather than denounce the faith of their mother in the court of the emperor Hadrian, these three young virgins 'submit willingly to their gruesome punishments.' Marks notes that 'their faith in God is absolute. In our time all such certainties have evaporated and may even be perceived as a kind of madness.' Collapsable Giraffe suggested to me that there could indeed be bridges built to span a one-thousand year abyss. But would it be necessary for those bridges to be suspended by cables of 'madness' in order for us to play the plays? Is madness yet another kind of wink at the audience? See also Jane Jeffrey's essay in this volume which treats specifically this production of *3 Virgins*.
4 See Wilson, *Florilegium*, 5–7, and Anderson and Zinsser, *A History of Their Own*, 186–7.
5 Case, 'Re-Viewing Hrotsvit,' 538.
6 I would like to thank the following actors and audience members who assisted me by recording their observations of the production process and

the performance for the purposes of this article: Roy Brooks, Thomas Garvey, Jean McCarron, Barbara Fraser, and Gregory Dale Schultz.

7 From the very beginning of the project I knew that sound would be critically important in producing these plays. I was fortunate to have the opportunity to work with Gregory Dale Schultz, M.Div., a composer who is the Director of Liturgy and Music at Santa Clara University. His soundscape proved one of the more striking elements of the production, creating aurally the emotional and spiritual terrain sketched by Hrotsvit and the performers. The sound design included plainchant, piano, and hand chimes.

8 The prologue included biblical readings from Genesis, Song of Songs, Luke, John, Galatians, and 1 Timothy. It also included excerpts from Tertullian's *On the Dress of Women*, Palladius's *The Lausiac History*, John Chrysostom's *Second Discourse on Genesis and Homilies on the Epistles of St. Paul*, Augustine's *City of God*, and Tertullian's *On the Spectacles*.

9 David Wiles's recent article in *Theatre History Studies* entitled 'Hrosvitha of Gandersheim: The Performance of Her Plays in the Tenth Century' proved a compelling source for me during the research phase of this project. He makes a fine case for the actual production of Hrotsvit's plays in the tenth century as, in his view, the plays remain skeletal and potentially confusing unless they are married to particular stage action and gesture. Yet he also asserts that 'the romantic vision of Hrosvitha and her comrades donning false beards behind the privacy of the cloister walls is one that we must reluctantly discard' (138). For Wiles, the production of the plays by the women religious at Gandersheim remains 'implausible on the grounds of social class as much as gender' (138); he suggests that the plays may have likely been performed by a male cast drawn from the population of the Gandersheim court/employees. See Janet Snyder's essay in this volume also.

10 Clark, *Women in the Early Church*, 88.

11 Ibid., 90.

12 Ibid., 89.

13 This is not to suggest that there is *no* humour in Hrotsvit's composition. For example, in *The Resurrection of Drusiana and Calimachus* the evil Fortunatus sits within the medieval comic devil tradition. His lines lend themselves to comic delivery; this coupled with a freer physicality provides a grotesque foil to the other characters. In this production, an unctuous and voyeuristic Fortunatus was ruled by earthy desires for money and food. At the time of his being bitten by the snake, he was ravenously eating an apple. When he died his second death after freely rejecting salvation in Christ, Fortunatus

dropped to the floor with histrionic gesture and contorted face. This death read more comically than any of the others.

14 During the funeral sequence for Drusiana, the *In Paradisum* was chanted; Andronicus and St John walked slowly to either side of Drusiana and faced upstage toward the high altar. Drusiana slowly rose and turned upstage as well. Andronicus picked up Drusiana's candle and the three processed to the high altar. Three chairs had been set on the top step. Drusiana walked up the steps and sat in the centre chair with her head bowed. Andronicus set her candle directly behind her on the altar. Andronicus and St John exited in a retiring procession as the chant concluded. Since Calimachus and Fortunatus were in the 'tomb' at the time of their deaths, they simply sat in the chairs on either side of Drusiana. At Drusiana's resurrection, the candle was lit as resurrection chimes sounded; she stood at her place with arms extended in the *orans* position. That is, she claimed the position and posture of the principal liturgical celebrant.

15 After Drusiana furiously rejects Calimachus's advances, Calimachus (with wounded pride) says, 'So far I have no reason to get angry or mad, because the reaction which my love elicited in you could very well make you turn red' (Wilson, *Florilegium*, 56).

16 Sticca, 'The Hagiographical and Monastic Context of Hrotswitha's Plays,' 15. Sticca mentions particularly St Nile of Rossano (910–1005) and St Romuald of Camaldoli (952–1027).

17 Ibid., 9.

18 See Wiles, 'Hrosvitha of Gandersheim,' 142–3. His argument concerning *The Fall and Repentance of Mary* is very compelling, especially as it builds upon his prior assertion that Hrotsvit's plays were written for performance. Wiles seems to be the first commentator on the play to question the received interpretation that 'the saintliness of Abraham is an unshakeable premise.' In all fairness, the 'commentators who have devoted much ink to this play' have tried to account seriously for the structural balance that Hrotsvit sets up. Mary 'falls' at the hands of a demon-lover who visits her at her cell disguised as a hermit. She is 'redeemed' at the hands of a hermit (the Christic Abraham) who visits her in a brothel disguised as a lover. Because this chiastic structure is typical of Hrotsvit's composition, the reading that sees Abraham as the seducer undercuts long-standing assumptions about Hrotsvit's style. Though I opted to follow Wiles in a reading that makes most dramatic sense to me, I do admit (thanks to Professor Phyllis Brown) that it remains possible to maintain the chiastic structure while critiquing (rather than destroying) Abraham's holiness: Abraham's education of Mary is insufficient and ineffective in keeping her safe from the

sin of despair, a far more serious sin in Hrotsvit than physical sin. Hence, though he may not be the actual seducer, Abraham and his friend Effrem still bear some responsibility for what happens to Mary.

19 Wiles notes that 'Abraham's behaviour was unorthodox in respect of normal hermit behaviour in the fourth century, for, as Aline Rouselle has demonstrated, the hermits of that era were reluctant even to take their young sons into the wilderness for fear of being smitten with sexual desire' ('Hrosvitha of Gandersheim,' 143).

Works Cited

Acta Sanctorum. Edited by Joannes Bollandus, Godefridus Henschenius, and Daniel Papenbrochius. Rev. ed. J. Carnandet. 68 vols. Paris: V. Palmé, 1863–1940. Reprint Brussels: Culture et Civilisation, 1965–70.

Adalbert. 'Continuatio Reginonis.' In *Quellen zur Geschichte der Sächsischen Kaiserzeit,* edited by Bauer and Rau, 184–243.

Airlie, Stuart. 'Review Article: 'After Empire – Recent Work on the Emergence of post-Carolingian Kingdoms.' *Early Medieval Europe* 2.2 (1993): 153–61.

Alford, John A. 'Literature and Law in Medieval England.' *PMLA* 92 (1977): 941–51.

Althoff, Gerd. 'Gandersheim und Quedlinburg: Ottonische Frauenklöster als Herrschafts- und Überlieferungszentren.' *Frühmittelalterliche Studien* 25 (1991): 123–44.

– 'Geschichtsschreibung in einer oralen Gesellschaft. Das Beispiel des 10. Jahrhunderts.' In *Ottonische Neuanfänge: Symposion zur Ausstellung 'Otto der Grosse, Magdeburg und Europa,'* edited by Bernd Schneidmüller and Stefan Weinfurter, 151–69. Mainz: Philipp von Zabern, 2001.

– *Die Ottonen: Königsherrschaft ohne Staat.* Stuttgart: W. Kohlhammer, 2000.

Anderson, Bonnie S., and Judith P. Zinsser. *A History of Their Own: Women in Europe from Prehistory to the Present.* Vol. 1. New York: Harper and Row, 1988.

The Anglo-Saxon Poetic Records. 6 vols. Edited by George Philip Krapp and Elliott Van Kirk Dobbie. New York: Columbia University Press, 1936.

Ashbach, Joseph von. *Roswitha und Conrad Celtes.* 2nd ed. Viena: Braumüller, 1868.

Atkinson, Clarissa. '"Precious Balm in a Fragile Glass": The Ideology of Virginity in the Later Middle Ages.' *Journal of Family History* 8 (1983): 131–43.

Augustine. *The City of God.* Translated by David Knowles. Harmondsworth: Penguin Books, 1972.

– *The City of God Against the Pagans.* 7 vols. Edited and translated by George E. McCracken. The Loeb Classical Library. Cambridge: Harvard University Press, 1957–72.

Baetke, Walter. *Das Heilige im Germanischen.* Tübingen: Mohr, 1942.

Bange, P. 'Women of the Nobility in the German Chronicles.' In *The Empress Theophano,* edited by Adelbert Davids, 150–68. New York: Cambridge University Press, 1995.

Bates, Paul A. *Faust: Sources, Works, Criticism.* New York: Harcourt, 1969.

Bauer, Albert, and Reinhold Rau, eds. *Quellen zur Geschichte der Sächsischen Kaiserzeit: Widukinds Sachsengeschichte, Adlaberts Fortsetzung der Chronik Reginos, Liudprands Werke.* Ausgewählte Quellen zur deutschen Geschite des Mittelalters, Freiherr vom Stein-Gedächtnisausgabe, 8. Darmstadt: Wissenschaftliche Buchgesellschaft, 1971.

Bäumer, Gertrud. *Adelheid, Mutter der Königreiche.* Tübingen: Rainer Wunderlich, 1936.

– *Die Frau und das geistige Leben.* Die Kulturaufgaben der Frau, 5. Leipzig: C.F. Amelang, 1911.

– *Männer und Frauen im geistigen Werden des deutschen Volkes.* Tübingen: Rainer Wunderlich, 1934.

Bede. In *Proverbia Salomonis.* Edited by D. Hurst. Turnholt: Brepols, 1983.

Bede's Ecclesiastical History of the English People. Edited and translated by Bertram Colgrave and R.A.B. Mynors. Oxford: Clarendon Press, 1969.

Bergman, Mary Bernardine. *Hrosvithae Liber Tertius: A Text with Translation, Introduction and Commentary.* Covington, KY: Sisters of St Benedict, 1943.

Bernhardt, John. *Itinerant Kingship and Royal Monasteries in Early Medieval Germany, c. 936–1075.* Cambridge: Cambridge University Press, 1993.

Berschin, Walter. 'Passio und Theater: Zur dramatischen Struktur einiger Vorlagen Hrotsvit von Gandersheim.' In *The Theatre in the Middle Ages,* edited by Herman Braet, Johan Nowe, and Gilbert Tournoy, 1–11. Leuven: Leuven University Press, 1985.

Bertini, Ferruccio. *Il 'Teatro' di Rosvita.* Genoa: Tilgher, 1979.

Bevington, David. 'Why Teach Medieval Drama?' In *Approaches to Teaching Medieval English Drama,* edited by Richard K. Emmerson, 151–6. Approaches to Teaching World Literature, 29. New York: MLA, 1990.

Beyreuther, Gerald. 'Kaiserin Adelheid: Mutter der Königreiche.' In *Herrscherinnen und Nonnen: Frauengestalten von der Ottonenzeit bis zu den Staufern,* edited by Erika Uitz, Barbara Pätzold, and Gerald Beyreuther, 43–80. Berlin: Deutscher Verlag der Wissenschaften, 1990.

Biblia Sacra Iuxta Vulgatam Versionem. Edited by Robert Weber. 2 Vols. Stuttgart: Württembergische Bibelanstalt, 1969.

Birks, Peter, and Grant McLeod, eds. and trans. *Justinian's Institutes.* Ithaca: Cornell University Press, 1987.

Birnes, W.J. 'Christ as Advocate: The Legal Metaphor of *Piers Plowman.*' *Annuale Mediaevale* 16 (1975): 71–93.

Bishop, Jane. 'Bishops as Marital Advisors in the Ninth Century.' In *Women of the Medieval World*, edited by Julius Kirshner and Suzanne F. Wemple, 54–85. Oxford: Basil Blackwell, 1985.

Black, Jonathan. 'The Use of Liturgical Texts in Hrotsvit's Works.' In *Hrotsvit of Gandersheim: Rara Avis in Saxonia?* 165–81.

Blenkinsopp, Joseph. 'The Social Context of the "Outsider Woman" in Proverbs 1–9.' *Biblica* 72 (1991): 457–73.

Boretius, Afred Edwin, ed. *Capitularia Regum Francorum.* MGH Leges, section 2, no. 26, 68–70. Hanover: Impensis Bibliopolii Hahniani, 1960.

Borch-Jacobsen, Mikkel. *The Freudian Subject.* Chicago: University of Chicago Press, 1988.

Bornscheuer, Lothar. *Miseriae Regum: Untersuchungen zum Krisen- und Todesgedanken in den herrschaftstheologischen Vorstellungen der ottonisch-salischen Zeit.* Arbeiten zur Frühmittelalterforschung, 4. Berlin: Walter de Gruyter, 1968.

Bosker, Margo R. *Sechs Stücke nach Stücken: Zu den Bearbeitungen von Peter Hacks.* Studies in Modern German Literature, 55. New York: Peter Lang, 1994.

Bossuat, Robert, Louis Pichard, and Guy Raynaud de Lage. *Dictionnaire des lettres françaises: Le Moyen Age.* Paris: Fayard, 1964.

Boswell, John. *Christianity, Social Tolerance, and Homosexuality.* Chicago: University of Chicago Press, 1980.

Bouchard, Constance Brittain. *Strong of Body, Brave and Noble: Chivalry and Society in Medieval France.* Ithaca: Cornell University Press, 1998.

Boyd, Beverly. *The Middle English Miracles of the Virgin.* San Marino, CA: Huntington Library, 1964.

Brown, Peter. *The Cult of the Saints: Its Rise and Function in Latin Christianity.* Chicago: University of Chicago Press, 1981.

Bruder, R. *Die germanische Frau im Lichte der Runenschriften und der antiken Historiographie.* Quellen und Forschungen zur Sprach- und Kulturgeschichte der germanischen Völker, 57. Berlin: Walter de Gruyter, 1974.

Brühl, Carlrichard. *Deutschland-Frankreich: Die Geburt zweier Völker.* Cologne: Böhlau, 1995.

Brühl, Carlrichard, and Bernd Schneidmüller. *Beiträge zur mittelalterlichen Reichs- und Nationsbildung in Deutschland und Frankreich.* Historische Zeitschrift, Beiheft N.F., 24. Munich: Oldenbourg, 1997.

Brundage, James A. *Medieval Canon Law*. London: Longman, 1995.

Burgess, Henry E. 'Hroswitha and Terence: A Study in Literary Imitation.' *Proceedings of the Pacific Northwest Conference on Foreign Languages* 19 (1968): 23–9.

Bynum, Caroline Walker. 'Did the Twelfth Century Discover the Individual?' In *Jesus as Mother*, 82–109. Berkeley: University of California Press, 1982.

– *The Resurrection of the Body in Western Christianity, 200–1330*. New York: Columbia University Press, 1995.

Bynum, Caroline Walker, ed. *Fragmentation and Redemption: Essays on Gender and the Human Body in Medieval Religion*. New York: Zone Books, 1991.

Cadden, Joan. *Meanings of Sex Difference in the Middle Ages: Medicine, Science, and Culture*. Cambridge: Cambridge University Press, 1993.

Camp, Claudia. 'The Strange Woman of Proverbs.' In *Wise, Strange and Holy: The Strange Woman and the Making of the Bible*, 40–71. Sheffield: Sheffield Academic Press, 2000.

– *Wisdom and the Feminine in the Book of Proverbs*. Sheffield: Almond, 1985.

Carlson, Marla. 'Impassive Bodies: Hrotsvit Stages Martyrdom.' *Theatre Journal* 50 (1998): 473–87.

Carlson, Marvin. *Theatre Semiotics: Signs of Life*. Bloomington: Indiana University Press, 1990.

Carruthers, Mary. *The Book of Memory: A Study of Memory in Medieval Culture*. New York and London: Cambridge University Press, 1990.

Case, Sue-Ellen. *Feminism and Theater*. New York: Methuen, 1988.

– 'Re-Viewing Hrotsvit.' *Theatre Journal* 35 (1983): 533–42.

Cazelles, Brigitte. *The Lady as Saint: A Collection of Hagiographic Romances of the Thirteenth Century*. Philadelphia: University of Pennsylvania Press, 1991.

Cerulli, Enrico. 'Le calife Abd al-Rahman III de Cordoue et le martyr Pelage dans un poème de Hrotsvitha.' *Studia Islamica* 22 (1970): 69–76.

Chamberlain, David. 'Musical Imagery and Musical Learning in Hrotsvit.' In *Hrotsvit of Gandersheim: Rara Avis in Saxonia?*

– 'Musical Learning and Dramatic Action in Hrotsvit's *Paphnutius*.' *Studies in Philology* 77.4 (1980): 319–43.

– *Woman as Hero in Old English Literature*. Syracuse: Syracuse University Press, 1986.

Cixous, Hélène. 'Sorties.' In *New French Feminisms*, edited by Elaine Marks and Isabelle de Courtivron, 90–8. University of Massachusetts Press, 1981.

Clark, Elizabeth A. *Women in the Early Church*. Message of the Fathers of the Church 13. 1983. Reprint Collegeville: Liturgical Press, 1990.

Colbert, Edward P. 'The Christians of Cordoba in the Tenth Century.' In *The Martyrs of Cordoba (850–859): A Study of the Sources*, 382–9. Washington, DC: Catholic University Press, 1962.

Colgrave, Bertram, and R.A.B. Mynors, eds. and trans. *Bede's Ecclesiastical History of the English People.* Oxford: Clarendon Press, 1969.

Colman, Rebecca. 'Reason and Unreason in Early Medieval Law.' *Journal of Interdisciplinary History* 4 (1974): 571–91.

Conner, Patrick. 'On Dating Cynewulf.' In *Cynewulf: Basic Readings,* edited by Robert Bjork, 23–55. New York: Garland, 1996.

Coulter, Claudia. 'The "Terentian" Comedies of a Tenth Century Nun.' *Classical Journal* 24 (1929): 515–29.

Curtius, Ernst Robert. *European Literature and the Latin Middle Ages.* Translated by Willard R. Trask. Princeton: Princeton University Press, 1973.

Davids, Adelbert, ed. *The Empress Theophano: Byzantium and the West at the Turn of the First Millennium.* Cambridge: Cambridge University Press, 1995.

Davidson, Clifford. *Saint Plays and Pageants of Medieval Britain.* http:// www.wmich.edu/medieval/research/eda/saint.html.

de Hamel, Christopher. *A History of Illuminated Manuscripts.* London: Phaidon Press, 1994.

de Luca, Kenneth. 'Hrotsvit's "Imitation" of Terence.' *Classical Folia* 28 (1974): 89–102.

Delany, Sheila. *Impolitic Bodies: Poetry, Saints, and Society in Fifteenth-Century England.* Oxford: Oxford University Press, 1998.

Demers, Patricia. '*In virginea forma*: The Salvific Feminine in the Plays of Hrotsvitha of Gandersheim and Hildegard of Bingen.' In *Reimagining Women: Representations of Women in Culture,* edited by Shirley Newman and Glennis Stephenson, 45–60. Toronto: University of Toronto Press, 1993.

Dhuoda. *Handbook for Her Warrior Son: Liber Manualis.* Edited and translated by Marcelle Thiebaux. Cambridge: Cambridge University Press, 1998

Díaz y Díaz, Manuel. 'La pasión de S. Pelayo y su difusión.' *Anuario de estudios medievales* 6 (1969): 97–116.

Dockray-Miller, Mary. *Motherhood and Mothering in Anglo-Saxon England.* New York: St Martin's Press, 2000.

Donovan, Leslie, trans. *Women Saints Lives in Old English Prose.* Woodbridge, Suffolk: Boydell and Brewer, 1999.

Dronke, Peter. *Women Writers of the Middle Ages: A Critical Study of Texts from Perpetua († 203) to Marguerite Porete († 1310).* Cambridge: Cambridge University Press, 1984.

Dumoulié, Camille. 'Formes théâtrales du délire: La Folie du pouvoir.' *Littératures* 31 (1994): 117–28.

– *Les Théâtres de la cruauté: Hommage à Antonin Artaud.* Paris: Desjonquères, 2000.

Eggert, Wolfgang. 'Das Wir-Gefühl bei fränkischen und deutschen Geschichts-schreibern bis zum Investiturstreit.' In *Wir-Gefühl und Regnum Saxonum bei frühmittelalterlichen Geschichtsschreibern,* by Wolfgang Eggert and Barbara Pätzold, 88–9. Forschungen zur mittelalterlichen Geschichte, 31. Weimar: Böhlau, 1984.

Elene. In *Anglo-Saxon Poetry.* Translated by Robert Kay Gordon. Rev. ed. London: Dent, 1954.

Elene. In *The Vercelli Book.* Vol. 2 of *The Anglo-Saxon Poetic Records.* Ed. George Philip Krapp and Elliott van Kirk Dobbie. New York: Columbia University Press, 1932.

Eliot, Marc. *Down 42nd Street: Sex, Money, Culture, and Politics at the Crossroads of the World.* New York: Warner, 2001.

Elm, Susanna. *Virgins of God: The Making of Asceticism in Late Antiquity.* Oxford: Clarendon, 1994.

Emmerson, Richard K., ed. *Approaches to Teaching Medieval English Drama.* Approaches to Teaching World Literature, 29. New York: MLA, 1990.

Enders, Jody. *The Medieval Theater of Cruelty: Rhetoric, Memory, Violence.* Ithaca: Cornell University Press, 1999.

– 'Of Miming and Signing: The Dramatic Rhetoric of Gesture.' In *Gesture in Medieval Drama and Art.* Edited by Clifford Davidson, 1–25. Kalamazoo, Michigan: The Medieval Institute, 2001.

Ericksen, Janet Schrunk. 'Offering the Forbidden Fruit in MS. Junius 11.' In *Gesture inMedieval Drama and Art,* edited by Clifford Davidson, 48–65. Kalamazoo, MI: Medieval Institute, 2001.

Farrell, Joseph. *Latin Language and Latin Culture: From Ancient to Modern Times.* Cambridge: University Press, 2001.

Fassler, Margot. 'Mary's Nativity, Fulbert of Chartres, and the *Stirps Jesse*: Liturgical Innovation circa 1000 and Its Afterlife.' *Speculum* 75.2 (April 2000): 389–414.

Fell, Christine E., with Cecily Clark and Elizabeth Williams. *Women in Anglo-Saxon England.* Oxford: Blackwell, 1984.

Ferrante, Joan M. *To the Glory of Her Sex: Women's Roles in the Composition of Medieval Texts.* Bloomington: Indiana University Press, 1997.

Fletcher, Richard. *The Barbarian Conversion: From Paganism to Christianity.* New York: Henry Holt, 1997.

Foucault, Michel. *Discipline and Punish: The Birth of the Prison.* Translated by Alan Sheridan. New York: Pantheon, 1977.

Fox, Robin Lane. *Pagans and Christians.* New York: Alfred Knopf, 1987.

France, Anatole. 'Hrotswitha aux marionnettes.' In *La Vie Littéraire.* 3rd series, 10–19. Paris: Calmann-Lévy, 1891.

– 'Les marionnettes de M. Signoret.' In *La Vie me Littéraire.* 2nd series, 145–50. Paris: Calmann-Lévy, 1890.

- *Oeuvres.* Vol. 1 of *Bibliothèque de la Pléiade.* Paris, 1890; Paris: Éditions Gallimard, 1984.
- *Thaïs.* Translated by Basia Gulati. Chicago: University of Chicago Press, 1976.

Franco, Emanuela. 'I drammi di Rosvita e *Rosie träumt* di Peter Hacks.' *Studi Medievali* 27 (1986): 225–39.

Frankforter, A. Daniel. 'Sexism and the Search for the Thematic Structure of the Plays of Hroswitha of Gandersheim.' *International Journal of Women's Studies* 2 (1979): 221–32.

Frenken, Goswin. 'Eine neue Hrotsvithandschrift.' *Gesellschaft für ältere deutsche Geschichtskunde* 44 (1922): 101–14.

Fried, Johannes. 'Die Königserhebung Heinrichs I: Erinnerung, Mündlichkeit und Traditionsbildung im 10. Jahrhundert.' In *Mittelalterforschung nach der Wende 1989*, edited by Michael Borgolte, 267–318. Historische Zeitschrift. Beiheft N.F., 20. Munich: R. Oldenbourg, 1995.

Frye, Northrop. *Anatomy of Criticism.* New York: Atheneum Press, 1967.

Gardner, Jane F. *Women in Roman Law and Society.* Bloomington: Indiana University Press, 1986.

Giesebrechte, Wilhelm von. 'Geschichte der deutschen Kaiserzeit.' In *Gründung des Kaiserthums*, 5th ed., 276–7. Leipzig: Duncker & Humblot, 1881.

Gilson, Etienne. *The Christian Philosophy of Saint Augustine.* New York: Random House, 1960.

Glew, Ellen Joan. 'From Brecht to "Socialist Classicism": The Aesthetic Theory of Peter Hacks.' PhD dissertation, Harvard University, 1980.

Glocker, Winfrid. *Die Verwandten der Ottonen und ihre Bedeutung in der Politik: Studien zur Familienpolitik und zur Genealogie des sächsischen Kaiserhauses.* Cologne: Böhlau, 1989.

Goetting, Hans. *Das Bistum Hildesheim 1: Das reichsunmittelbare Kanonissenstift Gandersheim.* Germania Sacra N.F., 7. Berlin: Walter de Gruyter, 1973.

Goez, Werner. *Translatio imperii: Ein Beitrag zur Geschichte des Geschichtsdenkens und der politischen Theorien im Mittelalter und in der frühen Neuzeit.* Tübingen: Mohr, 1958.

Gold, Barbara. 'Hrotsvitha Writes Herself: *Clamor Validus Gandeshemensis.*' In *Sex and Gender in Medieval and Renaissance Texts: The Latin Tradition*, edited by Barbara K. Gold, Paul Allen Miller, and Charles Platter, 41–70. Albany: State University of New York Press, 1997.

Gordon, Robert Kay, comp. and trans. *Anglo-Saxon Poetry.* Rev. ed. London: Dent; New York: Dutton, 1954.

Gottsched, Johann Christoph. *Nöthiger Vorrath zur Geschichte der deutschen Dramatischen Dichtkunst.* Leipzig, 1757–65. Reprint, Hildesheim and New York: Georg Olms, 1970.

– *Versuch einer Critischen Dichtkunst.* Leipzig, 1730.

Gout, Raoul. 'Anatole France et le théatre de Hrotsvitha.' *Mercure de France* 209 (1931): 595–611.

Greenberg, David F. *The Construction of Homosexuality.* Chicago: University of Chicago Press, 1988.

Gurr, Andrew. *The Shakespearean Stage, 1574–1642.* New York and Cambridge: Cambridge University Press, 1980.

Hacks, Peter. *Das Jahrmarktsfest zu Pfundersweilern. Rosie träumt: Zwei Bearbeitungen nach J.W. von Goethe und Hrosvith von Gandersheim.* Berlin and Weimar: Düsseldorf: Claassen, 1977.

– 'Zehn Zeilen über *Rosie träumt.*' In *Das Jahrmarktsfest zu Pfundersweilern,* 122–30.

Hagendahl, Harald. *Augustine and the Latin Classics.* Goteborg: Flanders Altiebolag, 1967.

Haight, Anne Lyon, ed. *Hroswitha of Gandersheim: Her Life, Times, and Works, and a Comprehensive Bibliography.* New York: Hroswitha Club, 1965.

Harris, John Wesley. *Medieval Theatre in Context.* London and New York: Routledge, 1992.

Hart, J.M. 'Allotria 2,5.' *Modern Language Notes* 17 (1902): 231–2.

Haskins, Susan. *Mary Magdalen: Myth and Metaphor.* London: HarperCollins, 1993.

Head, Thomas. 'Hrotsvit's *Primordia* and the Historical Traditions of Monastic Communities.' In *Hrotsvit of Gandersheim: Rara Avis in Saxonia?* 143–64.

Heffernan, Thomas J. *Sacred Biography: Saints and Their Biographers in the Middle Ages.* New York: Oxford University Press, 1988.

Helmholz, R.H. *The Spirit of Classical Canon Law.* Athens: University of Georgia Press, 1996.

Henel, Heinrich. *The Poetry of Conrad Ferdinand Meyer.* Madison: University of Wisconsin Press, 1954.

Hennecke, E., and W. Schneemelcher, eds. 'Christ's Descent into Hell.' In New Testament *Apocrypha.* Philadelphia: Westminster Press, 1963.

Herrin, Judith. *The Formation of Christendom.* Princeton: Princeton University Press, 1987.

Hill, Rosalind. 'The Christian View of the Muslims at the Time of the First Crusade.' In *The Eastern Mediterranean Lands in the Period of the Crusades,* edited by P.M. Holt, 1–8. Warminster, UK: Aris and Phillips, 1977.

Hlawitschka, Eduard, ed. *Königswahl und Thronfolge in ottonisch-frühdeutscher Zeit.* Wege der Forschung, 178. Darmstadt: Wissenschaftliche Buchgesellschaft, 1971.

Hollywood, Amy. *Sensible Ecstasy: Mysticism, Sexual Difference, and the Demands of History.* Chicago: University of Chicago Press, 2002.

The Holy Bible translated from the Latin Vulgate and diligently compared with other editions in divers languages. Rheims: 1582; Douai: 1609; London: Burns and Oates, 1964.

Homeyer, Helena, ed. *Hrotsvithae Opera.* Munich: Schoningh, 1970.

Hoof, Diane Van. 'The Saint and the Sinner: Hrotsvit's *Pafnutius* and Anatole France's *Thais.*' In *Hrotsvit of Gandersheim: Rara Avis in Saxonia?* 263–74.

Horner, Shari. 'The Violence of Exegesis: Reading the Bodies of Aelfric's Female Saints.' In *Violence Against Women in Medieval Texts,* edited by Anna Roberts, 22–43. Gainesville: University Press of Florida, 1998.

Hrotsvit of Gandersheim. *Opera Omnia.* Edited by Walter Berschin. Bibliotheca Teubneriana. Munich: K.G. Saur, 2001.

Hrotsvit of Gandersheim: Rara Avis in Saxonia? edited by Katharina M. Wilson. Medieval and Renaissance Monograph Series, 7. Edited by Guy R. Mermier. Ann Arbor, MI: Medieval and Renaissance Collegium, 1987.

Hubrich, Eduard. 'Fränkisches Wahl- und Erbkönigtum zur Merovingerzeit.' 1889. Reprinted in *Königswahl und Thronfolge in fränkisch-karolingischer Zeit,* edited by Eduard Hlawitschka, 3–58. Wege der Forschung, 247. Darmstadt: Wissenschaftliche Buchgesellschaft, 1975.

Huebner, Rudolph. *A History of Germanic Private Law.* Translated by Francis S. Philbrick. 1918. Reprint, New York: Augustus M. Kelley, 1968.

Hughes, Eril. 'Augustinian Elements in Hrotsvit's Plays.' In *Hrotsvit of Gandersheim: Rara Avis in Saxonia?* 63–70.

Hulme, W.H., ed. *The Middle English Harrowing of Hell and Gospel of Nicodemus.* Early English Text Society, Extra Series, 100. London: Oxford University Press, 1907.

Hutcheson, Gregory S. 'The Sodomitic Moor: Queerness in the Narrative of the *Reconquista.*' In *Queering the Middle Ages,* edited by Glenn Burger and Steven F. Kruger, 99–122. Minneapolis: University of Minnesota Press, 2001.

Jacobus de Voragine. *The Golden Legend: Readings on the Saints.* Translated by William Granger Ryan. Princeton: Princeton University Press, 1993.

Jaeger, C. Stephen. *The Envy of Angels: Cathedral Schools and Social Ideals in Medieval Europe 950–1200.* Philadelphia: University of Pennsylvania Press, 1994.

Jaeger, H. 'The Patristic Conception of Wisdom in the Light of Biblical and Rabbinical Research.' *Studia Patristica* 4 (1961): 90–106.

Jakobs, Hermann. 'Zum Thronfolgerecht der Ottonen.' 1971. Reprint in *Königswahl und Thronfolge in ottonisch-frühdeutscher Zeit,* edited by Eduard Hlawitschka, 509–28. Wege der Forschung, 178. Darmstadt: Wissenschaftliche Buchgesellschaft, 1971.

Jefferis, Sibylle. 'Hrotsvit and the *Magnum Legendarium Austriacum.*' In *Hrotsvit of Gandersheim: Rara Avis in Saxonia?* 239–52.

Jeffrey, Jane E. 'Virginal Allegories of Self Knowledge in Hrotsvit's *Sapientia*.' *Arachnē* 4 (1997): 160–81.

Jordan, Mark D. *The Invention of Sodomy in Christian Theology*. Chicago: University of Chicago Press, 1991.

Kadel, Andrew. *Matrology: A Bibliography of Writings by Christian Women from the First to the Fifteenth Centuries*. New York: Continuum, 1995.

Kamp, Hermann. 'Konflikte und Konfliktführung in der Anfängen der Regierung Otto I.' In *Otto der Grosse: Magdeburg und Europa*, edited by Matthias Puhle. Vol. 1, *Essays*, 168–78. Mainz: Philipp von Zabern, 2001.

Kaplan, Jeffrey P. *English Grammar: Principles and Facts*. Englewood Cliffs, NJ: Prentice-Hall, 1989.

Karpf, Ernst. *Herrscherlegitimation und Reichsbegriff in der ottonischen Geschichtsschreibung des 10. Jahrhunderts*. Historische Forschungen, 10. Stuttgart: Steiner, 1985.

Karras, Ruth Mazo. *Common Women: Prostitution and Sexuality in Medieval England*. New York: Oxford University Press, 1996.

Kedar, Benjamin Z. *Crusade and Mission*. Princeton: Princeton University Press, 1984.

Keller, Hagen. 'Entscheidungssituationen und Lernprozesse in den "Anfangen der deutschen Geschichte": Die "Italien- und Kaiserpolitik" Ottos des Grossen.' *Frühmittelalterliche Studien* 33 (1999): 20–48.

– 'Widukinds Bericht über die Aachener Wahl und Krönung Ottos I.' 1995. Reprinted in *Ottonische Königsherrschaft: Organisation und Legitimation königlicher Macht*, 91–130. Darmstadt: Wissenschaftliche Buchgesellschaft, 2002.

Keller, Hagen, and Gerd Althoff. *Heinrich I. und Otto der Grosse: Neubeginn auf karolingischem Erbe*. 2 vols. Göttingen: Muster-Schmidt, 1985.

Kettle, Ann J. 'Ruined Maids: Prostitutes and Servant Girls in Later Medieval England.' In *Matrons and Marginal Women in Medieval Society*, edited by Robert R. Edwards and Vickie Ziegler, 19–33. Woodbridge: Boydell Press, 1995.

Kirsch, Wolfgang. 'Hrotsvit von Gandersheim als Epikerin.' *Mittellateinisches Jahrbuch* 24/25 (1989/90): 215–24.

Kitchen, John. *Saints' Lives and the Rhetoric of Gender*. Oxford: Oxford University Press, 1998.

Kluckert, Ehrenfried. 'Romanesque Painting.' In *Romanesque, Architecture, Sculpture, Painting*, edited by Rolf Toman and Achim Bednorz, 400–25.

Knight, Alan E. *Aspects of Genre in Late Medieval French Drama*. Manchester: Manchester University Press, 1983.

Köpke, Rudolf. *Hrotsvit von Gandersheim: Zur Litteraturgeschichte des zehnten Jahrhunderts*. Berlin: Mittler, 1869.

Kraeger, Heinrich. *Conrad Ferdinand Meyer: Quellen und Wandlungen seiner Gedichte*. Palaestra, 16. Berlin: May & Müller, 1901.

Krapp, George Philip, and Elliott Van Kirk Dobbie, eds. *The Exeter Book.* Vol. 3, *Anglo-Saxon Poetic Records.* New York: Columbia University Press, 1936.

Kratz, Dennis M. 'The *Gesta Ottonis* in Its Context.' In *Hrotsvit of Gandersheim: Rara Avis in Saxonia?* 201–9.

– 'The Nun's Epic: Hroswitha on Christian Heroism.' In *Wege der Worte: Festschrift für Wolfgang Fleischhauer,* edited by Donald C. Riechel, 132–42. Cologne: Böhlau, 1978.

Kronenberg, Kurt. *Roswitha von Gandersheim: Leben und Werk.* Bad Gandersheim: C.F. Hertel, 1962.

Kuehne, Oswald Robert. *A Study of the Thais Legend with Special Reference to Hrothsvitha's 'Paphnutius.'* Philadelphia: University of Pennsylvania Press, 1922.

Kuhn, Annette, ed. *Frauen in Mittelalter.* Vol. 2, *Frauenbild und Frauenrechte in Kirche und Gesellschaft. Quellen und Materialien.* Düsseldorf: Schwann Verlag, 1984.

Lang, Bernhard. *Wisdom and the Book of Proverbs: An Israelite Goddess Redefined.* New York: Pilgrim Press, 1986.

Langland, William. *The Vision of Piers Plowman.* Edited by A.V.C. Schmidt. London: Everyman, 1978.

Lankewisch, Vincent A. 'Assault from Behind: Sodomy, Foreign Invasion, and Masculine Identity in the Roman d'Eneas.' In *Text and Territory: Geographical Imagination in the European Middle Ages,* edited by Sylvia Tomasch and Sealy Gilles, 207–47. Philadelphia: University of Pennsylvania Press, 1998.

Latham, R.E., and James Houston Baxter. *Revised Medieval Latin Word-List from British and Irish Sources.* Oxford: Oxford University Press, 1965.

Laudage, Johannes. 'Hausrecht und Thronfolge: Überlegungen zur Königserhebung Ottos des Großen und zu den Aufständen Thankmars, Heinrichs und Liudolfs.' *Historisches Jahrbuch* 112 (1992): 23–71.

– *Otto der Grosse (912–973): Eine Biographie.* Regensburg: Friedrich Pustet, 2001.

Le Bras, Gabriel. 'Canon Law.' In *The Legacy of the Middle Ages,* edited by C.G. Crump and E.F. Jacob, 321–61. Oxford: Clarendon, 1926.

Lees, Clare A., and Gillian R. Overing. 'Before History, Before Difference: Bodies, Metaphor, and the Church in Anglo-Saxon England.' *Yale Review of Criticism* 11 (1998): 315–34.

– 'Birthing Bishops and Fathering Poets: Bede, Hild, and the Relations of Cultural Production.' *Exemplaria* 6 (1994): 35–65.

– *Double Agents: Women and Clerical Culture in Anglo-Saxon England.* Philadelphia: University of Pennsylvania Press, 2001.

Lees, Jay T. 'Political and Dramatic Irony in the Portrayal of Women in the Beginning of Hrotsvit of Gandersheim's *Gesta Ottonis.*' In *Scripturus vitam: Lateinische Biographie von der Antike bis in die Gegenwart: Festgabe für Walter*

Berschin, edited by Dorothea Walz, 797–805. Heidelberg: Mattes Verlag, 2002.

Lenschen, Walter. 'Du drame religieux au théâtre socialiste: Hrotsvit de Gandersheim et Peter Hacks.' *Études de lettres* 3 (1983): 43–54.

Lerner, Gerda. *The Creation of Patriarchy*. New York: Oxford University Press, 1986.

Lévi-Provençal, E., and E. García Gómez, eds. and trans. *Crónica anónima de Abd al-Rahman III al-Nasir*. Madrid: Granada, 1950.

Leyser, Karl. *Medieval Germany and Its Neighbors, 900–1250*. London: Hambledon Press, 1982.

– *Rule and Conflict in an Early Medieval Society: Ottonian Saxony*. Oxford: Arnold, 1979.

'Life of St. Mary of Egypt.' Translated by Maria Kouli. In *Holy Women of Byzantium: Ten Saints' Lives in English Translation*, edited by Alice-Mary Talbot, 65–93. Washington, DC: Dumbarton Oaks, 1966.

'Life of St. Thomaïs of Lesbos.' Translated by Paul Halsall. In *Holy Women of Byzantium: Ten Saints' Lives in English Translation*, edited by Alice-Mary Talbot, 291–322. Washington, DC: Dumbarton Oaks, 1966.

Liudprand of Cremona. 'Antapodosis.' In *Quellen zur Geschichte der Sächsischen Kaiserzeit*, edited by Bauer and Rau, 244–495.

MacCulloch, J.A. *The Harrowing of Hell*. Edinburgh: T. & T. Clark, 1930.

'Marcionism.' *Encyclopaedia of Religion and Ethics*. Edited by James Hastings. New York: Scribner, 1928.

Marcus, Jacob R. *The Jew in the Medieval World*. New York: Harper and Row, 1938.

Marks, Peter. 'Girls in Deep Trouble, Not Just from Hadrian.' Review of *Three Virgins*, directed by Amy Huggans, performed by Collapsable Giraffe. *New York Times*, 19 July 1999, late edition E5.

Marsden, Richard. 'The Old Testament in Late Anglo-Saxon England: Preliminary Observations on the Textual Evidence.' In *The Early Medieval Bible: Its Production, Decoration and Use*, edited by Richard Gameson, 101–24. Cambridge Studies in Palaeography and Codicology. Cambridge: Cambridge University Press, 1994.

Marx, C.W. *The Devil's Rights and the Redemption in the Literature of Medieval England*. Cambridge: D.S. Brewer, 1995.

McKitterick, Rosamond, and Timothy Reuer, eds. *The New Cambridge Medieval History: c. 900–c. 1024*. Vol. 3. *The New Cambridge Medieval History*. Edited by Rosamond McKitterick. Cambridge: Cambridge University Press, 2000.

McNamara, Jo Ann Kay. *Sisters in Arms: Catholic Nuns through Two Millennia*. Cambridge, MA: Harvard University Press, 1996.

Menhardt, Hermann. 'Eine unbekannte Hrotsvitha-Handschrift.' *Zeitschrift für deutsches Altertum* 62 (1925): 233–6.

Miles, Margaret R. *Carnal Knowing: Female Nakedness and Religious Meaning in the Christian West.* New York: Vintage-Random House, 1991.

Miller, Thomas, ed. *The Old English Version of Bede's Ecclesiastical History of the English People.* Part 1, 2. EETS 96, 1891. Reprint, Oxford: Oxford University Press, 1959.

Mitchell, Michael. *Peter Hacks: Theatre for a Socialist Society*, 136–38. Glasgow: Scottish Papers in Germanic Studies, 1990.

Mommsen, Theodor, and Paul Krueger, eds. *The Digest of Justinian.* Translated by Alan Watson. Philadelphia: University of Pennsylvania Press, 1985.

Mühler, Heinrich von. 'Kaiser Otto I.' In *Gedichte von Heinrich von Mühler*, 313–15 Berlin: Vobßsche Buchhandlung, 1842.

Muir, Lynette R. *The Biblical Drama of Medieval Europe.* New York and Cambridge: Cambridge University Press, 1995.

Murphy, Roland E. 'The Personification of Wisdom.' In *Wisdom in Ancient Israel: Essays in Honour of J.A. Emerton*, edited by John Day, Robert P. Gordon, and H.G.M. Williamson, 222–33. Cambridge: Cambridge University Press, 1995.

– *The Tree of Life: An Exploration of Biblical Wisdom Literature.* 2nd ed. Grand Rapids, MI: Eerdmans, 1996.

Murray, Stephen. *Notre-Dame Cathedral of Amiens: The Power of Change in Gothic.* New York and London: Cambridge University Press, 1996.

Nagel, Bert. Introduction to *Sämtliche Dichtungen*, by Hrotsvitha. Edited by Otto Baumhauer. Munich: Winkler Verlag, 1966.

– *Hrotsvit von Gandersheim.* Stuttgart: Metzler, 1965.

Nelson, Charles. 'Hrotsvit von Gandersheim: Madwoman in the Abbey.' In *Women as Protagonists and Poets in the German Middle Ages: An Anthology of Feminist Approaches to Middle High German Literature*, edited by Albrecht Classen, Göppingen: Kümmerle, 1991.

Nelson, Janet. 'Rulers and Government.' In *The New Cambridge Medieval History.* Vol. 3, edited by Timothy Reuter, 43–55. Cambridge: Cambridge University Press, 1999.

Nentwig, Paul. 'Conrad Ferdinand Meyer: Der gleitende Purpur.' In *Wege zum Gedicht. II: Interpretation von Balladen*, edited by Rupert Hirschenauer and Albrecht Weber, 413–24. New ed. Munich and Zurich: Schnell and Steiner, 1964.

Newman, Barbara. *From Virile Woman to WomanChrist: Studies in Medieval Religion and Literature.* Philadelphia: University of Pennsylvania Press, 1995.

O'Callaghan, Joseph. *A History of Medieval Spain.* Ithaca: Cornell University Press, 1975.

The Old English Version of Bede's Ecclesiastical History of the English People. Edited by Thomas Miller, Part 1, 2, EETS 96. 1981. Reprint, Oxford: Oxford University Press, 1959.

Osterholz, Karl Heinz. '"Der gleitende Purpur." Versuch einer Deutung des C.F. Meyerschen Gedichtes.' *Muttersprache* (1954): 254–9.

Partner, Peter. *God of Battles: Holy Wars of Christianity and Islam.* Princeton: Princeton University Press, 1997.

Patterson, Lee. *Chaucer and the Subject of History.* Madison: University of Wisconsin Press, 1992.

Pätzold, Barbara. 'Die Auffassung des ostfränkisch-deutschen Reiches als "regnum Saxonum" in Quellen des 10. Jahrhunderts (vornehmlich bei sächsischen Geschichtsschreibern).' In *Wir-Gefühl und Regnum Saxonum bei frühmittelalterlichen Geschichtsschreibern,* edited by Wolfgang Eggert and Barbara Pätzold, 181–286. Forschungen zur mittelalterlichen Geschichte, 31. Weimar: Böhlau, 1984.

– 'Hrotsvit von Gandersheim: Lebensnormen und Wertvorstellungen.' In *Herrscherinnen und Nonnen: Frauengestalten von der Ottonenzeit bis zu den Staufern,* edited by Erika Uitz, Barbara Pätzold, and Gerald Beyreuther, 17–42. Berlin: Deutscher Verlag der Wissenschaften, 1990.

Payer, Pierre J. *Sex and the Penitentials: The Development of a Sexual Code, 550–1150.* Toronto: University of Toronto Press, 1984.

Pelikan, Jaroslav. 'Christ Crucified.' In *Jesus through the Centuries: His Place in the History of Culture,* 95–108. New Haven: Yale University Press, 1985.

Perkins, Pheme. *Jesus as Teacher.* Cambridge: Cambridge University Press, 1990.

Pertz, ed. *Vita Johannis Abbatis Gorziensis.* Monumenta Germaniae Historica. Scriptores rerum Germanicarum in usum scholarum separatim editi, 4, 335–77. Hanover, 1841.

Petroff, Elizabeth. *Body and Soul: Essays on Medieval Women and Mysticism.* Oxford: Oxford University Press, 1994.

– 'Eloquence and Heroic Virginity in Hrotsvit's Verse Legends.' In *Hrotsvit of Gandersheim: Rara Avis in Saxonia?* 229–38.

Petroff, Elizabeth, ed. *Medieval Women's Visionary Literature.* New York: Oxford University Press, 1986.

Plucknett, T.F.T. *A Concise History of the Common Law.* 2nd ed. Rochester, NY: Lawyers' Cooperative, 1936.

Pollock, Frederick, and Frederic William Maitland. *The History of English Law before the Time of Edward I.* 2nd ed. London: Cambridge University Press, 1968.

Power, Eileen. 'Bodo: A Frankish Peasant in the Time of Charlemagne.' In *Medieval People,* 18–38. Rev. ed. London: Methuen, 1963.

Preissl, Fritz. *Hrotsvit von Gandersheim und die Entstehung des mittelalterlichen Heldenbilds.* Erlangen: Palm and Enke, 1939.

Processus Satanae contra D. Virginem coram Judice Jesu in Processus juris joco-serius. Hanau, 1611.

Provost, William. 'The Boethian Voice in the Dramas of Hrotsvit.' In *Hrotsvit of Gandersheim: Rara Avis in Saxonia?* 71–8.

Rabanus Maurus. *Exposition in Proverbia Salomonis,* lib. I. Patrologiae Cursus Completus, Series Secunda Latina, vol. 111. Paris, 1851.

Rasmussen, Ann Marie. *Mothers and Daughters in Medieval German Literature.* Syracuse: Syracuse University Press, 1997.

Reid, Barbara E. *Choosing the Better Part? Women in the Gospel of Luke.* Collegeville, MN: Liturgical Press, 1996.

Reuter, Timothy. *Germany in the Early Middle Ages, c. 800–1056.* New York: Longman, 1991.

Richardson, Christine, and Jackie Johnston. *Medieval Drama.* New York: St Martin's Press, 1991.

Riedel, Volker. 'Utopien und Wirklichkeit: Soziale Entwürfe in den Antikestücken von Peter Hacks.' *Gymnasium* 109 (2002): 49–68.

Roberts, Arthur. 'Did Hrotswitha Imitate Terence?' *Modern Language Notes* 16 (1901): 478–81.

Robertson, Duncan. *Medieval Saints' Lives.* Lexington, KY: French Forum, 1995.

Rörig, Fritz. 'Geblütsrecht und freie Wahl in ihrer Auswirkung auf die deutsche Geschichte. Untersuchungen zur Geschichte der deutschen Königserhebung.' 1948. Reprinted in *Königswahl und Thronfolge in ottonisch-frühdeutscher Zeit,* edited by Eduard Hlawitschka, 71–147. Wege der Forschung, 178. Reprint, Darmstadt: Wissenschaftliche Buchgesellschaft, 1971.

Rosset, Clément. *Joyful Cruelty: Toward a Philosophy of the Real.* Translated by David F. Bell. New York: Oxford University Press, 1993.

Rudwin, Maximilian. *The Devil in Legend and Literature.* 1931. Reprint, LaSalle, IL: Open Court, 1959.

Russell, Jeffrey Burton. *Lucifer: The Devil in the Middle Ages.* Ithaca: Cornell University Press, 1984.

Rutebeuf. 'Le Miracle de Théophile.' In *Anthologie de la littérature française du moyen âge,* 3rd ed. edited by P. Groult, V. Émond, and G. Muraille, vol. 1, 227–33. Gembloux: Editions J. Duculot, 1967.

Salisbury, Joyce E. *Church Fathers, Independent Virgins.* London and New York: Verso, 1991.

Scarry, Elaine. *The Body in Pain: The Making and Unmaking of the World.* Oxford: Oxford University Press, 1987.

Schlesinger, Walter. 'Karolingische Königswahlen.' 1963. Reprinted in *Königswahl und Thronfolge in fränkisch-karolingischer Zeit,* Edited by Eduard Hlawitschka, 190–266. Wege der Forschung, 247. Reprint, Darmstadt: Wissenschaftliche Buchgesellschaft, 1975.

Schmid, Karl. 'Die Thronfolge Ottos des Großen.' 1964. Reprinted in *Königswahl und Thronfolge in ottonisch-frühdeutscher Zeit*, edited by Eduard Hlawitschka, 417–508. Wege der Forschung, 178. Reprint, Darmstadt: Wissenschaftliche Buchgesellschaft, 1971.

Schneidmüller, Bernd. 'Reich-Volk-Nation: Die Entstehung des deutschen Reiches und der deutschen Nation im Mittelalter.' In *Mittelalterliche nationes – neuzeitliche Nationen: Probleme der nationenbildung in Europa*, edited by Almut Bues and Rex Rexheuser, 73–101. Deutsches Historisches Institut Warschau Quellen und Studien, 2. Wiesbaden: Harrassowitz, 1995.

Schöffler, Heinz, ed. *Conrad Ferdinand Meyer: Werke*. Vol. 1. Berlin and Darmstadt: Tempel-Verlag, 1967.

Schroeder, Peter R. 'Hroswitha and the Feminization of Drama.' In *Women in Theatre*, edited by James Redmond, 49–58. Cambridge: Cambridge University Press, 1989.

Schröder, Rudolf Alexander. 'Roswitha von Gandersheim.' In *Die Aufsätze und Reden: Erster Band*. Vols 2 and 3 of *Gesammelte Werke*, vol. 3, 770–84. Berlin and Frankfurt: Suhrkamp, 1952.

Schütte, Bernd. *Untersuchungen zu den Lebensbeschreibungen der Königin Mathilde*. Monumenta Germaniae Historica. Studien und Texte, 9. Hanover: Hahnsche Buchhandlung, 1994.

Schütze-Pflugk, Marianne. *Herrscher- und Märtyrerauffassung bei Hrotsvit von Gandersheim*. Wiesbaden: Steiner, 1972.

Schwarz, Gerhard. *Die Heilige Ordnung der Männer: Patriarchalische Hierarchie und Gruppendynamik*. 2nd ed. Opladen, Germany: Westdeutscher Verlag, 1987.

Silber, Patricia. '"The Develis Perlament": Poetic Drama and a Dramatic Poem.' *Mediaevalia* 3 (1977) 215–28.

Simon, Eckehard. Preface to *The Theatre of Medieval Europe: New Research in Early Drama*, edited by Eckehard Simon, xi–xx. Cambridge: Cambridge University Press, 1991.

Southern, R.W. *Western Views of Islam in the Middle Ages*. Cambridge: Harvard University Press, 1962.

Sperberg-McQueen, M.R. 'Whose Body Is It? Chaste Strategies and the Reinforcement of Patriarchy in Three Plays by Hrotsvit von Gandersheim.' *Women in German Yearbook* 8 (1992): 47–71.

Springer, Matthias. 'Fragen zur Entstehung des mittelalterlichen deutschen Reiches.' *Zeitschrift für Geschichtswissenschaft* 43.5 (1995): 405–20.

Stewart, D.B., trans. *On Life and Letters by Anatole France*. 3rd ser. London: John Lane, 1922.

Sticca, Sandro. 'The Hagiographical and Monastic Context of Hrotswitha's Plays.' In *Hrotsvit of Gandersheim: Rara Avis in Saxonia?* 1–34.

- 'Hrotswitha's *Abraham* and Exegetical Tradition.' In *Fons Perennis: Saggi Critici di filologia in onore del prof. Vittorio D'Agostino*, 359–85. Turin, A cura della Aministrazione della Rivista di Studi. Classici, 1972.
- 'Hrotswitha's *Dulcitius* and Christian Symbolism.' *Mediaeval Studies* 32 (1970): 114–19.
- 'Italy: Liturgy and Christocentric Spirituality.' In *The Theatre of Medieval Europe*, edited by Eckehard Simon, 169–88. New York and London: Cambridge University Press, 1991.
- 'Sacred Drama and Comic Realism in the Plays of Hrotswitha of Gandersheim.' In *Acta VI: The Early Middle Ages*, edited by William Snyder, 124–5. Binghamton, NY: Center for Medieval and Early Renaissance Studies, 1979.
- 'Sacred Drama and Tragic Realism in Hroswitha's *Pafnutius.*' In *The Theatre in the Middle Ages*, edited by Herman Braet, Johan Nowé, and Gilbert Tournoy, 12–44. Leuven: Leuven University Press, 1985.
Stintzing, R. von. *Geschichte der popularen Literatur der romischkanonischen Rechts in Deutschland.* Stuttgart. 1867.
Sussman, Mark. 'New York's Facelift.' *Drama Review* 42 (1998): 34–42.
Tamerl, Alfred. *Hrotsvith von Gandersheim: Eine Entmystifizierung.* Fiktion dunkles Mittelalter, 2. Gräfelfing: Mantis-Verlag, 1999.
Tarr, Judith. 'Holy Virgins and Wanton Women: Hrotsvitha's Terence and "Anti-Terence."' *Dissertation Abstracts International* 50.11 (1990): 3582A.
- 'Terentian Elements in Hrotsvit.' In *Hrotsvit of Gandersheim: Rara Avis in Saxonia?* 55–62.
Tellenbach, Gerd. 'Die geistigen und politischen Grundlagen der karolingischen Thronfolge: Zugleich eine Studie über kollektive Willensbildung und kollektives Handeln im neunten Jahrhundert.' *Frühmittelalterlich Studien* 13 (1979): 184–302.
Terence. *Adelphoi.* Translated by Frank O. Copely. New York: Bobbs-Merrill, 1962.
- *The Comedies [of] Terence.* Translated by Betty Radice. Harmondsworth: Penguin, 1976.
- *The Phormio.* Translated by William Abbott Oldfather. In *An Anthology of Roman Drama*, edited by Philip Whaley Harsh, 105–53, New York: Holt Rinehart and Winston, 1965.
Thiébaux, Marcelle. *The Writings of Medieval Women.* 2nd ed. New York: Garland, 1994.
Thompson, Charlotte. '*Paphnutius* and the Cultural Vision.' In *Hrotsvit of Gandersheim: Rara Avis in Saxonia?* 111–25.
Tolan, John, ed. *Medieval Christian Perceptions of Islam.* New York: Garland, 1996.

–   *Saracens: Islam in the Medieval European Imagination.* New York: Columbia
    University Press, 2002.
Toman, Rolf, and Achim Bednorz, eds. *Romanesque: Architecture, Sculpture,
    Painting.* Cologne: Könemann, 1997.
Treggiari, Susan. *Roman Marriage: Iusti Coniuges from the Time of Cicero to the Time
    of Ulpian.* Oxford: Clarendon, 1991.
Trexler, Richard. Introduction to *Sex and Conquest: Gendered Violence, Political
    Order, and the European Conquest of the Americas.* Ithaca: Cornell University
    Press, 1995.
Trilse, Christoph. *Peter Hacks: Leben und Werk.* West Berlin: Verlag das
    europäische buch, 1980.
Vinogradoff, Paul. *Roman Law in Medieval Europe.* Oxford: Clarendon, 1929.
Vita Mathildis reginae posterior. In *Die Lebensbeschreibungen der Königin Mathilde,*
    edited by Bernd Schütte, 143–202. Monumenta Germaniae Historica.
    Scriptores rerum Germanicarum in usum scholarum separatim editi, 66.
    Hanover: Hansche Buchhandlung, 1994.
Vynckier, Henk. 'Arms-Talks in the Middle Ages: Hrotsvit, *Waltharius,* and the
    Heroic *Via.*' In *Hrotsvit of Gandersheim: Rara Avis in Saxonia?* 183–200.
Wagner, Fritz. 'Johann Christoph Gottsched und Hrotsvit von Gandersheim.'
    Mittellateinisches Jahrbuch 13 (1978): 253–66.
Wailes, Stephen L. 'Beyond Virginity: Flesh and Spirit in the Plays of Hrotsvit
    of Gandersheim.' *Speculum* 76 (2001): 1–27.
Waitz, Georg. Review of *Roswitha und Conrad Celtes* by Joseph Aschbach. *Göt-
    tingische Gelehrte Anzeigen* 2 (1867): 1261–70.
–   'Über das Verhältnis von Hrotsuits *Gesta Oddonis* zu Widukind.' *Forschungen
    zur deutschen Geschichte* 9 (1869): 335–42.
Wall, Glenda. 'Hrotsvit and the German Humanists.' In *Hrotsvit of Gandersheim:
    Rara Avis in Saxonia?* 253–61.
Wallach, Liutpold. 'Education and Culture in the Tenth Century,' *Medievalia et
    Humanistica* 9 (1955): 18–22.
Walz, Herbert. 'Die Rezeption von Hrotsvits "Paraiso Sancti Pelagii" im
    iberischen Raum.' *Iberoromania* 4 (1975): 19–40.
Ward, Benedicta. *Harlots of the Desert: A Study of Repentance in Early Monastic
    Sources.* Kalamazoo, MI: Cistercian Publications, 1987.
Warner, David A. 'Henry II at Magdeburg: Kingship, Ritual and the Cult of
    Saints.' *Early Medieval Europe* 3.2 (1994): 135–66.
Watson, Alan. *The State, Law and Religion: Pagan Rome.* Athens: University of
    Georgia Press, 1992.
Weber, Robert, ed. *Biblia Sacra Iuxta Vulgatam Versionem.* 2 vols. Stuttgart:
    Württembergische Bibelanstalt, 1969.

Wemple, Susanne. 'Monastic Life of Women from the Merovingians to the Ottonians.' In *Hrotsvit of Gandersheim: Rara Avis in Saxonia?* 35–54.

Widukind of Corvey. 'Res gestae Saxonicae.' In *Quellen zur Geschichte der Sächsischen Kaiserzeit,* edited by Bauer and Rau, 1–183.

Wiegand, M. Gonsalva, ed. 'The Non-Dramatic Works of Hrosvitha: Text, Translation, and Commentary.' PhD dissertation, St Louis University, MS, 1936.

Wiles, David. 'Hrotsvitha of Gandersheim: The Performance of Her Plays in the Tenth Century.' *Theatre History Studies* 19 (1999): 133–50.

Wilson, Katharina M. 'Hrotsvit and the *Artes*: Learning *Ad Usum Meliorem.*' In *The Worlds of Medieval Women: Creativity, Influence, Imagination,* edited by Constance Berman, Charles Connell, and Judith Rothschild, 3–14. Morgantown: West Virginia University Press, 1985.

– *Hrotsvit of Gandersheim: The Ethics of Authorial Stance.* Davis Medieval Texts and Studies, 7. Leiden: E.J. Brill, 1988.

– 'Mathematical Learning and Structural Composition in Hrotsvit's Works.' In *Hrotsvit of Gandersheim: Rara Avis in Saxonia?* 99–111.

– 'The Saxon Abbess: Hrotsvit of Gandersheim.' In *Medieval Women Writers,* edited by Katharina M. Wilson, 30–42. Athens: University of Georgia Press, 1984.

– 'Two Notes on Anatole France's Debt to Hrotsvit.' *University of South Florida Language Quarterly* 23.3–4 (1985): 18–19, 22.

– ed. *Medieval Women Writers.* Athens: University of Georgia Press, 1984.

– ed. and trans. *Hrotsvit of Gandersheim: A Florilegium of Her Works.* Cambridge: D.S. Brewer, 1998.

– trans. *The Plays of Hrostvit of Gandersheim.* Garland Library of Medieval Literature. Vol. 62, series B. New York: Garland, 1989.

Witherington, Ben, III. *Jesus the Sage: The Pilgrimage of Wisdom.* Minneapolis: Fortress Press, 1994.

Witt, Elizabeth Ann. 'Canonizing the Canoness: Anthologizing Hrotsvit.' *College Literature* 28 (2001): 85–91.

Wittig, Monique. 'The Mark of Gender.' In *The Poetics of Gender,* edited by Nancy K. Miller, 63–73. New York: Columbia University Press, 1986.

Wolf, Kenneth Baxter. *Christian Martyrs in Muslim Spain.* New York: Cambridge University Press, 1988.

Wolff, Hans Julius. *Roman Law: An Historical Introduction.* Norman: University of Oklahoma Press, 1951.

Woods, Marjorie Curry. 'Rape and the Pedagogical Rhetoric of Sexual Violence.' In *Criticism and Dissent in the Middle Ages,* edited by Rita Copeland, 56–87. Cambridge: Cambridge University Press, 1996.

Wright, Stephen K. 'The Durham Play of Mary and the Poor Knight: Sources and Analogues of a Lost English Miracle Play.' *Comparative Drama* 17 (1983) 254–65.

Zaenker, Karl A. 'Homage to Roswitha.' *Humanities Association Review* 29 (1978): 117–34.

– 'Hrotsvit and the Moderns: Her Impact on John Kennedy Toole and Peter Hacks.' In *Hrotsvit of Gandersheim: Rara Avis in Saxonia?* 275–85.

– 'The Metamorphosis of Roswitha von Gandersheim in Works by Anatole France and Peter Hacks.' *Proceedings of the Pacific Northwest Conference on Foreign Languages* 30. 1–2 (1979): 79–82.

Zeydel, Edwin H. 'Hrotsvit von Gandersheim and the Eternal Womanly.' *Studies in the German Drama: A Festschrift in Honor of Walter Silz*, edited by Donald H. Crosby and George C. Schoolfield, 1–14. University of North Carolina Studies in the Germanic Languages and Literatures, 76. Chapel Hill: University of North Carolina Press, 1974.

– 'Knowledge of Hrotsvitha's Works Prior to 1500.' *Modern Language Notes* 59 (1944): 382–5.

– 'The Reception of Hrotsvitha by the German Humanists after 1493.' *Journal of English and Germanic Philology* 44 (1945): 239–49.

– 'Were Hrotsvitha's Dramas Performed during Her Lifetime?' *Speculum* 20.4 (October 1945): 443–56.

Contributors

Phyllis R. Brown, Department of English, Santa Clara University
Jane Chance, Department of English, Rice University
David Day, Department of English, University of Houston, Clear Lake
Jane E. Jeffrey, Department of English, West Chester University
Daniel T. Kline, Department of English, University of Alaska, Anchorage
Jay T. Lees, Department of History, University of Northern Iowa
Linda A. McMillin, Department of History, Susquehanna University
Florence Newman, Department of English, Towson University
Patricia Silber, Department of English, Marymount College of Fordham University
Janet Snyder, Division of Art, West Virginia University
Ronald Stottlemyer, Department of English, Carroll College
Debra L. Stoudt, Department of Foreign Languages, University of Toledo
Robert Talbot, Department of English, Salem State College
Ulrike Wiethaus, Humanities Program, Wake Forest University
Katharina M. Wilson, Department of Comparative Literature, University of Georgia
Michael A. Zampelli, S.J., Department of Theatre, Santa Clara University

Index